Wills and Estates

FOURTH EDITION

Derek Fazakas

emond ▪ Toronto, Canada ▪ 2017

Emond Montgomery Publications Limited
60 Shaftesbury Avenue
Toronto ON M4T 1A3
http://www.emond.ca/highered

Printed in Canada.
Reprinted October 2018

We acknowledge the financial support of the Government of Canada.   Canadä

Emond Montgomery Publications has no responsibility for the persistence or accuracy of URLs for external or third-party Internet websites referred to in this publication, and does not guarantee that any content on such websites is, or will remain, accurate or appropriate.

Publisher: Mike Thompson
Managing editor, development: Kelly Dickson
Senior editor, production: Jim Lyons
Production supervisor: Laura Bast
Copy editor: Paula Pike
Typesetter: Tom Dart
Proofreader: Natalie Berchem
Indexer: Michael Bunn
Cover and text designer: Tara Agnerian
Cover image: Daniel Jedzura/Shutterstock

Library and Archives Canada Cataloguing in Publication

Fazakas, Derek, 1964-, author
   Wills and estates / Derek Fazakas. — Fourth edition.

Includes bibliographical references and index.
ISBN 978-1-77255-205-8 (paperback)

   1. Wills—Canada—Textbooks.   2. Executors and administrators—Canada—Textbooks.   3. Probate law and practice—Canada—Textbooks. I. Title.

KE808 F39 2017   346.71105'6   C2016-907195-2
KF753 F39 2017

Brief Contents

PART I   Estate Planning

PART II   Estate Administration

PART III   Estate Litigation

Contents

PART I

ESTATE PLANNING

1 Wills

2 Will Clauses

3 Interpretation of Wills

4 Intestacy

5 Powers of Attorney

6 Trusts

PART II

ESTATE ADMINISTRATION

7 **Proof of the Estate Trustee's Status as Estate Trustee**

8 **Preliminary Steps in Applying for a Certificate of Appointment of Estate Trustee**

9 **Applying for a Certificate of Appointment of Estate Trustee**

10　Collecting the Assets

11　Determining, Notifying, and Paying Creditors of the Estate

PART III

ESTATE LITIGATION

List of Figures

Preface

Wills and Estates is designed to assist law clerks in their understanding of the practice of estate law. The meaning of the word "estate" often refers to the property of a deceased person, but it can also refer to the total property held by a living person. This text is concerned with both meanings of the word.

The text is divided into three parts. Part I, Estate Planning, deals with estate planning documents—that is, wills, powers of attorney, and trusts—and with the creation and interpretation of these documents. It also discusses some of the legal implications of not having a will or a power of attorney. Part I is written from the point of view of a law office acting for persons attempting to put an estate plan in place.

Part II, Estate Administration, is written from the point of view of the law office acting for the estate trustee. This part covers all the tasks that are necessary in transferring the assets of a deceased person to the persons or entities entitled to them—namely, the beneficiaries and the creditors of the estate. These tasks fall into the following categories that, together, form a blueprint for the administration of any estate:

1. gather together (or secure) the assets;
2. notify and pay the creditors;
3. account to the beneficiaries (and the creditors); and
4. pay the beneficiaries.

Part II discusses the various tasks involved in completing each of these steps. The person who performs these tasks is called the "estate trustee," and the first three chapters of Part II discuss how a person becomes an estate trustee. This part also includes a chapter on the administration of powers of attorney and trusts, which, always in the case of powers of attorney and sometimes in the case of trusts, are functions that are performed prior to the death of the person who originally created the power of attorney or trust.

Part III, Estate Litigation, deals with the conflicts and resulting litigation that can arise during the course of the administration of an estate. It is written from the point of view of the law office acting for the estate trustee or for another party to the litigation. Litigation of this kind is loosely referred to as "estate litigation." In many ways, estate litigation overlaps with other types of civil litigation, but there are rules and procedures unique to estate litigation that are discussed here. Note that the *Rules of Civil Procedure* applicable to estate litigation are often available for use in a variety of other situations, including those pertaining to trusts and powers of attorney. Part III discusses how the rules apply in some common estate practice situations and points out some of the questions that may arise when using the rules. Part III also includes a chapter entitled "Statutory Forms of Estate Litigation," which deals with certain forms of litigation that are enabled by specific legislative provisions and a new chapter entitled "Mediation in Estate Litigation," which covers the important topic of conflict mediation as a way of solving estate-related disputes.

Keep in mind that the three parts to this text are interrelated and should be read as such. An understanding of all three is necessary for a complete understanding of any one area. For example, one cannot fully understand how to create a proper will without the knowledge of how to administer an estate and without some knowledge of the litigation that can arise when a will is not created properly.

I would like to thank John Grummett, Richard Shields, Judy Wolf, and Diane Jamieson, who provided me with excellent guidance in putting this fourth edition together. Thank you as well to the reviewers of the text: Jacqueline Asselin, Algonquin College; Anna Rolbin, Centennial College; Marie Sforza, Durham College; Judy Wolf, Seneca College; and Kenn C. Lui, Capilano College.

I would also like to thank Paul Emond and the people at Emond Publishing, specifically Sarah Fulton May, Kelly Dickson, Paula Pike, Mike Thompson, Laura Bast, David Handelsman, and Holly Penick, who aided in the development and production of this text.

About the Author

Derek Fazakas is a mediator of estate disputes as well as a practising lawyer whose law practice focuses on estate litigation matters. He has extensive experience in estate planning and estate administration and he is a past teacher of the estates course for law clerks and an occasional lecturer for the Hamilton Law Association.

PART I

Estate Planning

Wills

1

LEARNING OUTCOMES

After completing this chapter, you should be able to:

- List the formal requirements of a will

- List the legal requirements relating to a testator

- Identify the characteristics of a split will and other less-common wills

- Explain the two methods for amending a will

- Describe the processes for revoking or reviving a will

- Describe the best practices for storage of a client's will

Introduction

Estate planning is what people do to ensure that their bills are paid and their assets preserved and ultimately given to other people following their death. The most common form of estate planning is creating a will. A **will** is a document that sets out a person's wishes and directions with respect to the disposal of their property after their death. The person making the will was traditionally called the **testator** (male) or the **testatrix** (female). More recently, the term testator is used for all gender identities. When they sign the will, the testator is said to execute it.

Figure 1.1 is an example of a will. There are, as we shall see, many different ways to create a will, and no two wills are exactly alike. Notwithstanding the uniqueness of every will, all wills share some characteristics. This is due in part to the fact that, in order to be valid, all wills must be created and executed according to certain formal requirements. If a will is not valid, the wishes of the testator expressed in it will not be followed (unless those wishes correspond with the laws that come into play when a person dies without a will). It is the lawyer's and the law clerk's job to ensure that a client's will has been created and executed properly in accordance with the legal requirements. This is the case whether that will is created and executed under the direction and guidance of the lawyer and law clerk, or whether the client seeks the lawyer's opinion as to the validity of an existing will.

As an introduction to wills, this chapter discusses the basic legal requirements for creating and executing wills. It also explains some of the more common and less common ways in which wills are created, executed, and amended. Finally, the chapter deals with some practical issues facing a lawyer and a law clerk regarding the drafting and safekeeping of wills.

will
document that sets out a person's wishes and directions with respect to the disposal of his property after death

testator
person who makes a will (traditionally the male term; now used for all genders)

testatrix
the traditional term for a female person who makes a will

FIGURE 1.1 Will

THIS IS THE LAST WILL AND TESTAMENT of me, **John Doe**, whose current residence address is 99 Anywhere Street, Hamilton, Ontario, Q9Q 9Q9, retired bank manager.

1. REVOCATION

I revoke all previous wills.

2. INTERPRETATION

Where used in this document,

(a) "executor" shall be interchangeable with the term "estate trustee with a will," shall be deemed to include "trustee" if a trust fund has been established, to be pluralized if more than one executor has been named, and to include all genders as the context in each case requires;

(b) the singular, masculine, or personal pronoun shall be construed as meaning the plural, gender, or body corporate as the context in each case requires;

(c) paragraph headings are for reference purposes only and shall not define, limit, extend, or otherwise affect the meaning of any term or provision;

(d) "pay" shall be deemed to include "transfer" and "deliver" as the context in each case requires;

(e) "child" or "children" shall be deemed to include only my daughter, Jennifer Doe, and my sons, Steven Doe and John Doe Jr.

3. PAYMENT OF DEBTS AND TAXES

I direct my executor or executors to pay as soon as convenient after my death all debts, funeral and testamentary expenses and taxes that my estate is legally bound to pay, or to commute, prepay or defer payment of such debts or taxes as my executor or executors may in his, her, or their sole and absolute discretion consider advisable, and I hereby empower my executor or executors to make any election, determination, or designation pursuant to the *Income Tax Act* or any other taxing statute or any regulation pursuant thereto.

4. APPOINTMENT OF EXECUTOR

I appoint my spouse, JANE DOE, to be the sole executor of my estate. If my executor first named has not survived me by thirty days or is unable or unwilling to act, then I appoint as my executor my daughter, JENNIFER DOE. If my said daughter is unable or unwilling to act as my executor then I appoint as my executors my son, STEVEN DOE and my friend, JOHN DEW, acting jointly.

5. DISPOSITION

I give all the residue of my property, both real and personal, and including any property over which I may have a general power of appointment, to the executor or executors UPON THE FOLLOWING TRUSTS, namely:

(a) to divide all articles of a personal, domestic, or household use or ornament or works of art in accordance with a List or Memorandum signed by me, which I may leave among my personal papers or attached to a copy of this my Last Will;

(b) to give the entire residue of my estate to my spouse, JANE DOE, provided she survives me by thirty days;

(c) if my said spouse has failed to survive me by thirty days, to distribute my estate as follows:

(A) provided that she survives me by thirty days, to give to my daughter, JENNIFER DOE, the following:

(i) any real property which I may own at the time of my death, including houses and their respective contents;

(ii) any automobiles which I may own at the time of my death;

(B) to divide the residue of my estate equally between the following who survive me, share and share alike, subject to clauses 6 and 7, below;

(i) my son, JOHN DOE JR., provided he survives me by thirty days;

(ii) my son, STEVEN DOE, provided he survives me by thirty days.

6. LINEAL DESCENDANT OR DESCENDANTS OF DECEASED CHILD

If any child of mine who has been given a benefit herein dies before final distribution of my estate, leaving one or more lineal descendant or descendants then alive, such deceased child shall be considered alive for purposes of distribution hereunder and my executor or executors shall make the gift or distribution to which such deceased child would have been entitled, if she had not so died, to such lineal descendant or descendants by representation.

FIGURE 1.1 CONTINUED

7. AGE OR OTHER DISABILITY

If any person who becomes entitled to any share in my estate is under the age of majority or incapable of executing a release or under any other legal disability, my executor or executors shall hold and keep invested the share of such person and use the income and capital, or so much of either, as my executor or executors may in his, her, or their absolute discretion consider advisable for the maintenance, education, or benefit of such person until he or she is no longer incapable or under such age or disability and shall then distribute such share or the balance thereof remaining to such person, but in the meantime I authorize my executor or executors to make any payment for or on behalf of any such person which my executor or executors in his, her, or their sole discretion consider it advisable as a payment for the benefit, education, or general welfare of such person, and the receipt of any payee in those circumstances is a sufficient discharge to my executor or executors.

8. POWER TO INVEST

I authorize my executor or executors to make investments and otherwise deal with my estate (including property held for persons below a stipulated age or under any other legal disability) and to exercise any rights, powers, and privileges that may at any time exist with respect thereto to the same extent and as fully as I could if I were the living sole owner thereof as he, she, or they in his, her, or their absolute discretion consider to be in the best interests of my estate and the beneficiaries thereof.

9. POWER OF SALE

I authorize my executor or executors to use his, her, or their discretion in the realization of my estate with power to sell, call in, and convert into money any part of my estate not consisting of money at such time or times, in such manner and upon such terms and either for cash or credit or for part cash or part credit as he, she, or they may in his, her, or their uncontrolled discretion decide upon, or to postpone such conversion of my estate or any part or parts thereof for such length of time as he, she, or they may think best or to retain any portion of my estate in the form in which it may be at my death (notwithstanding that it may not be in the form of an investment in which executors are authorized to invest trust funds and whether or not there is a liability attached to any such portion of my estate) for such length of time as my executor or executors shall in his, her, or their complete discretion deem advisable, and my executor or executors shall not be held personally responsible for any loss that may occur to my estate by reason of his, her, or their so doing.

10. DISCRETION TO PAY OR DIVIDE

Except as herein expressly stated to the contrary, my executor or executors may make any division of my estate or set aside or pay any share or interest wholly or in part in the assets forming part of my estate at the time of my death or at the time of such division, setting aside, or payment, and I declare that where there may be some question of the value of any part of my estate my executor or executors may in his, her, or their absolute discretion fix the value of my estate or any part or parts thereof for the purpose of making any such division, setting aside, or payment, and his, her, or their decision shall be final and binding upon all persons concerned.

11. AUTHORITY BINDING

Any exercise by my executor or executors of the authority or discretion conferred on him, her, or them shall be binding on all beneficiaries of my estate whether or not such exercise would have the effect of conferring an advantage on any one or more of them at the expense of any other or could otherwise be considered but for the foregoing as not being an impartial exercise by my executor or executors of his, her, or their duties, powers, and discretions or as not maintaining an even hand among the beneficiaries.

12. EXCLUSION OF BENEFITS FROM COMMUNITY OF PROPERTY

All income from property given by me to any beneficiary who is, at my death, a spouse within the meaning of the *Family Law Act* or any similar legislation of another jurisdiction shall be excluded from the net family property of such beneficiary.

13. CUSTODY OF CHILDREN

If I die before all of my children are over the age of eighteen years and if my spouse has predeceased me or failed to survive me by thirty days, or if she has survived me but is deemed not competent to provide proper care and support for any of my surviving children under the *Mental Health Act* of Ontario, or any similar statute or law, I give custody of my surviving children to my sister, Mary Doe, and if my said sister is unable or unwilling to act as custodian of my said surviving children, I give custody of my surviving children to my friend, Ruth Smith. I wish it to be known that the custodians appointed above were chosen after a thorough and careful examination of all alternatives.

IN TESTIMONY WHEREOF I have to this my last will and testament written upon this and three preceding pages of paper hereunto subscribed my name this 1st day of January 2018.

SIGNED, PUBLISHED AND DECLARED	)
by **JOHN DOE**	)
as and for his last will and	)
testament, in the presence of	)
us, both present at the same	)
time, who at his request, in	)
his presence, and in the	)
presence of each other, have	)
hereunto subscribed our	)
names as witnesses:	)
	) *John Doe*
	) _____
	) John Doe
	)
Mary Breshney	)
_____	)
Mary Breshney	)
	)
Michael Finch	)
_____	)
Michael Finch	)

Formal Requirements of Wills

In Writing

The first requirement for a valid will is that it be in writing. An audio or video recorded will is not valid. An emailed or texted "will" that exists only on a computer or other digital device—or only in cyberspace—does in fact satisfy the writing requirement, but, as discussed below, other requirements make such a document invalid as a will.

Signed by the Testator

To be valid, a will must be signed by the testator. A hand-stamped signature does not satisfy this requirement, nor does a computer cut-and-paste version of the testator's signature. It is for this reason that a cyberspace will cannot be considered valid.

In the author's opinion, the lawyer should instruct the client to sign the will with his usual signature—that is, the way he would normally sign a cheque. If a client normally signs her cheques with her middle name rather than her first name, or with her first initial rather than her first name, that is the most appropriate way to sign the will. As will be seen later in this text, even though it is good practice for a lawyer or law clerk to generate an affidavit by one of the witnesses proving the genuineness of the testator's signature immediately upon the will's being signed, it may become necessary after the testator is deceased to prove that the testator in fact signed the will. In such a case, an authorized bank employee, or any other person who has knowledge or documentation of the testator's usual signature, could be called on to give her opinion as to the authenticity of the signature appearing on the will. Signing with the usual signature simply makes identification of the signature easier. Notwithstanding the above, signing with the usual signature is not a legal requirement.

It may happen that a hurried will has to be executed in circumstances that prevent the testator from using his usual signature. A testator, for example, may be in a hospital and may have suffered a stroke that prevents him from using his writing hand. A will of a right-handed testator signed with his left hand nevertheless satisfies the requirement of a signature.

It may be that the testator's signature is simply some form of mark or insignia as opposed to letters forming the testator's name, as, for example, in the case of a testator who does not know how to sign his name owing to illiteracy. In such a case, that mark or insignia would suffice as the testator's signature on the will. One common mark used in place of a written name is an "X." A will signed with an "X" is valid provided that the witnesses to the will are able to verify that the testator himself actually drew the "X." A will may also be signed by a person other than the testator in cases where the testator is physically prevented from signing his full signature because of weakness, blindness, or some other cause. In such cases, the person signing must do so on the instructions of the testator and in the presence of the testator and witnesses. As in all cases, it is essential that the testator be fully aware of what is contained in the will before it is signed.

One final requirement is that the signature must be at the foot or the end of the will. If the signature appears in the middle, the will is not invalidated, but all gifts and directions that appear after or below the signature are not considered part of the will. The *Succession*

Law Reform Act[1] does not indicate where the witnesses should sign the will (see below under "Witnessed"), but good practice dictates that they sign opposite or immediately below the signature of the testator.

While it is not a legal requirement, it is good practice to direct the testator and the witnesses to initial each page of the will except the last page, where the signatures appear. This provides some substantiation that one or more pages of the will were not altered or substituted after the will was executed. Although such a practice is advisable, it must be done carefully in case one page is missed, thus creating a presumption of mischief that would not otherwise have existed.

Exception to Signature Requirement

The *Succession Law Reform Act* allows for a situation in which, as indicated above, the testator does not sign her own will but instead has another person sign for her in her presence. In such a case, the testator must acknowledge, in the presence of the two witnesses (see the next section), that the other person has signed for her. It should be noted that under section 12(3) of the Act a gift in the will to a person who signs on behalf of the testator, or to that person's spouse, is considered void unless the Superior Court of Justice is satisfied that neither the person signing nor his spouse exercised any improper or undue influence on the testator. If the court is not so satisfied, the will is not invalidated but is interpreted as if the gift to the person had not been made.

Witnessed

A will must be witnessed by two witnesses, neither of whom should be a beneficiary named in the will (see below) or the spouse of such beneficiary. Both witnesses must be present while the testator signs, and they must themselves sign the will in the presence of the testator and should sign in the presence of each other as well.

The *Succession Law Reform Act* states that a will is not invalidated owing to the mental incompetence of the witnesses, but good practice dictates that witnesses be competent. At some later date, the witnesses will be asked to sign affidavits verifying that they witnessed the will. If a witness is mentally incompetent to swear such an affidavit, alternative means are available to prove the proper execution of the will (see Part II, Estate Administration), but it is much simpler to complete the affidavit.

Some lawyers ask the witnesses to sign such affidavits immediately after the will itself is signed. This is done so that the lawyer acting for the estate trustee will not have to track down the witnesses at some future date, perhaps many years later.

As in the case of a person signing on behalf of the testator, under section 12(3) of the *Succession Law Reform Act*, a gift to a witness of the will, or to the spouse of a witness, is considered void unless the Superior Court of Justice is satisfied that neither the witness nor her spouse exercised any improper or undue influence on the testator. Again, if the court is not so satisfied, the will is not invalidated but is interpreted as if the gift to the person had not been made.

In cases where the testator signs with a mark such as an "X," the witnesses must complete a special affidavit that affirms that the mark is that of the testator. In cases where the

---

1   RSO 1990, c S.26.

testator is blind, it is essential that the will be read to her in the presence of the witnesses because in such cases the witnesses must again complete a special affidavit affirming the testator's blindness and the fact that the will was read aloud in their presence.

Exceptions to Witnessing Requirement

holograph will
handwritten will

A will does not have to be witnessed if it is entirely in the handwriting of the testator and signed by him at the end or foot of the will. Such handwritten wills are called **holograph wills**. As a general rule, it may be professionally risky for lawyers or law clerks to advise clients to create holograph wills. This is due in part to the fact that the requirements are unyieldingly strict. (If any one of the requirements discussed below is not met, the document will not be considered a will.) Holograph wills have to be dealt with, however—for example, in an emergency situation, it may be necessary for a lawyer or law clerk to instruct a client on how to create such a document. A lawyer may also be acting for an estate in which the deceased has left only a holograph will.

Another exception to the witnessing requirement is the case of a member of the Canadian Forces placed on active service under the *National Defence Act*;[2] a member of any other naval, land, or air force while on active service; or a sailor when at sea or in the course of a voyage. In such situations, a person can create a valid will even if it is not wholly in her handwriting and/or witnessed. Provision is made in the *Succession Law Reform Act* for proving the proper execution of such wills through a certificate of active service signed by or on behalf of an officer who has custody of the records pertaining to the status of the testator as an active member of the forces. In a case where a certificate of active service is unavailable, the testator is deemed to be on active service after she has taken steps under the orders of a superior officer in preparation for serving with, being attached to, or being seconded to a component of the force she is serving under.

Disposing Intention

Perhaps the most important requirement of a valid will is that it have a disposing intention—that is, that the testator intends to give away her property by virtue of what is written in her will. If it can be proved, on the basis of the facts of the particular situation, that there was no intention to create a will on the part of the "testator," the "will" is not considered a valid will or even a will at all. Such a document, for example, might be made on behalf of a character in a role-playing online game.

Legal Requirements Relating to the Testator

Age of Testator

To make a valid will, a testator must be at least 18 years of age, subject to the exceptions specified in the *Succession Law Reform Act*.

---

2 RSC 1985, c N-5.

Exceptions to the Age Requirement

A will signed by a testator who is not 18 years of age can be considered valid in certain circumstances.

If the testator is a member of the Canadian Forces either as part of a regular force under the *National Defence Act* or while placed on active service under that Act (that is, presumably whether part of a "regular force" or not), or is a sailor and at sea or in the course of a voyage, she may be under the age of 18 and nevertheless make a valid will. Note that the provisions of the *Succession Law Reform Act* dealing with these exceptions to the age requirement are similar to the exceptions dealing with the witnessing requirement. Despite the similarity, the exception to the age requirement is more liberal in that it does not require that the testator be on active service if she is a member of a regular force in the Canadian Forces.

Another exception to the age requirement occurs where the testator is married or has been previously married. In such cases, the testator may make a valid will even though he is under 18. Again, if an underage person is contemplating marriage, he may make a valid will provided that the will states that it is being made in contemplation of marriage to a named person. In such a case, the will becomes valid only upon the testator's marriage to that named person.

Testamentary Capacity and Knowledge and Approval of Contents of the Will

A testator must have testamentary capacity and must know and approve the contents of the will. Otherwise, the will can be set aside by a court after the testator's death. The concepts of testamentary capacity and knowledge and approval by the testator (as well as the related topics of fraud and undue influence) are dealt with in Part III, Estate Litigation, Chapter 15, Challenging the Validity of the Will.

Testamentary capacity is related to the soundness of the testator's mind. In brief, a person lacks testamentary capacity if he lacks any one of the following four elements at the time of giving instructions for the will and at the time of signing the will:

1. an understanding of what it means to make a will;
2. an understanding of the extent of his own property;
3. an understanding of the relationships he has with those persons who might be expected to receive a portion of his estate; and
4. an understanding of the claims of the persons whom he is leaving out of his will.

While it may be difficult to prove a lack of the first three elements, the concepts are fairly straightforward. The fourth area of necessary understanding or knowledge (sometimes called "the testator's knowledge of the true objects of his bounty") can be difficult to grasp. It may seem to imply that a testator is obliged by law to make gifts of his estate to those relatives who are closest to him. With the exception of a legal spouse or dependants (dealt with in Part III, Chapter 16, Statutory Forms of Estate Litigation), however, there is no obligation in law to leave one's estate to those who are closely related by blood or marriage. That is, a will cannot be set aside merely because it does not provide for gifts to close relatives. Nevertheless, if a testator has close relatives and there is no apparent reason for leaving them out of the will, a court may consider the fact that they do not appear in the will in deciding whether it should be presumed that the testator lacked testamentary capacity. As will be seen in Chapter 16, this presumption may be rebutted with other evidence tending to show that the testator did indeed have testamentary capacity.

The test of "knowledge and approval" generally relates to the question of whether the testator was fully aware of the contents of the will, particularly the disposition section. Thus, for example, if a testator did not understand that certain gifts were going to certain persons, she would likely fail the test of knowledge and approval.

Clearly there can be many cases where the questions of testamentary capacity and knowledge and approval are interdependent. For the present, however, it should be noted that, while often related in practice, the question whether the testator had testamentary capacity and whether he knew and approved of the contents of the will are dealt with in the law as separate inquiries. Again, as will be seen in Chapter 15, the questions of fraud and undue influence are also closely related to testamentary capacity and knowledge and approval, but are treated in the law as a distinct category.

Appointment of Estate Trustee with a Will

estate trustee with a will
person chosen by testator to oversee the administration of her estate

The **estate trustee with a will**, formerly known as the executor or executrix (see Chapter 2, Will Clauses), is a person who is chosen by the testator to oversee the administration of her estate. The estate trustee's job is to protect or secure and gather together the assets of the deceased, determine and pay the creditors of the estate, and, ultimately, pay the beneficiaries their respective shares of the estate in accordance with the will.

A clause appointing an estate trustee is not a necessity for a valid will but is a practical requirement. Leaving it out creates unnecessary delay, expense, and uncertainty in the administration of the estate. An estate trustee must be at least 18 years old and must not be an undischarged bankrupt. These are the only legal qualifications, but for practical reasons estate trustees should be individuals who are fairly sophisticated in dealing with money and other valuable property. Whether the will appoints someone or not, the court will always have the final say as to who is given the role of estate trustee. This topic is dealt with in more detail in Chapter 9, Applying for a Certificate of Appointment of Estate Trustee.

Unusual Wills

Joint Wills

joint will
rare form of will that is signed by two persons with respect to the disposal of their property after death

The **joint will** is a rare form of will that is recognized as legal in most jurisdictions. Such a will is signed by two persons, usually a married couple, with respect to the disposal of their property after death. Joint wills used to be created with the intention of saving the time and expense involved in creating two separate wills. Most lawyers practising today, however, avoid creating joint wills because of the awkwardness and difficulties that can arise in interpreting their terms. Furthermore, word processing has eliminated most of the perceived benefit of creating a joint will.

Multiple Wills or Split Wills

Normally, a subsequent will revokes any previous will, so that a testator has at any one time only one valid will. Occasionally, however, a testator has two or more wills that are intended to govern the estate concurrently. Such wills are called **multiple** or **split wills**. Split wills are fairly common in the case of testators who have property in two or more countries or jurisdictions (although see the section below on international wills), with each will dealing with property within a specific jurisdiction. Following the 1998 decision in the case of *Granovsky Estate v Ontario*, however, lawyers in Ontario now routinely advise certain clients to create split wills even though all of their property is in Ontario. The rationale for this is explained in more detail in Part II, Chapter 8, Preliminary Steps in Applying for a Certificate of Appointment of Estate Trustee, but basically split wills are intended to save estate administration tax and are often used by testators whose estates are likely to include privately held corporate shares with significant value. The decision in *Granovsky Estate v Ontario*[3] allows such testators to avoid the estate administration tax that would otherwise be payable on the value of the corporate shares by having the corporate shares distributed by a separate will. Split wills must contain the necessary language to identify themselves as split wills (that is, wills intended to coexist with one another) so that one of the two will not be misinterpreted as revoking the other.

multiple or split wills
two or more wills that are intended to govern an estate concurrently

International Wills

If a testator signs a will that is valid under Ontario law and purports to deal with the testator's entire estate, as far as Ontario law is concerned that will is sufficient to deal with the testator's entire estate wherever it is situated—that is, even if some of the testator's assets are outside Canada. Nevertheless, a foreign jurisdiction may have its own laws related to estates that are inconsistent with Ontario law and may require a different form of will. Where the Ontario will is not valid under the foreign country's laws, the estate trustee may not be able to deal with the assets situated in that foreign country using only the Ontario will. This problem was addressed by an international treaty in which the signatory countries agreed to enact legislation that recognizes a certain standardized form of will. Canada is one of the signatories and, accordingly, section 42 of the *Succession Law Reform Act* sets out the requirements of an international will.

Wills Made Pursuant to the Indian Act

Special provisions in the federal *Indian Act*,[4] sections 45 to 50.1, relate to the wills and estates of Indigenous peoples. Essentially, the *Indian Act* allows the minister of Indigenous and northern affairs to allow any written document signed by an Indigenous person to be construed as a valid will, and provides powers and guidelines for the interpretation of such wills and for the distribution of such estates. This book does not cover such wills and estates because they fall under a unique set of rules that differ from the laws of Ontario.

---

3 *Granovsky Estate v Ontario*, 1998 CanLII 14913 (Ont Sup Ct J).
4 RSC 1985, c I-5.

Amending Wills

There are two ways to amend a will: by making the changes on the face of the will itself, and by making a formal amending document called a codicil. Both are discussed below.

Making Changes on the Face of the Will

Making changes on the face of the will is a fairly simple process if the changes are made before the will is executed and if each change is initialled by the testator and both of the witnesses. The amended will as signed is no different conceptually from a will that was not altered. If there are no initials beside the changes, the question may be raised in the future whether the will was signed with or without the alterations. As will be seen in Chapter 9, the proper execution of a will has to be proven by way of an affidavit of execution. If there are uninitialled changes on the face of the will, a special form of affidavit of execution is required, in which the witness states under oath that the will was in the changed state before it was signed.

If, on the other hand, the will has already been signed before the alterations are made, making a valid amendment requires both the testator and two witnesses to sign the will "in the margin or in some other part of the will opposite or near the alteration." The witnesses to the alteration do not have to be the same as the witnesses to the original will. Alternatively, the testator and the two witnesses may sign at the end of or opposite "a memorandum referring to the alteration and written in some part of the will" (*Succession Law Reform Act*, section 18(2)(b)). Note that signatures of witnesses are not technically required for alterations to a holograph will or a will of a member of the Canadian Forces placed on active service; a member of any other naval, land, or air force while on active service; or a sailor at sea or in the course of a voyage. Again, however, in practical terms, a question may arise as to whether the testator made the alterations in question.

If an amendment to a will does not satisfy the requirements discussed above, it is invalid. One exception to this rule occurs where the amendment on the face of the will renders part of the will "no longer apparent." In such a case, the part of the will that is rendered no longer apparent is invalidated. Depending on the circumstances, a court may consider extrinsic evidence, such as a photocopy of the unamended will, to uphold the provision that would otherwise be invalidated.

Amending a Will Formally by Way of Codicil

codicil
formal document
that amends a will

A will can also be amended by a **codicil**, a formal document that is created and executed after the will has been executed, and that refers to the will that it is amending. Figure 1.2 is an example of a codicil. For a codicil to be valid, it must be created in accordance with all of the legal requirements for a valid will. All rules and exceptions pertaining to a will also pertain to a codicil. As can be seen from the example, a codicil must be signed by the testator and witnessed by two witnesses, who do not have to be the same as the witnesses to the original will. If it is proven that the testator does not have knowledge and approval of the contents of the codicil, the codicil will not be valid.

The only difference between a will and a codicil is that a codicil cannot stand on its own. It must be interpreted alongside the will to which it refers.

As can be seen from Figure 1.2, a codicil generally looks like a will, except that it refers to a specific will that is being amended and contains instructions for the amendments. If a will is not referred to in a codicil, the risk may arise that what is intended to be a codicil could instead end up being interpreted as a will. In that case, the codicil may revoke the previous will rather than amend it.

A codicil can be written in holograph form—that is, wholly in the handwriting of the testator and signed—and a holograph codicil can amend a non-holograph will. Similarly, a non-holograph codicil can amend a holograph will.

While a codicil can amend a previous codicil, many lawyers consider reading a will with successive codicils awkward and confusing. In this day of computers that can easily store, open, and amend drafts of clients' wills, some lawyers avoid using codicils altogether.

FIGURE 1.2   Codicil

THIS IS A FIRST CODICIL to the Last Will of me, **John Doe**, whose current residence address is 99 Anywhere Street, Hamilton, Ontario, Q9Q 9Q9, retired bank manager, my said Last Will having been executed on the 1st day of January 2018.

1. I hereby delete subclause 5(c)(A)(ii) and substitute following therefor the following:

    "(ii) any automobiles and any watercraft which I may own at the time of my death;"

2. In all other respects I confirm my said Last Will.

IN TESTIMONY WHEREOF I have to this Codicil written upon this and one single preceding page of paper hereunto subscribed my name this 1st day of May 2018.

SIGNED, PUBLISHED AND DECLARED   )
by JOHN DOE   )
as and for his last will and   )
testament, in the presence of   )
us, both present at the same   )
time, who at his request, in   )
his presence, and in the   )
presence of each other, have   )
hereunto subscribed our   )
names as witnesses:)
)   *John Doe*
)   _____
)   John Doe
Anne Torrie   )
_____   )
Anne Torrie   )

Talon Chatelain   )
_____   )
Talon Chatelain

Revoking and Reviving Wills

As stated, except in the case of international wills and split wills, a subsequent will revokes a previous will, provided that the subsequent will is intended to deal with all of the property of the deceased. There is no rule preventing a holograph will from revoking a standard will, and vice versa. A will can also be revoked by physically destroying it—by tearing, burning, or other means of destruction—provided that two conditions are satisfied: the will must be physically destroyed by the testator or someone under his direction and in his presence; and the act of destroying the will is intended by the testator to revoke the will.

A will or part of a will that has been revoked can be revived by a valid will or codicil indicating the intention to revive the previously revoked will or the part of the will previously revoked. Such a will need not set out the gifts in the previous will but need only indicate the intention that the previous gifts be reinstated. While there may be occasions when using such a procedure is unavoidable, for practical purposes it is not advisable in normal circumstances owing to the inherent logistical complications of proving the gifts. The previous will intended to be revived, for example, may have been destroyed.

Note too that under section 19(2) of the *Succession Law Reform Act*, unless a contrary intention is shown, if a will has been partly revoked, then afterward wholly revoked, and then revived, the revival does not extend to the part of the will that was originally revoked. In other words, only the last revocation is cancelled.

Finally, as will be seen in Chapter 3, Interpretation of Wills, revocations of wills and parts of wills can occur by operation of law, for example in the case of marriage or divorce of the testator.

Safekeeping of Wills

After a will that is prepared by a lawyer or law clerk is signed, the question may arise as to what should be done with the original. While some lawyers hand the original will to the client with instructions to keep it safe, many lawyers consider that this practice is not in the best interests of the client. Often clients lose important documents, and losing an original will can lead to many complications in the future. Another potential problem is the possibility that a client may, on his own, attempt to make changes to his will on the face of the original itself and, in the process, inadvertently alter the disposition clauses in a way not intended. Accordingly, many lawyers make it a practice to keep the original signed will in a fireproof vault for safekeeping and give the client a photocopy.

Lawyers who keep clients' original wills incur two ongoing obligations with respect to their safekeeping. First, the lawyer has the duty of confidentiality (reflected in Section 3.3 of the Law Society of Upper Canada *Rules of Professional Conduct*, reproduced in Figure 1.3). Second, the lawyer must keep the will safe from physical harm or loss (Section 3.5, also reproduced in Figure 1.3). These duties of course extend to the lawyer's entire staff.

FIGURE 1.3   Rules of Professional Conduct Relevant to the Safekeeping of Wills, Law Society of Upper Canada

Section 3.3 Confidentiality

3.3-1 A lawyer at all times shall hold in strict confidence all information concerning the business and affairs of the client acquired in the course of the professional relationship and shall not divulge any such information unless
   (a) expressly or impliedly authorized by the client;
   (b) required by law or by order of a tribunal of competent jurisdiction to do so;
   (c) required to provide the information to the Law Society; or
   (d) otherwise permitted by rules 3.3-2 to 3.3-6.

Commentary

… A lawyer owes the duty of confidentiality to every client without exception and whether or not the client is a continuing or casual client. The duty survives the professional relationship and continues indefinitely after the lawyer has ceased to act for the client, whether or not differences have arisen between them.

… [I]t is implied that a lawyer may, unless the client directs otherwise, disclose the client's affairs to partners and associates in the law firm and, to the extent necessary, to administrative staff and to others whose services are used by the lawyer. But this implied authority to disclose places the lawyer under a duty to impress upon associates, employees, and students and other licensees engaged under contract with the lawyer or with the firm of the lawyer the importance of non-disclosure (both during their employment and afterwards) and requires the lawyer to take reasonable care to prevent their disclosing or using any information that the lawyer is bound to keep in confidence.

Section 3.5 Preservation of Client's Property

3.5-2 A lawyer shall care of a client's property as a careful and prudent owner would when dealing with like property and shall observe all relevant rules and law about the preservation of a client's property entrusted to a lawyer.

Commentary

… The lawyer should keep the client's papers and other property out of sight as well as out of reach of those not entitled to see them and should, subject to any rights of lien, promptly return them to the client upon request or at the conclusion of the lawyer's retainer.

3.5-4 A lawyer shall clearly label and identify the client's property and place it in safekeeping distinguishable from the lawyer's own property.

3.5-5 A lawyer shall maintain such records as necessary to identify a client's property that is in the lawyer's custody.

3.5-6 A lawyer shall account promptly for a client's property that is in the lawyer's custody and upon request shall deliver it to the order of the client or, if appropriate, at the conclusion of the retainer.

3.5-7 If a lawyer is unsure of the proper person to receive a client's property, the lawyer shall apply to a tribunal of competent jurisdiction for direction.

Although the rule of confidentiality is probably the most often-quoted rule of professional conduct for lawyers, it is an important rule that is worth discussing. The duty extends indefinitely, whether the lawyer continues to act for the client or not. It also extends beyond the death of the client, although at that point the lawyer may be obligated to deal with the deceased client's estate trustee. Before the client dies, however, the lawyer may find herself in a quandary if the client's attorney under a power of attorney for property (discussed in Chapter 5, Powers of Attorney) asks to see the client's will, especially if the client himself instructs or has instructed the lawyer not to disclose the will. While the lawyer must follow the instructions of the client, the client may no longer be of sound mind when instructing the lawyer not to deal with the client's attorney. In addition, the client, when of sound mind, may have included a clause in the power of attorney for property authorizing and directing the attorney to review the client's will. There is no easy answer to such situations, and when they do arise, it is usually best for the lawyer to consult with the Law Society of Upper Canada. Issues of legal capacity of clients are dealt with in more detail in Chapter 5.

Note that where an estate trustee requests the will of a deceased testator or even requests to read it, proof of death of the testator must be obtained by the lawyer or law clerk before that request can be honoured. In addition, if an attorney under a power of attorney for property or an estate trustee of the deceased testator requests that the lawyer holding the original will hand the will over, it is essential that the lawyer or law clerk first determine whether the attorney or estate trustee is named solely as such in the power of attorney or will, and that the attorney or estate trustee is the first in line. If he or she is not solely named, the lawyer must insist that all named attorneys or estate trustees request the document, preferably in writing. If the attorney or estate trustee is not the first in line, the lawyer must insist that the circumstances necessary for the next in line to take over as attorney or estate trustee be verified—for example, by a death certificate of the first-named person. In addition, the lawyer or law clerk receiving such instructions should insist on seeing and preserving appropriate identification of the attorney(s) or estate trustee(s) making the request.

When a lawyer or law clerk prepares a subsequent will for a client, it is usually considered good practice not to destroy the previous (now revoked) will. It is, however, also good practice to keep a photocopy of the previous will because there is always a possibility that, despite all the best efforts of the lawyer, the testator may later be found not to have had the required legal capacity to sign the subsequent will. In that case, the previous will may still be the last valid will of that testator. The foregoing is, of course, subject to the instructions of the client.

Finally, it should be noted that pursuant to section 2 of the *Estates Act*,[5] the office of the local registrar of the Superior Court of Justice (that is, the local court office) is an available depository for the safekeeping of wills. The rules pertaining to the depositing, inspecting, and safekeeping of wills on such premises are set out in rule 74.02 of the *Rules of Civil Procedure*.[6]

---

5 RSO 1990, c E.21.

6 RRO 1990, reg 194.

Will Kits

Lawyers and law clerks are often asked to discuss will kits or to review wills created with the help of will kits. A valid will can be created with a will kit provided that the instructions are correct and are followed. A review of a will created with the use of a will kit requires more than a cursory review of the clauses to see that "everything looks all right." That is, the lawyer would likely be held professionally negligent if there were any misunderstanding on the part of the testator regarding a material provision in the will, whether that provision was discussed or not. If such a review is undertaken, therefore, it is essential that it be done conscientiously and that each clause be discussed in detail. This clearly takes time and energy on the part of the lawyer or law clerk; consequently, unless the review is performed on a pro bono basis, any money saved by the client in using the will kit will likely be eliminated.

"Living Wills"

Lawyers and law clerks are often asked about so-called living wills. What these usually refer to is a health care directive to a treating doctor or personal representative of the client directing the doctor not to keep the client alive by artificial means in the event that the client is under an extreme mental or physical disability with no reasonable hope of recovery.

Living wills are not wills as such. Furthermore, a will is not the most appropriate place in which to put a "living will" clause. As in the case of the donation of organs or other living tissue, the intent of the clause will be thwarted if, as is often the case, the will is not consulted until perhaps days after the testator's death. Living wills are discussed in Chapter 5, because it is generally accepted in Ontario that the most appropriate place for a living will is within the body of a power of attorney for personal care.

Client Copy of Will

As indicated above, the lawyer usually keeps the original will and gives the client testator a photocopy. The testator can then review his will periodically without having to contact the lawyer. Whether the copy is kept in a safety deposit box or other safe place, it is a good practice to keep a list of assets (including any digital assets and possibly user names or passwords necessary to access them) and ongoing liabilities, and their particulars, with the copy of the will. These particulars include bank account information—the addresses of the banks where the testator has accounts and the account numbers. The lawyer often asks for this information from the client when preparing the will, but the list is merely a snapshot of the person's assets at that point in time. As will be seen in later chapters, the practice of keeping an up-to-date list of assets and liabilities can be very helpful to an estate trustee after the death of the testator.

Other papers that can be kept with the copy of the will include copies of any powers of attorney the client has made and the contact information of the lawyer who has possession of the original will and powers of attorney.

KEY TERMS

REVIEW QUESTIONS

1. What does it mean to administer an estate?

2. Define the following terms or concepts:

   a. will

   b. holograph will

   c. joint will

   d. multiple/split wills

   e. international will

   f. living will

   g. codicil

   h. testator/testatrix

   i. executor/executrix

   j. estate trustee with a will

3. What are the formal requirements of a valid will?

4. What form of signature is advisable?

5. Where does the signature have to be?

6. When can someone else sign a will for you?

7. Who can witness a will and how many witnesses should there be?

8. When are witnesses not required?

9. What are the legal requirements of a testator?

10. What is meant by the term "testamentary capacity"?

11. How does someone become an estate trustee with a will?

12. In what two ways can you amend a will?

13. Name three ways that a person can revoke her will?

14. How can a will be revived?

15. What are the lawyer's two main duties in the safekeeping of wills for clients?

16. What should be done with a will that has been revoked?

17. What government official will accept deposit of a will for safekeeping?

18. Are wills created with kits valid? Explain.

19. What should a client do with the original will and with a copy?

Will Clauses

2

LEARNING OUTCOMES

After completing this chapter, you should be able to:

- Explain the features of each clause in the sample will provided

- Explain the difference between a precatory and a mandatory memorandum

- Explain some unusual will clauses, including their limitations

Introduction

There is no single, preferable way to draft a will; in fact, wills take many forms. This chapter presents a clause-by-clause discussion of the sample will shown in Chapter 1, Wills (Figure 1.1). Keep in mind that this is only one form of will—for example, while each clause in this will has a heading, some wills have no headings. To a certain extent, the appearance of a will is the result of the personal choice of the lawyer or law clerk in charge of drafting it. The client, however, must always have the final say in what is contained in the will. Each client must be interviewed carefully to determine fully her circumstances and wishes before the will is drafted. Some lawyers use personal data sheets, which the client fills out and returns, to assist with the preparation of a will. Many lawyers and law clerks also use checklists to assist them in interviewing the client when taking instructions for the drafting of a will. Such checklists can be invaluable to the lawyer or law clerk to make sure that appropriate questions are asked, the answers to which might have a bearing on how the will is drafted. An example of one such checklist is reproduced in Figure 2.1. In any particular case, the so-called standard clauses in the client's will—such as the example included in this chapter—may be modified or left out depending on the client's individual wishes and instructions. Clients should be advised, however, that while some of the clauses may not seem to apply to their present circumstances, things may change in the future. The challenge for lawyers and law clerks in drafting a will is to attempt to preserve the client's basic estate plan in the light of future circumstances that are not yet known.

An area that can often be overlooked by clients is the potential for conflict between estate trustees and beneficiaries. For this reason, it is important to build safeguards into the will to deal with such potential conflict. As will be seen in Part II, Estate Administration, Chapter 9, Applying for a Certificate of Appointment of Estate Trustee, it is usually only during the administration of the estate—that is, after the testator dies and before the estate is distributed—that the beneficiaries named in the will have a chance to review its terms. With this in mind, many clauses in a well-drafted will are directed, at least partially, at those future beneficiaries.

Standard Will Clauses

Identification

Figure 2.2 reproduces the identification clause of the sample will in Chapter 1. Although not technically necessary for the validity of the will, this clause is useful in identifying the testator, setting out his address at the time of signing the will, and giving his occupation. As will be seen in Part II, such information can be useful to an estate trustee when administering the estate.

Revocation

A new, valid will automatically revokes any previous will made by the testator unless the new will explicitly states that it is not intended to revoke the previous will. Nevertheless, many wills contain a revocation clause. Figure 2.3 reproduces the revocation clause of the sample will in Chapter 1. Although this clause is not necessary if the will is drafted

FIGURE 2.1   Checklist

Will Instructions

Basic Information	☐ Previous Marriages:
Date: _____	How/When Terminated _____ _____
Name: _____	☐ Court Order Copy ☐ Separation Agreement Copy ☐ Children of
Address: _____	
Occupation: _____	☐ Children: Names, Ages, Residence
Marital Status: _____	

Executors and Custodians	Disposition

Executors: Name(s)
     Address ☐ outside of Ontario
     Age
     Occupation
	☐ Is there a contract respecting will
	
	 Specific Bequests:

Substitute Executors: Name(s)
     Address ☐ outside of Ontario
     Age
     Occupation
	Residue:
	
	 ☐ Gift Over to (family disaster) to:

Explain: ☐ Duties ☐ Executor's Year
          ☐ Compensation ☐ Debts
          ☐ Trust Clauses ☐ Sell, Invest
	☐ Born in Wedlock clause?
	 ☐ Spendthrift Trust
	          ☐ Age for Control of Gift: 18, 21, 25, other
	          ☐ Saunders v. Vautier (gift over)

☐ Custodians: Name(s)
     Address
     Age
     Occupation
     ☐ 90 day rule explained
	☐ Memorandum:
	          ☐ yes ☐ no ☐ precatory ☐ binding
	 ☐ FLA exclusion

Assets & Liabilities	

☐ Any Foreign Assets
 ☐ Home ☐ Mge _____
 ☐ Other Real Estate ☐ Mge _____
 ☐ Bank Assets
 ☐ Accounts
 ☐ Term Deposits/GICs
 ☐ CSBs
 ☐ Stocks/Bonds
 ☐ RRSP ☐ RRIF
 ☐ Pensions   ☐ CPP-H ☐ CPP-W
          ☐ Employment _____
          ☐ Veterans or Gov't_____
          ☐ Other _____
	☐ Insurance _____
	 ☐ Owner of Corporate Shares
	          ☐ All the Shares
	          ☐ Does the Corporation Own Assets
	 ☐ Joint assets
	 ☐ Safety Deposit Box _____
	 ☐ Pre-Paid Funeral _____
	 ☐ Burial Plot _____
	 ☐ Debts Owing to You _____
	 _____
	 ☐ Debts Owing by You _____
	 _____
	 ☐ Other Assets _____
	 ☐ Other Liabilities _____

FIGURE 2.2   Identification Clause

THIS IS THE LAST WILL AND TESTAMENT of me, **John Doe**, whose current residence address is 99 Anywhere Street, Hamilton, Ontario, Q9Q 9Q9, retired bank manager.

FIGURE 2.3   Revocation Clause

1. REVOCATION

I revoke all previous wills.

carefully, it is usually included as reassurance to the estate trustees and beneficiaries that the present will is the only will that needs to be consulted in the administration of the estate. Note that if the testator is attempting to create this will as one of two split wills (see Chapter 1), this clause will be amended to indicate that all previous wills except the other split will are to be revoked.

Interpretation Clause

Figure 2.4 reproduces the interpretation clause of the sample will. Like many other clauses included in this sample will, it is not necessary but is advisable because it minimizes the risk of disputes among beneficiaries, estate trustees, and third parties. This clause attempts to define as many as possible of the terms used in the will that may be open to more than one interpretation.

The interpretation clause states that the term "executor" may be used in place of "estate trustee with a will" and "trustee" as the context requires. Changes in Ontario law have replaced the terms "executor" and the female "executrix" with the term "estate trustee with a will." Despite this change, most other jurisdictions still use the term "executor" and indeed, most people and institutions in Ontario prefer this term.

This clause also states that "child" and "children" are to include only the named children of the testator. This statement can be valuable for a number of reasons. First, "child" can be interpreted as someone under the age of majority, but naming the adult children of the testator removes this possibility. Second, such a statement closes the door to anyone else claiming to be a child of the testator, perhaps born out of wedlock. This may be particularly relevant where the disposition clause of the will (discussed below) is worded in a generic way—for example, "to divide my estate equally among my children." In this connection, as will be seen in Chapter 3, Interpretation of Wills, the *Children's Law Reform Act*[1] specifies that, unless a contrary intention appears in the will, any reference to "children" shall be deemed to include, among other things, children of the person born out of wedlock. Of course, the testator may wish to include any children falling within this expanded definition of "child," in which case this clause would be amended or left out of the will. Note, too, that if there is any possibility that the testator may have more children born in wedlock in the future, whom he wishes to include in his will, but still wants to eliminate the

---

1 RSO 1990, c C.12.

possibility of paternal bloodline litigation, the definition of "children" can be altered to indicate something more general, such as "my children born in wedlock."

Direction to Estate Trustee to Pay Debts

Figure 2.5 reproduces the clause from the sample will dealing with the payment of debts. A direction to the estate trustees to pay the debts of the deceased and of the estate is not necessary given that this obligation exists in law whether or not it is contained in the will and despite anything written in the will to the contrary. Nevertheless, this clause serves to remind the estate trustees that they have this obligation and also reminds them that they have a general discretion to defer payment of debts and to make any decisions or elections under income tax law for the purpose of paying or deferring such debts. Again, these discretions do not depend on the will for their existence, but their presence in the will serves to notify everyone concerned that such discretions and obligations exist.

FIGURE 2.4 **Interpretation Section**

2. INTERPRETATION

Where used in this document,

(a) "executor" shall be interchangeable with the term "estate trustee with a will," shall be deemed to include "trustee" if a trust fund has been established, to be pluralized if more than one executor has been named, and to include all genders as the context in each case requires;

(b) the singular, masculine, or personal pronoun shall be construed as meaning the plural, gender, or body corporate as the context in each case requires;

(c) paragraph headings are for reference purposes only and shall not define, limit, extend, or otherwise affect the meaning of any term or provision;

(d) "pay" shall be deemed to include "transfer" and "deliver" as the context in each case requires;

(e) "child" or "children" shall be deemed to include only my daughter, Jennifer Doe, and my sons, Steven Doe and John Doe Jr.

FIGURE 2.5 **Payment of Debts Clause**

3. PAYMENT OF DEBTS AND TAXES

I direct my executor or executors to pay as soon as convenient after my death all debts, funeral and testamentary expenses and taxes that my estate is legally bound to pay, or to commute, prepay or defer payment of such debts or taxes as my executor or executors may in his, her, or their sole and absolute discretion consider advisable, and I hereby empower my executor or executors to make any election, determination, or designation pursuant to the *Income Tax Act* or any other taxing statute or any regulation pursuant thereto.

While the estate trustee does have the power to defer debts, any prejudice to the creditors of the estate that occurs as a result of such deferral may be actionable against the estate trustees personally. For a more thorough discussion of the estate trustee's obligation to pay debts of the estate and the consequences of not paying them, see Part II, Estate Administration, and Part III, Estate Litigation.

Appointment of Estate Trustee

Figure 2.6 reproduces the clause from the sample will nominating and appointing the estate trustees (referred to in this will as executors). As will be seen in Part II, Chapter 9, if a nomination of an estate trustee is left out of a will, the beneficiaries will most likely have to get together and decide which of them should be the estate trustee, keeping in mind priorities given to certain individuals under the *Estates Act*.[2] Even once that decision is made, however, there is little chance that the estate could be administered without the involvement of the court. This topic is covered in more detail under Part II.

In Figure 2.6, alternate estate trustees are named. This is because it cannot be known at the time of executing the will whether any particular estate trustee will be willing or able to act as trustee at the time of the death of the testator. Most lawyers therefore consider it advisable to name at least one alternate estate trustee, and sometimes more than one.

As can be seen, Figure 2.6 names two alternate estate trustees, and the second alternate is two persons acting jointly. When two or more estate trustees are named jointly, and both or all are willing and able to act, they act together.

FIGURE 2.6   Appointment of Trustee Clause

4.   APPOINTMENT OF EXECUTOR

I appoint my spouse, JANE DOE, to be the sole executor of my estate. If my executor first named has not survived me by thirty days or is unable or unwilling to act, then I appoint as my executor my daughter, JENNIFER DOE. If my said daughter is unable or unwilling to act as my executor then I appoint as my executors my son, STEVEN DOE and my friend, JOHN DEW, acting jointly.

Disposition

disposition clause
instructions regarding how an estate is to be distributed among the beneficiaries

Figure 2.7 reproduces the **disposition clause** of the sample will. This is an essential clause because a will is not considered a will unless it contains some form of disposition. The example indicates that a gift of the entire estate is to be made to the testator's spouse (clause 5(b)) and, in the alternative, such gift is to be distributed among the testator's three children (clause 5(c)). These gifts are stated to be subject to clauses 6 and 7, which appear later in the will and are explained below.

As can be seen, all of the gifts are subject to the condition that the beneficiary must survive the testator by at least 30 days. Many lawyers consider such a clause advisable

---

2   RSO 1990, c E.21.

because of the possibility that the testator and the beneficiary may die within a short period of each other, as in the case of a car accident. If an asset belongs to the testator and is gifted on her death to a beneficiary, who then dies shortly after, the asset has to be administered or transferred three times—first into the estate of the deceased, then to the beneficiary's estate, and then to that deceased beneficiary's own beneficiary. The clause in question is designed to minimize this risk.

Another risk that this clause is typically designed to eliminate is that of unequal distribution of assets of the collective estate of deceased spouses to their respective next of kin. Many spouses desire to leave gifts to their own siblings or other family members in the event that their spouse and children do not survive them. Without the 30-day clause, the families of the last of the two spouses to die would receive the entire collective estate of the two deceased spouses even if the two died a short time apart.

Some lawyers prefer to use a length of time greater than or less than 30 days. Such decisions must be made by balancing the above-noted risks against the risk that the beneficiary may be in need of the assets of the deceased very soon after the death of the deceased, even if that beneficiary continues to live for only a short time. In this regard, it is possible to include a provision in the will that gives the estate trustee the discretion to make payments to the surviving beneficiary for any needs that the beneficiary may have during the waiting period.

FIGURE 2.7   Disposition Clause

5. DISPOSITION

I give all the residue of my property, both real and personal, and including any property over which I may have a general power of appointment, to the executor or executors UPON THE FOLLOWING TRUSTS, namely:

    (a) to divide all articles of a personal, domestic, or household use or ornament or works of art in accordance with a List or Memorandum signed by me, which I may leave among my personal papers or attached to a copy of this my Last Will;

    (b) to give the entire residue of my estate to my spouse, JANE DOE, provided she survives me by thirty days;

    (c) if my said spouse has failed to survive me by thirty days, to distribute my estate as follows:

        (A) provided that she survives me by thirty days, to give to my daughter, JENNIFER DOE, the following:

            (i) any real property which I may own at the time of my death, including houses and their respective contents;

            (ii) any automobiles which I may own at the time of my death;

        (B) to divide the residue of my estate equally between the following who survive me, share and share alike, subject to clauses 6 and 7, below;

            (i) my son, JOHN DOE JR., provided he survives me by thirty days;

            (ii) my son, STEVEN DOE, provided he survives me by thirty days.

As will be seen in Chapter 3, even without the 30-day clause, there are provisions in the *Succession Law Reform Act*[3] that apply in a similar way in circumstances where two or more persons (not necessarily spouses) die at the same time or in circumstances where it is impossible to determine who died first. It is important to note, however, that such provisions are limited in that they apply only where the deaths are simultaneous or where it cannot be known which of the persons died first.

In the sample disposition clause, the gifts to the sons are **residual gifts**—that is, the sons share in everything that is left over in the estate after the debts and the gifts to the other beneficiaries are paid. The implications of giving residual gifts (and other kinds of gifts) are discussed in Chapter 3.

Clause (a) of the disposition clause in the sample will refers to a **memorandum** prepared by the testator that lists beneficiaries of specific items. If the memorandum is made before the date on which the will is executed and is referred to in the will, as here, it becomes part of the will. The estate trustee is then obligated to give the specified gifts to the beneficiaries named. In such a case, the memorandum is said to be a **mandatory memorandum** (or a "legal memorandum," as it is sometimes referred to).

If, on the other hand, the memorandum is created after the execution of the will, even if it is referred to in the will, as here, it is not binding on the estate trustee. In other words, the estate trustee cannot be held liable for not giving the specified items to the designated beneficiaries. In such a case, the memorandum is said to be a **precatory memorandum**. While a precatory memorandum is not binding, it can be helpful to an estate trustee when dealing with assets of a personal nature that are not gifted to any particular person under the will and that do not have significant financial value. An estate trustee could be liable if he follows a precatory memorandum to the financial prejudice of a creditor of the estate or a beneficiary under the will.

Figure 2.8 is an example of a precatory memorandum for the will discussed in this chapter. Although there is no legal requirement that a mandatory memorandum be signed and dated, both signing and dating it are advisable. The signing of the memorandum allows it to be proven as the testator's memorandum, and the dating helps to establish whether the memorandum is mandatory or precatory. A memorandum with nothing written on it but the names of beneficiaries and their gifts will likely be considered binding if it is left with the will and if it is proven to have been prepared before the execution of the will. Nevertheless, to avoid uncertainty, it is advisable to instruct a client preparing a memorandum to put her name and the words "this is the memorandum referred to in my will dated [so and so]" somewhere on the document.

Lineal Descendants

Figure 2.9 reproduces the lineal descendants clause. As indicated in the disposition clause, the gifts to the beneficiaries are subject to this clause and clause 7. This clause is an extension of the disposition clause, and it could have been included under the heading "Disposition" in the will. For ease of reading of the disposition clause, however, this clause is kept separate. It simply specifies that if any children of the testator predecease the testator, leaving children of their own, the deceased child's own children will divide the share that

residual gift gift to a beneficiary that is left over in the estate after the debts and the gifts to other beneficiaries are paid

memorandum document added to the will that lists beneficiaries of specific items

mandatory memorandum binding memorandum that is made before the will is executed and is referred to in the will

precatory memorandum non-binding memorandum that is made after the will is executed and may or may not be referred to in the will

3   RSO 1990, c S.26.

otherwise would have gone to the parent (the child of the testator). If a child of the testator dies without leaving children, only then will the directions set out in the disposition clause take effect to leave that deceased child's share to the surviving children of the testator.

FIGURE 2.8   Precatory Memorandum

This is the memorandum referred to in my will dated January 1, 2018.

> I want my granddaughter, Lisa, to receive my gold watch that I got from the bank.
> I want my granddaughter, Susan, to receive my woodworking tools.
> I want my grandson, John, to receive my aquarium equipment.

Dated March 10, 2018.

John Doe
_____
John Doe

FIGURE 2.9   Lineal Descendants Clause

6.   LINEAL DESCENDANT OR DESCENDANTS OF DECEASED CHILD

If any child of mine who has been given a benefit herein dies before final distribution of my estate, leaving one or more lineal descendant or descendants then alive, such deceased child shall be considered alive for purposes of distribution hereunder and my executor or executors shall make the gift or distribution to which such deceased child would have been entitled, if she had not so died, to such lineal descendant or descendants by representation.

Testamentary Trust

The clause reproduced in Figure 2.10 creates what is called a testamentary trust for any beneficiaries who may be under the age of 18 or mentally incapacitated. Trusts are discussed in more detail in Chapter 6, Trusts. A **testamentary trust** is one that is set up by the will of the testator and commences after the death of the testator, provided that the preconditions under which the trust is set up exist. In Figure 2.10, the precondition for the trust is that any particular beneficiary is under the age of 18 or mentally incapacitated at the time of the testator's death.

Briefly, a **trust** is a means by which money or property can be held by an individual or an institution (the trustee) for the benefit of another (the beneficiary) according to the rules governing the trust. In Figure 2.10, the estate trustee is also appointed the trustee of the testamentary trust. In other words, the estate trustee is the person who must administer the estate but must also administer or manage the trust funds in accordance with the rules of the trust. The rules in the sample will are fairly simple: the trustee is to hold the trust money

testamentary trust
trust that is set up by the will of a testator and commences after the death of the testator, provided that the preconditions under which the trust is to be set up exist

trust
means by which money or property can be held by an individual or an institution (the trustee) for the benefit of another (the beneficiary) according to the rules governing the trust

(the amount of the gift that would have gone to the beneficiary of the will but for the fact that the beneficiary is under 18 or mentally incapacitated), and to pay to any person or institution on behalf of the beneficiary the income from that money, or a portion of the principal amount of that money, provided that the trustee considers that the payment is advisable for the benefit, education, or general welfare of the beneficiary. In this particular testamentary trust, the decision whether to pay the income or part of the principal is left to the trustee. Other clauses of the will, discussed below, provide additional guidelines.

FIGURE 2.10   Testamentary Trust

7. AGE OR OTHER DISABILITY

If any person who becomes entitled to any share in my estate is under the age of majority or incapable of executing a release or under any other legal disability, my executor or executors shall hold and keep invested the share of such person and use the income and capital, or so much of either, as my executor or executors may in his, her, or their absolute discretion consider advisable for the maintenance, education, or benefit of such person until he or she is no longer incapable or under such age or disability and shall then distribute such share or the balance thereof remaining to such person, but in the meantime I authorize my executor or executors to make any payment for or on behalf of any such person which my executor or executors in his, her, or their sole discretion consider it advisable as a payment for the benefit, education, or general welfare of such person, and the receipt of any payee in those circumstances is a sufficient discharge to my executor or executors.

The reason for this trust is that a beneficiary under the age of 18 does not have the legal capacity to give a receipt for a gift under a will. If an estate trustee were to simply deliver a gift to a beneficiary under the age of 18, the beneficiary could make a valid claim for receipt of her gift once again upon reaching the age of 18. In such a case, the estate trustee would likely be held personally liable for the amount of the gift. The trust clause establishes a mechanism for the gift to be held until the beneficiary attains the age of 18. As discussed in more detail in Chapter 6, Trusts, this clause can specify an age beyond 18 for the final gift to take place but in such a case, care must be taken to structure the trust correctly in order to obtain the intended result.

Similarly, a beneficiary who is mentally incapacitated is unable to legally receive a gift under a will. In the absence of a testamentary trust in a will, where there is a gift to an underage or to a mentally incapacitated beneficiary who does not already have an attorney under a power of attorney or a person appointed by the court as guardian of his property, the Office of the Attorney General would likely assume control of the gift for the benefit of that beneficiary. In the case of an underage beneficiary, the branch of the Office of the Attorney General involved would be the Office of the Children's Lawyer, and in the case of a mentally incapacitated beneficiary, the branch would be the Office of the Public Guardian and Trustee.

As will be seen in Chapter 6, trusts are set up for reasons other than avoiding the involvement of the Children's Lawyer or the Public Guardian and Trustee. For example, a person may wish to have a trustee look after funds that are gifted to a beneficiary who is over 18. Although such trust arrangements can be made, if not done properly they may not have their intended effect.

Note that the testator does not have to appoint the same person to be the estate trustee with a will and the trustee of the testamentary trust. They often are the same person, however, because many lawyers feel that nominating separate individuals or entities can become difficult and cumbersome in the administration of the estate and the trust.

Power to Invest

Figure 2.11 reproduces the power to invest clause. This clause provides a general discretion to the estate trustee when dealing with assets that are held in the estate or in a testamentary trust. Generally, the assets of the deceased may be held in the estate for approximately one year while the estate trustee is administering the estate. This is known as "the executor's year." In the case of a testamentary trust, the assets may be held for a considerably longer period, and as in the case of a mentally incapacitated beneficiary, they may be held indefinitely—that is, for the lifetime of the beneficiary.

FIGURE 2.11   Power to Invest Clause

8. POWER TO INVEST

I authorize my executor or executors to make investments and otherwise deal with my estate (including property held for persons below a stipulated age or under any other legal disability) and to exercise any rights, powers, and privileges that may at any time exist with respect thereto to the same extent and as fully as I could if I were the living sole owner thereof as he, she, or they in his, her, or their absolute discretion consider to be in the best interests of my estate and the beneficiaries thereof.

As will be seen in Part II, during this period of time that the assets are held, the estate trustee has an obligation to the beneficiaries of the estate and of any testamentary trusts to see that the funds are reasonably invested. This clause, then, serves to remind estate trustees that they have such obligations toward the beneficiaries. The clause also reminds the beneficiaries and third parties that the estate trustee has the same rights to invest the assets as the deceased would have had if she were alive.

As with many clauses in this will, this particular clause is not technically necessary, but because the will is made at a time when it is impossible to know what circumstances will exist at the time of the testator's death, such clauses are usually considered advisable.

Power of Sale

Figure 2.12 reproduces the power of sale clause. This clause is a response to section 17 of the *Estates Administration Act*,[4] which states that real estate owned by an estate cannot be sold unless it is for the purpose of paying the debts of the estate or unless a majority of the beneficiaries representing at least a one-half interest in the real estate who are entitled to a portion of that real estate, by way of residual gift or otherwise, consent in writing. Section 17 goes on, however, to allow this requirement of obtaining consent to be overridden with

---

4   RSO 1990, c E.22.

a power of sale clause in the will such as the example provided. Most lawyers therefore consider it to be inadvisable to leave a clause similar to this one out of a will. The reason, of course, is that the estate is much more difficult, time-consuming, and expensive to administer when consent of the beneficiaries is required at any particular stage. It will be seen in Part II, Chapter 12, Accounting to the Beneficiaries and Paying the Beneficiaries, that releases from the beneficiaries are usually sought as well, but this is only toward the end of the administration, when most or all of the estate trustee's work has been completed.

FIGURE 2.12   Power of Sale Clause

9. POWER OF SALE

I authorize my executor or executors to use his, her, or their discretion in the realization of my estate with power to sell, call in, and convert into money any part of my estate not consisting of money at such time or times, in such manner and upon such terms and either for cash or credit or for part cash or part credit as he, she, or they may in his, her, or their uncontrolled discretion decide upon, or to postpone such conversion of my estate or any part or parts thereof for such length of time as he, she, or they may think best or to retain any portion of my estate in the form in which it may be at my death (notwithstanding that it may not be in the form of an investment in which executors are authorized to invest trust funds and whether or not there is a liability attached to any such portion of my estate) for such length of time as my executor or executors shall in his, her, or their complete discretion deem advisable, and my executor or executors shall not be held personally responsible for any loss that may occur to my estate by reason of his, her, or their so doing.

A client may indicate to the lawyer that this clause is not needed. Either the client does not own real estate or she may be giving—"devising"—any real estate that she does own to a specific beneficiary. In either case, the client may say that there is no need for any real estate to be sold by the estate. Although the client always has the final say on how her will shall read, it should be pointed out to her that a will is an attempt to lay down rules and guidelines that will take effect at some future time, when unforeseen events and circumstances may have intervened. For example, it may be that the client acquires real estate after executing the will, either intentionally or by inheritance, or the intended devisee of the real estate may have predeceased the testator. For these reasons, then, it is usually advisable to have a power of sale clause in almost every will.

Discretion to Pay or Divide

Figure 2.13 reproduces the discretion to pay or divide clause. This clause, like many others giving discretion to the estate trustee, is designed to prevent any disputes among estate trustees, beneficiaries, and third parties. Although very generally worded, it is designed to address the very specific situation where a number of items in an estate belong together— for example, a table and chairs. The clause gives an estate trustee the discretion to keep the set together to retain its value—that is, to insist that it be given to one particular person.

This clause can be very comforting to an estate trustee in circumstances where disputes may arise among beneficiaries who are given the contents of a house and must decide among themselves as to their division. It is, incidentally, usually inadvisable to make a gift of "the contents of my house" because many disputes can arise about the meaning of "contents"—or example, does "contents" include cash or securities? A good will is much more specific.

FIGURE 2.13 Discretion to Pay Clause

10. DISCRETION TO PAY OR DIVIDE

Except as herein expressly stated to the contrary, my executor or executors may make any division of my estate or set aside or pay any share or interest wholly or in part in the assets forming part of my estate at the time of my death or at the time of such division, setting aside, or payment, and I declare that where there may be some question of the value of any part of my estate my executor or executors may in his, her, or their absolute discretion fix the value of my estate or any part or parts thereof for the purpose of making any such division, setting aside, or payment, and his, her, or their decision shall be final and binding upon all persons concerned.

Authority Binding

The authority binding clause, reproduced in Figure 2.14, is included as a final catchall clause to establish further that the estate trustee is to be given maximum discretion in administering the estate. As will be seen in Part II, however, despite what is said in clauses granting discretion, such as this one, the estate trustee does have limits on exercising such discretion in administering the estate. The estate trustee must follow proper procedures and must not take advantage of unsophisticated beneficiaries. Where questions arise about the proper exercise of discretion by the estate trustee, a court will use common sense, legislation, and case law to decide whether he or she has crossed the line. Nevertheless, it is generally considered to be good estate planning to give an estate trustee, once he or she has been carefully chosen, the greatest discretion possible so that the estate can be administered as efficiently as possible.

FIGURE 2.14 Authority Binding Clause

11. AUTHORITY BINDING

Any exercise by my executor or executors of the authority or discretion conferred on him, her, or them shall be binding on all beneficiaries of my estate whether or not such exercise would have the effect of conferring an advantage on any one or more of them at the expense of any other or could otherwise be considered but for the foregoing as not being an impartial exercise by my executor or executors of his, her, or their duties, powers, and discretions or as not maintaining an even hand among the beneficiaries.

Family Law Act

Figure 2.15 reproduces the clause entitled "Exclusion of Benefits from Community of Property" from the sample will. This clause, which can also be called the *Family Law Act* clause, is included for the purpose of protecting beneficiaries who may be undergoing or contemplating divorce proceedings or who may be facing such proceedings in the future. The *Family Law Act*[5] sets out a scheme for dividing up matrimonial property upon the breakdown of a marriage.

FIGURE 2.15 Family Law Act Clause

12. EXCLUSION OF BENEFITS FROM COMMUNITY OF PROPERTY

All income from property given by me to any beneficiary who is, at my death, a spouse within the meaning of the *Family Law Act* or any similar legislation of another jurisdiction shall be excluded from the net family property of such beneficiary.

The scheme is outlined in detail in Part III, Chapter 16, Statutory Forms of Estate Litigation, under the topic of the *Family Law Act* election for the surviving spouse of the testator. Briefly, however, it is as follows: in the absence of a valid domestic contract to the contrary, the matrimonial property of a married couple is divided upon breakdown of the marriage by adding up the net value of the assets and liabilities that each spouse owns and owes on the date of the breakdown and subtracting from that sum the net value of all of the assets and liabilities that each spouse brought into the marriage.

Excluded from the calculation is the value of any real estate brought into the marriage that becomes the matrimonial home and is such on the date of separation. That is, if a spouse owned a home on the date of marriage and it became the matrimonial home, that spouse is not entitled to take credit for owning it before the marriage. The result of the calculation is the spouse's net value. When the calculations of net family property are completed, the spouse whose net value is greater pays to the other spouse whatever amount is necessary to make their net values equal—that is, one-half of the difference between their two values.

The important point here is that before each spouse's net value is determined, she or he is entitled to deduct certain items. One such deduction is the value of any property received by way of gift or bequest, provided that such property remains identifiable and is not subsequently mixed with jointly owned property. For example, if a spouse inherits $100,000 during the marriage and keeps it in her own separate bank account, upon a division of matrimonial property she does not have to include it in the calculation of her net value. If the spouse did have to include such money in the calculation, she would, in a sense, be sharing it with her spouse upon the breakdown of the marriage.

The *Family Law Act* goes on to state that, while gifts and bequests are to be excluded from the calculation of net family property, any income from such gifts or bequests is to be factored in unless the gifts or bequests are given with the expressed intention that such income be excluded. In other words, using the above example, if a spouse inherits $100,000

---

5 RSO 1990, c F.3.

and puts it in a separate bank account, while she does not have to include the $100,000 in calculating her net family property, she will have to include the interest earned on that amount unless the will under which she inherited states otherwise. This clause in the sample will indicates that the income from any gift given to any beneficiaries is to be excluded from the calculation of net family property.

Custody

The custody clause, reproduced in Figure 2.16, is discussed in more detail in Chapter 3. Such a clause is not considered binding because custody of children is not proprietary but is entirely within the jurisdiction of the court. Nevertheless, this kind of clause is often included because it can be helpful to a court in deciding who will be custodian in the event that a child's natural parents are deceased or unable to act as custodians and there is a dispute over custody. It should be noted that there is a distinction to be drawn between custody of a child, as referred to in this clause, and guardianship of a child's property, which is a form of trust.

Generally, custody clauses in wills are considered binding for 90 days only, and even during this period a court can overrule such a clause if in the opinion of the court it is in the best interests of the children to do so.

FIGURE 2.16   Custody Clause

13. CUSTODY OF CHILDREN

If I die before all of my children are over the age of eighteen years and if my spouse has predeceased me or failed to survive me by thirty days, or if she has survived me but is deemed not competent to provide proper care and support for any of my surviving children under the *Mental Health Act* of Ontario, or any similar statute or law, I give custody of my surviving children to my sister, Mary Doe, and if my said sister is unable or unwilling to act as custodian of my said surviving children, I give custody of my surviving children to my friend, Ruth Smith. I wish it to be known that the custodians appointed above were chosen after a thorough and careful examination of all alternatives.

Testimonium

This part of the will, reproduced in Figure 2.17, is also not technically necessary, although it is useful because it helps to establish that the document in question is intended to be a will. The clause also provides a convenient place to put the date of the will, which is useful in determining whether it is the latest will or not.

FIGURE 2.17   Testimonium

IN TESTIMONY WHEREOF I have to this my last will and testament written upon this and three preceding pages of paper hereunto subscribed my name this 1st day of January 2018.

Signatures

The signature clause from the sample will is reproduced in Figure 2.18. While the signature of the testator and the signatures of the witnesses are necessary for the validity of the will (unless the will is a holograph will, in which case the latter are not necessary), the signatures need not be set out in the way indicated in this clause. As explained in Chapter 1, the signature of the testator must be at the foot or end of the will, but the *Succession Law Reform Act* is silent as to where the signatures of the witnesses should appear. Nevertheless, it is considered good practice to have the witnesses sign beside or underneath the signature of the testator. This clause helps to ensure that the signatures end up in the correct place.

FIGURE 2.18   Signatures

SIGNED, PUBLISHED AND DECLARED)
by **JOHN DOE**)
as and for his last will and)
testament, in the presence of)
us, both present at the same)
time, who at his request, in)
his presence, and in the)
presence of each other, have)
hereunto subscribed our)
names as witnesses:)
)
) *John Doe*
) _____
) John Doe
)
Mary Breshney)
_____)
Mary Breshney)
)
)
Michael Finch)
_____)
Michael Finch)

Unusual Will Clauses

Clauses Gifting Body Parts

Some wills contain clauses donating body parts to science or to people awaiting transplants. In the past, the legality of such gifts was considered suspect by legal scholars, since body parts may or may not be personal property. The *Trillium Gift of Life Network Act*[6] (formerly the *Human Tissue Gift Act*) now authorizes such donations in a will or other document. One example of another such document is the organ donor card attached to Ontario driver's licences.

---

6   RSO 1990, c H.20.

As in the case of living wills, many lawyers feel that putting gifts of human tissue in wills is not advisable, because wills are often not consulted until after the time during which human tissue can be safely transplanted in a recipient. Many lawyers feel that the most appropriate place to make a directive for a gift of human tissue is on the organ donor portion of the driver's licence or attached to a power of attorney for personal care (discussed in Chapter 5, Powers of Attorney). It should also be noted that Service Ontario is encouraging people to register their consent to organ and tissue donation at <www.ontario.ca/page/organ-and-tissue-donor-registration>.

Such documents are more likely to be immediately on hand when a person dies.

Clauses Setting Out Burial Instructions

Similarly, many lawyers consider clauses setting out burial instructions inappropriate in a will. Although, strictly speaking, it is up to the estate trustee to arrange the funeral of a deceased person, it is common for funeral arrangements to be made, perhaps by the immediate family of the deceased, before the will is even consulted. Most lawyers advise clients who have specific directions about their funeral either to put such directions in a power of attorney for personal care or to communicate such instructions in some other way to the people most likely to be involved with the funeral. The same considerations apply to a prepaid funeral: notice of this fact should be brought to the attention of the same people and the documentation kept in a safe place. Note that putting burial or funeral instructions in a power of attorney for personal care is only for the purpose of bringing the deceased person's wishes to the forefront as early as possible following the death rather than for the purpose of granting authority with respect to the person's remains. As will be seen later in this book, when a person dies, any legal authority granted by a power of attorney (either for personal care or property) ceases.

Family Pet Beneficiaries

Some wills contain gifts to animals. Because animals are not considered persons in law, such gifts are void and should not be included in any will. The client may nevertheless want to create a testamentary trust in which the income or capital of the trust is to be used for the benefit of a particular pet, with the remainder going to a third party when the pet dies. The client should be made aware, however, that such trusts are not enforceable for practical reasons. That is, if the trustee fails to live up to his obligations under the trust, there is no person to bring proceedings in a court against the trustee.

KEY TERMS

disposition clause, 26
mandatory memorandum, 28
memorandum, 28
precatory memorandum, 28

residual gift, 28
testamentary trust, 29
trust, 29

REVIEW QUESTIONS

1. Define the following terms or concepts:

    a. mandatory memorandum;

    b. precatory memorandum;

    c. trust;

    d. testamentary trust;

    e. residual gift;

    f. executor's year.

2. Who has the final say in what a will contains?

3. Explain whether the following elements of a will are (a) necessary, or (b) useful:

    a. an identification clause;

    b. a revocation clause;

    c. an interpretation clause;

    d. a direction to pay debts.

4. What is the result if a will does not name an estate trustee?

5. Is a disposition clause in a will necessary?

6. What is the purpose of a 30-day survival clause?

7. What is a "lineal descendants" clause?

8. What difficulty arises when making a gift to an underage person?

9. What happens when a gift is made to a person who is mentally incapacitated?

10. What is the purpose of an investment clause?

11. Why is it advisable to have a "power of sale" clause in almost every will?

12. Why is it advisable to have a "discretion to pay or divide" clause in a will?

13. Why is it advisable to avoid the phrase "contents of my house"?

14. What is the purpose of an "authority binding" clause in a will and what are its limitations?

15. What is the purpose of including a *Family Law Act* clause in a will?

16. How binding is a "custody of children" clause in a will? Is it useful?

17. Is a "testimonium clause" necessary? Why is it useful?

18. Where must the signature of the witnesses be?

19. Explain whether or not it is advisable to make a gift of body parts in a will.

20. Is it advisable to set out burial instructions in a will? Why or why not?

21. What is the problem with making a gift to, or setting up a trust for, a family pet?

22. Why is it important to carefully interview a client before drafting his will?

Interpretation of Wills

3

LEARNING OUTCOMES

After reading this chapter, you should be able to:

- Explain the rules governing the order of distribution of the assets in an estate

- Explain ademption and lapse

- Explain the anti-lapse provisions of the *Succession Law Reform Act*

- Explain the rules relating to simultaneous deaths and presumption of death

- Explain the special treatment the law gives to named beneficiary assets

- Explain the effect of marriage, divorce, and domestic contracts on a will

- Explain the expanded definition of "children" for interpreting wills and trusts

Introduction

While a will is interpreted by estate trustees and courts after the testator's death, it is important for lawyers and law clerks to look ahead and pre-interpret the will instructions that are proposed by a client. This is to ensure that any reasonably possible future set of facts does not lead to undesired results. Rules regarding the interpretation of wills after the testator's death are therefore relevant in a discussion about estate planning.

One fundamental rule is that the will is to be interpreted as of the date of death rather than the date on which it is signed. For example, if a testator has two nephews at the time of executing his will and has three nephews at the time of his death, any provision in the will making a gift "to my nephews" will be deemed to refer to all three nephews. The same principle applies to assets owned by a testator. If the testator owns two gold rings at the time of signing her will but five at the time of her death, a gift in the will of "my gold rings" will include all five rings.

Despite the above, a will can be worded in such a way as to bypass this rule of interpretation. In the example of the three nephews at the time of death, the testator could have made the gift to "my nephews who are alive at the time that I sign this will." Any nephews born after the date of execution of the will would then not share in the gift. Similarly, in the example of the gold rings, the testator could have made the gift of "those gold rings that I currently own." The specified beneficiaries may only be entitled to receive the two gold rings that she owned on the day the will was signed. Such a gift, however, might well raise other problems, such as the non-existence of the rings at the time of death (see the "Ademption" section below) or the difficulties of proving which rings were owned at a particular time.

Interpreting Gifts

Terminology

This text uses the term "gift" to describe that which is given to a beneficiary under a will. Many wills and judgments, however, use more traditional terminology. For example, the words "bequest" and "**legacy**" have often been used to describe gifts of personal property or money. Similarly, the word "devise" is traditionally used to describe gifts of real estate.

The word "issue" is often used in wills to refer to children or other lineal descendants of the testator. Besides the fact that it includes grandchildren and great grandchildren, the word "issue" is often preferable because the words "children" or "child" typically refer to persons under the age of majority, whereas wills are usually intended to include adult children of the testator under the term "children."

Another term important in the interpretation of wills is "*per stirpes*," which is illustrated in clause 6 of the sample will in Chapter 1. **Per stirpes** is a phrase used to describe a particular pattern of distribution whereby a gift to a predeceased beneficiary flows downward to that beneficiary's children or to that beneficiary's children's children (and so on) so that each child receives a share or all of his parent's share, as the case may be. An example of a gift using a *per stirpes* distribution would appear in a will as follows: "I give $90,000 to be

legacy
gift under a will of personal property or money

per stirpes
form of distribution to surviving descendants of a predeceased beneficiary whereby the original gift flows downward by representation

divided among my lineal descendants in equal shares *per stirpes*." If the testator in this example has two children, A and B, and if B is deceased leaving children C, D, and E, and if E is deceased leaving children F and G, the distribution will be as follows:

- A gets $45,000.
- C gets $15,000.
- D gets $15,000.
- F gets $7,500.
- G gets $7,500.

Per stirpes is often contrasted to **per capita**, which describes a different pattern of distribution whereby each survivor receives an equal share regardless of how far removed each is from the original beneficiary. In the above example, if the phrase "per capita" appeared in the will instead of *per stirpes*, each of the surviving beneficiaries would receive $18,000.

Creditors Paid First

Despite what may be stated in the will to the contrary, it is an implied term of every will that beneficiaries are paid only if there are sufficient funds in the estate to satisfy all of the debts of the estate. Those to whom debts are owed are called **creditors of the estate**. Although it is sometimes said that the creditors of the estate are paid first or "off the top" before beneficiaries are paid, this may be misleading in that it implies that creditors are always paid on an earlier date than beneficiaries. In fact, estate trustees often give beneficiaries an advance payment toward their gifts before all of the creditors' claims are fully paid. As will be seen in Part II, Estate Administration, however, a prudent estate trustee will make such an advance only after he is certain of all the creditors of the estate and has verified that there are sufficient funds to cover such debts.

The rule that creditors are paid first is an extension of a deeply entrenched policy in our legal system that, in general, a person who incurs debt must not put his money to other uses to the prejudice of the creditor. If the estate trustee in charge of the funds of the estate ignores this rule, he may well be held personally liable to the creditors of the estate.

Debts of the estate include debts of the deceased that arose during her lifetime as well as debts that arose after her death. Examples of the former are credit card balances, utility bills that were unpaid at the time of death, mortgage payments that came due before the date of death and remained unpaid, and income taxes owing before the date of death. Examples of the latter include utility bills on a house held in the name of the estate, mortgage payments and income taxes coming due for a period following the date of death, and funeral expenses.

By virtue of section 32(1) of the *Succession Law Reform Act*,[1] debts do not include mortgages owed on property that is specifically gifted to a beneficiary, unless the will states otherwise. In other words, if a parcel of real estate on which there is a mortgage is given by will to a beneficiary, and the will does not specifically state that the estate is to bear the

per capita
form of distribution to surviving descendants of a predeceased beneficiary whereby each survivor receives an equal share of the original gift

creditors of the estate
those to whom debts of the estate are owed

---

1   RSO 1990, c S.26.

responsibility for the mortgage, the beneficiary takes only the equity in the property, the parcel subject to the mortgage, or the value of the property minus the amount required to pay out the mortgage.

In the event that the estate is insolvent—that is, if there are insufficient assets to cover all of the debts of the estate—there are certain procedures for the estate trustee to follow. These procedures will be discussed later, in Part II, Chapter 11, Determining, Notifying, and Paying Creditors of the Estate.

Order of Payment of Beneficiaries

Occasionally an estate has sufficient funds to pay all of the creditors of the estate but insufficient funds to cover all of the gifts in the will. In such a case, the law provides a default scheme that determines which beneficiaries, if any, are fully paid and which are partially paid, if at all. The determining factor as to which beneficiary will lose all or part of her gift is the category of gift that is provided for in the will to that beneficiary. Most lawyers feel that it is best to fully inform the client at the time the will is drafted about the default scheme that would come into play should there be insufficient assets to cover all of the gifts in the anticipated will. In this way, the will can be drafted to coincide as closely as possible with the client's estate plan, keeping in mind the possibility that there may be insufficient assets to cover all of the anticipated gifts.

The categories of gifts that determine the priority of payment of beneficiaries in the event that there are insufficient assets are as follows:

1. gifts of residue that, on their face, consist of a share of everything that is left over after creditors and all other beneficiaries are paid (known as "residual gifts" or "residue");

2. gifts of specific amounts of money from no particular source (known as "general gifts" or "general legacies");

3. gifts of specific amounts of money from a specified source (known as "demonstrative gifts" or "demonstrative legacies");

4. gifts of specific items (known as "specific gifts," "specific bequests," or "specific legacies"); and

5. gifts of real estate (known as "devises").

The five categories described above are listed in the order in which the gifts are to be diminished or eliminated in the event that there are insufficient assets to cover all of the gifts in the will. Thus, if there are insufficient assets, the first category of gift that will be diminished and possibly eliminated is the residual gift. This does not mean that a residual gift is necessarily a lesser gift than other gifts. On the contrary, in many estates, beneficiaries who receive a residual gift ultimately receive a larger share of the estate than the other beneficiaries because such gifts expand with the expansion of the assets of the testator. On the other hand, not only do residual gifts diminish as the assets of the testator diminish, but they are completely eliminated if there are insufficient assets in the estate to pay the creditors and the other gifts. Figures 3.1 and 3.2 show two examples of how an estate is distributed where a beneficiary is granted a residual gift.

The next category of gift that will be diminished or eliminated is a gift of a sum of money that specifies no particular source, as in Figure 3.3 (that is, the gift of $10,000 to the testator's friend Kelly). A gift of this nature is called a "general gift" or a "general legacy." If there are insufficient assets to completely satisfy a general gift but there are enough to partially pay the gift, the gift will be diminished or will "**abate**." If there are several general gifts in the will and insufficient assets to pay them, all of the general gifts will abate ratably—that is, proportionally.

The next category of gift that will be diminished or eliminated after the residual gifts and the general gifts is a gift of a sum of money from a specified source. A gift of this kind is called a "**demonstrative gift**" or a "demonstrative legacy." An example of a demonstrative gift is a gift of $500 from a specific bank account owned by the deceased or a gift of $10,000 from a specific mutual fund. Again, if there are insufficient assets to cover the demonstrative gift after paying creditors, it will abate. Figure 3.4 is an example of an abatement of a demonstrative gift.

abatement
diminishment of a gift under a will to satisfy debts of an estate

demonstrative gift
gift of a sum of money from a specifically identified source

FIGURE 3.1   Residual Gift: Example One

Deceased: single, no dependants

Assets: car worth $5,000
                 bank account containing $10,000
                 gold in safety deposit box worth $100,000

Debts: credit card debt $1,000

Will: car to friend Steve
                 gift of $20,000 to friend Kelly
                 residue to friend Anne

How is the estate distributed?

                 $1,000 to credit card company

                 car to Steve
                 $20,000 to Kelly
                 $89,000 to Anne

FIGURE 3.2   Residual Gift: Example Two

Deceased: single, no dependants

Assets: car worth $5,000
                   bank account containing $10,000
                   gold in safety deposit box worth $100,000

Debts: credit card debt $1,000
                   student loan $38,000
                   line of credit $50,000

Will: car to friend Steve
                   gift of $20,000 to friend Kelly
                   residue to friend Anne

How is the estate distributed?

                   $1,000 to credit card company
                   $38,000 to student loan bank
                   $50,000 to line of credit bank

                   car to Steve
                   $20,000 to Kelly
                   $1,000 to Anne

**FIGURE 3.3   Abatement of Gift of Money with No Particular
Source with No Abatement of Demonstrative Gift**

Deceased: single, no dependants

Assets: car worth $5,000
                   Bank of Grimsby account containing $10,000
                   loose cash $10,000

Debts: credit card debt $9,000

Will: car to friend Steve
                   $8,000 from Bank of Grimsby account to friend Joe
                   $10,000 to friend Kelly
                   residue to friend Anne

How is the estate distributed?

                   $9,000 to credit card company

                   car to Steve
                   $8,000 to Joe
                   $3,000 to Kelly
                   $0 to Anne

FIGURE 3.4   Demonstrative Gift

Deceased: single, no dependants

Assets: car worth $5,000
Bank of Grimsby account containing $10,000
loose cash $10,000

Debts: credit card debt $9,000
line of credit $5,000

Will: car to friend Steve
$8,000 from Bank of Grimsby account to friend Joe
$9,000 to credit card company
$10,000 to friend Kelly
residue to friend Anne

How is the estate distributed?

$9,000 to credit card company
$5,000 to line of credit

car to Steve
$6,000 to Joe
$0 to Kelly
$0 to Anne

If a gift is a demonstrative gift and the specified source is not owned by the testator at the time of his death, case law would suggest that the gift does not disappear. Instead, the gift will be treated as a general gift and will be paid (or diminished) as if it were a gift of money from no specified source. Figure 3.5 is an example of this principle. It should be noted that in such a situation, the question could arise whether the gift of money from a specified source is a gift of the source or a demonstrative gift. For example, if the will states "all of the money in my savings account to X" and the deceased has no savings account at the time of his death, the gift will likely be found to be a specific gift (that is, a gift of the specific bank account) rather than a demonstrative gift. In such a case, the gift will disappear (see the discussion of ademption below).

FIGURE 3.5   Demonstrative Gift Not Owned by Testator

Deceased: single, no dependants

Assets: car worth $5,000
                 loose cash $10,000

Debts: credit card debt $9,000

Will: car to friend Steve
                 $8,000 from Bank of Grimsby account to friend Joe
                 $2,000 to friend Kelly
                 residue to friend Anne

How is the estate distributed?

                 $9,000 to credit card company

                 car to Steve
                 $800 to Joe
                 $200 to Kelly
                 $0 to Anne

specific gift
gift of a particular object of personal property, lease, or assignment of debt

The second-to-last category of gift that will be eliminated is the specific gift. As indicated above, a **specific gift** is a gift of a particular object of personal property. The subject matter of the specific gift includes things like paintings and vehicles, and also leases and assignments of debts, such as a mortgage that was owned by the deceased on the date of death.

It may happen that, to pay the creditors, the object of a specific gift in a will has to be sold to pay the creditors. In such a situation, unless a contrary intention appears in the will, the remainder of such funds will go to the beneficiary of the specific gift as opposed to the beneficiary of the residue. Figure 3.6 illustrates such a situation.

The last category of gift that will be eliminated if there are insufficient assets in the estate is the specific gift of land or real estate. Such gifts, called devises, are the last to go toward payments of creditors. Again, if a piece of land that was specifically gifted to a beneficiary has to be sold to pay creditors and there are funds remaining, the funds remaining will go to the beneficiary of that devise rather than the residual beneficiary or beneficiaries of the estate.

FIGURE 3.6   Specific Gift

Deceased:	single, no dependants
Assets	car worth $5,000 bank account containing $10,000
Debts:	credit card debt $1,000 line of credit $10,000
Will:	car to friend Steve gift of $20,000 to friend Kelly residue to friend Anne

How is the estate distributed?

$1,000 to credit card company
$10,000 to line of credit bank

$4,000 to Steve
$0 to Kelly
$0 to Anne

Ademption

Ademption arises when the object of a specific gift, whether it is personal property or land, does not exist or is not owned by the testator at the time of his death. In such a case, the gift of the specific item fails, and the gift is said to have adeemed. Figure 3.7 illustrates ademption.

ademption
situation that occurs when the object of a specific gift does not exist or is not owned by the testator at the time of his death

FIGURE 3.7   Ademption

Deceased:	single, no dependants
Assets:	bank account containing $10,000
Debts:	credit card debt $1,000
Will:	car to friend Steve gift of $5,000 to friend Kelly residue to friend Anne

How is the estate distributed?

$1,000 to credit card company

nothing to Steve
$5,000 to Kelly
$4,000 to Anne

Lapse

Lapse occurs when a beneficiary named in a will is not alive at the time of the testator's death and there is no alternate beneficiary named. In such a case, the gift will fail or "**lapse.**" If the gift is other than a residual gift, it will fall into the residue of the estate and be distributed to the residual beneficiaries. Figure 3.8 illustrates this situation.

If the gift is one of residue, the result of the lapse is an intestacy (that is, the gift is treated as if the testator had not made a will for that gift—see Chapter 4, Intestacy), unless the court construes the intention of the testator otherwise. A general rule used by courts in the interpretation of wills is that a testator is assumed to have made his will in such a way as to avoid an intestacy. On this basis, courts strive to construe a gift that would otherwise have resulted in a lapse of residue as a gift to a member or class of beneficiaries resulting in no lapse. This kind of construction is possible only if there are other surviving residual beneficiaries and the court is satisfied that the intention of the testator was to treat the surviving residual beneficiaries as belonging to the same class as the deceased beneficiary.

In determining how to distribute an estate in the event of a lapse, it is important to consider the so-called anti-lapse rules of the *Succession Law Reform Act* (see the next section). These provisions set out the rules for distribution of gifts that would otherwise lapse but for the fact that the beneficiary belongs to a specified category of beneficiaries.

One exception to the rule of lapse applies to gifts to charities. If the charity is non-existent at the time of the testator's death, the gift can be made to a charity with a similar object or purpose according to a doctrine known as *cy-près*, which is Latin for "near there."

lapse

fail; the situation that occurs when a beneficiary specified in a will is not alive at the time of the testator's death

FIGURE 3.8   Lapse

Deceased: single, no dependants

Assets: car worth $5,000
                 bank account containing $10,000

Debts: credit card debt $1,000

Will: car to friend Steve
                 gift of $5,000 to friend Kelly
                 residue to friend Anne

Steve has predeceased

How is the estate distributed?

       $1,000 to credit card company
       $5,000 to Kelly
       $4,000 to Anne
       car to Anne

Anti-Lapse Provisions

Section 31 of the *Succession Law Reform Act* contains the rules known as the **anti-lapse provisions**. They are designed to allow gifts to certain relatives of deceased beneficiaries that would otherwise lapse. The anti-lapse provisions do not apply if a contrary intention appears in the will, and they apply only to gifts made to the children, grandchildren, or siblings of the deceased testator. If gifts to such beneficiaries lapse—that is, if those beneficiaries predecease the deceased and no alternate beneficiaries are named in the will—those gifts are given to the spouse and children of that deceased beneficiary as if that beneficiary had died without a will and without debts, and as if there were no laws giving what is called the "preferential share" to the spouse of that person. The preferential share is a device built into Part II of the *Succession Law Reform Act* to protect the spouse of a person who dies without a will. It will be explained in more detail in Chapter 4, Intestacy.

anti-lapse provisions rules designed to allow gifts to certain relatives of deceased beneficiaries that would otherwise lapse

Simultaneous Deaths

Section 55 of the *Succession Law Reform Act* sets out the rules that apply to multiple estates in cases where two or more persons die at the same time or in circumstances where it is impossible to determine which of them died first. The rule, in section 55(1) of the Act, states that in those circumstances the property of each person is treated as if that person had survived the others. Such a rule is required in a situation where one of the deceased persons is the other deceased person's beneficiary. Without this provision, forensic investigations would have to be performed in order to decide whether one deceased person's surviving beneficiaries were entitled to gifts made in the other deceased person's will.

Similarly, section 55(2) of the Act states that where two persons who are joint owners of property (real estate or otherwise) die simultaneously or in circumstances where it is impossible to determine which died first, they are deemed to have held the property in common rather than jointly. The holding of property "in common" means that, upon death of one of the common owners, the property passes not to the other common owner but to the deceased owner's beneficiaries. Section 55(2) operates only if no contrary intention appears in the will.

Presumption of Death

Sometimes the question arises whether a missing person—be she a testator, an intestate person, or a beneficiary of an estate—is still alive. In such a situation, the *Declarations of Death Act, 2002*[2] specifies that an "interested" person may apply to the court for a declaration that the person is deceased. An "interested person" is defined in section 1 of the Act as

> any person who is or would be affected by an order declaring that an individual is dead, including,
>> (a) a person named as executor or estate trustee in the individual's will,

---

2 SO 2002, c 14.

(b) a person who may be entitled to apply to be appointed administrator of the individual's estate on intestacy,

(c) the individual's spouse,

(d) the individual's next of kin,

(e) the individual's guardian or attorney for personal care or property under the *Substitute Decisions Act, 1992,*

(f) a person who is in possession of property owned by the individual,

(g) if there is a contract of life insurance or group insurance insuring the individual's life,

    (i) the insurer, and

    (ii) any potential claimant under the contract, and

(h) if the individual has been declared an absentee under the *Absentees Act*, the committee of his or her estate.

The conditions necessary for a successful application under the Act are as follows (from section 2 of the Act):

(a) the individual has disappeared in circumstances of peril or has been absent for at least seven years;

(b) the applicant has not heard of or from the individual since the disappearance or, in the case of a seven-year absence, the applicant has not heard of or from the individual during the seven-year period;

(c) to the applicant's knowledge, after making reasonable inquiries, no other person has heard of or from the individual since the disappearance or, in the case of a seven-year absence, no other person has heard of or from the individual during the seven-year period;

(d) the applicant has no reason to believe that the individual is alive; and

(e) there is sufficient evidence to find that the individual is dead.

The Act specifies that the person applying for the order must serve notice to all other interested persons "of whom the applicant is aware." The Act also sets out provisions allowing the court discretion in the applicability of an order declaring somebody deceased. Of particular note is the fact that, under section 6, if a distribution of the absentee's property is made after an order is granted declaring him deceased, "the distribution is final even if the individual is afterwards discovered to be alive, and the individual is not entitled to recover the distributed property." Section 6(3), however, does provide that in such circumstances, "the court may, if it is of the opinion that it would be just to do so, make an order requiring a person to whom property was distributed to reconvey all or part of it to the individual or to pay a specified amount to the individual."

It should be noted that if a person is missing but the situation does not meet the requirements necessary for her to be declared deceased, another person can apply to the court under the *Absentees Act*[3] to be a committee—that is, guardian—of a missing person's property. Under the Act, a committee has the same rights over the missing person's

---

3 RSO 1990, c A.3.

property as a guardian of property appointed under the *Substitute Decisions Act, 1992.*[4] Guardianships of property are dealt with in Part III, Estate Litigation, Chapter 16, Statutory Forms of Estate Litigation. The powers of a guardian of property are similar to the powers of an attorney under a continuing power of attorney for property (discussed in Chapter 5, Powers of Attorney).

Named Beneficiary Assets

Notwithstanding the fact that creditors are paid first in the administration of an estate, certain assets, including bank accounts and real property, can be set up to bypass the estate altogether and go directly to a survivor. For such assets to bypass the estate, and thereby bypass creditors, certain conditions must be satisfied.

Bank Accounts

Where a person dies with a bank account that has more than one owner, the account will transfer to the survivor(s), provided it can be established that it was the intention of the account holders for the account to pass to the survivor. For practical purposes, it is the deceased's intention that is important in this context. The question becomes whether the deceased intended the surviving account holder(s) to obtain ultimate ownership of the account or whether the deceased simply added that person or persons to the account for convenience. An example of the latter would be an elderly parent who adds a child to his bank account with the sole intention of making it more convenient for the child to pay the parent's bills. Bank records often provide the necessary evidence to determine the intention of the deceased account holder. Sometimes, however, the intention of the deceased cannot be determined with evidence and in such cases the law imposes presumptions which determine the issue. For example, the law presumes that a parent who places a minor child (but not an adult child) as an owner on a bank account, has done so with the intention of passing ownership in the account to the minor child upon the parent's death. Similarly, section 14(b) of the *Family Law Act*[5] provides that married spouses are presumed to have intended joint accounts to pass to the surviving spouse.

Real Property

For real property to pass to a survivor, the survivor and the deceased must be registered as owners of the property and must own the property as "joint tenants" (as opposed to "tenants in common"). If the deceased and the survivor own the property as tenants in common, the deceased's share of the property will fall into her estate.

It should be noted that sometimes, real property can be held in complex combinations of joint tenancy and tenancy in common. For example, a person may hold one share of the real property in joint tenancy with another group of persons who hold the remaining share as tenants in common as between themselves.

For the purpose of the present inquiry, the relevant relationship is that between the deceased and the other owners. It should also be noted that even in cases where real

---

4 SO 1992, c 30.
5 RSO 1990, c F.3.

property is owned in joint tenancy with a person who has died, it is possible for a creditor of the deceased or other interested person to challenge the direct transfer of the property to the surviving joint tenant upon the deceased's death. In other words, it is possible in some circumstances for the property to pass into the estate. Such inquiries are beyond the scope of this text but, briefly, the court will look at the intention of the deceased in placing the property in joint tenancy and, where the evidence fails to provide an answer, the court will apply presumptions to determine the issue. Again, the *Family Law Act* at section 14(a) provides a statutory presumption (though rebuttable with evidence to the contrary) that real property owned by married spouses in joint tenancy is intended to pass directly to the surviving spouse.

Funds or Plans

There are other assets, besides joint bank accounts and real property, that can bypass a deceased's estate and go directly to a survivor. Such assets are referred to as "funds or plans" and include pensions, profit-sharing plans, trusts funds, registered retirement savings plans (RRSPs), and registered income funds (RRIFs). Sometimes funds or plans are only payable to certain individuals and, as in the case of RRSPs and RRIFs, there are always tax consequences for transferring them except insofar as the tax is deferred if the designated beneficiary is a surviving spouse or a spousal trust. One characteristic that funds or plans have in common is that the designation of a beneficiary of such assets (or the revocation of a beneficiary) can be done either in a will or in a signed instrument. "Instrument" in this context means a document signed by the owner of the asset that formally expresses the intention to designate a certain individual as the recipient of the asset (or formally revokes a previous designation).

Part III of the *Succession Law Reform Act* specifically addresses the interaction of wills and instruments designating beneficiaries of funds or plans (or revoking previously made designations). Section 52(1), for example, provides that a will can only revoke a designation made in a previous instrument if the will "relates expressly to a plan, either generally or specifically." In other words, the residue clause of a will simply gifting the testator's "remaining assets" to a certain beneficiary would be insufficient to revoke a previously executed instrument designating a different beneficiary because it does not refer to the fund or plan.

Section 52 of the Act also provides the following rules pertaining to the revocation or designation of beneficiaries of funds or plans:

(a) a later designation of a beneficiary of a fund or plan revokes a previous designation (s 52(2));

(b) a revocation of a will containing a designation of a beneficiary of a fund or plan revokes the designation (s 52(3));

(c) a revocation of a designation of a beneficiary of a fund or plan does not revive an earlier designation (s 52(6));

(d) a designation or revocation of a beneficiary of a fund or plan in a will is effective from the moment the will is signed (which is an exception to the rule that the will speaks from the date of death) (s 52(7));

(e) a revocation or designation of a beneficiary of a fund or plan in a will, which is found to be an invalid will, is not invalid by reason of the invalidity of the will (s 52(4)); and

(f) an act purporting to revoke an invalid will containing a designation of a beneficiary of a fund or plan is considered to be a revocation of the designation, if the act purporting to revoke the will is a proper revocation of a valid will (s 52(5)).

Life Insurance

Life insurance, although technically not an asset, can also designate a specific beneficiary. In such a case, the proceeds do not fall into the estate unless there is no surviving named beneficiary or the specific beneficiary named is the estate itself.

It is worth noting in reference to funds or plans, discussed in the previous section, that if the fund or plan in question is an insurance product (life insurance for example, or certain investment plans administered by life insurance companies), the rules applicable to the designation of beneficiaries in Part III of the *Succession Law Reform Act* do not apply. In such cases, the validity of any designations of beneficiaries is governed by the *Insurance Act*.[6]

Privately Held Corporations

If a prospective testator owns shares in a corporation with other persons, it is incumbent on the lawyer or law clerk, prior to drafting the will, to make further inquiries into the existence of a shareholder agreement respecting the transfer of the testator's shares upon her death. If such an agreements exists, and if it is properly drafted and executed, it will supersede the provisions of a will purporting to deal with the shares in a way that is inconsistent with the agreement.

Problems with will drafting can also arise where someone is the sole owner of a corporation that itself owns assets. The prospective testator may forget that it is his corporation and not he personally who owns the assets and may instruct the lawyer to prepare a will that gifts the assets to one beneficiary while gifting the shares of the corporation to another beneficiary. In such a case, the beneficiary of the shares of the corporation, not the intended beneficiary, will end up with the assets. The current state of the law indicates that the lawyer could be held liable to the intended beneficiary in such a case for failing to inquire into the structure of ownership of the testator's assets. It is therefore incumbent on a lawyer or law clerk, when receiving instructions for the preparation of a will, to make inquiries into these issues.

---

6 RSO 1990, c I.8.

Interpreting Wills in the Light of Family Law Issues

Effect of Marriage

If a person is married after signing a will, the will is automatically void or voidable. An exception to this rule arises where the will states that it is made in contemplation of that particular marriage. A will that is made before a marriage and that does not state that it was made in contemplation of the marriage, however, can be upheld if the spouse of the testator elects to allow the will to stand. The election is to be made in writing and must be filed in the Office of the Estate Registrar for Ontario within one year of the date of death of the testator.

Effect of Divorce

Unlike a marriage, a divorce does not entirely revoke the wills of the divorced couple, but it does have an effect on their wills to the extent that each will be read as if the will had been revoked and the divorced spouses had predeceased each other. In other words, if a testator executed a will before she was divorced and then died after a divorce judgment was granted but before executing a new will, any gifts to her spouse in her will are treated as if her spouse had already died. Similarly, the appointment of her ex-spouse as estate trustee in her will is void. None of these consequences apply, however, if a contrary intention appears in the will.

This rule applies only to divorce and not to separation. If a couple is merely separated, unless they have a separation agreement that speaks to their respective wills or estates, their wills will stand as they are.

Domestic Contracts

A domestic or marriage contract or a separation agreement will take precedence over the statutory rules pertaining to a couple's wills and estates if those matters are addressed by the domestic contract. As will be expanded on in Part II, this principle underscores the importance of the estate trustee's making inquiries, upon undertaking the administration of an estate, as to whether a deceased testator who was married or divorced was party to a domestic contract.

Domestic contracts have very stringent formal requirements and will not likely be held to be valid and binding if they are not in writing, witnessed, and entered into with full financial disclosure and independent legal advice.

Definition of "Children"

Another important family law issue in the context of wills is the expanded definition of "child" or "children" as it occurs in the *Children's Law Reform Act*.[7] The Act provides that

---

7   RSO 1990, c C.12.

any reference to "child" or "children" in a will or trust document automatically includes children born outside marriage and adopted children. This rule applies to references to the testator's own children and to the children of a beneficiary. While the Act provides that this rule of interpretation does not apply if a contrary intention appears in the will or trust document, case law has held that merely using the words "blood" or "marriage" to describe the relationship with the child is not sufficient to establish a contrary intention.

In addition to the above, section 8 of the Act sets out a series of circumstances in which a man is presumed to be the father of a particular child. These rules are relevant in that gifts in a will may be made by a man "to my children," or it may be necessary to determine who the children of a deceased male beneficiary are for the purposes of giving that beneficiary's share to his children pursuant to the terms of the will or the statutory anti-lapse provisions. The section 8 rules can be summarized as follows:

Unless it is proven otherwise on a balance of probabilities, a man is presumed to be the father of a child if

1. he is married to the mother of the child at the time of the birth of the child;

2. he was married to the mother of the child and the marriage was terminated by:
   (a) the death of the father within 300 days before the birth of the child;
   (b) judgment of nullity of marriage within 300 days before the birth of the child; or
   (c) divorce where the decree nisi was granted within 300 days before the birth of the child;

3. he marries the mother of the child after the birth of the child and acknowledges that he is the natural father;

4. he was cohabiting with the mother of the child in a relationship of some permanence;
   (a) at the time of the birth of the child; or
   (b) within 300 days before the birth of the child;

5. he has certified himself as the child's father when registering the birth under the *Vital Statistics Act*[8] or a similar Act; or

6. he has been found or recognized in his lifetime by a court in Canada to be the father of the child.

Any reference to marriage in the above guidelines includes a void marriage if it was entered into in good faith and the two spouses cohabit. In such a case, the time during which the two spouses cohabit is deemed to be the time during which they are married for the purposes of the above guidelines.

As well, the *Succession Law Reform Act* defines "child" and "children" to include children conceived before but born after their parent's death.

---

8 RSO 1990, c V.4.

Custody Clauses

As seen in the sample will in Chapter 2, Will Clauses, one common clause gives custody of underage children to named custodians. It is important to point out to clients that such a clause is not binding in law, since any decisions pertaining to children are always subject to the direction of the court. Although the general rule is that such clauses are valid for only 90 days, if a testator names a custodian who is not appropriate, a court has the power to override the clause even within the 90-day period.

Despite the above, a custody clause can be valuable because it represents the recommendation of the deceased testator (presumably the parent) as to whom he thinks is an appropriate custodian. Such clauses will likely be considered by a court when making a determination as to custody.

Family Law Act Right of Election

Section 6 of the *Family Law Act*[9] contains provisions that allow for protection of a married spouse who does not receive a fair share of the estate of his or her deceased spouse. The rule states that a married spouse is entitled to elect to set aside the will of his or her deceased spouse and receive a division of matrimonial property (similar to that which would be available on a marriage breakdown) rather than receiving what is given under the will. The election must be made within six months of the date of death of the deceased spouse or within such further time period as the court may allow.

Although this right of election is discussed more thoroughly in Part III, it is relevant in the present context. At the time of taking instructions for a will that appears to fail to adequately provide for a client's married spouse, the lawyer or law clerk is obligated to point out to the testator that the proposed will could possibly be set aside by the surviving spouse on this ground after the death of the testator.

Rule Against Double Portions

In the case of gifts in wills from parents to their children, the common law rule against double portions (sometimes called "the hotch pot rule") has to be considered. According to this rule, a gift to a particular child may be reduced or even eliminated. The rule holds that a child of a testator may not be entitled to her full bequest if, subsequent to executing the will, the testator gives a large gift of money, or presumably anything of value, to that child. This rule, followed in the case of *Christmas Estate v. Tuck*,[10] operates on the logic that the gift given during the parent's lifetime is a pre-inheritance and is meant to be deducted from the share of the parent's estate that the recipient would otherwise have taken. The presumption can be rebutted with evidence to the contrary—that is, evidence showing that the subsequent gift made by the parent was meant to be taken in addition to the child's entitlement under the will.

---

9 RSO 1990, c F.3.

10 (1995), 10 ETR 47 (Ont Gen Div).

KEY TERMS

abatement, 43
ademption, 47
anti-lapse provisions, 49
creditors of the estate, 41
demonstrative gift, 43

lapse, 48
legacy, 40
per capita, 41
per stirpes, 40
specific gift, 46

REVIEW QUESTIONS

1. Define the following terms or concepts:
   a. ademption;
   b. abatement;
   c. lapse;
   d. hotch pot rule.

2. As of what date is a will interpreted? Provide an example of where this might make a difference in the distribution of the deceased's assets?

3. Compare and contrast a "gift," "bequest," "legacy," and "devise" under the terms of a will.

4. Explain the difference between a "*per stirpes*" form of distribution and one made "per capita"?

5. What priority do creditors take in the distribution of an estate? Explain your answer.

6. Identify the five categories of gifts in a will and the order in which they are eliminated or diminished when there is a shortfall.

7. Provide an example of an application of the *cy-près* doctrine?

8. To which beneficiaries do the anti-lapse provisions of the *Succession Law Reform Act* apply?

9. What would exclude the application of the anti-lapse provisions?

10. What rule applies where two persons die simultaneously or in circumstances where it is impossible to determine who died first and each is a beneficiary under the other's will.

11. In those same circumstances, what happens if the two deceased persons own property jointly with the right of survivorship?

12. What statute can one resort to where a person involved in an estate is missing? What is the relevant period of time for the person to be missing?

13. What are at least two types of assets owned by a deceased person that do not fall into the estate?

14. Describe two situations where the proceeds of a life insurance policy would not fall into the estate assets.

15. If a registered retirement savings plan is left to A in a will but B is later designated in an instrument as the beneficiary, who is entitled to the proceeds?

16. What is the effect of marriage on a pre-existing will? What are the two exceptions?

17. What is the effect of a divorce on a pre-existing will? What will exclude these results?

18. What is the effect of a domestic contract in the administration of an estate?

19. By virtue of which statute does the word "children" in a will include those born outside the marriage or adopted?

20. What is the effect of putting a "custody of children" clause in a will?

21. What remedy is available to a spouse who feels that he or she has not received a fair share of the other spouse's estate under the will, and within what time frame must the remedy be enacted?

Intestacy

4

LEARNING OUTCOMES

After reading this chapter, you should be able to:

- Describe the concept of intestacy

- Describe the concept of "escheating to the Crown" and when it occurs

- Explain the rules governing the distribution of an estate where there is no legally valid will

- Explain what partial intestacy is and how the law deals with it

- Describe how an estate trustee is appointed in cases of intestacy

Introduction

intestacy
state of dying
without a valid will

Intestacy arises when a person dies without a valid will. In such a case, the deceased is said to have died "intestate" and is often referred to as "the intestate." Intestacy also arises when a person dies with a will but the will fails to dispose of all the property belonging to the deceased. The latter situation is referred to as a "partial intestacy" because the deceased has died testate with respect to some property and intestate with respect to other property. A partial intestacy usually occurs only when the will of the deceased person is drafted poorly. That is, if the deceased has a valid will that names a residual beneficiary and a reasonable number of alternate residual beneficiaries, a situation of partial intestacy will not likely occur. In both a full or partial intestacy, the laws of intestate succession (set out in Part II of the *Succession Law Reform Act*[1]) govern. They must be consulted in order to determine who is entitled to the assets with respect to which the deceased died intestate.

It is important to determine which relatives of the intestate have survived her in order to determine how her net estate (or the intestate property if it is a partial intestacy) is to be distributed. In the unusual case where the intestate is not survived by any next of kin, her net estate will **escheat** to the provincial Crown—that is, the estate will be paid or delivered to the government.

escheat
the forfeiting of
ownership to
the Crown for
lack of heirs

While the question of who is entitled to a share of the estate on an intestacy is for an estate trustee to answer just before administering the estate, the subject is often discussed with clients in the context of estate planning so that they are fully informed about why a will is or is not needed. For this reason, the rules of distribution on an intestacy are discussed in Part I, Estate Planning, rather than in Part II, Estate Administration.

Two points should be kept in mind when reading this chapter. First, the word "net" in the phrase "net estate" refers to the principle that the creditors of the estate will be fully paid "off the top" before any distributions are made. As discussed in Chapter 3, Interpretation of Wills, this does not necessarily mean that the creditors are paid earlier in time than the beneficiaries; rather, assets sufficient to pay the debts must be set aside before the beneficiaries are paid. Second, as will be seen in Part II, the deceased may own assets that fall outside the estate, such as real estate held jointly. In other words, the rules of intestate succession do not affect creditors' rights and do not affect those who own property jointly with the deceased with right of survivorship.

Distribution of Estate Where There Is No Legally Valid Will

Overview of Intestate Succession

The rules of intestate succession, set out in Part II of the *Succession Law Reform Act*, put the intestate's surviving relatives into classes that are based loosely on the degree of closeness of the members of the class to the deceased. These classes can be likened to widening circles around the deceased. Distribution of the deceased's estate is made to the innermost

---

1   RSO 1990, c S.26.

circle first and then outward by steps. Only when the innermost circle is empty—when there are no surviving relatives in that circle—will the next innermost circle be looked to for beneficiaries. If that circle also does not have surviving relatives, the next circle will be looked to, and so on.

- The first, innermost, class of relatives consists of the spouse, children, and other issue (defined below) of the deceased.
- The second class consists of the parents of the deceased.
- The third class consists of the siblings of the deceased.
- The fourth class consists of the nieces and nephews of the deceased.
- The fifth class consists of the uncles and aunts and other relatives of the deceased.

When distributing among one class of relatives, whichever class that may be, particular rules come into play for distribution among the members of that class. Furthermore, other rules apply in some circumstances that will allow a person who would normally appear in one class of relatives—that is, in a farther circle—to stand in the place of a deceased member of a closer class or circle. Such a situation occurs when a member of a particular class has predeceased the intestate, leaving surviving relatives of her own at the same time that other members of that particular class have survived. These rules apply only in certain situations, which are discussed below. The rest of this part of the chapter deals with the rules pertaining to the distribution among the members of the particular classes of relatives and the rules allowing for a member of one class to be substituted for a member of another class.

Spouse and Issue

Definition of "Spouse" and "Issue"

The innermost circle of beneficiaries in an intestate estate is made up of the spouse and issue of the deceased. "Spouse" is defined in section 1(1) of the *Succession Law Reform Act*.

> In this Act, ...
>> "spouse" means either of two persons who,
>>> (a) are married to each other, or
>>> (b) have together entered into a marriage that is voidable or void, in good
>> faith on the part of the person asserting a right under this Act.

This definition of "spouse" mirrors the one in Part I of the *Family Law Act*[2] that deals with the division of matrimonial property on the breakdown of a marriage. That is, for the purpose of interpreting the rules of intestate succession, "spouse" does not include what is most often referred to as a "common law" spouse. Also note that in the discussion of intestacy, a person who is married but separated from the intestate at the time of the intestate's death is not prevented from asserting his or her rights as a spouse under the laws of intestate succession.

---

2 RSO 1990, c F.3.

Furthermore, section 1(2) of the *Succession Law Reform Act* states:

> In the definition of "spouse," a reference to marriage includes a marriage that is actually or potentially polygamous, if it was celebrated in a jurisdiction whose system of law recognizes it as valid.

In other words, if a person dies intestate and has more than one spouse, provided that the marriages took place in a jurisdiction where polygamy is legal, each of the spouses may be able to assert rights under the laws of intestate succession. Presumably the spouses would share equally in the distribution that would otherwise have gone to an only spouse, although, depending on the particular facts of each case, arguments may be made for unequal distribution.

A person's issue includes his or her children, grandchildren, great-grandchildren, and so on. In this context, reference should be made to the *Children's Law Reform Act*,[3] discussed in Chapter 3, Interpretation of Wills. For the purposes of the present discussion, note that not only wills but also statutes are to be interpreted in accordance with the expanded definition of "child" and "children." In other words, adopted children and children born out of wedlock fall into the definition of "issue" as it appears in the *Succession Law Reform Act*. In addition, section 47(9) of the Act states that "descendants and relatives of the deceased conceived before and born alive after the death of the deceased shall inherit as if they had been born in the lifetime of the deceased and had survived him or her."

Intestate Dies with Surviving Spouse but No Surviving Issue

If a person dies intestate with no issue and has a spouse who falls within the definition of "spouse" set out in section 1(1) of the *Succession Law Reform Act*, the spouse is entitled to the entire net estate of the deceased—that is, after sufficient assets to pay the creditors are set aside. Figure 4.1 is an example of this kind of distribution.

FIGURE 4.1 Distribution to Spouse

Deceased died intestate:

Spouse:	Alice
Other next of kin and descendants:	none
Assets:	$300,000
Debts:	credit card debt $10,000

How is the estate distributed?

$10,000 to credit card company
$290,000 to Alice

---

3 RSO 1990, c C.12.

Intestate Dies with Issue but No Surviving Spouse

If a person dies intestate without a spouse but has some surviving issue, the issue receives the deceased's entire net estate. The estate is first divided evenly among the children of the intestate. If any of those children have predeceased the intestate, leaving children of their own, the deceased child's own children receive the share that would otherwise have gone to their parent. In dividing that share among themselves, the grandchildren take equal shares. If, in turn, any of the grandchildren have also predeceased, leaving children of their own, those great-grandchildren of the intestate receive a share of the share of the original share. In other words, each beneficiary receives a share by representation. Figure 4.2 illustrates distribution by representation in a situation of intestacy.

FIGURE 4.2   Distribution by Representation

Deceased died intestate:

Spouse:	Alice (predeceased)
Other next of kin and descendants:	daughter, Monique
	Monique's daughter, Jill
	Monique's son, William
	deceased son, James
	James's son, Paul
	James's daughter, Susan
Assets:	$20,000
Debts:	credit card debt $10,000
How is the estate distributed?	
	$10,000 to credit card company
	$5,000 to Monique
	$2,500 to Paul
	$2,500 to Susan

Intestate Dies with Spouse and Issue, and Net Estate Is Worth Less Than $200,000

If a person dies intestate with a spouse and some issue but the net estate is worth $200,000 or less, the spouse is entitled to the entire net estate according to what is called the spouse's preferential share. The preferential share is a concept provided for in section 45 of the *Succession Law Reform Act*, which states that the surviving spouse of a deceased person is entitled to a certain amount (set by regulation under the *Succession Law Reform Act*) "off the top" of the estate before any other distributions are made. The current amount of the preferential share, as set by Ontario Regulation 54/95, is $200,000. Accordingly, if the net estate is worth less than $200,000, the spouse is entitled to all of the net estate. Figure 4.3 is an example of this kind of distribution.

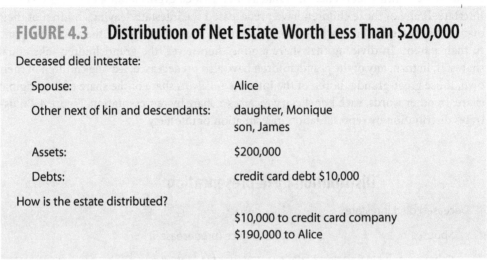

FIGURE 4.3   **Distribution of Net Estate Worth Less Than $200,000**

Deceased died intestate:

Spouse:	Alice
Other next of kin and descendants:	daughter, Monique son, James
Assets:	$200,000
Debts:	credit card debt $10,000

How is the estate distributed?

$10,000 to credit card company
$190,000 to Alice

Intestate Dies with Surviving Spouse and One Child, or, If Child Has Predeceased, with Any Issue of Child, and Net Estate Is Worth More Than $200,000

If the intestate had one child during his or her life and a spouse at the time of his or her death, the spouse is entitled to the preferential share of $200,000—that is, the first $200,000 available in the net estate. The excess, known as the "distributive share," is divided equally between the intestate's spouse and the intestate's child. Figure 4.4 is an example of this kind of distribution.

If the intestate's one child has predeceased the intestate and left no children or other issue, the intestate's spouse receives the entire estate. If, however, the intestate's child has predeceased the intestate and left surviving children—that is, grandchildren of the intestate—or if the grandchildren have predeceased and left surviving great-grandchildren of the intestate, for the purposes of distribution, the predeceased child or grandchild is treated as if alive, and his children equally share the part of the estate that would have gone to their parent had that parent not predeceased the intestate. Figure 4.5 is an example of such a distribution.

FIGURE 4.4   Distribution of Net Estate Worth More Than $200,000

Deceased died intestate:

Spouse:	Alice
Other next of kin and descendants:	daughter, Monique
Assets:	$250,000
Debts:	credit card debt $10,000

How is the estate distributed?

$10,000 to credit card company
$220,000 to Alice
$20,000 to Monique

FIGURE 4.5   Distribution with Predeceased Child

Deceased died intestate:

Spouse:	Alice
Other next of kin and descendants:	deceased daughter, Monique
	Monique's daughter, Elizabeth
	Monique's son, Frank
Assets:	$250,000
Debts:	credit card debt $10,000

How is the estate distributed?

$10,000 to credit card company

$220,000 to Alice
$10,000 to Elizabeth
$10,000 to Frank

Intestate Dies with Surviving Spouse and More Than One Child, More Than One Child Either Survives the Intestate or Leaves Issue Who Survive the Intestate, and Net Estate Is Worth More Than $200,000

If a person dies intestate with a surviving spouse and has more than one surviving child, the intestate's spouse receives the first $200,000 of the net estate. The excess is then divided into three equal parts. One part goes to the spouse, and the other two parts are divided evenly among the surviving children. This is the case no matter how many children survive the deceased. Thus, for example, if the intestate had a spouse and eight surviving children, each child would receive one-eighth of two-thirds (or one-twelfth) of the excess over $200,000. Figure 4.6 is an example of such a distribution.

FIGURE 4.6   Distribution with Children and Net Estate Worth More Than $200,000

Deceased died intestate:

Spouse:	Alice
Other next of kin and descendants:	daughter Monique
	son James
	son Steve
	daughter Joanne
	daughter Penny
	son William
	son Kenneth
	daughter Mary
Assets:	$510,000
Debts:	credit card debt $10,000

How is the estate distributed?

$10,000 to credit card company

$300,000 to Alice
$25,000 to Monique
$25,000 to James
$25,000 to Steve
$25,000 to Joanne
$25,000 to Penny
$25,000 to William
$25,000 to Kenneth
$25,000 to Mary

If one or more of the children have predeceased the intestate, leaving children of their own (the grandchildren of the intestate), these grandchildren receive the share that would otherwise have gone to their parent. If, in turn, one of those grandchildren of the intestate has died leaving children of his own (great-grandchildren of the intestate), these great-grandchildren receive the share that would otherwise have gone to their parent. Figure 4.7 is an example of this kind of distribution.

If a child or any other issue of the intestate predeceases the intestate without leaving any surviving issue, that person is treated as if he or she had not existed for the purposes of the rules of intestate succession.

FIGURE 4.7   Distribution to Grandchildren and Great-Grandchildren

Deceased died intestate:

Spouse:	Alice
Other next of kin and descendants:	daughter, Monique
	deceased son, James
	James's deceased son, Paul
	Paul's son, John
	Paul's daughter Amy
	Paul's daughter Diane
	James's daughter, Susan
Assets:	$510,000
Debts:	credit card debt $10,000

How is the estate distributed?

$10,000 to credit card company

$300,000.00 to Alice
$100,000.00 to Monique
$50,000.00 to Susan
$16,666.66 to John
$16,666.67 to Amy
$16,666.67 to Diane

No Surviving Spouse or Issue, but Surviving Parent

If a person dies intestate leaving no surviving spouse or issue, the next class of relatives to be looked to comprises the parents of the deceased. In such circumstances, the parents share equally in the intestate's entire net estate. This rule applies whether the parents are together, separated, or divorced at the time of death of the intestate. If only one parent survives the intestate, this parent receives the entire net estate. Figure 4.8 is an example of this kind of distribution.

No Surviving Spouse, Issue, or Parent, but at Least One Surviving Sibling

If a person dies intestate with no surviving spouse, no children or other issue, and no parents, but has surviving siblings, the siblings share equally in the distribution of the net estate. If the intestate had only one sibling and that sibling survives the intestate, he or she receives the entire net estate. If there were two or more siblings but only one survives the intestate, and the predeceased sibling(s) left no surviving children, again the surviving sibling receives the entire net estate.

If there are one or more surviving siblings, and one or more predeceased siblings are survived by children (nieces and nephews of the intestate), the surviving siblings share the estate with the surviving children of the deceased siblings. The nieces and nephews of the intestate share equally in the part of the net estate that would otherwise have gone to their parent; in other words, the distribution is by representation. Figure 4.9 is an example of such a distribution. In contrast to the situation outlined above dealing with the issue of the intestate, if the children of the predeceased siblings of the intestate (his or her nieces and nephews) also predecease the intestate, their share of the estate does not pass to their children (the great-nieces and great-nephews of the intestate). In other words, in the case of siblings of the intestate, inheriting by representation stops after the second generation. Figure 4.10 illustrates this principle.

The definitions of "brother" and "sister" include all siblings, including half-siblings and adopted siblings.

FIGURE 4.8   Distribution to Parent

Deceased died intestate:

Spouse:	Alice (predeceased)
Other next of kin and descendants:	mother, Muriel
	deceased father, Richard
	aunt, Thelma
	uncle, Gordon
Assets:	$300,000
Debts:	credit card debt $10,000

How is the estate distributed?

$10,000 to credit card company

$290,000 to Muriel

FIGURE 4.9   Distribution to Sibling and Niece and Nephew by Representation

Deceased died intestate:

Spouse:	Alice (predeceased)
Other next of kin and descendants:	sister, Sarah
	Sarah's daughter, June
	deceased brother, Jordan
	Jordan's son, James
	Jordan's daughter, Millie
Assets:	$210,000
Debts:	credit card debt $10,000

How is the estate distributed?

$10,000 to credit card company

$100,000 to Sarah
$50,000 to James
$50,000 to Millie

FIGURE 4.10   **Distribution to Sibling and Nephew (No Distribution to Child of Predeceased Niece)**

Deceased died intestate:

Spouse:	Alice (predeceased)
Other next of kin and descendants:	sister, Sarah
	deceased brother, Jordan
	Jordan's son, James
	Jordan's deceased daughter, Millie
	Millie's son, Ryan
Assets:	$210,000
Debts:	credit card debt $10,000

How is the estate distributed?

$10,000 to credit card company

$100,000 to Sarah
$100,000 to James

No Surviving Spouse, Issue, Parent, or Sibling, but at Least One Surviving Niece or Nephew

If a person dies intestate with no surviving spouse, issue, parent, or sibling, but has one surviving niece or nephew, she receives the entire net estate of the intestate. If there are two or more surviving nieces and/or nephews, these nieces and/or nephews share equally in the distribution of the net estate. Figure 4.11 illustrates such a situation. Again, at this stage of distribution, there is no representation. In other words, any nieces or nephews who predecease the intestate do not notionally pass on any inheritance that they would otherwise have received from the estate. The result is that the surviving nieces and nephews share equally, regardless of how many or how few come from each brother or sister of the deceased intestate.

No Surviving Spouse, Issue, Parent, Sibling, or Niece or Nephew, but at Least One Surviving Other Blood Relative

If a person dies intestate with no surviving spouse, issue, parent, sibling, or niece or nephew, but has one or more surviving blood relatives, the estate is distributed according to the table of consanguinity or bloodlines (Figure 4.12). This table sets out the progressively distant classes of relatives of an intestate person. Each kind of blood relative is given a designated number that defines his or her class. Grand nephew (sometimes referred to as "great nephew"), for example, is designated number 4, which is also shared by grand uncle (sometimes referred to as "great uncle") and first cousin. Thus, if the intestate is survived only by a grand nephew (number 4), a grand uncle (number 4), and a second cousin (number 5), the grand nephew and the grand uncle will share equally in the distribution of the net estate. If the intestate is survived only by a second cousin, the second cousin will receive the entire net estate.

FIGURE 4.11   Distribution to Nieces and Nephew (No Distribution by Representation)

Deceased died intestate:

Spouse:	Alice (predeceased)

Other next of kin and descendants:	deceased sister, Sarah
	    Sarah's daughter, June
	deceased brother, Jordan
	    Jordan's son, James
	    Jordan's daughter, Millie

Assets:	$310,000
Debts:	credit card debt $10,000

How is the estate distributed?

$10,000 to credit card company

$100,000 to June
$100,000 to James
$100,000 to Millie

The table of consanguinity should not be consulted for any situation in which the intestate is survived by a spouse, issue, parent, sibling, or niece or nephew because the numbers on this table do not correspond with the rules set out in the *Succession Law Reform Act*. It is only when the rules for a spouse, issue, parent, sibling, or niece or nephew are exhausted that the table of consanguinity applies.

No Surviving Relative

If a person dies intestate and has no surviving relative, the government assumes ownership of the net estate under the *Escheats Act*.[4] As noted in the introduction to this chapter, the terminology in such a case is "the estate escheats to the Crown."

Simultaneous Deaths

In intestate estates, as in testate estates where the will does not contain a common disaster clause, where two or more persons who would otherwise be beneficiaries of one another's estate die simultaneously or in circumstances where it is impossible to determine who died

---

4   RSO 1990, c E.20.

first, section 55 of the *Succession Law Reform Act* applies. Section 55(1) states that for the purposes of determining the beneficiaries of the estate of each person who died, each person is deemed to be the survivor of the other(s). Section 55(2) indicates that joint tenancies owned by persons dying in such circumstances are deemed tenancies in common—that is, the joint tenants' respective estates each receive a share of the joint tenancy.

FIGURE 4.12   Table of Consanguinity

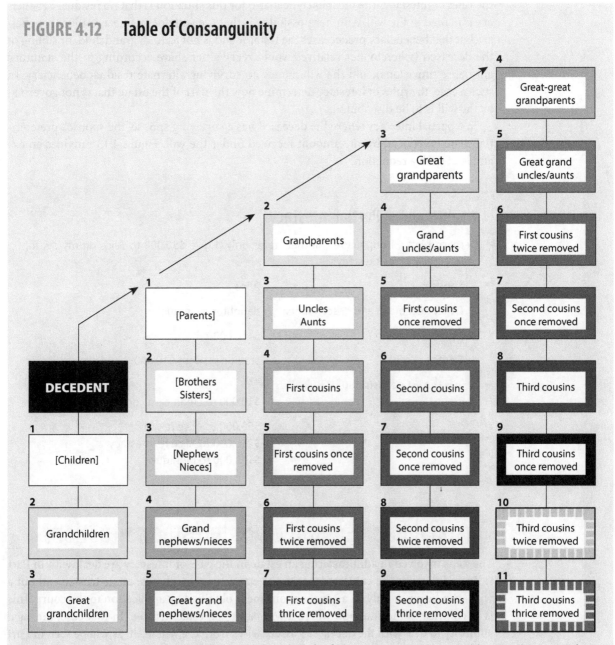

Note: The table of consanguinity applies only when the rules for a spouse, issue, parent, sibling, or niece or nephew (indicated by square brackets) are exhausted.

Intestacy Distribution Where There Is a Will

As explained in the introduction to this chapter, intestacy can occur even where the deceased had a valid will. If, for example, property owned by the deceased is not in some way given to a surviving person by the deceased's will, that property must be dealt with under the rules of intestacy. The most likely scenario for this situation is that no residual beneficiary is named in the will. Another possibility is that the will does name a residual beneficiary but that beneficiary predeceases the testator and is not a child, grandchild, or sibling of the deceased (whereby her relatives would receive her share according to the statutory anti-lapse provisions), and the will names no surviving alternate residual beneficiary. In such a case, the rules of intestacy determine how the part of the estate that is not governed by the will is to be distributed.

In a partial intestacy where the deceased has a surviving spouse, the spouse's preferential share is reduced by any amount received under the will. Figure 4.13 provides an example of such a reduction.

FIGURE 4.13 **Partial Intestacy**

Deceased left a homemade will that states only "I give $50,000 to Alice on my death," resulting in partial intestacy:

Spouse:	Alice
Other next of kin and descendants:	daughter, Monique
Assets:	$410,000
Debts:	credit card debt $10,000

How is the estate distributed?

$10,000 to credit card company

$50,000 to Alice re will
$250,000 to Alice re intestacy
$100,000 to Monique

Personal Representatives in Intestacy Situations

The steps involved in administering an estate in the case of intestacy are dealt with in Part II. In an intestacy, the entitlement to act as estate trustee—that is, estate trustee without a will—can be given only by a court appointment obtained by application to the court. This is in contrast to the situation where a will names an estate trustee. In that case, the legal authority to deal with the deceased's assets arises from the will itself, as will be seen in Part II. Despite this authority arising from the will, it may turn out that because of the legitimate requirements of third parties (such as transfer agents of publicly traded securities or land registry office requirements), such assets cannot be dealt with or transferred to the beneficiaries without a court appointment of the estate trustee.

In an intestacy, the appropriate person to apply to the court for an appointment as estate trustee without a will is set out in section 29(1) of the *Estates Act*[5]—namely, the deceased's spouse (which is defined either as the person to whom the deceased was married immediately before death or the person with whom the deceased "was living in a conjugal relationship outside marriage immediately before death"), "the next of kin of the deceased," or the spouse and the next of kin together. Some have interpreted section 29(1) as containing a priority whereby the spouse has priority over the next of kin. The section does not, however, set out such a hierarchy. Instead, reference is made in section 29(1) to the "discretion of the court" as the deciding factor in the event of competing claims. In addition, section 29(2) allows a majority of the beneficiaries of the estate (provided they are residents of Ontario) to request that the court appoint a person other than the spouse or next of kin as estate trustee. Section 29(3) also gives discretion to the court when other special circumstances arise. In the case of a partial intestacy with no estate trustee named in the will, the court reviews the appropriateness of any applicant for the role of estate trustee with a will, considering all of the circumstances of the particular case. For example, where the part of the estate that is not governed by the will is small in relation to the part that is governed by the will, the court is more likely to grant the appointment to the major beneficiary under the will than to the major beneficiary under the part of the estate governed by the laws of intestate succession (assuming that these are different persons).

---

5 RSO 1990, c E.21.

KEY TERMS

escheat, 60

intestacy, 60

REVIEW QUESTIONS

1. Define the following terms or concepts:
   a. intestacy
   b. escheat

2. When does a partial intestacy usually occur?

3. The rules of intestate succession do not affect the rights of which two groups?

4. What are the five "rings" or classes of intestate successors?

5. What is the standing of a "common law spouse" on intestate succession?

6. What does the "expanded definition" of children include?

7. What is the standing of a child born after the deceased's death?

8. Who inherits when the deceased dies without a will or issue but leaving a spouse and what, if anything, does that spouse inherit?

9. Who inherits if the intestate deceased leaves a net estate of $300,000 without a spouse, issue, or other next of kin?

10. Who inherits if the intestate deceased leaves a net estate of $300,000, with no spouse but leaving issue and siblings?

11. Who inherits if the intestate deceased leaves a net estate of $200,000 with a spouse and issue?

12. Who inherits what if the intestate deceased leaves a net estate of $300,000 with a spouse and issue?

13. Who inherits what if the intestate deceased leaves a net estate of $300,000 with no spouse, issue, or parents but leaves siblings?

14. How might grandchildren or great grandchildren be included in the above examples?

15. How might nephews and nieces be included in the above examples?

16. How do you divide the net remainder of the estate of an intestate after paying the spouse's preferential share where the deceased left (a) one child, and (b) more than one child?

17. Under what circumstances would divorced parents of an intestate deceased inherit, and what would they inherit?

18. When do siblings of an intestate deceased inherit?

19. Under what circumstances might nephews and nieces of an intestate deceased inherit?

20. When do half-brothers and half-sisters of an intestate deceased inherit?

21. Describe when the table of consanguinity would apply to intestate succession.

22. Who is the appropriate person to apply for a certificate of appointment in the estate of an intestate?

Powers of Attorney

5

LEARNING OUTCOMES

After completing this chapter, you should be able to:

- Explain the difference between a power of attorney for property and a power of attorney for personal care

- List the formal requirements of a power of attorney for property or for personal care, including who can be a witness

- Explain who can be an attorney for property or for personal care

- Explain the advantages and disadvantages of joint attorneys for property and for personal care

- Explain the mental capacity requirements for a person granting a power of attorney for property or for personal care

- Explain how a power of attorney for property or for personal care can be revoked or how an attorney can resign

- Explain the accounting requirements of an attorney for property and for personal care

- Describe the best practices for safekeeping original powers of attorney

- Explain the difference between restricted and general powers of attorney for property

- Explain what a bank power of attorney is

- Explain specific instructions (including a "living will" clause) or "special provisions" as they might appear in a power of attorney for personal care

Introduction

As part of the estate planning process, a person can create powers of attorney. The **power of attorney** concept has evolved considerably over the past 200 years. Historically it was a document in which a person ("the grantor") granted power over his assets to another person ("the attorney"). The power granted would cease upon the grantor's becoming mentally incapable of managing his affairs. Eventually the law changed to allow the attorney's authority over the grantor's assets to continue beyond the time at which the grantor became mentally incapacitated, provided that the power of attorney specifically stated that it was so intended and was witnessed by a person other than the attorney or the spouse of the attorney.

In the early 1990s, Ontario enacted a set of statutes that reflected a dramatic new direction in the law related to powers of attorney and mental incapacity. Most notable among these statutes was the *Substitute Decisions Act, 1992*.[1]

The *Substitute Decisions Act, 1992* brought into being a new kind of power of attorney known as the power of attorney for personal care. This was created for the purpose of appointing an attorney to make decisions regarding the grantor's health care, nutrition, shelter, clothing, hygiene, or safety—that is, personal care decisions—when the grantor becomes unable to make such decisions for himself or herself.

The Act also modified the law as it applies to continuing powers of attorney for property—that is, powers of attorney for property that continue after the grantor has become mentally incapacitated. (Powers of attorney for property that are not intended to continue beyond a subsequent legal incapacity of the grantor, theoretically, are still governed by the old *Powers of Attorney Act*,[2] which remains in existence.) The Act uses the term "continuing power of attorney" and "continuing power of attorney for property" interchangeably to denote a continuing power of attorney for property. This nomenclature has led to some confusion because a power of attorney for personal care is also a form of continuing power of attorney and yet is never referred to in the Act as a "continuing power of attorney" or even a "continuing power of attorney for personal care."

Also note that the word "attorney" in Canada is not synonymous with the word "lawyer" as it is in the United States. Clients are sometimes understandably confused about the term "power of attorney" and think, for example, that the document gives power to a lawyer over the grantor's assets or person. To avoid such confusion, it is sometimes appropriate to point out to the client that "attorney" in this context does not mean "lawyer."

Finally, the attorney named in a power of attorney is the substitute decision-maker for a live person. At no time past or present has the law allowed an attorney to act beyond the death of the grantor. When the grantor of a power of attorney dies, the power of attorney ceases to be effective. If, after the death of the grantor, the attorney knowingly continues to act under the apparent authority in the power of attorney, he could face civil, or even criminal, liability.

The rest of this chapter deals with some of the practicalities of and requirements for valid continuing powers of attorney for property and personal care.

---

1   SO 1992, c 30.
2   RSO 1990, c P.20.

Formal Requirements of Powers of Attorney

Power of Attorney for Property

A continuing power of attorney for property must be in writing and must be signed by the grantor and two witnesses. The legal requirements relating to the named attorney and the witnesses are discussed below. Interestingly, neither the old *Powers of Attorney Act* nor the *Substitute Decisions Act, 1992* sets out the formal requirements for a power of attorney for property that is non-continuing—that is, not intended to be used during a subsequent legal incapacity of the grantor. Practicality, however, dictates that the formal requirements set out in the *Substitute Decisions Act, 1992* should be followed in creating any power of attorney for property, be it continuing or non-continuing.

Under the *Substitute Decisions Act, 1992*, if the power of attorney for property is intended to be a continuing power of attorney for property, then the document must state either that it is a continuing power of attorney or that it is the grantor's intention that the power of attorney for property be exercised during the grantor's subsequent legal incapacity.

The *Substitute Decisions Act, 1992* mentions a "prescribed form" of power of attorney for property that can be used. Although a prescribed form does not appear in the statute or its regulations, the government has published brochures that include a sample blank power of attorney for property. The Act also states that the prescribed form need not be followed for the power of attorney for property to be valid. Figure 5.1 is a lawyer's draft of a continuing power of attorney.

FIGURE 5.1   Power of Attorney for Property

POWER OF ATTORNEY FOR PROPERTY

THIS IS A POWER OF ATTORNEY FOR PROPERTY made pursuant to the *Substitute Decisions Act, 1992*, SO 1992, c. 30, as amended.

1. This continuing power of attorney for property is given by **JOHN DOE**, whose current residence address is 99 Anywhere Street, Hamilton, Ontario, Q9Q 9Q9, retired bank manager.

2. I hereby appoint either my wife, JANE DOE, acting alone, or my three children, JENNIFER DOE, JOHN DOE JR. and STEVEN DOE, acting jointly, to be my attorney(s) for property.

3. I declare that this power of attorney may be exercised during any subsequent legal incapacity on my part to manage property and that I intend this document to be a continuing power of attorney for property pursuant to the *Substitute Decisions Act, 1992*.

4. In making this power of attorney I am aware:

   (a)   of the nature and extent of my property;

   (b)   of the obligations I owe to my dependants;

   (c)   that my attorney(s) will be able to do on my behalf anything in respect of property that I could do if capable, except make a will and except to the extent that this power of attorney sets out conditions and restrictions on the powers of my attorney(s);

FIGURE 5.1 CONTINUED

    (d)   that my attorney(s) must account for his or her or their dealings with my property;

    (e)   that I may, while capable, revoke this power of attorney;

    (f)   that the value of my property administered by my attorney(s) may decline unless my attorney(s) manage(s) it prudently; and

    (g)   that there is a possibility that my attorney(s) could misuse the authority given to him or her or them by this power of attorney.

5.   I recognize that by making this power of attorney I hereby revoke any other power of attorney for property previously made by me.

6.   This power of attorney is subject to the following conditions, restrictions and supplementary powers:

    (a)   I authorize my attorney(s) to bind and to secure information on behalf of my estate in respect of its dealings with any person, institution, government or legal entity;

    (b)   I authorize my attorney(s) to delegate any act my attorney(s) may exercise to some other person or legal entity and to revoke or suspend such delegation;

    (c)   I authorize my attorney(s) to revoke, suspend or reinstate (if it has been revoked) any power of attorney for property previously given by me;

    (d)   I authorize my attorney(s) to receive and draw on an interim basis fair and reasonable compensation or such amount as may be prescribed by the *Substitute Decisions Act, 1992* or any regulation made thereunder for his, her, or their care, pains, trouble and time expended in and about the administration of my estate;

    (e)   I authorize my attorney(s) to manage my estate for my benefit, for the benefit of any person, including my attorney(s), to whom I am under a legal obligation to provide a benefit, to the extent that my attorney(s) consider(s) it necessary to fulfill such obligation and for the benefit of any charitable purpose or any person, including my attorney(s), which or whom my attorney(s) consider(s) I would have wished to benefit were I acting personally instead of through my attorney(s);

    (f)   I authorize my attorney(s) to take physical possession of all my property, including property held in a safety deposit box, property held in safekeeping by others on my behalf, and property held by others subject to some professional privilege, which privilege I waive for this purpose, and for greater certainty I hereby specifically authorize my attorney(s) to have the right to review my will in order to be able to manage my estate in a manner that is sensitive to its provisions;

    (g)   I authorize my attorney(s) to exercise all my rights with respect to the disposition or encumbrance of a matrimonial home including those dealt with by the *Family Law Act*;

    (h)   I authorize my attorney(s) to pay my attorney(s) for personal care fair and reasonable compensation for his, her or their care, pain, time and trouble expended pursuant to a power of attorney for personal care and to allocate such compensation between or among them if there be more than one.

I have executed this power of attorney in the presence of both of the witnesses and on the date set out below.

Date: January 1, 2018

John Doe
_____

John Doe

We are the subscribing witnesses to this power of attorney for property and were both present together and saw it executed by the person whose name appears above on the date shown above. Neither of us has any reason to believe that the grantor is incapable of giving a power of attorney for property or instructions therein contained. Each of us is of the full age of 18 years and neither of us is the attorney's or grantor's spouse or partner, a child of the grantor or considered in law as such, or a person whose property is under guardianship or has a guardian of the person.

Mary Breshney
_____
Mary Breshney

Michael Finch
_____
Michael Finch

Power of Attorney for Personal Care

An example of a power of attorney for personal care is reproduced in Figure 5.2. Like the continuing power of attorney for property, a power of attorney for personal care must be in writing and must be signed by the grantor and two witnesses. The legal requirements for the named attorney and the witnesses for power of attorney for personal care are discussed below. Again, while the *Substitute Decisions Act, 1992* mentions a prescribed form of power of attorney for personal care, such a form does not appear in the statute or regulations, although government publications set out suggested forms. The Act also indicates that the prescribed form need not be followed in order for the power of attorney for personal care to be valid.

FIGURE 5.2 Power of Attorney for Personal Care

POWER OF ATTORNEY FOR PERSONAL CARE

THIS POWER OF ATTORNEY FOR PERSONAL CARE is given pursuant to the *Substitute Decisions Act, 1992*, by **JOHN DOE**, whose current residence address is 99 Anywhere Street, Hamilton, Ontario, Q9Q 9Q9, retired bank manager.

1. **Appointment.** I hereby appoint my wife, JANE DOE, acting alone, or my three children, JENNIFER DOE, JOHN DOE JR. and STEVEN DOE, acting jointly, to be my attorney(s) for personal care.

2. **Authorization.** I authorize my attorney(s) to make decisions concerning my personal care subject only to any conditions and restrictions or specific instructions contained herein.

3. **Age, Mental Capacity, Awareness and Qualification.** In executing this document, I acknowledge that (a) I am of the full age of sixteen years, (b) I am aware that this power of attorney relates to my personal care including, but not limited to, my health care, nutrition, shelter, clothing, hygiene or safety, (c) I believe that the attorney(s) named herein has (have) a genuine concern for my welfare and I appreciate and understand that I may need to have her or them make personal care decisions for me, and (d) no person or persons named herein as my attorney(s) provide(s) health care, residential, social, training or support services to me for compensation, unless she or they is (are) my spouse, partner or relative.

FIGURE 5.2 CONTINUED

4. **Specific Conditions or Restrictions.** Except as herein stated, there are no specific conditions or restrictions.

5. **Specific Instructions.** In the event that my circumstances of health are such that there is no reasonable expectation of my recovery from extreme physical or mental disability, I direct my attorney(s) to allow me to die and not be kept alive by medications, artificial means, life-support equipment, cardiopulmonary resuscitation or heroic measures, but I do ask that medication be mercifully administered to me to alleviate suffering even though this may shorten my remaining life.

6. **Consent to Treatment.** I authorize my attorney(s), on my behalf, to give consent or refuse to consent to treatment to which the *Health Care Consent Act, 1996* applies.

7. **Indemnification.** I indemnify from any liability to me, to my estate or to any third party, any person who, in reliance on this power of attorney, acts consistently with my wishes herein expressed even though such action is considered by such person not to be in my best interests.

8. **Headings.** Paragraph headings are for reference purposes only and shall not define, limit or extend any provision.

I have executed this power of attorney in the presence of both of the witnesses and on the date set out below.

Date: January 1, 2018

John Doe
_____
John Doe

We are the subscribing witnesses to this power of attorney for personal care and were both present together and saw it executed by the person whose name appears above on the date shown above. Neither of us has any reason to believe that the grantor is incapable of giving a power of attorney for personal care or instructions therein contained. Each of us is of the full age of 18 years and neither of us is the attorney's or grantor's spouse or partner, a child of the grantor or considered in law as such, or a person whose property is under guardianship or has a guardian of the person.

Mary Breshney
_____
Mary Breshney

Michael Finch
_____
Michael Finch

When Is the Power of Attorney Effective?

Power of Attorney for Property

An important preliminary issue in preparing powers of attorney for property is whether a particular power of attorney should be made effective immediately or whether it should be made effective at some future time. If the power of attorney for property does not indicate when it is to become effective, it is deemed to be effective from the moment it is signed. In such a case, the named attorney will be able to deal with the grantor's assets from the moment the power of attorney for property is signed (provided that he has the power of attorney document in his possession). It is fairly common for a power of attorney for property to be drawn to become effective upon the grantor's becoming legally incapacitated. The lawyer and the law clerk, however, should consider carefully whether such a condition to a certain extent defeats the purpose of the power of attorney for property by having its effectiveness depend on an event that cannot easily be established. If, for example, the power of attorney for property is being created for the purpose of bypassing the "red tape" and uncertainty that arises when a person appears to be incapable of managing her property, unless the power of attorney cites a specific triggering event that is a relatively simple one to establish, it may create an additional layer of red tape. A finding of incapacity can often be difficult to obtain, particularly when a person is obviously capable in some ways and yet appears incapable in other ways. In addition, because of the serious legal repercussions of a finding of legal incapacity, medical practitioners are understandably reluctant to make such a diagnosis without a full-scale assessment.

Nevertheless, if the grantor's wishes are that the power of attorney for property is to be effective only on the subsequent incapacity of the grantor, it will be necessary to establish what constitutes legal incapacity. The *Substitute Decisions Act, 1992* allows for a power of attorney to provide its own test for making this determination. If, however, the power of attorney does not provide its own test, under section 9(3) of the Act, the power of attorney does not come into effect until

> (a) the attorney is notified in the prescribed form by an assessor that the assessor has performed an assessment of the grantor's incapacity and has found that the grantor is incapable of managing property; or
> (b) the attorney is notified that a certificate of incapacity has been issued in respect of the grantor under the *Mental Health Act*.

An assessor is defined in the regulations to the *Substitute Decisions Act, 1992*[3] as a person who is a member of

- the College of Physicians and Surgeons of Ontario,
- the College of Psychologists of Ontario,
- the Ontario College of Certified Social Workers,
- the College of Occupational Therapists of Ontario, or
- the College of Nurses of Ontario

and who has successfully completed a training course as described in the regulations. It is also a requirement of an assessor that he or she have professional liability insurance of at least $1,000,000.

The assessment of whether the grantor is incapable of managing property, or the certificate of incapacity, is based on section 6 of the Act, which states:

> A person is incapable of managing property if the person is not able to understand information that is relevant to making a decision in the management of his or her property, or is not able to appreciate the reasonably foreseeable consequences of a decision or lack of decision.

---

3 O Reg 238/00, s 1(1).

Power of Attorney for Personal Care

Unlike the power of attorney for property, which is deemed to be effective from the moment it is signed unless otherwise stated in the document, the power of attorney for personal care is effective only upon the incapacity of the grantor. The difference is logical because if a grantor has mental capacity, she will be able to directly instruct those around her about her care.

Incapacity to make decisions regarding personal care can vary depending on the decision to be made. A person may be deemed capable of making one kind of decision regarding personal care but not another kind. For example, a decision on what to eat for dinner may be within a person's capacity, while a decision as to whether to undergo heart surgery may not be. In this regard, it should be noted that, in the past, mental incapacity was treated in the law as a discrete state of mind that meant a person was either incapable or not, with no gradations in between.

If the personal-care decision facing the grantor is in respect of medical treatment, the question whether he has the requisite mental capacity to make the decision is answered with reference to the *Health Care Consent Act, 1996*.[4] That is, section 49 of the *Substitute Decisions Act, 1992* holds that the power of attorney for personal care becomes effective when the decision to be made relates to treatment of the grantor, and the attorney is authorized under the *Health Care Consent Act, 1996* to make the decision on behalf of the grantor. Although "treatment" is defined very broadly under the *Health Care Consent Act, 1996*, it is generally meant to encompass positive action on the part of a health care provider for the benefit of the person in question. Section 4(1) of the *Health Care Consent Act, 1996* contains the following test regarding the question whether a person has the requisite mental capacity to make a decision regarding treatment:

> A person is capable with respect to a treatment, admission to a care facility or a personal assistance service if the person is able to understand the information that is relevant to making a decision about the treatment, admission or personal assistance service, as the case may be, and able to appreciate the reasonably foreseeable consequences of a decision or lack of decision.

The Act goes on to state in section 20 that when a person is incapable with respect to a treatment decision, the person's attorney under a power of attorney for personal care can make the decision. In a somewhat circular way, these sections together grant the attorney the legal authority to act with respect to treatment. In the event that the *Health Care Consent Act, 1996* does not authorize the attorney to give consent with respect to a particular decision—for example, in the case of a treatment that does not fall under the wide definition of "treatment" in the Act—the attorney may nevertheless act if he has reasonable grounds to believe that the grantor of the power of attorney is incapable of making a particular personal care decision. The default test for capacity for personal care is contained in section 45 of the Act, which states:

> A person is incapable of personal care if the person is not able to understand information that is relevant to making a decision concerning his or her own health care, nutrition, shelter, clothing, hygiene or safety, or is not able to appreciate the reasonably foreseeable consequences of a decision or a lack of decision.

---

4 SO 1996, c 2 (Sched A).

This ability of the attorney to decide on reasonable grounds whether the power of attorney for personal care is effective is subject to one exception, where the power of attorney document itself indicates that there must be a confirmation of incapacity before the power of attorney is effective. As in the case of the continuing power of attorney for property, such confirmation can be made according to a test set out in the power of attorney document itself or can be based on the finding of an assessor.

If the test for the grantor's incapacity is given by an assessor, the power of attorney for personal care document may require the assessor to consider certain factors in coming to a decision. Where an assessor has performed an assessment and has concluded that the grantor is incapacitated with respect to the decision in question, the power of attorney for personal care becomes effective when the assessor provides the attorney with a form indicating that the grantor is incapacitated (unless another method is specified in the power of attorney). This form, referred to in section 49(2) of the *Substitute Decisions Act, 1992*, is set out in the regulations under the Act. The finding by an assessor that a person is incapable with respect to making decisions about treatment of personal assistance can be appealed under the *Health Care Consent Act, 1996*, and a grantor of a power of attorney can pre-waive this right to appeal. Such a waiver, however, is considered to be a "special provision" in the Act. If such a special provision is contained in the power of attorney for personal care, fairly onerous requirements must be satisfied (as discussed below under "Special Provisions of a Power of Attorney for Personal Care").

Who Can Be an Attorney?

Power of Attorney for Property

The first requirement for a valid continuing power of attorney (and also, it is assumed, as stated above, for a non-continuing power of attorney for property) is contained in section 5 of the *Substitute Decisions Act, 1992*, which states that the attorney must be at least 18 years of age. A practical requirement, of course, is that the attorney be of sound mind. Another practical requirement is that he or she must be willing to assume the role of attorney. As can be seen from the example of the continuing power of attorney in Figure 5.1, the only persons to actually sign the document are the grantor and the two witnesses (whose qualifications are discussed below). It is therefore possible for an attorney so appointed to not even know that he or she has been named, and it may turn out that he or she is not willing or able to assume the role. (See below under "Resignation of Attorney(s)" for property.) It goes without saying that the proposed attorney should be approached beforehand to see whether he or she is willing to act when needed.

A person who does not wish to act as the attorney is not obligated by law to act and can refuse the role without the risk of civil liability, provided that he or she has not already taken some steps to assume the role. If the attorney has decided not to assume the role, the power of attorney for property is not technically invalid, but it is invalid for all practical purposes. In such a case, if the grantor is incapacitated, her property may be taken over by an interested party, perhaps a friend or relative, upon successful application to the Superior Court of Justice to be appointed guardian of the person's property (as covered in Part III, Estate Litigation, Chapter 16, Statutory Forms of Estate Litigation). In the alternative, and perhaps as a last resort, the Office of the Public Guardian and Trustee, a branch of the Office of the Attorney General, may assume control of the person's property.

In addition to consulting the proposed attorney for property beforehand, it is usually advisable, subject to the comments below under "Substitute or Joint Attorneys" for property, to name more than one attorney.

Power of Attorney for Personal Care

In contrast to powers of attorney for property, which require the attorney to be at least 18 years of age, an attorney for personal care can be 16 years of age or older. Again, it is a practical requirement that the attorney be of sound mind.

There are other, special restrictions on who can be an attorney for personal care. Under section 46(3) of the *Substitute Decisions Act, 1992*, a person cannot be an attorney for personal care if he or she provides health care or residential, social, training, or support services to the grantor for compensation. These restrictions do not apply, however, if the person providing such care for compensation is the grantor's spouse, partner, or relative. As in the case of the power of attorney for property, a person appointed attorney for personal care is not obligated to accept the role. Again, for that reason, lawyers and law clerks should advise their clients to consult with the proposed attorney to determine whether that person is likely to be willing to accept the role should the necessity arise.

Requirements of Capacity of the Grantor

Power of Attorney for Property

As indicated above, section 6 of the *Substitute Decisions Act, 1992* sets out the test for deciding whether a person is capable of managing property. This is not the same as the test used to determine whether a person is capable of granting a continuing power of attorney for property. In fact, section 9(1) of the *Substitute Decisions Act, 1992* states explicitly that a person may be incapable of managing property and yet may be capable of granting a continuing power of attorney for property.

The test for deciding the latter is set out in section 8(1) of the Act:

> A person is capable of giving a continuing power of attorney if he or she,
>
> (a) knows what kind of property he or she has and its approximate value;
>
> (b) is aware of obligations owed to his or her dependants;
>
> (c) knows that the attorney will be able to do on the person's behalf anything in respect of property that the person could do if capable, except make a will, subject to the conditions and restrictions set out in the power of attorney;
>
> (d) knows that the attorney must account for his or her dealings with the person's property;
>
> (e) knows that he or she may, if capable, revoke the continuing power of attorney;
>
> (f) appreciates that unless the attorney manages the property prudently its value may decline; and
>
> (g) appreciates the possibility that the attorney could misuse the authority given to him or her.

This test is also the test for revoking an existing continuing power of attorney for property (see below under "Termination and Revocation of Power of Attorney" for property). If a grantor has executed a valid continuing power of attorney for property and subsequently becomes mentally incapable to the point where he or she is unable to meet the test set out in section 8(1), he or she may be powerless to prevent the attorney from continuing to act as attorney even if the grantor is unhappy with the attorney's actions.

Power of Attorney for Personal Care

Similar to the case of the power of attorney for property, the grantor may give a valid power of attorney for personal care even if, at the time of giving it, he himself is incapable of personal care. The test is contained in section 47(1) of the *Substitute Decisions Act, 1992*, which reads as follows:

> A person is capable of giving a power of attorney for personal care if the person,
> (a)   has the ability to understand whether the proposed attorney has a genuine concern for the person's welfare; and
> (b)   appreciates that the person may need to have the proposed attorney make decisions for the person.

As can be seen, the threshold is considerably lower for the power of attorney for personal care than for the power of attorney for property. Note, however, that a higher degree of mental capacity is required for a power of attorney for personal care containing specific personal care instructions or special provisions (both discussed below). As will be seen, if the grantor wishes to include specific instructions or special provisions in his power of attorney for personal care, he must have the requisite mental capacity to make the relevant personal care decisions when granting the power of attorney.

Requirements of Witnesses

Power of Attorney for Property

A final requirement of a valid continuing power of attorney for property is that it be witnessed by two legally valid witnesses who are both present when the grantor signs and who both sign the document in the presence of each other. As stated above, while it is not entirely clear what the corresponding requirement for a non-continuing power of attorney for property is, practicality dictates that the same requirements ought to be followed for the latter.

To be a valid witness for a continuing power of attorney for property, the witness must not be one of the persons specified in section 10(2) of the *Substitute Decisions Act, 1992*:

> The following persons shall not be witnesses:
>
> 1. The attorney or the attorney's spouse or partner.
> 2. The grantor's spouse or partner.
> 3. A child of the grantor or a person whom the grantor has demonstrated a settled intention to treat as his or her child.

4. A person whose property is under guardianship or who has a guardian of the person.
5. A person who is less than eighteen years old.

Again, apart from these restrictions, practicality dictates that the witnesses be of sound mind. Note as well that section 10(4) states that if the continuing power of attorney is not properly witnessed in accordance with the requirements of the Act, a court may nevertheless declare the power of attorney to be effective if the court is of the opinion that it is in the best interests of the grantor, or the grantor's dependants, to do so.

Power of Attorney for Personal Care

The requirements for the witnesses of a power of attorney for personal care are set out in section 48(2) of the *Substitute Decisions Act, 1992*. This section indicates that the equivalent section for powers of attorney for property (s 10(2)) applies in the case of powers of attorney for personal care. In addition, similar to section 10(4) for powers of attorney for property, section 48(4) provides that a court may uphold a power of attorney for personal care despite non-compliance with the witness requirement if it is in the best interests of the grantor to do so. Again, from a practical standpoint, the witnesses should be of sound mind.

Substitute or Joint Attorneys

Power of Attorney for Property

If a client creates a continuing power of attorney for property and names only one attorney, the power of attorney ceases to be useful or valid if the attorney named dies, becomes mentally incapacitated with no reasonable hope of recovery, or ceases to act as attorney. For this reason, a client will often decide to name two or more attorneys in the power of attorney. There are several ways to go about doing this, all of which have their own advantages and disadvantages.

One way is to specify that both or all named attorneys must act jointly—that is, together. Such an arrangement necessitates both or all such joint attorneys' signatures on all documents executed under the power, such as transfers of land, mortgages, cheques, and so on. Requiring all to sign allows each attorney to know what is being done on behalf of the grantor of the power. For this reason, many clients believe that their affairs will be more conscientiously managed. A disadvantage to this arrangement is that if one of the named attorneys is unavailable to sign a document, the power of attorney for property cannot be used. The document can, of course, specify that the attorneys named must act together, and that if one is deceased or incapacitated, the other(s) can act alone. The disadvantage to this solution is that the surviving mentally capable attorney(s) may have to provide documentation to a third party that the other attorney is deceased or mentally incapable. While evidence of death is usually fairly easy to provide—a funeral director's statement of death would probably suffice—evidence of incapacity may be much more difficult to obtain.

Another approach is to name two or more attorneys who can act jointly and severally. This phrase is commonly used in legal documents. Contrary to what one might think at first, "jointly" means "together" and "severally" means "alone." In such an arrangement, the third party requiring the continuing power of attorney for property can legally deal with any attorney named in the power of attorney, whether acting alone or in conjunction with the other(s). Although this arrangement has the advantage of ease of use, it does create additional risk to the grantor in that the attorneys may disagree or act contrary to one another's wishes or plans and thus cause financial harm. This option also eliminates the safeguard of a bilateral (or multilateral) "watchdog" that exists if the attorneys must act together. Despite the disadvantages of this approach, in the author's view it is usually the best one. The problems that such an arrangement creates can be minimized by careful selection of the attorneys. Indeed, if a client thinks that a particular individual needs another to keep him in check with respect to the client's financial affairs, the client should perhaps reconsider naming that individual as attorney in the first place.

It is also possible to have a combination of the above solutions. For example, a grantor could name as attorney either the grantor's spouse on the one hand or his children, acting jointly, on the other. All in all, the client's particular circumstances must be examined carefully to come up with an arrangement that best suits her situation. At all times, a client should be reminded that the power of attorney for property is a very powerful document, and that, particularly in view of the fact that future circumstances may render it irrevocable, the decision of who should be the attorney should not be made lightly. It is often a good idea for a lawyer or law clerk to ask a client to imagine not getting along with the proposed attorney to see whether the client truly believes that the proposed attorney will make sound and fair decisions concerning the client's property.

Note that the *Substitute Decisions Act, 1992* uses the term "substitute attorney," although, in practice, many lawyers and law clerks use the term "alternate attorney."

Power of Attorney for Personal Care

A power of attorney for personal care can also have substitute attorneys or joint attorneys. The considerations regarding the best choices for a particular client are similar to those arising in the case of continuing powers of attorney for property, although the particular kinds of decisions to be made in the case of a power of attorney for personal care obviously have to be taken into account when assessing the best candidate for the role of attorney.

Termination and Revocation of Power of Attorney

Power of Attorney for Property

Section 12(1) of the *Substitute Decisions Act, 1992* sets out the situations in which a continuing power of attorney for property is terminated:

1. the attorney dies or becomes incapable of managing property and there is no other joint attorney and there is no substitute attorney;
2. the court appoints a guardian of the grantor's property;
3. the grantor creates a new power of attorney for property (unless the grantor provides for multiple co-existing powers of attorney);
4. the grantor revokes the power of attorney; or
5. the grantor dies.

Section 12(2) indicates that a revocation of a continuing power of attorney must be in writing and executed "in the same way as a continuing power of attorney." Presumably this section means that a revocation must be witnessed by two witnesses who qualify under section 10(2). It is also presumed that in order to revoke a continuing power of attorney, the grantor must have the same mental capacity as that required to grant the power of attorney in the first place. In addition, it is presumed that the person whose power is being revoked would or should be notified of such revocation.

Power of Attorney for Personal Care

Under section 53(1) of the *Substitute Decisions Act, 1992*, a power of attorney for personal care terminates when one of the following occurs:

1. the attorney dies or becomes incapable of making personal care decisions, and there is no other joint attorney or alternate attorney;
2. the court appoints a guardian of the grantor;
3. the grantor creates a new power of attorney for personal care (unless the grantor provides for multiple co-existing powers of attorney); or
4. the grantor revokes the power of attorney.

This section closely resembles section 12(1), which deals with the termination of a power of attorney for property. Although the latter section includes the additional circumstance of the death of the grantor, it goes without saying that the power of attorney for personal care automatically terminates on the death of the grantor because there is no longer a living person to care for.

As with the power of attorney for property, the power of attorney for personal care can be revoked by the grantor if she has the capacity to grant one. Section 53(2) of the Act states that the revocation must be in writing and executed in the same way as the power of attorney for personal care although, if the power of attorney contains "special provisions," there are special requirements for a revocation (see below).

Resignation of Attorney(s)

Power of Attorney for Property

Under section 11 of the *Substitute Decisions Act, 1992*, an attorney named under a continuing power of attorney for property may resign. If, however, the attorney has already acted in his capacity as attorney, he must put the resignation in writing and deliver it to the following persons:

1. the grantor of the power of attorney;
2. any co-attorneys under the power of attorney; and
3. any substitute attorneys named in the power of attorney.

Furthermore, if the continuing power of attorney does not provide for any alternate attorneys and, presumably, there are no other co-attorneys, and if the attorney is of the opinion that the grantor is incapable of managing property, the resignation is also to be delivered to the following persons:

4. the grantor's spouse or partner;

5. the relatives of the grantor who are known to the attorney and who reside in Ontario; and

6. persons with whom the attorney previously dealt on behalf of the grantor and with whom further dealings are likely to be required on behalf of the grantor.

The resigning attorney need only make reasonable efforts to serve the persons referred to in point 6 above. In addition, there are two situations in which the notice of resignation does not have to be served on the grantor's spouse or partner and relatives. The first is when the power of attorney itself indicates that the notice is not to be sent to these persons. The second is when the grantor and her spouse are separated within the meaning of the *Divorce Act*.[5] In such a case, the *Substitute Decisions Act, 1992* provides that the spouse and any relatives of the grantor who are related to the grantor by marriage do not have to be served.

Note that "partner" is defined in section 1(1) of the *Substitute Decisions Act, 1992* as "either of two persons who have lived together for at least one year and have a close personal relationship that is of primary importance in both persons' lives." The word "partner" as it is used in the Act should not be confused with the word as it appears in most other areas of the common law world to denote a specific business entity. Note also that the term "relative" is not defined in the Act.

Power of Attorney for Personal Care

The procedure for resignation by an attorney for personal care (set out in section 52 of the *Substitute Decisions Act, 1992*) is similar to that for the resignation of an attorney for property. The resignation must be in writing and delivered to the following persons:

1. the grantor of the power of attorney;

2. any co-attorneys under the power of attorney; and

3. any substitute attorneys named in the power of attorney.

If the power of attorney does not provide for substitute attorneys or, presumably, any co-attorneys, and unless the power of attorney provides otherwise, the resignation is to be delivered to the following persons:

4. the grantor's spouse or partner (unless separated within the meaning of the *Divorce Act*);

5. the relatives of the grantor who are known to the attorney and who reside in Ontario (unless such relatives are related to the grantor by marriage, and the grantor and his or her spouse are separated within the meaning of the *Divorce Act*); and

---

5   RSC 1985, c 3 (2d Supp).

6. persons with whom the attorney previously dealt on behalf of the grantor and with whom further dealings are likely to be required on behalf of the grantor.

Again, the resigning attorney need only make reasonable efforts to serve the persons referred to in point 6 above. Note that, in the case of a resigning attorney for property, the persons referred to in points 4 to 6 above are to be served only if the attorney is of the opinion that the grantor is incapable of managing property; whereas, in the case of a resigning attorney for personal care, those persons are to be served regardless. Again, "relative" is not defined in the Act.

Restricted and General Powers of Attorney

Power of Attorney for Property

A power of attorney for property can be drawn in a form that gives power over the grantor's assets in whatever way is desired. That is to say, the attorney can be given specific powers with specific restrictions over the grantor's assets, or the attorney can be given general powers over the grantor's assets. In the latter case, the power of attorney for property is sometimes called a "general power of attorney for property" or a "general power of attorney." The distinction between a continuing power of attorney and a non-continuing power of attorney for property should be kept in mind in this context. A **general power of attorney for property** can be continuing or non-continuing. If it is a general continuing power of attorney for property, it gives unrestricted powers over the grantor's assets to the attorney or attorneys both before and after the grantor becomes legally incapacitated. If it is a general non-continuing power of attorney for property, it gives unrestricted powers over the grantor's assets up until the time when the grantor becomes legally incapacitated.

Powers of attorney for property (either continuing or non-continuing) that are not general can be very useful, as in the case, for example, of a person who will not be in the country when a transaction (such as the sale of real estate) is to take place. A power of attorney for property can be used in such a situation by naming an attorney to sign any necessary papers to complete the transaction. The power of attorney for property can be drafted to apply only to that particular transaction or that particular piece of property. Such a power of attorney typically does not need to be a continuing power of attorney.

Figure 5.3 is an example of such a restricted continuing power of attorney for property. As can be seen from this example, there is no clause indicating that the power of attorney for property can be used during a subsequent legal incapacity of the grantor. In other words, it is not a continuing power of attorney. It is important in cases of powers of attorney that are tailor-made for specific situations that lawyers and law clerks not draft the document too broadly and give more power to the attorney than was intended. On the other hand, it is also important for lawyers and law clerks to be sure that the power of attorney is drafted broadly enough to have the intended effect. That is, a continuing power of attorney for property is often created for the purpose of preventing the Public Guardian and Trustee from assuming control of the grantor's assets when the grantor becomes mentally incompetent. The *Substitute Decisions Act, 1992*, however, makes it clear in section

general power of attorney for property power of attorney for property that gives unrestricted powers over the grantor's assets to the attorney(s)

16.1 that if the grantor is incapable and has not given a continuing power of attorney over all of his assets to another person, the Public Guardian and Trustee will have the authority to assume control of the assets. In other words, for example, it may not be possible to have a continuing restricted power of attorney that can be relied on to the same extent as a continuing general power of attorney with respect to the Public Guardian and Trustee. As in all other cases of estate planning, it is important for the lawyer and the law clerk to get clear instructions from the client and to confirm these instructions in writing.

FIGURE 5.3 Restricted Power of Attorney for Property

POWER OF ATTORNEY FOR PROPERTY

THIS POWER OF ATTORNEY FOR PROPERTY is to be interpreted in accordance with the restrictions set out below:

1. This power of attorney for property is given by **JOHN DOE**, whose current residence address is 99 Anywhere Street, Hamilton, Ontario, Q9Q 9Q9, retired bank manager.

2. I hereby appoint my sister-in-law, MARIE JETT, to be my attorney solely and only with respect to the sale, encumbrance, transfer and other dealings with my property known municipally as 331 Britanzia Road, Selkirk, Ontario, N0A 1A0.

3. In making this power of attorney I am aware:

    (a) of the nature and extent of my property;

    (b) of the obligations I owe to my dependants;

    (c) that my attorney will be able to do on my behalf anything in respect of the specified real property that I could do except to the extent that this power of attorney sets out conditions and restrictions on the powers of my attorney;

    (d) that my attorney must account for her dealings with my property;

    (e) that I may, while capable, revoke this power of attorney;

    (f) that the value of my property administered by my attorney may decline unless my attorney manages it prudently; and

    (g) that there is a possibility that my attorney could misuse the authority given to her by this power of attorney.

4. This power of attorney is subject to the following conditions, restrictions and supplementary powers:

    (a) This power of attorney is restricted solely to dealings with the real property described above and applies to no other property, whether real or personal, currently in my possession, ownership or control;

    (b) I authorize my attorney to bind and to secure information on my behalf in respect of dealings with any person, institution, government or legal entity;

    (c) I authorize my attorney to delegate any act my attorney may exercise to some other person or legal entity and to revoke or suspend such delegation;

    (d) I authorize my attorney to sign on my behalf any disclaimer with regard to executions, liens or other encumbrances purported to be filed against myself or the above-described property should she, after examining such executions, liens or other encumbrances, believe them not to apply to me or the above-described property.

FIGURE 5.3 CONTINUED

I have executed this power of attorney in the presence of both of the witnesses and on the date set out below.

Date: March 10, 2018

John Doe
_____
John Doe

We are the subscribing witnesses to this power of attorney for property and were both present together and saw it executed by the person whose name appears above on the date shown above. Neither of us has any reason to believe that the grantor is incapable of giving a power of attorney for property or instructions therein contained. Each of us is of the full age of 18 years and neither of us is the attorney's or grantor's spouse or partner, a child of the grantor or considered in law as such, or a person whose property is under guardianship or has a guardian of the person.

Miranda Douglas
_____
Miranda Douglas

Shinquay Pertell
_____
Shinquay Pertell

The authority for creating restricted continuing powers of attorney for property is contained in section 7(6) of the *Substitute Decisions Act, 1992*. The authority for creating restricted non-continuing powers of attorney for property is contained in section 2 of the old *Powers of Attorney Act*.

Note, however, that even under a general continuing power of attorney for property, an attorney can never be given the power to create a new will for the grantor. The latter rule is set out in section 7(2) of the *Substitute Decisions Act, 1992*, and it presumably restricts an attorney from revoking the grantor's existing will as well. If a power of attorney for property does contain a provision purporting to allow the attorney to make a will for the grantor, that provision will be invalid—any document purporting to be the will of the grantor but signed by the attorney will be an invalid will. The old *Powers of Attorney Act* does not specifically address will drafting by an attorney but does include the proviso in section 2 that a power of attorney (for property) can authorize an attorney only "to do on behalf of the [grantor] anything that the [grantor] can lawfully do by an attorney," and it is safe to assume that drafting a will is not one of the things a person can lawfully do by an attorney.

Power of Attorney for Personal Care

The *Substitute Decisions Act, 1992* provides in section 46(6) that the power of attorney for personal care can be subject to the conditions and restrictions contained in the document itself, although such conditions and restrictions are not valid if they are inconsistent with the Act. Such conditions and restrictions may include a provision that, before making a decision, the attorney must first consult with certain family members to determine their wishes. Unless the client insists on onerous conditions and restrictions, a lawyer or law clerk should be careful not to create any conditions that make the attorney's job too difficult and thereby defeat the purpose of the power of attorney.

Requirement for Attorney to Account for Actions as Attorney

Power of Attorney for Property

The *Substitute Decisions Act, 1992* requires that attorneys for property be in a position to account for their actions as attorneys—that is, they must maintain accounts. This certainly applies to attorneys under non-continuing powers of attorney as well. This accounting procedure is further examined in Part II, Chapter 12, Accounting to the Beneficiaries and Paying the Beneficiaries. However, two points should be noted about accounting with respect to powers of attorney for property in the estate planning stage. The first is that attorneys for property are entitled to take compensation for their actions as attorneys. The compensation is subject to a court's ruling on a passing of accounts, but is defined in the regulations as amounting to 3 percent of the capital and income receipts, 3 percent of the capital and income disbursements, and three-fifths of 1 percent of the annual average value of the assets. If there is more than one attorney, they would typically share the compensation. The concepts of income and capital receipts and disbursements will be discussed in more detail in Chapter 12.

The second point in this connection is that even though the law allows for civil sanctions of liability against an attorney, the requirement that the attorney be accountable for her actions while managing the property of a grantor under a power of attorney for property is an ineffective tool in recovering assets that may have been squandered by the attorney. In other words, if an inappropriate attorney is chosen and the grantor's assets diminish in value owing to the attorney's imprudence or dishonesty, it is quite possible, if not likely, that the grantor or the grantor's estate will not be able to recover those assets. Recovery may be impossible even if a court order is issued requiring the attorney to reimburse the grantor. This limitation further underscores the degree of power that is being granted in a power of attorney for property and the necessity of choosing an attorney carefully.

Power of Attorney for Personal Care

The regulations to the *Substitute Decisions Act, 1992*[6] require an attorney under a power of attorney for personal care to keep records pertaining to personal care decisions made. These records include:

- a list of all decisions regarding health care, safety, and shelter made on behalf of the incapable person, including the nature of each decision, the reason for it, and the date;
- a copy of medical reports or other documents, if any, relating to each decision;
- the names of any persons consulted, including the incapable person, in respect of each decision and the date;

---

6   O Reg 100/96, s 3(1).

- a description of the incapable person's wishes, if any, relevant to each decision, that he or she expressed when capable and the manner in which they were expressed;

- a description of the incapable person's current wishes, if ascertainable and if relevant to the decision;

- for each decision taken, the attorney's opinion on each of the factors listed in section 66(4) of the Act that relate to the values and beliefs the grantor held when capable, as well as factors relating to the preservation of, or the prevention of the deterioration of, the grantor's quality of life and factors, weighing the risks of actions against the expected benefits.

Requirement for Attorney to Use Original Document

Power of Attorney for Property

As indicated above, a power of attorney is used when a third party or an institution such as a bank requires a signature of the grantor of the power of attorney for property in the course of dealing with the grantor's property. At such time, the attorney's signature is put on the document (usually with the words "as attorney for [grantor's name])." The third party or institution is legally obligated to accept the attorney's signature in place of the grantor's. Accompanying this obligation, however, is the entitlement of the institution to satisfy itself that the person signing as attorney for the grantor is indeed the attorney for property of the grantor.

The accepted form of confirmation is to present the institution with the power of attorney document itself, along with proof of identification of the attorney. Sometimes the institution requires the original document, in which case it must be produced for inspection; a photocopy can be made by the institution. Occasionally, production of a notarial copy is sufficient, but this cannot be relied on. For this reason, it is sometimes advisable for the lawyer or law clerk to have the client sign two or three original power of attorney for property documents for future use. It may happen that two originals have to be filed with two different institutions.

Power of Attorney for Personal Care

The considerations regarding the use by the attorney of the original power of attorney for personal care are similar to those regarding the power of attorney for property, except that the institutions and individuals to be dealt with in the former case are usually medical practitioners and social workers.

The Role of the Lawyer and the Law Clerk in Safekeeping Original Powers of Attorney

Power of Attorney for Property

As indicated above, grantors of powers of attorney for property often execute more than one original document. Because the power given to the attorney is often effective immediately, unless the document states that it becomes effective only upon the grantor's incapacity or some other future event, putting several originals in circulation could pose considerable risk to the grantor. For this reason, the lawyer often recommends that the original powers of attorney for property be kept in the lawyer's office. In that case, the lawyer is obligated to keep the documents safe in the same way that he or she keeps original wills safe (see Chapter 1, Wills).

There are, however, additional concerns for lawyers and law clerks. In the case of safeguarding an original will, a lawyer or law clerk knows that he or she can release the original will to the named estate trustee upon the death of the client. In the case of original powers of attorney for property, however, the client is still alive but may be incapacitated. It may be that the lawyer or law clerk is receiving instructions from the client not to release the original document to the named attorney at the same time that the attorney is requesting it. Although one way of avoiding this dilemma is for the lawyer or law clerk to refuse to keep the original documents, in the author's view this may not be the best service to the client because the client is put at some risk in keeping the originals. A better solution would be to have clear written instructions from the client at the time she signs the power of attorney for property as to when, how, and to whom the original powers of attorney should be released from the custody of the lawyer or law clerk. Such instructions could perhaps contain an indemnity to save the lawyer or law clerk harm from any decisions made according to the written instructions that may lead to unfavourable results.

Power of Attorney for Personal Care

The practical requirements with respect to the safekeeping of original powers of attorney for personal care are not as onerous as those for powers of attorney for property. Generally, it is less likely that mischief can result if the original power of attorney for personal care is available to others. In fact, many lawyers make it a practice to ensure that their clients have at least one original power of attorney for personal care at home and on hand in case of a medical emergency.

Particular Issues Relating to Powers of Attorney

Power of Attorney for Property

Powers of Attorney Executed Before the Substitute Decisions Act, 1992

As indicated above, continuing powers of attorney for property existed long before the *Substitute Decisions Act, 1992*, although they were referred to simply as "powers of attorney" and were created under the *Powers of Attorney Act*. One notable difference between continuing powers of attorney for property under the *Substitute Decisions Act, 1992* and the old continuing powers of attorney is that the old continuing powers of attorney required only one witness.

Section 14 of the *Substitute Decisions Act, 1992* specifically allows for such older continuing powers of attorney that predated the Act, or that were made within six months of the Act's coming into force, to be valid continuing powers of attorney for property notwithstanding that they do not have the requisite number of witnesses, pursuant to what is often called a "grandfather clause." Because the Act came into force on April 3, 1995, the threshold date is October 3, 1995 (six months later). Thus, any continuing power of attorney executed (signed) on or before October 3, 1995 is valid even if it has only one witness's signature.

As in the case of a power of attorney created under the *Substitute Decisions Act, 1992*, a power of attorney created under the old regime, with one witness, is not a continuing power of attorney for property unless it is stated in the document itself that it is intended to operate during a subsequent legal incapacity of the grantor.

Finally, while a power of attorney falling within the grandfather clause may be valid, as time goes on, fewer and fewer of such powers of attorney will be circulated, and fewer and fewer employees of financial institutions will see such documents. The result is that an attorney or a lawyer or law clerk acting for an attorney may have to spend more time attempting to convince a financial institution employee that such a power of attorney is valid. In the light of this, it is often advisable for a grantor of a power of attorney drafted under the old regime to set it aside and sign a new power using the new form. The old power of attorney should nonetheless be kept safe, in case an allegation is later made that the grantor did not have the requisite capacity to sign a valid power of attorney for property at the time of signing the new one.

Bank Powers of Attorney

Occasionally, banks and trust companies insist that their customers use the institution's own form of power of attorney in granting a power of attorney over the assets held by the bank or trust company. These powers of attorney are usually drafted in such a way as to grant the power only with respect to those specific assets.

It is questionable whether a bank could insist on its own form of power of attorney or whether it would be entitled to follow a previously executed bank form of power of attorney when a subsequent valid power of attorney for property is granted that is inconsistent with the terms of the bank's power of attorney (for example, one that names a different attorney).

A bank may take the position that it is a federal entity under the Constitution of Canada and is therefore not bound by a power of attorney for property that is a provincially sanctioned document. In the author's view, such an argument would fail because authority to legislate over the subject matter of the power of attorney for property—property and property rights—under that same Constitution is granted to the provinces. That being said, it is probably preferable to ensure that the two documents are not inconsistent.

Power of Attorney for Personal Care
Specific Instructions and the Living Will Clause

As indicated above, section 46(6) of the *Substitute Decisions Act, 1992* allows the power of attorney for personal care to contain conditions and restrictions regarding the powers granted under the power of attorney. Section 46(7) goes on to state that the power of attorney for personal care may contain specific instructions to the attorney as well. Specific instructions could relate to anything within the realm of personal care. The most common specific instruction in a personal care power of attorney is known as a "living will" clause.

An example is provided in clause 5 of Figure 5.2. The living will clause usually states that the grantor does not wish to be kept alive in circumstances where he is under an extreme mental or physical disability and there is no reasonable hope of recovery. As in the example, this living will clause usually goes on to request that medications nevertheless continue to be administered in order to alleviate suffering. Some living will clauses contain instructions relating to specific disabilities and treatments to be administered or avoided. If a client wishes such clauses to be included in a power of attorney for personal care, it is essential that the lawyer or law clerk take instructions carefully and review them thoroughly with the client. Some lawyers consider that setting out too detailed a directive to the attorney can cause difficulties at a later date because of the ever-changing nature of medical science and practice and because of the unpredictability of a person's health. As in all other areas of estate planning, the client should be made aware of the options and asked to make the ultimate decision.

Special Provisions

Section 50 of the *Substitute Decisions Act, 1992* sets out the rules under which the grantor of the power of attorney for personal care can authorize the use of necessary and reasonable force against her at some future date for the purpose of determining whether the grantor lacks the capacity for personal care or for the purpose of caring for the grantor. This section also allows a grantor to include a provision that pre-waives the grantor's right to appeal a finding of incapacity by an assessor. The Act refers to such provisions as "special provisions."

Special provisions in a power of attorney for personal care are invalid unless all of the following requirements are met:

1. Within 30 days of executing the power of attorney, the grantor makes a statement in the prescribed form indicating that she understands the special provision and the effect of section 50(4), which provides that a power of attorney with the special provision can be revoked only if within 30 days before the revocation an assessor completes an assessment of the grantor and makes a statement in the form prescribed by the regulations under the Act that the grantor is capable of personal care.

2. Within 30 days of executing the power of attorney, an assessor completes an assessment of the grantor and makes a statement in the prescribed form that the grantor is capable of personal care.

From the point of view of the lawyer or law clerk, in the event that a client wants to include a special provision in her power of attorney for personal care, it is essential that she be fully informed of the procedural requirements.

Human Tissue Gift Statements

The *Trillium Gift of Life Network Act*[7] (formerly the *Human Tissue Gift Act*) states in section 4(1) that a person who is 16 years of age or older may direct that his body parts be

---

7 RSO 1990, c H.20.

used after his death "for therapeutic purposes, medical education or scientific research" and that such directions are to be "in a writing signed by the person at any time." As indicated in Chapter 2, Will Clauses, many lawyers consider that the most appropriate place for a person to put a statement donating body parts is on the Ontario driver's licence or possibly in a power of attorney for personal care, because that document is most likely to be on hand at the time a person dies.

In the latter case, however, the question arises whether such a donation would, if contested, be upheld in light of the fact that a power of attorney for personal care is considered to be terminated upon the death of the grantor. A possible solution may be for such directions to be contained in a separate document that is attached to the power of attorney for personal care. Note, too, that the *Trillium Gift of Life Network Act* does not specifically prohibit multiple statements donating body parts, indicating that a person can sign more than one such statement. For example, one statement may be in the person's will, one in her power of attorney for personal care, one on her driver's licence, and one in her online registration with Service Ontario. Such multiple statements should, of course, be consistent with one another.

KEY TERMS

general power of attorney for property, 90   power of attorney, 76

REVIEW QUESTIONS

1. What is the significance of the word "continuing" as it relates to a power of attorney for property and why is it not used in connection with a power of attorney for personal care?

2. What happens to a power of attorney when the grantor of a power of attorney dies?

3. Do powers of attorney for property or personal care have to be in a "prescribed form" to be valid in Ontario?

4. What are the formal requirements of a power of attorney for property and a power of attorney for personal care?

5. When does a power of attorney for property normally take effect?

6. Why may it be inadvisable to provide in a power of attorney for property that it is to take effect if the grantor becomes incapable of managing her property?

7. Can a person named as an attorney refuse to act?

8. Is it possible that a person who is incapable of managing property is still capable of granting a power of attorney for property? Explain.

9. What five categories of persons cannot be a witness to a power of attorney for property or personal care?

10. If two or more attorneys are named to act "jointly and severally" what does "jointly" mean and what does "severally" mean?

11. How is a power of attorney for property revoked?

12. Explain the procedure for a person who has acted as an attorney under a power of attorney for property to resign.

13. If the power of attorney so authorizes, can an attorney make a new will for the grantor?

14. Describe the difference between a general power of attorney for property and a restricted power of attorney for property, and provide three examples of conditions or restrictions.

15. What records should an attorney for property keep? Explain.

16. If a lawyer holds an original power of attorney for safekeeping, when and to whom can it be released?

17. Under what circumstances is a power of attorney for property with only one witness valid?

18. What is a power of attorney for personal care and when does it become effective?

19. At what age can a person give a power of attorney for personal care and at what age can a person act as an attorney for personal care?

20. What categories of persons are barred from acting as attorneys for personal care and what are the exceptions?

21. What is a "living will" clause in a power of attorney for personal care?

22. Can a grantor of a power of attorney for personal care authorize use of force against him in the future and, if so, for what purpose?

6

Trusts

LEARNING OUTCOMES

After completing this chapter, you should be able to:

- Explain the roles of the various persons involved in the creation and execution of trusts, including the *settlor*, the *trustee,* and the *beneficiary*

- Describe the differences between beneficiaries, contingent beneficiaries, alternate beneficiaries, and unascertained beneficiaries

- Briefly explain the rule contained in the case of *Saunders v Vautier* in relation to unascertained beneficiaries

- Understand that a trust is not a legal entity, but a legal relationship

- List the three certainties that must be included in a trust document to ensure its validity

- Describe the rule against perpetuities

- Describe the rule against accumulations

- Distinguish between, and understand the reasons for setting up, spendthrift trusts, Henson trusts, qualifying spousal trusts, alter ego trusts, and joint partner trusts

- Explain the requirements that must be met before a court will consider a variation of a trust

Introduction

The sample will discussed in Chapter 2, Will Clauses, provided for a trust that was to come into being in the event that the beneficiary of any gift was under the age of majority or mentally incapacitated at the time of the testator's death. Recall that this kind of trust, the rules of which are contained in a person's will and which is activated upon his death, is called a testamentary trust. Many wills contain such trusts owing to the fact that a person who is under the age of majority or mentally incapacitated is legally unable to accept a gift outright. The gift must be held in a trust either until such time as the beneficiary has attained the age of majority or until the beneficiary is no longer mentally incapacitated. If the beneficiary is permanently mentally incapacitated, the trust usually remains active until the beneficiary is deceased or until the trust funds are fully depleted.

A testamentary trust allows the testator to decide who will be the trustee of the gift under the will and what rules will govern the distribution of the gift during the time that the trust remains active. In the Chapter 2 example, the trustee is obligated to make payments from the income or capital as the trustee in her sole discretion deems advisable for the "maintenance, education or benefit" of the beneficiary.

Many testators go further than the trust provided in the example and extend the age at which the beneficiary acquires the gift to 21 or 25 years, or beyond. Some testators, particularly in a situation where the intended beneficiary of a gift under the will is mentally incompetent, set up a trust that is to be in force for the beneficiary's lifetime.

inter vivos trust
trust that is
activated while the
person setting up
the trust is still alive

This chapter discusses trusts in more detail. As will be seen, a testamentary trust is not the only kind of trust that is used for estate planning purposes. An ***inter vivos* trust** can be set up in a document often called a "deed of trust" and activated while the person setting up the trust is still alive. *Inter vivos* trusts, which get their name from the Latin words meaning "between the living," are often used by people to acquire an income tax advantage through the pre-death disbursement of property. For this reason, as well as the fact that testamentary trusts and *inter vivos* trusts share many characteristics, *inter vivos* trusts are often studied in the context of an estates course.

Although the law allows for the existence of many different kinds of trust—such as written, unwritten, express, unintentional, implied, revocable, irrevocable, and so on—the trusts used for estate planning purposes are usually either testamentary trusts, which are written and irrevocable because they are contained in wills and take effect upon the death of the testator, or written irrevocable *inter vivos* trusts. Unless otherwise stated, this part of the text is concerned only with such written intended irrevocable trusts.

Terminology

As with many other topics in the field of law, understanding and recognizing the terminology associated with the law of trusts is an important part of understanding the subject itself.

Settlor/Testator

In basic terms, a trust is an arrangement in which property is transferred from one person to a second person who agrees to hold it for the benefit of a third person (although, as will be seen below, persons can play dual roles in some circumstances). The person who transfers the property is the person who sets up the trust. In the case of a testamentary trust, this person is called simply the "testator" or the "deceased." In the case of an *inter vivos* trust, the person who sets up the trust is called the **settlor**.

A testamentary trust is activated by the death of the testator. An *inter vivos* trust is activated by the settlor's signing the declaration or deed of trust and delivering the trust property to the trustee.

settlor
person who sets up an *inter vivos* trust

Trustee

The person to whom the trust property is transferred is called the **trustee**. The trustee becomes the legal owner of the trust property but is not legally in a position to obtain a benefit from it. Instead, the property must be held for the benefit of the beneficiary (defined in the next section). It is the trustee's job to hold the property and administer the trust in accordance with the rules of the trust.

trustee
person to whom trust property is transferred

A trustee's specific rights and obligations with respect to the trust property—that is, the rules of the trust—are set out in the trust document, which is either the will of the deceased or the deed of trust. A trustee is also subject to the provisions of the *Trustee Act*[1] and the rules for trusts laid down in case law. An overriding principle of trust law is that the trustee is obligated to act in the best interests of the beneficiaries. The terminology used to describe the relationship between trustee and beneficiary with respect to this obligation is "fiduciary." The Latin root of this word is *fides*, meaning "faith"; hence, the trustee must be faithful to the trust obligations. The trustee is said to have a fiduciary duty to the beneficiary. If a trustee breaches her fiduciary relationship, she may face civil or even criminal liability.

In the sample clause from the will in Chapter 2 (Figure 2.10), the estate trustee is also the trustee of the testamentary trust; however, they do not have to be the same person.

While the estate trustee is sometimes described as a trustee of the estate (and, as discussed in Chapter 2, Ontario legislation has changed the traditional common law term "executor" to "estate trustee"), strictly speaking, the estate trustee's role has not historically been equated with that of trustee proper. In other words, the subject matter of a gift made through a testamentary trust can be transferred, if the will so provides, to a separate trustee named in the will in the same way that the subject matter of any other gift made in the will can be transferred to the beneficiary of a gift. In many cases, however, it is considered to be unduly complicated for the estate trustee and the trustee of the testamentary trust to be different people. Accordingly, wills often appoint the same person for both roles.

Beneficiary

As indicated above, the person for whom the trust property is held is called the **beneficiary** of the trust, sometimes referred to by the partially Latin term "*cestui que* trust." There can be one beneficiary or several.

Sometimes there are **contingent beneficiaries** who, if a particular condition is satisfied, become beneficiaries of the trust. For example, a clause in a testamentary or *inter vivos* trust might provide as follows:

beneficiary
person for whom trust property is held

contingent beneficiary
person who, if a particular condition is satisfied, becomes a beneficiary of a trust

---

1 RSO 1990, c T.23.

> My nephew Rajif is to receive $50,000.00 of the trust fund upon his 25th birthday if and only if he has obtained a bachelor of science degree from an accredited university by that date.

In this example, Rajif is a contingent beneficiary.

A particular kind of contingent beneficiary is an **alternate beneficiary**. An alternate beneficiary becomes a beneficiary if the first-named beneficiary either dies or ceases to be a beneficiary by not satisfying a specified condition. In essence, an alternate beneficiary is one that takes the place of a previously named beneficiary. An example of this kind of arrangement would be a trust, again either testamentary or *inter vivos*, in which there is a provision stating that if the beneficiary dies before reaching a certain age, her share is to be gifted to another named beneficiary. This arrangement is often called a **gift over**. As will be seen under "Variation of Trusts" below, a gift over creating alternate beneficiaries can have an important effect on the rights of the main beneficiary of a trust.

If a trust has an open-ended group of beneficiaries that could expand over time, the trust is said to have **unascertained beneficiaries**. Unascertained beneficiaries are, in a sense, theoretical place holders in the trust. They can be presently non-existent persons (for example, where the trust provides money to the settlor's "future grandchildren") or persons who already exist but who become beneficiaries only upon the occurrence of a specified event (for example, where the trust gifts money to "any Stoney Creek Little League player who hits a home run during the next regular season"). Though unascertained beneficiaries are theoretical individuals until they join the class of beneficiaries proper, they can be important in the administration of a trust. That is, where a trust has unascertained beneficiaries, the trustee is obligated to consider their interests in addition to the interests of the existing, known, or ascertained beneficiaries. Similarly, the court must take into account the interests of unascertained beneficiaries when called upon to make a decision regarding the administration of a trust involving such beneficiaries.

Trust as Legal Entity or Relationship?

Trusts are often referred to as legal entities, similar to corporations, although, strictly speaking, this terminology is incorrect. While corporations can, among other things, own property and conduct lawsuits, trusts in and of themselves cannot do these things. Property that falls into a trust actually becomes legally owned by the trustee rather than by the trust itself. Similarly, any lawsuits conducted for the trust will be conducted in the name of the trustee rather than the trust.

A trust, then, is not a legal entity but a legal relationship between people, and in this respect is more akin to a contract than to a corporation. The analogy to a contract, however, should not be taken too far because a contract usually involves some sort of bargaining between the parties, whereas a trust rarely involves such bargaining. Furthermore, contracts may or may not involve assets, whereas trusts always involve assets of some kind.

Nonetheless, for income tax purposes, trusts are treated as legal entities. As will be seen in Part II, Chapter 13, Administering Testamentary and Inter Vivos Trusts and Powers of Attorney, trustees usually have to file a separate tax return for the trust (called a T3 Trust Income Tax and Information Return); in other words, trusts, like corporations, are

alternate beneficiary
a beneficiary who becomes a beneficiary by taking the place of a previously named beneficiary, most commonly as a result of the death of the previously named beneficiary

gift over
alternate gift to another beneficiary in the event that the first beneficiary predeceases

unascertained beneficiary
a theoretical beneficiary who does not yet exist—or who does not exist as a beneficiary—but who would become a beneficiary of a trust upon being born or upon the happening of a specified event

themselves taxpayers. It is probably because of this that a trust is sometimes incorrectly characterized as a legal entity.

Vested and Contingent

An important term in trust law is the term "vest" or "vesting." At the time a beneficiary obtains an existing or definite future right to benefit from the trust property, the trust is said to have **vested**—that is, the benefit of the property has been conferred on the beneficiary. If a person may or may not enjoy the benefits of the trust property in the future, depending on whether a particular event occurs, the trust has not vested in that person but remains **contingent**.

vested
settled upon

contingent
conditional

Drafting Trust Documents

As indicated in the introduction to this chapter, the trustee must hold the trust property for the benefit of the beneficiary of the trust and in accordance with the rules of the trust. The rules are set out in the trust document, which is either a will (in the case of a testamentary trust) or a declaration or deed of trust (in the case of an *inter vivos* trust). Lawyers are often retained by clients to prepare wills and, perhaps less often, deeds of *inter vivos* trusts. It is essential that the lawyer or law clerk involved draft the trust document in accordance with both the client's intentions and the law of trusts.

The consequences of not drafting a trust document properly can be many, and an exhaustive discussion of the topic is beyond the scope of this text. This section discusses the fundamental rules of trusts that are the starting point for the proper drafting of trusts. Such basic requirements must be understood before the more precise requirements for a particular kind of trust are considered.

Three Certainties

In order for a trust to be valid, the declaration of trust (either the deed of trust or the part of the will setting up the testamentary trust) must create certainty—that is, it must be absolutely clear, in the following three ways:

1. certainty of words or intention;
2. certainty of subject matter; and
3. certainty of purpose or objects.

Certainty of words or intention means that it must be certain from the words in the trust document that the testator or settlor clearly intends to transfer the legal ownership in the property to the trustee and the *beneficial* ownership to the beneficiary. It is not an absolute requirement that the trust document use the words "trust," "deed of trust," "trustee," or "beneficiary" as long as the intention of the testator or settlor is clear.

Certainty of subject matter means that it must be certain and clear from the words in the trust document exactly what property is being transferred to the trustee.

Certainty of purpose or objects means that it must be certain and clear from the words of the trust document who the beneficiary or beneficiaries of the trust are. An individual beneficiary may be an unascertainable beneficiary, but the rule is satisfied as long as the class of beneficiary itself is certain. In this connection, a class described as "friends" would probably not qualify. As will be seen below, the rule requiring certainty of objects has an important exception in the case of charitable trusts.

Apart from the three certainties, the trust document should indicate the rules under which the trust is administered. These rules, of course, should not undermine the three certainties.

Rule Against Perpetuities

As a very general rule, the law is averse to uncertainty. This aversion gave rise to the rule against perpetuities, which should be kept in mind in the drafting of trusts. The rule comes from the common law and is modified to a certain extent by the *Perpetuities Act*. The various subrules relating to the rule against perpetuities are very complex and beyond the scope of this text. This section, however, attempts to describe the rule in basic terms so that a perpetuities problem will be recognized if it arises. As will be seen below under "Different Kinds of Trust," charitable trusts are exempt from the rule against perpetuities in some circumstances.

rule against perpetuities
rule that prevents a trust from being open-ended indefinitely with respect to its potential beneficiaries

In basic terms, the **rule against perpetuities** prevents a trust from being open-ended indefinitely with respect to its potential beneficiaries. The rule holds that a trust must vest within 21 years (plus the period of human gestation, or 9 months) of the death of a person who is alive at the time the trust is created and is referred to in the trust document (called a "life in being"). Thus, for example, a trust that attempts to name as beneficiaries "every first-born male child in direct lineage to me" will, most likely, eventually offend the rule against perpetuities. The result is that the trust will be forced to vest in the beneficiaries who happen to be alive 21 years (plus 9 months) after the death of the life in being (any person referred to in the will or the deed of trust). If no life in being is explicitly cited in the trust document, a court will decide who that person is on the basis of a reading of the trust document. After the cut-off date, there can be no new beneficiaries to receive the benefit of the trust moneys. Naturally, such a situation is not a problem for the last surviving beneficiaries because they acquire the full benefit of the trust property by operation of the rule against perpetuities. The situation may, however, go directly against the wishes of the testator or the settlor of the trust, who may have arranged the trust differently had he contemplated its inevitable end.

For present purposes, note that a lawyer or law clerk must take care to verify the validity of the trust if the trust has unascertained beneficiaries who might be born later than 21 years (plus 9 months) from the death of a person who is alive at the time the trust is created and who is referred to in the trust document.

The rule against perpetuities is more often an issue for testamentary trusts than for *inter vivos* trusts. This is so because the life in being at the time of setting up the *inter vivos* trust can be a newborn baby (or even a person conceived but not yet born), thereby extending the time for vesting as long as possible. The same arrangement cannot assuredly be made in the case of a testamentary trust simply because the date of death of the testator cannot be known with certainty.

If there is no life in being specifically named, the maximum length of time for the vesting of the trust property is 21 years (plus 9 months).

The rule against perpetuities should not be confused with the 21-year deemed-disposition rule for trusts that appears in the *Income Tax Act*.[2] This rule relates to capital gains tax payable by trusts and is covered in greater detail in Part II, Chapter 13. Neither rule should be confused with the rule against accumulations, discussed below, which is also based on a 21-year period.

Rule Against Accumulations

The *Accumulations Act*[3] prohibits a trust from accumulating income indefinitely—that is, allowing income from investments or interest income to build up in the trust without distribution. Generally, the period allowed for accumulations under the Act is 21 years. Section 2 of the Act specifies that the Act does not apply to "any provision for raising portions for a child" of a settlor or testator "or for a child of a person taking an interest under any such conveyance, settlement or devise."

If the *Accumulations Act* is breached, section 1(6) of the Act provides that the income accumulated after the allowed period is to be given to the persons who would have been entitled to the income had it been distributed.

Section 3 of the Act specifies that the rule against accumulations does not apply to a trust fund established for work pensions, retirement allowances, or employee benefits.

Overlapping Roles

As will be seen below in the brief discussion on different kinds of trusts, it is possible in certain circumstances for the roles of settlor and trustee to overlap to a certain extent. If the client intends to create such a trust, as in all other cases it is important for the lawyer or law clerk drafting the trust document to ascertain whether the purposes intended will be achieved. In this connection, for example, a trust designed to avoid income tax must also satisfy the requirements of the *Income Tax Act*.

Trusts in the context of income tax are discussed in Chapter 13.

Different Kinds of Trusts

This section discusses different kinds of trusts that (with the exception of the secret trust) are fairly common. It should be noted that, while the trusts discussed below have names, not all trusts are identified by a particular name.

Spendthrift Trust

Parents of minor children are often concerned that they will die before their children are of a sensible age and that their children will spend their inheritance frivolously. A common solution to this concern is the creation of a so-called spendthrift trust. A

---

2 RSC 1985, c 1 (5th Supp).
3 RSO 1990, c A.5.

spendthrift trust names a trustee who will manage the trust money and make decisions as to what purchases and expenditures are appropriate for the beneficiary until the beneficiary reaches a specified age. When the beneficiary reaches the specified age (commonly 21 or 25 years), he or she receives the gift outright. Some spendthrift trusts specify that a portion of the beneficiary's share is to be received outright at a certain age and the remainder at a later age.

A spendthrift trust need not be drafted so that it comes to an end during the lifetime of the beneficiary (although note the rule against accumulations discussed above). Similarly, a spendthrift trust may, in some circumstances, occur in an *inter vivos* trust.

Henson Trust

A so-called **Henson trust** is often created to protect a beneficiary of an estate who is receiving regular government assistance under the Ontario Disability Support Program (ODSP). The ODSP does not provide payments to individuals who own assets over a certain value or who have a certain income level. Thus, gifting a portion of an estate to such an individual would normally disqualify him from further government assistance, at least for a time. A Henson trust, if properly drafted, will allow the beneficiary to continue receiving assistance from the ODSP and to receive additional amounts from the trust as needed and as calculated to avoid disqualification of the beneficiary under the ODSP. The essence of the Henson trust is that the beneficiary never acquires a legal right to acquire the trust funds, insofar as the distribution of those funds remains entirely within the discretion of the trustee.

While the original Henson trust (from which the name came) was a testamentary trust, Henson trusts can also be *inter vivos* trusts. *Inter vivos* Henson trusts are sometimes set up by a litigation guardian at the conclusion of a court action where the plaintiff is in receipt of disability assistance and receives a lump-sum award of damages that would otherwise disqualify him from continued government assistance.

Qualifying Spousal Trust

A **qualifying spousal trust** is a trust that qualifies for advantageous tax treatment under the *Income Tax Act*. Generally speaking, a qualifying spousal trust does not have to pay periodic capital gains tax as do other trusts and can be set up without capital gains consequences to the settlor. Qualifying spousal trusts, which can be either testamentary or *inter vivos*, are discussed in more detail in Part II, Chapter 13.

Charitable Trust

A **charitable trust**—a trust that is set up for a charitable purpose—is, for public policy reasons, able to bypass some of the rules restricting trusts. For example, with respect to the certainty of objects (one of the three certainties normally required in a trust document), the objects of the trust can be expressed to be for a charitable purpose rather than a specific charity. This exception is based on the *cy-près* doctrine, which comes from the Latin phrase meaning "as close as possible". The *cy-près* doctrine also comes into play in interpreting wills to charities that are non-existent or unreasonably difficult to locate. In the case of such gifts in a will, a court is allowed to make a ruling that gives the gift to a charity that has the same charitable purpose as the one named in the will. Such a result hinges to a certain extent on the court's finding as to the intention of the testator.

Somewhat similarly, but in this case related to the rule against perpetuities, while the trust must vest in a charity within the perpetuity period, the charity receiving the benefit of the trust may change or be superseded by a different charity outside the perpetuity period. In other words, if a charity named as beneficiary in a will ceases to exist, even if the cessation of existence is outside the period of the life in being plus 21 years, the benefit can vest in the new charity notwithstanding the lapse of time as long as the new charity has the same charitable purpose as the previous one.

The above is by no means a complete treatment of the subject of charitable trusts, but is intended to provide some familiarity with the more relevant issues involved in trusts.

Alter Ego Trust

There are some advantages to passing property to beneficiaries through a trust—that is, by transferring property first to an *inter vivos* trust and then to the beneficiaries upon the death of the settlor—rather than through an estate by virtue of a will. These advantages include avoiding estate administration tax, also known as "probate fees" (discussed in more detail in Part II, Chapter 8, Preliminary Steps in Applying for a Certificate of Appointment of Estate Trustee), and generally ensuring that assets end up in the hands of the beneficiaries faster than when passing through an estate.

Nevertheless, transferring assets through *inter vivos* trusts was not common prior to 2001, largely due to the fact that a person who transferred property to an *inter vivos* trust would immediately become liable for capital gains tax on the property; the trust would also be subject to the 21-year deemed disposition rule, which requires capital gains tax to be paid every 21 years regardless of whether it is transferred to anybody else. In 2001, however, the *Income Tax Act* was amended to allow so-called alter ego trusts, which, if the requirements were met, deferred the capital gains tax until the death of the settlor and suspended the 21-year deemed disposition rule. The requirements of an **alter ego trust** are that the settlor must be at least 65 years of age; the trust must have been created after 1999; the trust must be drafted such that the settlor is entitled to all of the income from the trust while the settlor is alive; only the settlor is entitled to the capital of the trust while the settlor is alive; and the settlor must be resident of Canada.

Joint Partner Trust

The 2001 amendments to the *Income Tax Act*, referred to above under Alter Ego Trust, also allow for **joint partner trusts**, which are essentially alter ego trusts for spouses, whether married or common law, for their collective benefit. Joint partner trusts require that the settlor be at least 65 years of age and a resident of Canada; that the trust be set up after 1999; and that the trust allow only the settlor or her spouse to be entitled to all of the income and capital of the trust while at least one of them is alive. If these requirements are met, capital gains tax is not triggered when the property is transferred to the trust and the deemed disposition rule does not apply.

alter ego trust a particular kind of *inter vivos* trust, which is used to suspend the 21-year deemed-disposition rule in the *Income Tax Act* and to suspend capital gains tax until the death of the settlor

joint partner trust essentially, alter ego trusts for spouses

Secret Trust

A **secret trust** under the common law is a form of testamentary trust, but one that does not appear in the will. A secret trust may or may not be in writing. It usually involves a gift to a person in a will (who appears to be a beneficiary) along with a statement, oral or written, by the testator to that apparent beneficiary to the effect that the gift is to be held in trust for other individuals or another person. For the secret trust to be valid, there must be an acceptance of the role of trustee by the person named as beneficiary in the will. The communication by the testator to that person and the acceptance by that person need not use the words "trust," "trustee," or "beneficiary" as long as the intention is clear. As with many common law rules, exceptions and subrules modify the original rule related to secret trusts. Such permutations are outside the scope of this text. Note that secret trusts are rare and usually difficult to prove.

Variation of Trusts

The terms of a trust can be varied by an application to the court under the *Variation of Trusts Act*.[4] This short piece of legislation, consisting of two subsections, indicates that a court may approve and allow a proposed variation of a trust on behalf of any person related to the trust, including unascertained beneficiaries. An important requirement of the approval, however, appears in section 1(2) of the Act, which states that the court "shall not approve" a proposed variation if it is not in the best interests of, among others, the beneficiaries of the trust, including the unascertained beneficiaries. In other words, the court must protect all of the beneficiaries of the trust, including those who do not yet exist. A court will not likely grant a variation of a trust unless it is in the best interests of all such beneficiaries to do so.

When drafting a testamentary trust clause in a will, if it is a trust that is to remain in existence for a beneficiary past the age of 18 years, it is generally considered appropriate to provide for a gift over in the event that the beneficiary dies before the trust is to be distributed. As discussed above, a gift over is an alternate gift to another beneficiary in the event that the first beneficiary predeceases. It has been held that without such a gift over, the beneficiary, upon reaching the age of 18, may apply to the court to have the trust "broken up" and distributed early. The gift over prevents the breaking of the trust because the court is required to consider the best interests of any alternate beneficiaries before allowing the trust to be broken. Only if there are no other beneficiaries whose interests could be prejudiced by the early distribution will the court distribute early. A clause giving the gift over is often referred to as a *Saunders v Vautier* clause, in reference to the well-known British case from 1841 in which this issue was pointedly decided. Briefly, in *Saunders v Vautier*,[5] a testator died leaving a will in which the beneficiary (Vautier) was given a gift of some stock in a company but in a spendthrift trust. In this regard the will provided that the gift was to be held in trust for him until he reached the age of 25. Key to the case, however, was the fact that the will did not specify an alternate beneficiary in the event that Vautier did not

---

4   RSO 1990, c V.1.

5   (1841), 4 Beav 115.

reach that age. Upon reaching the age of adulthood (21 years), Vautier applied to the court to have the gift given to him outright, notwithstanding the terms of the will. The court ruled that because Vautier had an absolute indefeasible interest in the gift—that is, there was no gift over—the laws of equity (or fairness) allowed him to obtain the gift as soon as he reached the age of legal competence, which in this case was 21 years.

KEY TERMS

alter ego trust, 109
alternate beneficiary, 104
beneficiary, 103
charitable trust, 108
contingent, 105
contingent beneficiary, 103
gift over, 104
Henson trust, 108
inter vivos trust, 102

joint partner trust, 109
qualifying spousal trust, 108
rule against perpetuities, 106
secret trust, 110
settlor, 103
spendthrift trust, 108
trustee, 103
unascertained beneficiary, 104
vested, 105

REVIEW QUESTIONS

1. Define the following terms or concepts:

    a. *inter vivos*

    b. settlor

    c. fiduciary

    d. *cestui que* trust

    e. vested

    f. contingent beneficiary

    g. unascertained beneficiary

2. When it comes to income tax law, why is a trust usually, but incorrectly, characterized as a legal entity?

3. Who is the legal owner of the trust property?

4. Who is the beneficial owner of the trust property?

5. Identify two types of trust documents.

6. A trustee is said to have a fiduciary duty to a beneficiary. Explain.

7. Describe the three "certainties" of a trust.

8. What, stated very generally, is the purpose of the "rule against perpetuities"?

9. What is meant by the term "life in being"?

10. What, stated very generally, is the purpose of the "rule against accumulations"?

11. Explain the differences between a testamentary trust and an *inter vivos* trust.

12. Describe the purpose of the following types of trusts:

    a. spendthrift trust

    b. Henson trust

    c. qualifying spousal trust

    d. alter ego trust

    e. charitable trust

    f. secret trust

13. What "certainty" may be relaxed in the case of a charitable trust?

14. If assets are to remain in trust form for a beneficiary past the age of 18 years, what will prevent the trust from being broken after the beneficiary reaches 18?

15. How is an *inter vivos* trust activated?

16. When does a testamentary trust become activated?

17. Why is the existence of a "secret" trust difficult to prove?

18. Identify four requirements under the *Income Tax Act* for a tax-deferred transfer of assets to a joint partner trust.

19. When is the rule in *Saunders v Vautier* most often applied?

PART II

Estate Administration

Proof of the Estate Trustee's Status as Estate Trustee

7

LEARNING OUTCOMES

After completing this chapter, you should be able to:

- Understand why proof of the estate trustee's appointment would be needed for the estate to be administered

- Understand the situations in which the will of the deceased is sufficient proof of the estate trustee's appointment and when it is insufficient

- Understand why an estate trustee in an intestate estate must receive her appointment from the court

- Identify the key differences among the following forms of proof of appointment of a person as estate trustee:
  - Certificate of appointment of estate trustee with a will
  - Certificate of appointment of estate trustee without a will
  - Certificate of appointment of estate trustee with a will limited to the assets referred to in the will

- Identify the situations where some less common court certificates are required, including:
  - Confirmation by resealing of appointment of estate trustee with or without a will
  - Certificate of ancillary appointment of estate trustee with a will
  - Certificate of appointment of succeeding estate trustee with a will
  - Certificate of appointment of succeeding estate trustee without a will
  - Certificate of appointment of estate trustee during litigation

- Describe the circumstances in which financial institutions, transfer agents, and the Bank of Canada will release the assets of an estate with or without additional forms of proof

- Recount outdated terminology relating to estate trustees and know why it is important to maintain familiarity with it

Introduction

Administering an estate requires the estate trustee to carry out a number of procedural steps. The first step is gathering together the assets of the deceased—ascertaining, securing, taking possession of, and preserving all that was owned by the deceased at the time of his death, excluding those assets that bypass the estate by way of joint ownership with a survivor.

Ascertaining the assets may involve meticulously inspecting the personal papers and personal effects of the deceased, including incoming mail, with a view to finding financial statements, tax bills, income tax returns, and the like that would lead to disclosure of the assets held by the deceased. In the case of movable objects such as vehicles, jewelry, and other valuables, it means physically taking possession of them and putting them in a safe place. In the case of real estate, "gathering together the assets" means securing any structures on the property such as a house and its furniture, furnishings, and appliances; gathering up the access keys; and perhaps changing the locks. It may mean a trip to the summer cottage to ascertain its contents and equipment such as boats and motors, securing them, and perhaps closing the cottage for the winter. It also means amending the fire insurance policy and changing the land title records to reflect ownership by the estate trustee. In the case of objects of personal property, the ownership of which is registered with third parties, such as shares in a corporation, "gathering together the assets" means both physically taking possession of the share certificates and putting them in a safe place, and performing whatever tasks are necessary to change the registration to show the estate trustee as owner. In the case of assets held by banks and other financial institutions, "gathering together the assets" means instructing such institutions to change their records to reflect ownership by the estate trustee.

For all of the different kinds of assets, usually some form of proof is required by the person or institution holding the assets or in possession of the records indicating ownership that the person claiming to be the estate trustee is in fact the estate trustee and that her instructions ought to be followed. This chapter provides an introduction to the various forms of proof that are typically required by institutions and others holding assets of the deceased. Depending on the asset and the particulars of the estate, different forms and degrees of proof are required that, from the estate's point of view, vary in cost. Generally, estate trustees have a duty to the beneficiaries of the estate to minimize the cost. It is the lawyer's job to determine what form of proof is most appropriate in the situation and to advise the client—the actual or prospective estate trustee—accordingly. The tasks involved in ensuring that such proof is obtained are discussed in Chapter 9, Applying for a Certificate of Appointment of Estate Trustee, and Chapter 10, Collecting the Assets.

Common Forms of Proof of the Appointment of an Estate Trustee

The Deceased's Will

Theoretically, once the fact of the death of the deceased is established, if the deceased left a valid will appointing an estate trustee, the estate trustee would simply have to show the original will, and perhaps proof of his own identity, to people and institutions holding assets of the deceased in order to prove that he is legally able to take possession of them. If, for example, the deceased had shared an apartment with a roommate and all of the deceased's assets consisted of objects in the apartment, it would probably be sufficient for the estate trustee to show the deceased's roommate the original will in order to gain access to the apartment and take possession of the deceased's belongings.

Looking at the situation from the roommate's point of view, however, while the roommate is legally obligated to give the deceased's belongings to the person or entity legally entitled to them (that is, the estate trustee), if the roommate handed over the belongings to someone who, it turned out, was not entitled to them, she could be held personally liable for their value. In other words, if the roommate handed over the belongings to a person posing as the estate trustee, or whom she falsely believed to be the estate trustee, the roommate could be held liable to the estate. This raises the question whether the will itself provides adequate protection to any person or entity holding assets of the deceased or records indicating ownership of assets by the deceased.

The answer is no. Even if the signature on the will can be verified as that of the deceased, the deceased may have made a more recent will appointing someone else as the estate trustee.

A further problem may arise from the fact that many wills name two or more persons, acting jointly, as estate trustees. If only one of them is willing and able to act, any institution or person looking at the will would want to receive instructions from not just one but all of them. It may be recalled from Chapter 1, Wills, where the duties of the lawyer in safekeeping the will were discussed, that the lawyer must be sure not to release the original will to one of the named estate trustees unless written confirmation from all estate trustees is received. The same principle applies in situations where one of two or three estate trustees approaches an institution holding assets of the deceased. Notwithstanding all the other reasons discussed above, the institution would be justified, and perhaps even obligated, to refuse to act on the instructions of just one estate trustee.

Finally, many wills name alternate estate trustees in case the first-named person is unable or unwilling to act. If the person willing and able to act as estate trustee is not the first-named estate trustee, and the proof of his status is the will itself, any person or institution holding assets of the deceased would be justified in refusing to take instructions from the second-named person.

The solution to this problem of proof of status is the certificate of appointment of estate trustee with a will, a document obtained from the court. Although, as suggested above, a person who is first named in a will can legally present herself as the estate trustee from the moment of the death of the testator, without obtaining a certificate of appointment, third parties such as financial institutions holding assets of the deceased often insist on the higher degree of proof provided by such a certificate. A certificate of appointment also deals with the problem of proof that arises when the deceased's will does not name anyone as estate trustee, as sometimes happens in the case of homemade wills, or where none of the named estate trustees are able or willing to act.

Certificate of Appointment of Estate Trustee with a Will

certificate of appointment of estate trustee with a will
document from the court setting out the name of a deceased with a will, identifying the estate, and giving the name and address of the estate trustee

The **certificate of appointment of estate trustee with a will** is a document from the court signed by a judge or the court registrar and imprinted with the court's seal. It sets out the name of the deceased, identifies the estate, and gives the name and address of the estate trustee. An example of a certificate of appointment is shown in Figure 7.1. As can be seen from the example, a copy of the last will (as well as any codicils to the will) of the deceased is part of the certificate. This incidentally provides assurance to the estate trustee that she can rely on that will as the last will—that is, that the gifts and other terms set out therein can be relied on without concern that they may have been revoked in a subsequent will.

Ontario courts are organized in jurisdictions based on a district or regional basis. The procedure within the court upon receipt of an application for a certificate of appointment in any such jurisdiction requires the estate registrar for Ontario to check a central, province-wide database to see whether any other wills of the deceased have been presented in any other jurisdiction. This internal request for clearance is done by the court prior to the issuance of the certificate. Once the clearance is obtained and the certificate of appointment is signed and stamped by the court, the estate trustee can take the certificate and show it, or provide notarial copies of it, to any institutions holding assets of the deceased. Any person, financial institution, land registry office, or other entity that holds assets of the deceased and that is presented with a certificate of appointment of estate trustee is legally obligated to deal with the estate trustee as if such estate trustee were the deceased. No further proof of the appointment is required, although the estate trustee may have to prove her identity as well. Also, if the certificate is more than one year old, confirmation from the court that the certificate has not been revoked may legitimately be requested by any person or entity still holding assets of the deceased.

The procedure for obtaining a certificate of appointment of estate trustee with a will is discussed in detail in Chapters 9 and 10. For now, it should be noted that the court will ask for its own proof of certain matters, such as whether the person making an application for the certificate is the appropriate candidate, whether the will presented is the last will, the value of the assets of the deceased, and confirmation of the deceased's death. For almost all of these questions, the court relies on an affidavit of the estate trustee. Furthermore, as indicated above, the court conducts its own inquiry by checking the provincial database to see whether any other wills have been presented to a court in Ontario for that same deceased person. It is, of course, possible for a new will to surface after the certificate of appointment of estate trustee with a will has been granted and relied on by third-party persons and institutions. Such legal quandaries are, however, rare and would usually be settled by parties through actions that are outside the scope of this text.

FIGURE 7.1   **Certificate of Appointment of Estate Trustee With a Will**

Court File No. 3456/12

ONTARIO
SUPERIOR COURT OF JUSTICE

IN THE ESTATE OF JACQUELINE STICK, deceased.

late of   34 Thistle Street, Toronto, Ontario, M5A 9Q9
occupation   retired security guard
who died on   January 12, 2018

CERTIFICATE OF APPOINTMENT OF ESTATE TRUSTEE WITH A WILL

Applicant	Address	Occupation
Robert Larise	345 Needlebrook Avenue, Oakville, Ontario, L6J Q9Q	auto manufacturer

This CERTIFICATE OF APPOINTMENT OF ESTATE TRUSTEE WITH A WILL is hereby issued under the seal of the court to the applicant named above. A copy of the deceased's last will (and codicil(s), if any) is attached.

DATE: May 25, 2018

"Seal"

Gilda Hendrickson
_____
Registrar
Gilda Hendrickson

Address of court office:

393 University Avenue
10th Floor
Toronto, Ontario
M5G 1E6

THIS IS THE LAST WILL AND TESTAMENT of me, **JACQUELINE STICK**, whose current residence address is 34 Thistle Street, Toronto, Ontario, M5A 9Q9, retired security guard.

I appoint my friend ROBERT LARISE to be the sole estate trustee of my estate. In the event that my first-named estate trustee is unable or unwilling to act, I appoint my friend GRITTA GABLE to be the sole estate trustee of my estate.

FIGURE 7.1 CONTINUED

I give all the residue of my property, both real and personal, and including any property over which I may have a general power of appointment, to my estate trustee UPON THE FOLLOWING TRUSTS: (A) to pay the amount of $5,000 to my friend RAOUL THURGOOD; (B) to pay the amount of $25,000 to THE HUMAN FUND in Toronto, Ontario; and (C) to hold the entire residue of my estate in a trust fund, the beneficiary of which is to be my friend GORDON PONNER, and I direct my estate trustee to pay the income from such fund to GORDON PONNER for his lifetime, the frequency of such payments to be in the entire discretion of my estate trustee, and in the event that GORDON PONNER fails to survive me, or upon the death of GORDON PONNER, I direct that the capital portion of the said trust fund be paid to THE HUMAN FUND as aforesaid.

IN TESTIMONY WHEREOF I have to this my last will and testament written upon this page of paper hereunto subscribed my name this 15th day of December, 2009.

SIGNED, PUBLISHED AND DECLARED)
by JACQUELINE STICK)
as and for her last will and)
testament, in the presence of)
us, both present at the same)
time, who at her request, in)
her presence, and in the)
presence of each other, have)
hereunto subscribed our)
names as witnesses:)
)
)   *Jacqueline Stick*
)   ‾‾‾‾‾‾‾‾‾‾‾‾‾‾‾‾‾‾‾‾‾
)   Jacqueline Stick
)
Jill Clifford)
‾‾‾‾‾‾‾‾‾‾‾‾‾‾‾‾)
Jill Clifford)
Darren McDowell)
‾‾‾‾‾‾‾‾‾‾‾‾‾‾‾‾)
Darren McDowell)

Court File No. 3456/18

In the estate of JACQUELINE STICK, deceased

ONTARIO

SUPERIOR COURT OF JUSTICE

PROCEEDING COMMENCED AT Toronto

Certificate of Appointment

of Estate Trustee With a Will

Grit, Grat & Groot

Barristers & Solicitors

15 Cross Street

Toronto, Ontario

M5A 1Q1

Telephone: 416-555-5555

Facsimile: 416-555-5556

GWENDOLYN GRAT

Solicitor for the Applicant

If two or more estate trustees are named in the will and not all of them are applying for the certificate of appointment, before granting the certificate of appointment the court requires proof by way of sworn statement that the other named estate trustees are unable or unwilling to act. Again, while these forms of proof are not without the possibility of error or mischief, practicalities dictate the need for reliable proof to third parties of the appointment of the estate trustee, which is provided by the certificate of appointment. Note that the *Rules of Civil Procedure* allow for a special kind of certificate of appointment of estate trustee with a will—namely, a "certificate of appointment of estate trustee with a will limited to the assets referred to in the will." This latter form of certificate of appointment is to be obtained in the situation where there are split wills.

Certificate of Appointment of Estate Trustee Without a Will

If the deceased died intestate, even if a person is willing and able to assume the role of estate trustee and all of the beneficiaries of the estate under the laws of intestate succession are agreeable, that person cannot be the estate trustee without the involvement of the court. As indicated above, in the case of a testate estate, application is made to the court for a certificate of appointment of estate trustee with a will. In the case of an intestate estate, the certificate of appointment is called the **certificate of appointment of estate trustee without a will**.

certificate of appointment of estate trustee without a will document from the court setting out the name of a deceased without a will, identifying the estate, and giving the name and address of the estate trustee

The procedure for obtaining a certificate of appointment of estate trustee without a will is outlined in Chapters 9 and 10. It is conceptually similar to that for obtaining a certificate of appointment with a will, except that, because there is no will, there is no sworn statement pertaining to the proper execution of the will. Instead, the sworn statement lists the deceased's next of kin to make the court aware of the hierarchy of beneficiaries in the particular estate. Depending on the proposed estate trustee's placement in the hierarchy, consents of persons beneficially entitled to the estate may also have to be submitted. An applicant for a certificate of appointment as estate trustee without a will must be a resident of Ontario. As discussed below, third parties dealing with the estate are considered insufficiently protected unless the estate trustee falls under the jurisdiction of the Ontario courts.

Less Common Forms of Proof of Appointment of Estate Trustee

The certificates of appointment of estate trustee with a will and without a will are the most common forms of proof of the appointment of the estate trustee. However, other forms of proof apply in some less common situations. These other forms of proof are discussed below.

Confirmation by Resealing of Appointment of Estate Trustee With or Without a Will

If a non-resident of Ontario (but a resident of Canada, the United Kingdom, or a British possession) dies with or without a will while owning assets in Ontario, that person's estate representative in the outside jurisdiction—the estate trustee or executor, or administrator (where there is no will), as she probably would be called—would most likely be a resident of the outside jurisdiction and would most likely have been appointed by a court of that jurisdiction as the estate representative in that jurisdiction. It is not considered adequate protection, however, for the person or institution holding the assets in Ontario to rely on the certificate of appointment of estate trustee, or its equivalent, from the court of the outside jurisdiction. The reason is that, for example, the certificate of appointment might not be in a recognizable form, and more important, on its face the estate trustee is not subject to the jurisdiction of the Ontario court.

The solution is for the estate trustee from the outside jurisdiction to apply to the Ontario court for a resealing of the outside certificate of appointment or its equivalent. The Ontario court will put its own seal or stamp on the outside certificate, thus communicating to third parties in Ontario that the certificate can be relied on.

The confirmation by resealing of appointment of estate trustee with or without a will cannot be obtained unless the outside estate trustee has first obtained the equivalent of the certificate of appointment in the outside jurisdiction, which itself must be another part of Canada, the United Kingdom, or a British possession.

Certificate of Ancillary Appointment of Estate Trustee With a Will

Where a resident of a foreign country—that is, outside Canada or outside a country within the United Kingdom or a British possession—dies with a will while owning assets in Ontario, the appropriate certificate of appointment of estate trustee to obtain is the certificate of ancillary appointment of estate trustee with a will. This certificate, like the confirmation by resealing of appointment of estate trustee with or without a will, is the Ontario version of the foreign jurisdiction's appointment of estate trustee. It is important to note that this document is obtainable only if the deceased died with a will and if the foreign estate trustee obtained the equivalent of a certificate of appointment of estate trustee with a will from the foreign jurisdiction.

Certificate of Appointment of Foreign Estate Trustee's Nominee as Estate Trustee Without a Will

Where a resident of a foreign country that is not in the United Kingdom or a British possession dies without a will while owning assets in Ontario, the protection afforded to the third parties holding those assets is diminished by three factors. First, the estate trustee likely will not be an Ontario resident and therefore will not be under the jurisdiction of the Ontario courts. Second, the estate trustee likely will not be under the jurisdiction of a court in the United Kingdom or a British possession. Third, the estate trustee will not have a will from which he derives his authority. Accordingly, the requirements for an appointment of estate trustee by the Ontario court in this situation are the most stringent. The applicant in Ontario must first be appointed the estate trustee (or its equivalent) in the foreign jurisdiction—that is, in the jurisdiction where the deceased was resident—and then must designate an Ontario resident, who is called "the nominee" and who acts in place of the estate trustee without a will. The nominee is a person under the jurisdiction of the Ontario court who can be made the subject of a court action if the estate is mishandled.

Certificate of Appointment of Succeeding Estate Trustee With a Will

If one of two or several estate trustees dies, the one or those remaining proceed to administer the estate. With respect to dealings with third parties, it is only necessary that the trustee(s) provide proof of death of the deceased trustee. If, however, the trustee who dies is the sole or last surviving trustee, that deceased person's own estate trustee assumes the obligations of the unadministered estate—that is, she becomes the trustee of both estates. This process is known as **devolution**—that is, the legal transfer of rights or powers from one person to another. In cases of devolution, the deceased estate trustee's own trustee would normally prove her appointment as estate trustee to third parties by presenting a copy of the original certificate of appointment, proof of death of the other estate trustee or trustees, and a copy of her own certificate of appointment.

devolution
the legal transfer
of rights or powers
from one person
to another

If, however, the sole or last deceased estate trustee died intestate or with a will appointing an estate trustee who is unable or unwilling to assume the role, some interested party such as a beneficiary or creditor would have to make application to the court for an appointment in order to complete the job of administering the original estate. There is, however, a need to prove the new estate trustee's status as succeeding estate trustee to third parties holding unadministered assets of the deceased. The certificate of appointment of succeeding estate trustee with a will fulfills this need.

In the situation where there are two or more estate trustees, one of whom falls ill and is no longer able to act as estate trustee although still alive, the appropriate course of action would be a motion to the court by the remaining estate trustee(s) for removal of that estate trustee. This procedure is dealt with in more detail in Part III, Estate Litigation, Chapter 14, Challenging the Conduct of the Estate Trustees.

Certificate of Appointment of Succeeding Estate Trustee Without a Will

Similar to the certificate of appointment of succeeding estate trustee with a will, the certificate of appointment of succeeding estate trustee without a will is granted where the estate trustee in an intestate situation dies. There is, however, no devolution in intestate estates. Accordingly, whether the estate trustee without a will herself dies testate or intestate, a certificate of succeeding estate trustee without a will is required.

Certificate of Appointment of Estate Trustee During Litigation

Finally, if there is litigation in relation to the estate that affects the ability of the estate trustee to administer the estate, the question may arise—perhaps incidental to the litigation itself—as to who should be the estate trustee during the course of the litigation. This person, perhaps after the parties have reached some consensus themselves on the appropriate person, will be appointed by a judge to act as the estate trustee during litigation.

Under section 28 of the *Estates Act*,[1] and subject to the direction of the court, the estate trustee during litigation has the same powers as an estate trustee without a will except that he cannot distribute the estate to beneficiaries. This, of course, still allows the estate trustee during litigation to pay the debts of the estate on an ongoing basis. The remuneration for acting as the estate trustee during litigation is "such reasonable remuneration as the court considers proper."

---

1 RSO 1990, c E.21.

Determining Whether a Certificate of Appointment Is Necessary

As will be seen in Chapter 8, Preliminary Steps in Applying for a Certificate of Appointment of Estate Trustee, except in special circumstances, an application for a certificate of appointment must be accompanied by a cheque or bank draft representing a deposit toward the estate administration tax owing pursuant to the provincial *Estate Administration Tax Act*.[2] The amount of estate administration tax owing, based on the value of all the assets falling into the estate with some exceptions and modifications, is discussed in more detail in Chapter 8. Because obtaining a certificate of appointment can be costly and, as a general rule, an estate trustee is under an obligation to incur only reasonable expenses on behalf of the estate, the estate trustee may wish to consider whether an application to the court should be made at all. The lawyer's job is to advise when such a step can be safely skipped and when it cannot.

The question to be asked is, will every asset belonging to the deceased be transferable without a certificate? While the actual process of transferring assets will be dealt with in Chapter 10, for now note that, even if all assets but one do not require a certificate of appointment for their transfer, the value of all assets must nevertheless be included in the calculation of the estate administration tax when making the application to the court, except assets covered by valid or accepted split wills.

Finally, it should be stated that while the certificate of appointment provides some assurance to third parties holding assets of the deceased that they can deliver such assets to the named estate trustee, it also provides assurance to the estate trustee himself that the appointment is secure. In other words, notwithstanding that the third parties may waive the need for a certificate of appointment, the circumstances might be such that the estate trustee will reasonably want a certificate for his own reassurance. One such circumstance might be in the case of a document that may or may not be a valid holograph will.

Assets Held by Financial Institutions

Assets held by financial institutions include bank accounts, registered retirement savings plans (RRSPs), registered retirement income funds (RRIFs), annuities, mutual funds, and term deposits. Financial institutions include banks, trust companies, credit unions, and private investment brokerages. Whether to release such assets to the estate trustee without the production of a certificate of appointment of estate trustee is solely within the discretion of the financial institution holding the assets. Most financial institutions have a policy waiving the need for the certificate of appointment where the deceased died with a will and the value of the assets held by the financial institution is a relatively small amount—for example, less than $10,000 or $15,000. The determination of the threshold of asset value, and the waiver itself, are entirely the prerogative of the institution holding the assets or in charge of the records showing ownership of the assets.

The lawyer will typically write a letter to the financial institution indicating the circumstances and requesting that the assets be transferred without the need to obtain a

---

2   RSO 1990, c E.22.

certificate of appointment. Figure 7.2 is an example of such a letter. The letter normally includes a notarial copy of the deceased's will (the front page of which is reproduced in Figure 7.3) and an authorization and direction from the estate trustee(s) (as in Figure 7.4).

FIGURE 7.2   Lawyer's Letter Requesting Transfer of Funds

February 2, 2018
My File: B8-1237

Bank of Dundas
450 Thistle Street
Toronto, Ontario
M5A Q8Q

Dear Madam or Sir,

Re: Estate of Jacqueline Stick
who died January 12, 2018

Please be advised that we act for Robert Larise, the estate trustee in the above-noted estate.

I understand that you hold assets of Ms. Stick at your branch.

Please advise whether you would agree to transferring such assets into the name of the estate without a certificate of appointment of estate trustee with a will.

I have enclosed, for your records, a funeral director's statement of death, an authorization and direction from Mr. Larise and a notarial copy of Ms. Stick's will.

Thank you for your consideration of this matter.

Yours Truly,

GRIT, GRAT & GROOT

Mary Ross

Mary Ross, Law Clerk

As indicated above, if the deceased died intestate, it is unlikely that a financial institution will transfer the assets without a certificate of appointment of estate trustee. Where there is no will, the financial institution has a limited ability to determine who are the deceased's next of kin and therefore the appropriate recipients of her assets.

An exception may occur where the intestate is survived by a married spouse and the estate is worth less than the spousal preferential share of $200,000. In such a case, the financial institution may reasonably conclude that the surviving spouse is the beneficiary at law and may simply require proof of his married status. On the other hand, it cannot know whether another financial institution is also holding assets of the deceased that raise the total net value of the estate above the threshold for the spousal preferential share. That is, a release of assets can still be risky in that other beneficiaries may have a claim on them.

Also, while the spouse may be entitled to the first $200,000 of the intestate's net estate, there may be creditors of the estate to whom part or all of that sum is owed. If the financial institution transfers the assets it holds to the surviving spouse without a certificate of appointment, it may be held liable to such creditors.

FIGURE 7.3   Notarial Copy of the Will

NOTARIAL CERTIFICATE

Province of Ontario	)
	) TO ALL WHOM THESE PRESENTS MAY
To Wit:	) COME, BE SEEN OR KNOWN

I, GWENDOLYN GRAT,

a Notary Public, in and for the Province of Ontario, by Royal Authority duly appointed, residing at the City of Toronto, in said Province, DO CERTIFY AND ATTEST that the paper writing hereto annexed is a true copy of a document purporting to be

the last will and testament of Jacqueline Stick;

the said copy having been compared by me with the said original document which does not appear to have been altered in any way, except in size, an act whereof being requested I have granted under my Notarial Form and Seal of Office to serve and avail as occasion shall or may require.

IN TESTIMONY WHEREOF I have hereunto subscribed my name and affixed my Notarial Seal of Office at Toronto, Ontario this 30th day of January, 2018.

Gwendolyn Grat
_____
Gwendolyn Grat
A Notary Public in and for the
Province of Ontario, Canada.

Issued from the office of GRIT, GRAT & GROOT, Barristers & Solicitors, 15 Cross Street, Toronto, Ontario, M5A 1Q1.

Publicly Traded Stocks

Many people own publicly traded stocks or shares of corporations. Such assets are often called "equities," a term that has, in our society, come to mean a form of partial ownership. Equities in publicly traded companies can be owned in many different ways but are commonly owned in mutual funds or investment plans or by direct ownership of stock or shares in a particular corporation. Mutual funds are collections of equities (or other vehicles of investment, such as bonds, mortgages, and the like) that are maintained within investment plans by financial institutions. The financial institutions purchase and sell investments, including equities in companies, within the funds and sell shares of the funds themselves. An individual may also directly have equity in a publicly traded company by owning stock or shares of the corporation. Such stock, which is represented by share certificates, can be purchased and sold through a stockbroker, an online service, or an employment stock option plan. Every publicly held corporation has a stock register listing owners of all its shares and a transfer agent whose job it is to administer the ever-changing ownership of the corporation. The transfer agent of a publicly traded company is often a branch of a chartered bank or a trust company. When assisting an estate trustee in transferring share certificates, the lawyer may have to make inquiries to determine who is the transfer agent of a particular stock.

FIGURE 7.4   Trustee Authorization: Provision of Requested Information

AUTHORIZATION AND DIRECTION

TO: Bank of Dundas
       450 Thistle Street
       Toronto, Ontario
       M5A Q8Q

RE: Estate of Jacqueline Stick
       who died January 12, 2018

I, Robert Larise, the estate trustee in the estate of Jacqueline Stick, deceased, hereby authorize and direct you to provide my lawyer—namely, Gwendolyn Grat, of

       GRIT, GRAT & GROOT
       Barristers & Solicitors
       15 Cross Street
       Toronto, Ontario
       M5A 1Q1

or any agent of my said lawyer, with any requested information or documentation pertaining to the estate of Jacqueline Stick or the assets of Jacqueline Stick.

This shall be your good and sufficient authority for so doing.

Signed this 30th day of January, 2018.

Robert Larise

———————————————
Robert Larise

Again, it is solely within the discretion of the transfer agent whether to transfer shares of a corporation owned by a deceased when there is no certificate of appointment. Each transfer agent has its own set of policies. As will be seen in Chapter 10, if the transfer agent agrees to transfer the shares without a certificate of appointment, it will typically have its own procedures to be followed and forms to be completed. A letter similar to that in Figure 7.2 should be sent to the transfer agent to determine whether a certificate of appointment is required and, if not, what the requirements are.

Again, it is unlikely that the transfer agent will agree to transfer shares in a publicly traded corporation if the deceased died intestate and there is no certificate of appointment of estate trustee. This is because where there is no will, there can be no estate trustee without a certificate. Nevertheless, as in the other cases, the decision is left to the transfer agent.

In very rare instances, the ownership of shares in a corporation may not be handled by a transfer agent but by the corporation itself. In that case, the corporation has to be contacted to determine whether the stocks can be transferred without a certificate of appointment and, if so, what documentation is required.

Canada Savings Bonds

Canada savings bonds are issued by the government of Canada. Under current Bank of Canada policy, such bonds can be distributed without a certificate of appointment if the recipient is the married spouse of the deceased owner and the total value of the bonds is less than $200,000, or if the recipient is not the married spouse of the deceased and the total value of the bonds is $20,000 or less. These rules are the same whether the estate is testate or intestate.

The Bank of Canada posts its policy as to the face value of Canada savings bonds that can be transferred without a certificate of appointment on its website, which can be accessed at www.csb.gc.ca. (Click on "Resources" and then "Services"; then scroll through the results to find "Transfer or Redeem from a Deceased Owner." Click on it, and select "Bank of Canada Business Rules." The precise link, for now, is <http://csb.gc.ca/wp-content/uploads/2009/04/bank-of-canada-business-rules.pdf>.) The face value depends on the face value of the bonds and the structure of the estate. Currently the policy is as follows: If there is a specific bequest of bonds to a beneficiary in a will, all of the bonds can be transferred without obtaining a certificate of appointment. If the married spouse of the deceased person is the sole beneficiary under the will, up to $75,000 worth of Canada savings bonds can be transferred without obtaining a certificate of appointment. If the deceased's children or the deceased's married spouse and children are the sole beneficiaries under the will, up to $50,000 worth can be transferred without a certificate of appointment. If the deceased's parents, siblings, or other family members are the sole beneficiaries of the estate (and where there are no surviving spouse or children of the deceased), up to $20,000 worth can be transferred without a certificate. If the common law spouse, same-sex partner, or friend of the deceased is the sole beneficiary under the will, up to $20,000 worth can be transferred without a certificate. In the case of double estates between spouses, where the bond owner and his spouse are both deceased and the children are the beneficiaries, up to $50,000 can be transferred without a certificate. If the sole beneficiary under the will is an organization (such as a charity or a church) or a trust, a certificate of appointment of estate trustee is required.

Other Personal Property

"Other personal property" includes everything except real property, such as personal effects, household furniture, cars, loans, debts owing to the deceased, and business assets. As a general rule, when determining whether a certificate of appointment is needed to transfer such assets, the relevant person or institution to consult is the one in possession of the asset or holding the official register that records the ownership of the asset.

Land (Real Property)

Real property can be owned in one name alone, or with another person or other persons. If the property is owned with another person or other persons, it can be owned in joint tenancy or in tenancy in common. It is only in cases of sole ownership or tenancy in common that the property will pass into the estate. When property is owned jointly with another person, it passes directly to the survivor or survivors upon the deceased's death and is not subject to the claims of the deceased's beneficiaries or creditors (except those creditors whose debts are secured against the real property itself). Where property is owned as a tenancy in common, the deceased's share of the real property will be an asset of the estate.

It is still possible in some instances to sell real property from an estate or transfer real property to a beneficiary of the estate where there is no certificate of appointment of estate trustee. Nevertheless, the situations in which such transfers are possible are rare, and, even if possible, they are not always advisable.

The documentation required to transfer real property to and from an estate trustee where there is no certificate of appointment is dealt with in Chapter 10. In brief and in very general terms, real property that has been converted by the Ontario government from Ontario's (now outdated) registry system to the newer "land titles conversion qualified" system can be transferred without a certificate of appointment if the transfer is a "first dealing" with the property since it was converted.

Where the Deceased Resided Outside Ontario

If the deceased did not normally reside in Ontario, the estate trustee may need to apply for one of the certificates of appointment relating to estates of individuals residing in other jurisdictions, as described above. It should be emphasized that, for all of those certificates, it is a precondition that the estate trustee from the outside jurisdiction be already appointed in the jurisdiction where the deceased resided.

Old Terminology

Estate trustees of whatever type are often referred to, in statutes and other legal documents, as "personal representatives." Until approximately 1995, a certificate of appointment of estate trustee with a will was called "letters probate" or simply "probate," and a certificate of appointment of estate trustee without a will was called "letters of administration." Similarly, until recently, an estate trustee with a will was called an "executor" (or the female "executrix"), and an estate trustee without a will was called an "administrator" (or the female "administratrix"). The old terminology is mentioned because in most other jurisdictions in the world, it is still current. Even in Ontario, the majority of bank employees, bank managers, financial planners, land registry office staff, estate lawyers, and members of the general public still know, recognize, and use the old terminology over the newer and more cumbersome terminology. Because of this, a lawyer is still often called upon to clear up confusion on the part of both clients and financial institutions resulting from the new terminology. It is not uncommon, for example, for a client to be told by a bank employee that she needs to bring in a "probated certificate of appointment" or a "certificate of probate trustee," or some other currently non-existent document.

KEY TERMS

REVIEW QUESTIONS

1. From what document does an estate trustee with a will derive his or her authority?

2. What are the first steps that the estate trustee named in the will must take regarding the assets of the deceased?

3. What must the estate trustee do with the deceased's personal property such as vehicles and jewellery; real property such as a home and a cottage; shares in a corporation; and bank assets?

4. When is proof of an estate trustee's authority required?

5. When is a will naming the executor satisfactory proof of her authority, and when is it unsatisfactory?

6. What is a certificate of appointment of estate trustee with a will?

7. What certificate of appointment is applied for when there is no will?

8. Who assumes administration of an estate where the appointed estate trustee of that estate dies?

9. When is a certificate of ancillary appointment of estate trustee with a will applied for?

10. When is a certificate of appointment of foreign estate trustee's nominee as estate trustee without a will applied for?

11. Under what circumstances might a certificate of appointment of succeeding estate trustee with a will be required?

12. Under what circumstances would a certificate of appointment of succeeding estate trustee without a will be required?

13. What certificate is applied for if litigation arises relating to the estate, which affects the ability of the estate trustee to administer the estate?

14. Describe a situation where a confirmation by resealing of appointment of estate trustee with or without a will would be required.

15. When can a financial institution insist that a certificate of the court be produced before complying with the estate trustee's request to deal with assets that the financial institution holds?

16. In what circumstances do financial institutions sometimes waive the strict requirement for a certificate of appointment?

17. Will a certificate of appointment of estate trustee always be required to transfer assets held in publicly traded stocks?

18. When can Canada savings bonds be transferred without a certificate?

19. What happens with real property of the deceased owned jointly with another person?

20. Why should a lawyer or law clerk be familiar with old forms of terminology such as "probate," "administration," "executor," and "administratrix"?

Preliminary Steps in Applying for a Certificate of Appointment of Estate Trustee

8

Contents

LEARNING OUTCOMES

After reading this chapter, you should be able to:

- Explain the importance of due diligence in identifying and evaluating the assets of the deceased

- Understand how estate administration tax is calculated and paid

- Describe what an administration bond of indemnity is, when it is required, and who is allowed to provide such a bond

- Understand the amount of a bond required with different types of sureties

Introduction

Once it has been determined that a certificate of appointment of estate trustee is required, it is usually the job of the lawyer to prepare and submit the application to the court. This chapter deals with the steps that must be taken before the application is submitted.

Valuation of the Assets

The first step is to arrive at a valuation of the assets of the estate. This is done for the purpose of calculating the estate administration tax (discussed below). As indicated in Chapter 7, Proof of the Estate Trustee's Status as Estate Trustee, this tax is normally deposited with the court at the time of making the application for the certificate of appointment and paid by the court to the minister of finance upon issuance of the certificate of appointment. As discussed below, the total value of the deceased's assets falling into the estate must be stated on the application form in two categories: personal property and real property. The personal property category includes all property except real property that does not bypass the estate by way of right of survivorship (for example, joint bank accounts or RRSPs that name a direct beneficiary). Similarly, the real property category includes all real estate within Ontario that was solely owned by the deceased or owned by the deceased as a tenant in common. If the real property was owned by the deceased as a joint tenant, ownership in the property automatically passes to the surviving joint owner(s).

Also, as discussed below, the personal property category on the application form is not to include any property that is dealt with in a valid split will and the real property listed on the form is to be reduced by the amount of any mortgages owing on the real property.

Note that it often falls on the law clerk to conduct a preliminary investigation into the assets of the estate by interviewing the client and/or the estate trustee (or prospective estate trustee). Lawyers and law clerks often employ an estate information form that serves as a checklist of sorts to begin the process of determining the deceased's assets and liabilities. Figure 8.1 is an example of such a form. While the client sometimes knows little about the deceased's assets, it is important to stress to the client that as an estate trustee she has a legal obligation to be duly diligent in tracking down and properly evaluating the deceased's assets. As will be seen in detail in Chapter 11, Determining, Notifying, and Paying Creditors of the Estate, as of January 1, 2015, the *Estate Administration Tax Act, 1998*[1] requires that the estate trustee complete and file a special tax return after receiving the certificate of appointment. This tax return, called the estate information return, requires details of the various assets belonging to the estate, including their respective fair market values.

Valuing Personal Property

Assets Held by Financial Institutions

To obtain the value of assets held by financial institutions—for example, banks, trust companies, credit unions, and investment brokerages—it is necessary to contact those

---

1 SO 1998, c 34, Sched.

institutions to request that they provide particulars of all accounts, investments, mortgages, loans, credit cards, lines of credit, and safety deposit boxes held by the deceased at their institution. Such information should include the value of assets as of the date of death but will also include information such as account numbers for the various assets and the interest earned by each following the date of death. This information will be needed for completing the estate information form. Also, as will be seen in Chapter 12, Accounting to the Beneficiaries and Paying the Beneficiaries, it will be necessary to have such information later when accounting to the beneficiaries. When such contact is made, it is also convenient at that time to ask the financial institution (as explained in Chapter 7) whether it will require a certificate of appointment for the transfer of assets. Figure 8.2 is an example of a letter requesting this information.

In seeking confirmation of the value of assets held by financial institutions, there are two potential problems: (1) there is no sure way to determine which financial institutions, if any, held assets of the deceased; and (2) a financial institution may not provide information on the deceased's assets to someone who has not been appointed estate trustee.

The first problem is solved by carefully reviewing the information obtained in the client interview as well as from the deceased's personal papers, including bank books, online bank accounts, financial statements, income tax returns, mail, and email, to determine his habits of banking and making investments. As discussed in Chapter 1, Wills, if the deceased kept an accurate list of his assets and liabilities, this task is significantly easier for the estate trustee. Even if there is a list, however, it is important for the estate trustee to make sure that the list is accurate and up to date. It can never be known for certain that all of the deceased's assets have been found, and it sometimes happens that assets surface after the estate has been administered and wound up.

The second problem may be solved in a number of ways, depending on the circumstances. If the deceased died with a will appointing an estate trustee, the value of the assets can usually be obtained by writing a letter to each of the financial institutions where the deceased is thought to have had assets. The letter (as in the example in Figure 8.2) would include proof of death (usually the funeral director's statement), a notarial copy of the will (see Chapter 7, Figure 7.3), and a direction signed by the estate trustee requesting that the financial institution communicate with the estate trustee's lawyer on the valuation of the assets (see Chapter 7, Figure 7.4). Typically, the lawyer or law clerk prepares such documentation to be included with the letter.

In the case of an estate without a will, a financial institution may be unwilling to provide any information. It is then the lawyer's job to attempt to persuade the institution to provide the information, although if the institution does not do so, its decision before a certificate of appointment is obtained must be respected. If a financial institution does not make disclosure, the estate trustee must simply provide her best estimate of the value of the assets held by that institution along with an undertaking to the court to make up the difference (discussed below). Past tax returns of the deceased may provide clues about the value of some assets.

FIGURE 8.1   Preliminary Estate Assets and Liabilities Checklist

Canvass these items with your client and record any known particulars:

Assets

- ☐ Real estate
  - ☐ owned with others (names and percentages): _____
  - ☐ joint or   ☐ tenancy in common
- ☐ Bank accounts
  - ☐ owned with others (names): _____
  - ☐ convenience   ☐ right of survivorship
- ☐ Life insurance (particulars): _____
- ☐ RSP (particulars): _____
- ☐ RIF
  - ☐ named beneficiary (names): _____
- ☐ Receiving old age security
- ☐ Receiving Canada Pension Plan
- ☐ Receiving private pension (particulars): _____
  - ☐ named beneficiary (particulars): _____
- ☐ Receiving foreign country pension (particulars): _____
- ☐ Investments held by investor(s) (particulars): _____
- ☐ Loosely held stocks (particulars): _____
- ☐ Canada savings bonds (particulars): _____
- ☐ Other bonds (particulars): _____
- ☐ Bank securities (term deposits, etc.) (particulars): _____
  - ☐ named beneficiary (particulars): _____
- ☐ Cash (amount): _____
- ☐ Uncashed cheques (particulars): _____
- ☐ Jewellery (particulars): _____
- ☐ Personal effects (particulars if more than nominal value): _____
- ☐ Works of art (particulars if more than nominal value): _____
- ☐ Collections (particulars if more than nominal value): _____
- ☐ Furniture (particulars if possibly more than nominal value): _____
- ☐ Other named beneficiary (particulars): _____
- ☐ Other (particulars): _____

Debts

- ☐ Funeral account (amount): _____
- ☐ Mortgages (particulars): _____
- ☐ Line(s) of credit (particulars): _____
- ☐ Credit cards (particulars): _____
- ☐ Other bank loans (particulars): _____
- ☐ Other loans (family, etc.) (particulars): _____
- ☐ Contractual obligations (particulars): _____
- ☐ Income tax (particulars): _____
- ☐ Ongoing litigation (particulars): _____
- ☐ Other (particulars): _____

FIGURE 8.2   Lawyer's Letter Requesting Account Valuation

February 27, 2018

My File: B8-1237

Bank of Dundas

450 Thistle Street

Toronto, Ontario

M5A 8Q8

Dear Madam or Sir,

Re: Estate of Jacqueline Stick
who died January 12, 2018

I am writing further to my letter dated February 2, 2018. I confirm that we act for Mr. Robert Larise, the estate trustee in the above-noted estate, and that you have indicated that a certificate of appointment of estate trustee is required to transfer Ms. Stick's term deposit and chequing account into the name of the estate.

We are in the process of preparing the application for a certificate of appointment, and, in that regard, we must obtain a valuation of all of Ms. Stick's assets as of her date of death, which was January 12, 2018. I would therefore ask you to please provide me with the account numbers and respective values (currently and as of the date of death) of all assets held by you in Ms. Stick's name, including all accounts and investments. Also, if Ms. Stick had one or more safety deposit boxes at your bank, I would ask you to please provide us with the particulars.

Further to the above, any information you can provide us as to the amounts paid in interest with respect to any such assets in the last year as well as the applicable rates and how the interest was paid (i.e., whether it was rolled into the principal or paid out to another bank account) would be very helpful at this time.

In addition, if you have any particulars of mortgages, lines of credit, credit cards, or other loans owing by Ms. Stick, I would ask you to please provide particulars.

I refer you to the enclosures in my last letter—namely, the notarial copy of the will, the funeral director's statement of death, and an authorization and direction from Mr. Larise.

Thank you for your consideration and please do not hesitate to contact me if you have any questions or concerns.

Yours truly,

GRIT, GRAT & GROOT

Mary Ross

Mary Ross, Law Clerk

Publicly Traded Stocks

As indicated in Chapter 7, people often own stock or shares in corporations. The Internet (querying TSX historical values) can provide a way in which to verify the value of these assets as of the date of death. The value of publicly traded shares can also be ascertained by checking online or in a newspaper as close as possible to the date of death to obtain the traded value for the shares at that time, or by consulting a stockbroker. Newspaper stock listings or online databases would also of course list the current market value of mutual funds, but if such funds were purchased through a financial institution, the institution may be a more convenient or reliable source of information.

Canada Savings Bonds and Other Interest-Bearing Securities

The valuation of Canada savings bonds and other interest-bearing securities is based on the combined face value and the accrued or accumulated interest to the date of death.

Personal Effects and Household Furniture

The deceased's personal effects and household furniture normally fall into the estate. Personal effects such as clothing and well-used furniture and furnishings are often given a nominal value for the purpose of the application. The deceased may, however, have owned items such as objects of art that appear to have a high value, and in those cases a professional valuation should be obtained. If the deceased was cohabiting with another person at the time of his death, the estate trustee must determine as well as she can which assets belonged solely to the deceased, and which were owned jointly with the survivor and therefore may bypass the estate.

If there is any possibility of dispute about the value of any particular asset, it is always advisable to obtain a professional valuation. It is also a wise practice for the estate trustee to make, as soon as possible, a list of every item of value in the deceased's permanent residence and other premises, such as a summer cottage. As previously mentioned, the estate trustee must in any event immediately take steps to secure and preserve the assets. In this connection, she may have to restrict access to the assets to prevent conversion by third parties. Such steps may include changing the locks of the premises and removing some or all of the items and placing them in storage.

If the deceased was renting his premises, sections 91 and 92 of the *Residential Tenancies Act, 2006*[2] may be relevant. Section 91 states that, upon the death of the tenant, the tenancy is deemed to be terminated after 30 days, and the landlord is obligated until the 30 days have expired to preserve the property of the deceased with the exception of property that is unsafe or unhygienic. The landlord must also allow the estate trustee to have reasonable access to the premises. Section 92 gives the landlord certain rights to dispose of a deceased person's property if it is unsafe or unhygienic or if the 30-day period has expired. In such a case, the estate can claim the proceeds of any sale less the cost of storing and selling the property and less any arrears of rent for a period of six months.

---

2 SO 2006, c 1.

Vehicles

The estate trustee must take immediate possession of any vehicles and notify the insurance company of the death. It is also important to note the particulars of any vehicles, such as the make, model, and vehicle identification number. As will be seen, the estate information return requires this information along with the vehicle's fair market value. Although a professional appraisal may be obtained, a dealer-suggested retail price or the value included in the used vehicle information package would normally be sufficient, unless the value is obviously lower or higher than such estimates. The used vehicle information package, which is required to transfer the vehicle, can be purchased from the Ministry of Transportation at a reasonable price.

Business Assets

Business assets or holdings owned by a deceased person can vary from simple to very complex. Any such assets falling into the estate also must be assigned a value. Business assets or holdings may have been owned by the deceased as a sole proprietor, through a partnership, or by means of a private corporation. Subject to any partnership, shareholders', or other agreements entered into by the deceased, which often deal specifically with the death of a partner or shareholder, such assets become part of the estate. Typically, shareholders' agreements provide that the survivor or survivors among them will retain ownership and control of the corporation with a predetermined procedure for compensating the deceased's beneficiaries for the value of the partnership interest or shares. In such cases, partners are often obligated by virtue of the agreement to hold life insurance policies (sometimes referred to as "key-person policies") on each other for this purpose. If such compensation is owing to the estate itself, it must be included in the valuation of the estate for the purpose of the application. Otherwise, the compensation is not part of the estate but is more like life insurance payable to a named beneficiary.

In the case of valuing business assets, the lawyer or estate trustee may have to thoroughly review any shareholders' or partnership agreements, as well as any corporate books containing the articles of incorporation and resolutions of the directors, in order to ensure that assets are secured and their proper value has been ascertained. This information is necessary for completion of the estate information return and also for determining capital gains tax that may be owing by the estate. If the business holdings of the deceased are considerable or complex, an auditor, often a chartered accountant, is usually retained for an opinion as to the value of the business assets.

Loans Owing to the Deceased

As indicated in Chapter 7, any loans owing to the deceased become assets of the estate. Such loans may be formal, such as a registered mortgage, or less formal, perhaps even unwritten, as in the case of some family loans. For the purposes of the application for a certificate of appointment and the estate information return, these loans are considered property and must be given an accurate value.

Strictly speaking, the value of a loan is the principal owing, plus the interest to be paid over time, less an amount calculated to represent the present unavailability of the money and the possibility that the full payment will not be received. This kind of calculation is known as a "present value" calculation and is normally undertaken by an actuary or a similarly qualified expert.

Many lawyers recommend that the value placed on a loan owing to the deceased, for the purpose of the application for a certificate of appointment, be the amount that could be collected if the loan were called in as of the date of death. Loans and mortgages, however, cannot always be called in simply because the deceased died.

As will be seen in Chapter 10, Collecting the Assets, if the estate trustee puts a value on a loan owing that subsequent events prove was too high, perhaps because the loan cannot be collected, the estate trustee has some recourse in that any overpayment of estate administration tax based on the incorrectly high valuation can be recovered upon application to the court.

Other Debts Owing to the Deceased

Other debts owing to the deceased can include such items as the deceased's deposit paid to a landlord toward the last month's rent, the interest owing on that deposit, and unpaid wages and benefits from an employer. In all cases, the estate trustee must contact the person or institution that owes the debt to the deceased to confirm the amount owing. Such amounts are then added to the calculation of the value of the estate.

Valuing Real Property

Chapter 7 explained that only property that is solely owned by the deceased or owned by the deceased as a tenant in common will fall into the estate. If such real property does fall into the estate it too must be valued by the estate trustee for the purpose of calculating estate administration tax. The rules that came into play on January 1, 2015 under the *Estate Administration Tax Act, 1998*, clearly make it inappropriate for an estate trustee to simply base the value of real estate on his own estimate. It is now considered to be standard practice for an estate trustee to obtain the assistance of an expert in the valuation of real property. Such valuation can be done by way of a formal appraisal or by a letter of opinion. A formal appraisal is done by a qualified real estate appraiser, who must have access to the premises, and usually costs between $500 and $2,000. A letter of opinion, on the other hand, is often given by a real estate broker or even an agent or sales representative and usually costs between $200 and $400. It should, however, be from a person who is qualified to give an opinion on the value of the kind of real estate in question—residential, commercial, industrial, and so on. Access to the structures on the property is not necessary, although the opinion will be more accurate if such access is given. An estate trustee named in a will usually has such access as of right, subject to any tenancies. A prospective estate trustee without a will, on the other hand, does not generally have such access because of the requirement for a court-approved appointment. It is generally considered appropriate for the prospective estate trustee to obtain two or three letters of opinion from independent real estate brokers or agents and to take the average of them as the estimated value.

If there is any uncertainty or, for example, a foreseen dispute among beneficiaries concerning the value, a formal appraisal is a better approach. Such a dispute may arise where an estate trustee decides to sell the real property to an acquaintance or relative rather than selling it on the open market. Aside from the estate trustee's obligation to the beneficiaries to obtain the highest price possible for that asset, the agreed-upon value on that sale may not be the proper value to put on the probate application.

Note that under section 1 of the *Estate Administration Tax Act, 1998*, the value of real property owned by the deceased is reduced by the amount of any mortgage secured against the property. For this reason, the valuation of real property submitted on the certificate of appointment is likewise reduced by the amount owing on a mortgage.

Estate Administration Tax

As indicated above, the valuation of the property owned by the deceased is done for the purpose of calculating estate administration tax, formerly called, and often still referred to as, "probate fees." The amount of the estate administration tax is based on the value of the estate assets, with some exceptions as discussed below.

Calculation of the Estate Administration Tax

Under the *Estate Administration Tax Act, 1998*, the amount of tax is $5 per thousand of assets up to $50,000 and $15 per thousand thereafter. The thousands are rounded up to the next nearest thousand. A quick formula for calculating the tax is to take the number of thousands rounded up, multiply this number by 15, and subtract 500. The result is the estate administration tax to be paid in dollars. Figures 8.3 and 8.4 are two examples of calculating the estate administration tax.

As will be seen below, in certain situations the value to be used for the estate is not the full value of the estate as of the date of death. Also, as discussed in Chapter 7, jointly held property with right of survivorship is not included in the value of the estate, and assets with a direct beneficiary (such as life insurance that names a beneficiary other than the estate itself) is similarly excluded. An example is shown in Figure 8.5.

Under section 2(2) of the *Estate Administration Tax Act, 1998*, the estate is exempt from the tax if the value of the estate is not over $1,000.

Split Wills

In some situations, estate administration tax is not paid on the entire estate within Ontario. In this regard, section 32(3) of the *Estates Act* states:

> [W]here the application or grant is limited to part only of the property of the deceased, it is sufficient to set forth in the statement of value only the property and value thereof intended to be affected by such application or grant.

This section of the Act is used to support the availability of multiple or split wills to reduce estate administration tax.

FIGURE 8.3 Calculating Estate Administration Tax: Example 1

Assets as of date of death:

Term deposit at Bank of Dundas	$16,000.00
Savings account at Bank of Grimsby	1,012.15
2015 Honda Accord	21,000.00
Personal effects	5,000.00
Total	$43,012.15

Calculation:

Total assets: $43,012.15 (round up to $44,000.00)

44 × $5 = $220 estate administration tax

FIGURE 8.4 Calculating Estate Administration Tax: Example 2

Assets as of date of death:

Real property

House at 2031 Princess Court, Hagersville	$110,000.00
Less mortgage to Bank of Geneva	(49,745.23)
Total	$ 60,254.77

Personal property

20 common shares in Moments Inc.	$ 10,000.00
Gold bar	5,923.00
2016 Fifth Wheel Camper	40,000.00
2016 Ford F150 truck	30,000.00
antique dining table and chairs	12,000.00
Personal effects	4,000.00
Total	$101,923.00

Calculation:

Total assets: $162,177.77 (round up to $163,000.00)

50 × $5 = $250

113 × $15 = $1,695

Total = $1,945 estate administration tax

FIGURE 8.5 Calculating Estate Administration Tax: Example 3

Assets as of date of death:

Real property

House at 21 East First Street, Sudbury, Ontario owned jointly with Jack Frost	$500,000.00
Total	0.00

Personal property

Painting by Fibro Alimo.	$ 500.00
Joint bank account with right of survivorship with Jack Frost	299,678.37
Personal effects	2,000.00
Total	$ 2,500.00

Calculation:

Total assets: $2,500

3 × $5 = $15 estate administration tax

As you may recall from Chapter 1, some lawyers advise testators to create two coexisting wills, each dealing with separate assets within Ontario. The intention is to create one will making gifts of items that require a certificate of appointment (such as real property and shares of publicly held corporations) and another will making gifts of items that may not require a certificate of appointment (such as art objects and privately held business interests).

As we will see in Chapter 9, Applying for a Certificate of Appointment of Estate Trustee, when an application for a certificate of appointment is submitted to the court office, it is accompanied by the original will. When the certificate is issued, a copy of the will forms part of the certificate itself (see Chapter 7, Figure 7.1). The theory behind the concept of split wills is that estate administration tax will be payable only on the items that are covered in the will submitted with the application.

This practice of creating split wills can fairly be said to arise out of the 1998 decision in the case of *Granovsky Estate v Ontario*[3] in which a deceased person with substantial assets left two wills that were executed at the same time. One will disposed of the deceased's assets (totalling approximately $3 million) for which letters probate (that is, a certificate of appointment) would be necessary before transferring such assets to the beneficiaries. The other will included assets (totalling approximately $25 million) for which letters probate would not likely be necessary. The government of Ontario contested this proposed

---

3 *Granovsky Estate v Ontario*, 1998 CanLII 14913 (Ont SC).

split-will arrangement, essentially claiming that it should be entitled to the extra $375,000 in probate fees (now called "estate administration tax"). After considering the history of probate fees and multiple wills (which had often been used to deal with assets in different jurisdictions), the court agreed with the Granovsky estate and allowed the split wills to stand.

It is possible that, in some circumstances, a court could be persuaded that section 32(3) of the *Estates Act*[4] applies to some of the other, less common certificates of appointment described in Chapter 7, thereby allowing the estate to reduce the estate administration tax payable on certain foreign assets. This topic is discussed in Chapter 9.

Estate Administration Tax Based on an Estimated Value of the Estate

As explained in Chapter 7, there are occasions where an applicant for a certificate of appointment of estate trustee must estimate the value of certain assets of the estate. This is particularly likely in the case of an application for a certificate of appointment without a will, where the applicant has no authority to act in the capacity of estate trustee, and therefore has no authority to ask financial institutions for information relating to the estate until the certificate is issued. Where an estimate is given, section 3(4) of the *Estate Administration Tax Act, 1998* requires that the application for a certificate of appointment be accompanied by a written undertaking.

In the undertaking, the estate trustee must agree to file an affidavit regarding the true value of the estate within six months of the date of the application and to pay any additional estate administration tax that might be owing at that time. Under the regulation to the Act, an estate trustee must also file a revised estate information return respecting the true value of the assets within 30 days after fulfilling the undertaking. Under section 3(7) of the Act, any overpayment of tax based on an estimate will be refunded upon application to the court. As we will see in Chapter 10, Collecting the Assets, such overpayment becomes an asset of the estate that the estate trustee is obligated to collect. Similarly, as will be seen in Chapter 11, an underpayment of estate administration tax becomes a debt of the estate that the estate trustee is obligated to pay.

Obtaining the Funds for Payment of the Estate Administration Tax

A cheque or bank draft made payable to the minister of finance will normally need to be attached to the application for a certificate of appointment. Sometimes obtaining the funds at this stage in the administration of the estate can be a challenge. If there are funds on deposit in the name of the deceased, a draft can usually be obtained by submitting a letter with an authorization and direction to the financial institution. The letter and authorization (examples of which are shown in Figures 8.6 and 8.7) request a particular sum, with an explanation that it is required in order to obtain the certificate of appointment. The letter should enclose a notarial copy of the will, if there is one, and a death certificate.

If no bank assets are available, a financial institution, such as an investment broker, may be able to obtain access to funds by liquidating sufficient investments for this purpose. If that and other possible sources are unavailable, the estate trustee may have to pay the

---

4   RSO 1990, c E.21.

estate administration tax out of his own pocket and be reimbursed when estate funds are available.

Section 4 of the *Estate Administration Tax Act, 1998* provides for obtaining a certificate of appointment of estate trustee without paying the estate administration tax in advance. For an applicant to use this procedure, the court must first be satisfied that the matter is urgent, that financial hardship will result from the court's insistence on the tax in advance, and that sufficient assurance for the due payment of the tax has been provided to the court. Such assurance would be by way of affidavit or upon "such other material as the judge may require."

FIGURE 8.6   Letter Requesting Payment of Estate Administration Tax

March 15, 2018
My File: B8-1237

Bank of Dundas
450 Thistle Street
Toronto, Ontario
M5A Q8Q

Dear Sir or Madam

Re: Estate of Jacqueline Stick
who died January 12, 2018

I am writing further to my letters dated February 2, 2018 and February 27, 2018 to request your assistance in obtaining the certificate of appointment of estate trustee with a will in the above-noted estate.

Specifically, we would ask that you provide us with a bank draft, drawn from Ms Stick's chequing account, payable to the minister of finance, in the amount of $2,725. Our calculations indicate that this is the amount required for the estate administration tax (i.e. probate fees) payable in this case.

I have enclosed herewith an authorization and direction from Mr. Robert Larise, the estate trustee, pertaining to this amount. If you are in agreement with providing us with the said bank draft, please mail it to us in accordance with the authorization and direction.

Thank you again and please feel free to contact me if you require any additional information or documentation.

Yours truly,
GRIT, GRAT & GROOT

Mary Ross

Mary Ross, Law Clerk

FIGURE 8.7   Trustee Authorization: Payment of Estate Administration Tax

AUTHORIZATION AND DIRECTION

TO: Bank of Dundas
               450 Thistle Street
               Toronto, Ontario
               M5A Q8Q

RE: Estate of Jacqueline Stick
               who died January 12, 2018

I, Robert Larise, the estate trustee in the estate of Jacqueline Stick, deceased, hereby authorize and direct you to prepare a bank draft payable to the minister of finance in the amount of $2,725, for the purpose of my application to the Superior Court of Justice for a certificate of appointment of estate trustee with a will, and I further direct you to deliver the said cheque to my lawyer, namely:

               GRIT, GRAT & GROOT
               15 Cross Street
               Toronto, Ontario
               M5A 1Q1
               <u>Attention: Ms Gwendolyn Grat</u>

This shall be your good and sufficient authority for so doing.

Signed this 12th day of March, 2018.

Robert Larise

Administration Bonds of Indemnity

administration bond of indemnity
promise by the estate trustee to administer the estate properly and promise by the estate trustee and a third party, such as an insurance company, to indemnify any creditors or beneficiaries prejudiced by the failure to do so

In some situations, an application for a certificate of appointment of estate trustee must be accompanied by an **administration bond of indemnity** ("administration bond"). Generally, an administration bond is a promise that the person tendering the bond will conduct herself in the prescribed manner, and a bond of indemnity contains an additional promise to indemnify (compensate) anyone who suffers a loss as a result of the breaking of the promise. A bond of indemnity usually binds a third party to compensate any parties who may suffer losses in such circumstances. In the present context, an administration bond is a promise by the estate trustee to administer the estate properly and a promise by the estate trustee and a third party to indemnify any creditors or beneficiaries prejudiced by the failure to do so.

The general rule, under section 35 of the *Estates Act*, is that an administration bond is always required before the court issues any certificate of appointment. This rule is subject to exceptions. Section 36(1) of the Act, for example, indicates that government bodies, such as the Public Guardian and Trustee, do not have to submit a bond if they are acting as estate trustee. In addition to the statutory exceptions, the practice has arisen for the court to waive the need for a bond in an application for a certificate of appointment of estate trustee with a will where the applicant is named in the will as estate trustee, unless she is not a resident of Ontario or unless there is a reason in the particular case for a bond to be ordered.

In other cases, as explained below, the amount of the bond may be reduced or increased if the application has been made to the court.

Form of Bond

An example of a bond is in Figure 8.8. The third party agreeing to indemnify the beneficiaries and creditors is called the **surety**. The surety can be a private person, several private persons or a bonding company. A bonding company is usually an insurance company, licensed under the *Insurance Act*[5] to write surety and fidelity insurance in Ontario. If the surety is one or more private persons, the form of the bond is Form 74.33 of the *Rules of Civil Procedure* (as in the example provided in Figure 8.8). If the surety is a bonding company, the form of the bond is Form 74.32. A bonding company will agree to act as surety in exchange for a premium that is paid annually for as long as the bond remains active.

surety
third party to an administration bond of indemnity

The bond names the estate trustee as principal and specifies that the entity to which the bond is owed—the **obligee**—is the court. In the event that the estate trustee fails to administer the estate properly, section 38 of the *Estates Act* applies. This section states that a prejudiced party may make a summary application to the court, and if the judge is satisfied that prejudice has resulted from the estate trustee's failure to administer the estate properly, the judge may order the registrar to assign the bond to the prejudiced party with the effect that that party can then take legal action against any of the sureties named in the bond. If the surety is called on to pay in accordance with the bond, the surety himself (or itself) is entitled to bring an action against the estate trustee to recover his (or its) own losses.

obligee
entity to which an administration bond of indemnity is owed (the court)

Number of Sureties and Amount of Bond

Section 37(1) of the *Estates Act* requires that the amount of the bond "shall be in a penalty of double the amount under which the property of the deceased has been sworn, and the judge may direct that more than one bond be given so as to limit the liability of any surety to such amount as the judge considers proper." This section is somewhat modified by section 37(2), which indicates that a judge may reduce or waive the need for the bond. In this regard, the practice has arisen that if the bond is from a bonding company, it need only be in an amount equal to the value of the estate; but if, on the other hand, the surety is not a bonding company—that is, it is a personal surety—the estate trustee must provide two sureties, each posting a bond equal to the value of the estate, so that the total bond amount submitted is double the estate value. The amount of the bond may be further modified through the operation of the *Rules of Civil Procedure*,[6] discussed below.

A personal surety must be a resident of Ontario and must not be a minor.

---

5   RSO 1990, c I.8.
6   RRO 1990, Reg 194.

FIGURE 8.8 Form 74.33: Example of a Bond

FORM 74.33

Courts of Justice Act

BOND — PERSONAL SURETIES

ONTARIO

SUPERIOR COURT OF JUSTICE

BOND NO.   AMOUNT: $428,016

IN THE ESTATE OF JACQUELINE STICK, deceased.

The principal in this bond is Robert Larise

The sureties in this bond are Stephanie Booth and William Moon

The obligee in this bond is the Accountant of the Superior Court of Justice acting for the benefit of creditors and persons entitled to share in the estate of the deceased.

The principal and the sureties bind themselves, their heirs, executors, successors and assigns jointly and severally to the Accountant of the Superior Court of Justice in the amount of Four Hundred and Twenty Eight Thousand and Sixteen Dollars ($428,016).

The principal as an estate trustee is required to prepare a complete and true inventory of all the property of the deceased, collect the assets of the estate, pay the debts of the estate, distribute the property of the deceased according to law, and render a complete and true accounting of these activities when lawfully required.

The primary obligation under this bond belongs to the principal. The principal is liable under this bond for any amount found by the court to be owing to any creditors of the estate and persons entitled to share in the estate to whom proper payment has not been made.

The sureties, provided they have been given reasonable notice of any proceeding in which judgment may be given against the principal for failure to perform the obligations of this bond shall, on order of the court, and on default of the principal to pay any final judgment made against the principal in the proceeding, pay to the obligee the amount of any deficiency in the payment by the principal, but the sureties shall not be liable to pay more than the amount of the bond.

The amount of this bond shall be reduced by and to the extent of any payment made under the bond pursuant to an order of the court.

The sureties are entitled to an assignment of the rights of any person who receives payment or benefit from the proceeds of this bond, to the extent of such payment or benefit received.

DATE   March 12, 2018

SIGNED, SEALED AND DELIVERED
in the presence of:

....   *Robert Larise*
                                                    ....
                                                    Principal   Robert Larise

                                                    Stephanie Booth
                                                    ....
                                                    Surety   Stephanie Booth

                                                    William Moon
                                                    ....
                                                    Surety   William Moon

AFFIDAVIT OF SURETY

I, Stephanie Booth, of the City of Toronto, make oath and say/affirm:

I am a proposed surety on behalf of the intended estate trustees of the property of Jacqueline Stick, deceased, named in the attached bond.

I am eighteen years of age or over and own property worth $1,000,000.00 over and above all encumbrances, and over and above what will pay my just debts and every sum for which I am now bail or for which I am liable as surety or endorser or otherwise.

SWORN/AFFIRMED BEFORE me at the City of Toronto in the province of Ontario this 12th day of March , 20 18.	))))) *Stephanie Booth*) ....)))

Gwendolyn Grat
....
A Commissioner for Taking Affidavits *(or as may be)*

AFFIDAVIT OF SURETY

I, William Moon, of the City of Hamilton, make oath and say/affirm:

I am a proposed surety on behalf of the intended estate trustees of the property of Jacqueline Stick, deceased, named in the attached bond.

I am eighteen years of age or over and own property worth $500,000 over and above all encumbrances, and over and above what will pay my just debts and every sum for which I am now bail or for which I am liable as surety or endorser or otherwise.

SWORN/AFFIRMED BEFORE me at the City of Toronto in the province of Ontario this 12th day of March , 20 18.	))))) *William Moon*) ....)))

Gwendolyn Grat
....
A Commissioner for Taking Affidavits *(or as may be)*

RCP-E 74.33 (November 1, 2005)

Reducing or Increasing the Amount of the Bond Under the Rules of Civil Procedure

Rule 74.11(2) provides that any person who has a vested or contingent interest in the estate, including a creditor of the estate, can apply to the court for an order that the administration bond be increased or reduced. Such an application would normally be accompanied by affidavit evidence providing the basis for the claim. If the court is satisfied that sufficient grounds have been provided for the request, it will order that the bond be increased or reduced accordingly. Some additional rules in the *Rules of Civil Procedure* pertaining to bonds are discussed below.

Rule 74.11(1)(d) of the *Rules of Civil Procedure* states that if the value of the estate does not exceed $100,000, one personal surety is sufficient.

Rule 74.11(1)(e) provides that, in the case of a certificate of appointment of succeeding estate trustee with a will, the bond required is to be based on the value of the unadministered assets—that is, those assets not already collected and distributed. For example, if the value of the estate was originally $400,000 and the value of the unadministered assets in the estate is now $150,000, and if there are personal sureties, each surety will post a bond in the amount of $150,000.

Rule 74.11(1)(f) provides that, in the case of a confirmation by resealing of the appointment of estate trustee and an ancillary appointment of estate trustee, the value of the bond "shall be based on the value of the assets of the estate over which the estate trustee seeks jurisdiction in Ontario."

Cancellation of Bond

A bond is cancelled, and the estate trustee and surety are released from the obligation to pay, when the administration of the estate is complete and an accounting has been rendered. As we will see in Chapter 12, the accounting can be formal or informal, depending on whether the beneficiaries are all mentally competent adults and whether all agree to an informal accounting. Under section 43 of the *Estates Act*, if a beneficiary is a minor or mentally incompetent, the bond will not be cancelled "until after such notice as the judge may direct" has been given to the Children's Lawyer or the Public Guardian and Trustee, as the case may be. Upon completion of administration, an application to deliver up the bond for cancellation is usually made. Such delivery is important because, if a surety company bond is not delivered up for cancellation, the annual premium on it will continue to be payable.

Application to Waive the Need for a Bond of Indemnity

Section 36(2) of the *Estates Act* specifies that if the deceased died intestate and is survived by a spouse, the spouse does not have to obtain an administration bond provided that the net value of the estate does not exceed the spouse's preferential share under section 45 of the *Succession Law Reform Act*[7]—$200,000—and "there is filed with the application for administration an affidavit setting forth the debts of the estate."

---

7   RSO 1990, c S.26.

It is also possible to apply for an order of the court to waive the necessity of submitting an administration bond. The application includes an affidavit of the estate trustee setting out the relevant facts and a draft in triplicate of the order sought. An application to waive the need for an administration bond should be made only where there appears to be sufficiently good reason, from the court's point of view, to allow such a waiver. A sufficiently good reason might be that the estate trustee is the sole beneficiary of the estate and there are no or very few debts. In such a case, even if the estate trustee resides outside Ontario or Canada, it might be successfully argued that there is little risk to third parties in waiving the bond.

KEY TERMS

administration bond of indemnity, 146
obligee, 147

surety, 147

REVIEW QUESTIONS

1. Why do you value the assets of an estate?

2. How do you ascertain the value of assets held by financial institutions and how can you be sure you are dealing with the appropriate financial institutions?

3. Explain why it is a good idea to ask each financial institution holding assets of the deceased whether or not it will require a certificate of appointment in order to transfer the assets.

4. How do you ascertain the value of publicly traded stocks?

5. What do you have to add to the face value of interest-bearing securities such as Canada savings bonds when valuing the assets?

6. What is the solution where there is the possibility of dispute about the value of any item of personal property?

7. Why is the used vehicle information package issued by the Ministry of Transportation useful?

8. What should the estate trustee do with respect to vehicle insurance?

9. Why might an accountant be retained by the estate trustee with respect to business assets of the deceased?

10. Why might an actuary or other expert be retained by an estate trustee with respect to family loans made by the deceased?

11. Identify typical debts that may be owing to a deceased at the time of death and explain how the estate trustee should deal with these debts.

12. In what circumstances is it advisable for an estate trustee to obtain a formal evaluation of real property as opposed to a letter of opinion?

13. What is the significance in Ontario of an outstanding mortgage on real property that forms part of the estate?

14. Explain what is meant by the term "probate fees."

15. What is a quick formula for calculating estate administration tax?

16. When is estate administration tax paid and on what is it based?

17. How are the funds obtained to pay the estate administration tax?

18. How can a prospective estate trustee obtain a certificate of appointment when the value of the estate cannot be ascertained?

19. Describe one situation where an estate trustee would file an undertaking with the court to provide an affidavit as to the true value of the estate within six months of the filing of an application for a certificate of appointment.

20. What is an administration bond of indemnity?

21. When would an administration bond be required on an application for a certificate of appointment of estate trustee?

22. Identify the principal, surety, and obligee in an administration bond.

23. What is the normal amount of the bond where the surety is:
   a. an insurance company?
   b. private persons?

24. How is an administration bond ultimately cancelled?

25. What is required to have the court consider waiving the requirement of filing an administration bond?

LEARNING OUTCOMES

After reading this chapter, you should be able to:

- List the basic materials required to apply for a certificate of appointment of estate trustee with a will

- List the basic materials required to apply for a certificate of appointment of estate trustee without a will

- List the basic materials required when applying for less common certificates of appointment, including confirmation by resealing of appointment of estate trustee with or without a will; certificate of ancillary appointment of estate trustee with a will; certificate of appointment of foreign estate trustee's nominee as estate trustee without a will; certificate of appointment of succeeding estate trustee with a will; certificate of appointment of succeeding estate trustee without a will; and certificate of appointment of estate trustee during litigation

Introduction

This chapter discusses the documents that must be submitted for each different kind of application for certificate of appointment.

The application and other material are usually filed by leaving them at the court registrar's office. If the application and the material are complete and in order—that is, properly prepared—the certificate is usually issued as a matter of course and is available for pickup at the court office within four to six weeks, depending on the current workload of the court employees and officials.

The *Rules of Civil Procedure*[1] relating to the application must be seen as guidelines only, because the court always has the right to require that various other documents be submitted or other procedures be followed in granting any particular certificate of appointment. Rigidity cannot be insisted on because, in some circumstances, it could lead to injustice for certain parties.

Throughout this chapter, forms referred to by number (such as "Form 74.17") are found in the *Rules of Civil Procedure*.

Proof of Death

It should be noted that the court has recently begun to require proof of death to be supplied along with applications for certificates of appointment, though this change has yet to appear in the *Rules of Civil Procedure*. In the past, the court has relied on the sworn statement in the application for the certificate of appointment which indicates date of death, place of death, etc. as proof of the deceased's death. Acceptable forms of proof of death would be a funeral director's certificate of death or an official death certificate from the province of Ontario. If a person is presumed deceased by a court pursuant to the *Declarations of Death Act, 2002*[2]—for example, where a person has disappeared in circumstances of peril or where a person has been absent for seven years and there is sufficient evidence for a court to find that the person is deceased—an order from the court declaring the person deceased would be sufficient proof of death.

Applying for a Certificate of Appointment of Estate Trustee With a Will

Basic Material to Be Submitted

The application is made at the court office in the courthouse for the jurisdiction in Ontario where the deceased had her permanent residence—that is, the jurisdictional county, district, or region in which the deceased lived. In addition to the cheque or bank draft for the

---

1 RRO 1990, reg 194.
2 SO 2002, c 14, Sch.

estate administration tax payable (and an undertaking to pay the proper amount if the value of the estate is estimated) and proof of death, the basic documents to be submitted are as follows (assuming that all applicants are appointed in the will as estate trustees and all are residents of Canada):

- completed application for a certificate of appointment of estate trustee with a will (Form 74.4 for an individual applicant or several individuals, or Form 74.5 for a corporate applicant);
- draft certificate of appointment of estate trustee with a will (Form 74.13);
- affidavit of service of notice of the application on appropriate parties (Form 74.6), with a copy of the notice of application (Form 74.7) attached as an exhibit to the application;
- original will and original codicils (if any), and two photocopies of the will and each codicil (if any) (which are marked as exhibits to the application); and
- affidavit of execution (Form 74.8) of the will and codicils (if any), with the original will and codicils (if any) again submitted as an exhibit to the affidavit of execution.

These documents, and others that must be submitted in special circumstances, are discussed below.

Application Form

The application is made on Form 74.4 if the applicant is an individual or a group of individuals, and on Form 74.5 if the applicant is a corporation, such as a trust company. An example of a completed Form 74.4 is shown in Figure 9.1. As can be seen, the form asks various questions about the deceased and the estate that are designed to help the court determine whether the application should be granted. The application form must be signed by all of the applicants—that is, the estate trustees—and the information provided on the form must be sworn to as true at the same time.

Note that the application refers to the will as "Exhibit A" and any codicils as "Exhibit B" and "Exhibit C." As explained in more detail below, the original will (and codicils, if any) must be submitted with the application, and as in the example in Figure 9.1, the will must contain a **jurat**, or attestation, signed by the person who administered the oath—that is, either the lawyer, as notary public or commissioner for oaths, or the law clerk, if the latter is a commissioner for oaths. Figure 9.2 is an example of a jurat.

jurat
attestation paragraph

If any estate trustee named in the will is in priority to the applicant or applicants and is deceased, the fact of his death must be stated on the form under the words "explain why that person [the applicant] is entitled to apply" (see Figure 9.1). This is also the appropriate place to indicate that any living person named as estate trustee in the will is not applying and has executed (signed) a renunciation. The renunciation is provided in Form 74.18 and must be signed by any living person named as estate trustee in priority or equal in priority to the applicant, and then must be filed along with the application. If the person named as estate trustee refuses or is unable to sign, the applicant is left with the remedy of an order to accept or refuse appointment (discussed in Part III, Estate Litigation, Chapter 14, Challenging the Conduct of the Estate Trustees).

FIGURE 9.1 **Completed Form 74.4: Application for Certificate of Appointment of Estate Trustee With a Will (Individual Applicant)**

FORM 74.4

Courts of Justice Act

APPLICATION FOR CERTIFICATE OF APPOINTMENT OF ESTATE TRUSTEE WITH A WILL (INDIVIDUAL APPLICANT)

ONTARIO

SUPERIOR COURT OF JUSTICE

at   Toronto

This application is filed by *(insert name and address)* Gwendolyn Grat
Grit, Grat & Groot, Barristers & Solicitors, 15 Cross Street, Toronto, ON M5A 1Q1
Telephone: 416-555-5555; Facsimile 416-555-5556

DETAILS ABOUT THE DECEASED PERSON

Complete in full as applicable

First given name	Second given name	Third given name	Surname
Jacqueline			Stick

And if the deceased was known by any other name(s), state below the full name(s) used including surname.

First given name	Second given name	Third given name	Surname
Jackie			

Date of birth of the deceased person, if known: *(day, month, year)*
27/07/1940

Address of fixed place of abode *(street or postal address) (city or town)* 34 Thistle Street, Toronto, ON M5A 9Q9	*(county or district)* Municipality of Metropolitan Toronto
If the deceased person had no fixed place of abode in Ontario, did he or she have property in Ontario? . ☐ No ☐ Yes	**Last occupation of deceased person** Security Guard

Place of death *(city or town; county or district)* City of Toronto	**Date of death** *(day, month, year)* 12/01/2018	**Date of last will** (marked as Exhibit "A") *(day, month, year)* 15/12/2017

Was the deceased person 18 years of age or older at the date of the will (or 21 years of age or older if the will is dated earlier than September 1, 1971)?   ☐ No   ☒ Yes

If not, explain why certificate is being sought. Give details in an attached schedule.

Date of codicil (marked as Exhibit "B") *(day, month, year)*	**Date of codicil** (marked as Exhibit "C") *(day, month, year)*

Marital Status ☒ Unmarried ☐ Married ☐ Widowed ☐ Divorced

Did the deceased person marry after the date of the will?	☒ No ☐ Yes

If yes, explain why certificate is being sought. Give details in an attached schedule.

Was a marriage of the deceased person terminated by a judgment absolute of divorce, or declared a nullity, after the date of the will?	☒ No ☐ Yes

If yes, give details in an attached schedule.

Is any person who signed the will or a codicil as witness or for the testator, or the spouse of such person, a beneficiary under the will?	☒ No ☐ Yes

If yes, give details in an attached schedule.

VALUE OF ASSETS OF ESTATE

Do not include in the total amount: insurance payable to a named beneficiary or assigned for value, property held jointly and passing by survivorship, or real estate outside Ontario.

Personal Property	Real estate, net of encumbrances	Total
$ 54,007.12	$ 160,000.00	$ 214,007.12

Is there any person entitled to an interest in the estate who is not an applicant?	☒ No ☐ Yes

If a person named in the will or a codicil as estate trustee is not an applicant, explain.

If a person not named in the will or a codicil as estate trustee is an applicant, explain why that person is entitled to apply.

If the spouse of the deceased is an applicant, has the spouse elected to receive the entitlement under section 5 of the *Family Law Act*?	☐ No ☐ Yes

If yes, explain why the spouse is entitled to apply.

FIGURE 9.1 CONTINUED

AFFIDAVIT(S) OF APPLICANT(S)
(Attach a separate sheet for additional affidavits, if necessary)

I, an applicant named in this application, make oath and say/affirm:

1. I am 18 years of age or older.
2. The exhibit(s) referred to in this application are the last will and each codicil (where applicable) of the deceased person and I do not know of any later will or codicil.
3. I will faithfully administer the deceased person's property according to law and render a complete and true account of my administration when lawfully required.
4. If I am not named as estate trustee in the will or codicil, consents of persons who together have a majority interest in the value of the assets of the estate at the date of death are attached.
5. The information contained in this application and in any attached schedules is true, to the best of my knowledge and belief.

Name *(surname and forename(s))*	Occupation
Larise, Robert	auto manufacturer

Address *(street or postal address)*	*(city or town)*	*(province)*	*(postal code)*
345 Needlebrook Avenue	Oakville	Ontario	L6J Q9Q

Sworn/Affirmed before me at the City

of Toronto

in the Municipality

of Metro Toronto

this 12th   day of March   , 20 18

Robert Larise
Signature of applicant

Gwendolyn Grat
A Commissioner for taking Affidavits *(or as may be)*

Name *(surname and forename(s))*	**Occupation**	
Address *(street or postal address)* *(city or town)*	*(province)*	*(postal code)*

Sworn/Affirmed before me at the _____

of _____

in the _____

of _____

this _____ day of _____ , 20 _____

_____
Signature of applicant

_____
A Commissioner for taking Affidavits *(or as may be)*

Notice to applicant: Information provided on this form related to the payment of estate administration tax may be forwarded to the Ministry of Finance pursuant to clause 39(1)(b) and 42(1)(c) of the *Freedom of Information and Protection of Privacy Act.* This includes the name of the deceased, name and address of estate trustee(s), value of the estate and any undertakings and tax payments made or refunded. This information will be used by the Ministry of Finance to determine the value of estates and the amount of estate administration tax payable. Questions about the collection of this information should be directed to the Senior Manager – Audit, Advisory and Compliance Branch, 33 King Street West, PO Box 625, Oshawa ON L1H 8H9, 1-866-668-8297.

FIGURE 9.2 **Jurat (on the Back of the Will) for Application for Certificate of Appointment of Estate Trustee With a Will**

This is "Exhibit A" to the affidavit of Robert Larise, sworn before me this 12th day of March, 2018.

Gwendolyn Grat
A commissioner, etc.

Another situation that requires additional documentation occurs when the applicant is not named as the estate trustee in the will. In that case, along with any renunciations from living persons appointed but not acting, the applicant must file consents of the beneficiaries to the applicant's appointment. The consent form is Form 74.12 and, by virtue of rule 74.04(1)(g), enough consents must be submitted with the application that the persons consenting represent a majority interest in the deceased's estate as of the date of death. Note that the consent contains a line (to be deleted if inapplicable) that relates to the signatory's consent to an order dispensing with the filing of an administration bond. The line is included in the form because, if one of the applicants is not named in the will as an estate trustee, or if one of the applicants is not a resident of Ontario, an administration bond may be required. As in other cases where an administration bond is required, it is possible to apply for an order dispensing with the necessity to file a bond (see Chapter 8, Preliminary Steps in Applying for a Certificate of Appointment of Estate Trustee). If the beneficiaries consent, such consents will be included with the application.

It should be noted that if the named estate trustees are unable or unwilling to assume the role (or if there are no named estate trustees) and the beneficiaries do not agree as to who will assume the role, section 29 of the *Estates Act*,[3] taken as a whole, indicates that in normal circumstances and subject to the discretion of the court, the spouse of the deceased (either married or common law and including same-sex spouses) is to be considered first, followed by the various next of kin of the deceased according to the degree of kinship to the deceased. Section 29 also indicates that when an estate is insolvent, a creditor or several creditors can be given the appointment as estate trustee.

In addition to the above, if all of the applicants for the certificate of appointment of estate trustee with a will are normally resident outside Canada, a bond of indemnity (or multiple bonds) has to be submitted along with the application unless the court agrees on application to waive the requirement (see Chapter 8). In these circumstances, a bond is normally from an insurance or guarantee company and has a net value equal to the value of the assets in the estate (Form 74.32); from a personal surety and has a net value at least double the value of the assets in the estate (Form 74.33); or, more commonly than the latter, from two personal sureties, each of whom posts a bond with a net value at least equal to the value of the assets in the estate (Form 74.33).

An application for a certificate of appointment of estate trustee with a will limited to the assets referred to in the will, for use in estates where the deceased left split wills, is identical

---

3 RSO 1990, c E.21.

to an application for a standard certificate of appointment of estate trustee with a will except that the application form used is 74.4.1 for individual applicants and 74.5.1 for corporate applicants.

Draft Certificate of Appointment

A draft certificate of appointment of estate trustee with a will (Form 74.13) is to be provided with the application. The word "draft" refers to the fact that it is unsigned and not impressed with the seal of the court. If the application is granted, it will be signed by a judge or the court registrar and sealed. An example of a certificate of appointment is reproduced in Chapter 7 as Figure 7.1. The certificate has a front and a back page and the draft is usually submitted as a single piece of 11 × 17 inch paper. Some courts request an extra copy of the front page of the certificate for their own records.

Affidavit of Service of Notice of Application

An affidavit that notice of application has been "sent or caused to be sent" to all interested parties must be submitted with the application package. An example is shown in Figure 9.3. The affidavit of service (Form 74.6) must be signed by the applicant, or one of the applicants if there is more than one. Naturally, the affidavit of service of notice cannot be sworn unless the notice has in fact been served on the appropriate parties. It is therefore necessary for the lawyer to ensure that the notice is in fact served before the meeting with the applicant (estate trustee) to sign the affidavit of service of notice. Although the applicant signs the affidavit of service and swears to the truth of its contents, it is not necessary that he actually serve (mail) the document. Usually the lawyer (or an employee under her direction) serves the notice. The applicant can nevertheless sign the affidavit because he swears that he has sent the notice or "caused [it] to be sent."

The affidavit of service refers to "Exhibit A," which is also reproduced in Figure 9.3. "Exhibit A" is a copy of the notice of application that was actually sent (Form 74.7), and a jurat is required as in the case of the will submitted with the application.

As to the question "Who are the appropriate parties to serve?" rule 74.04(2) states:

> Notice of the application shall be served on all persons entitled to share in the distribution of the estate, including charities and contingent beneficiaries …

All beneficiaries, then, are served, whether their individual gifts are contingent on the occurrence of some future event or not. The group includes children, beneficiaries who would have received a share of the estate if it were not for the fact that another beneficiary has survived, and even unborn beneficiaries (if the will provides that persons not yet alive may be future beneficiaries if certain other persons die before the administration of the estate is completed). The last-mentioned case of unborn beneficiaries often occurs where there is a testamentary trust, with the income payable to a named beneficiary who may be an infant, and the remainder to go to the beneficiary's children (in accordance with *Saunders v Vautier*,[4] discussed in Part I, Estate Planning, Chapter 6, Trusts).

---

4 (1841), 4 Beav 115.

FIGURE 9.3 **Form 74.6: Affidavit of Service of Notice of Application**

FORM 74.6

Courts of Justice Act

AFFIDAVIT OF SERVICE OF NOTICE

ONTARIO

SUPERIOR COURT OF JUSTICE

IN THE ESTATE OF   JACQUELINE STICK   , deceased.

AFFIDAVIT OF SERVICE OF NOTICE

I,   Robert Larise, of the City of Oakville in the Region of Halton   , make oath and say/affirm:

1.   I am an applicant for a certificate of appointment of estate trustee with a will in the estate.

2.   I have sent or caused to be sent a notice in Form 74.7, a copy of which is marked as Exhibit "A" to this affidavit, to all adult persons and charities named in the notice (except to an applicant who is entitled to share in the distribution of the estate), to the Public Guardian and Trustee if paragraph 6 of the notice applies, to a parent or guardian of the minor and to the Children's Lawyer if paragraph 4 applies, to the guardian or attorney if paragraph 5 applies, and to the Children's Lawyer if paragraph 7 applies, all by regular lettermail sent to the person's last known address.

3.   I have attached or caused to be attached to each notice the following:

   (A)   In the case of a notice sent to or in respect of a person entitled only to a specified item of property or stated amount of money, an extract of the part or parts of the will or codicil relating to the gift, or a copy of the will (and codicil(s), if any).

   (B)   In the case of a notice sent to or in respect of any other beneficiary, a copy of the will (and codicil(s), if any).

   (C)   In the case of a notice sent to the Children's Lawyer or the Public Guardian and Trustee, a copy of the will (and codicil(s), if any) and a statement of the estimated value of the interest of the person represented.

4.   The following persons and charities specifically named in the Will are not entitled to be served for the reasons shown:

Name of person (as it appears in will, if applicable)	**Reason not served**
Not Applicable	

   If paragraph 4 does not apply insert "Not Applicable."

5.   The following persons named in the Will or being a member of a class of beneficiaries under the Will may be entitled to be served but have not been served for the reasons shown below:

Name of person (as it appears in will, if applicable)	**Reason not served**
Not Applicable	

   If paragraph 5 does not apply insert "Not Applicable."

6.   To the best of my knowledge and belief, subject to paragraph 5 (if applicable), the persons named in the notice are all the persons who are entitled to share in the distribution of the estate.

Sworn/Affirmed before me at the ...... City ....)

of .... Toronto ....)

in the .... Province ....)

of........... Ontario ....)   _____

                                                                                                  Robert Larise

this ...... 12th ..... day of .... March .... , 2018 ....)   Signature of applicant

_____
                Gwendolyn Grat
A Commissioner for taking Affidavits *(or as may be)*

FORM 74.7

Court of Justice Act

NOTICE OF AN APPLICATION FOR A CERTIFICATE OF APPOINTMENT OF
ESTATE TRUSTEE WITH A WILL

ONTARIO

SUPERIOR COURT OF JUSTICE

IN THE ESTATE OF _____ JACQUELINE STICK _____ , deceased.
(insert name)

**NOTICE OF AN APPLICATION FOR A CERTIFICATE OF APPOINTMENT OF ESTATE
TRUSTEE WITH A WILL**

1. The deceased died on January 12, 2018. _____.
    (insert date)

2. Attached to this notice are:

    (A) If the notice is sent to or in respect of a person entitled only to a specified item of
         property or stated amount of money, an extract of the part or parts of the will or codicil
         relating to the gift, or a copy of the will (and codicil(s), if any).

    (B) If the notice is sent to or in respect of any other beneficiary, a copy of the will (and
         codicil(s), if any).

    (C) If the notice is sent to the Children's Lawyer or the Public Guardian and Trustee, a copy of
         the will (and codicil(s), if any), and if it is not included in the notice, a statement of the
         estimated value of the interest of the person represented.

3. The applicant named in this notice is applying for a certificate of appointment of estate
    trustee with a will.

APPLICANT

Name	Address
Robert Larise	345 Needlebrook Avenue, Oakville ON, L6J Q9Q

4. The following persons who are less than 18 years of age are entitled, whether their interest
    is contingent or vested, to share in the distribution of the estate:

Name	Date of Birth *(day, month, year)*	Name and Address of Parent or Guardian	Estimated Value of Interest in Estate*
Not applicable.			

* Note: *The Estimated Value of Interest in Estate may be omitted in the form if it is included in a separate
schedule attached to the notice sent to the Children's Lawyer.*

FIGURE 9.3 CONTINUED

5. The following persons who are mentally incapable within the meaning of section 6 of the *Substitute Decisions Act, 1992* in respect of an issue in the proceeding, and who have guardians or attorneys acting under powers of attorney with authority to act in the proceeding, are entitled, whether their interest is contingent or vested, to share in the distribution of the estate:

Name and Address of Person	Name and Address of Guardian or Attorney*
Not applicable.	

* Specify whether guardian or attorney.

6. The following persons who are mentally incapable within the meaning of section 6 of the *Substitute Decisions Act, 1992* in respect of an issue in the proceeding, and who do not have guardians or attorneys acting under powers of attorney with authority to act in the proceeding, are entitled, whether their interest is contingent or vested, to share in the distribution of the estate:

Name and Address of Person	Estimated Value of Interest in Estate *
Gordon Ponner 36 Fountain Street, Toronto, ON, M5A Q2Q	The estimated value of the interest of Gordon Ponner in the estate is included in a separate schedule attached to the notice sent to the Public Guardian and Trustee.

* Note: The Estimated Value of Interest in Estate may be omitted in the form if it is included in a separate schedule attached to the notice sent to the Public Guardian and Trustee.

7. ~~Unborn or unascertained persons may be entitled to share in the distribution of the estate~~.
    (Delete if not applicable)

8. All other persons and charities entitled, whether their interest is contingent or vested, to share in the distribution of the estate are as follows:

Name	Address
1. Raoul Thurgood	1. 1396 Giga Street Hamilton, ON, L8S Q9Q
2. The Human Fund	2. 20 Beller Street Toronto, ON, M5A Q8Q

9. This notice is being sent, by regular lettermail, to all adult persons and charities named above in this notice (except to an applicant who is entitled to share in the distribution of the estate), to the Public Guardian and Trustee if paragraph 6 applies, to a parent or guardian of the minor and to the Children's Lawyer if paragraph 4 applies, to the guardian or attorney if paragraph 5 applies, and to the Children's Lawyer if paragraph 7 applies.

10. The following persons named in the Will or being a member of a class of beneficiaries under the Will may be entitled to be served but have not been served for the reasons shown below:

Name of person (as it appears in will, if applicable)	Reason not served
Not applicable	

If paragraph 10 does not apply insert "Not Applicable."

DATE: March 12, 2018.

The notice of application asks for a breakdown of the various kinds of beneficiaries (see Figure 9.3, page 2 of the form). Thus, underage beneficiaries are listed under paragraph 4; mentally incapable beneficiaries who have an attorney under a power of attorney are listed under paragraph 5; mentally incapable beneficiaries who do not have an attorney under a power of attorney are listed under paragraph 6; unborn or unascertained beneficiaries are listed under paragraph 7; and all other beneficiaries, including adult persons of sound mind and charities, are listed under paragraph 8. Although all are to be served, each may be served in a different way depending on the category into which each falls.

Service on an underage beneficiary is made by serving the child's guardian as well as the Office of the Children's Lawyer.

Service on mentally incapable beneficiaries is made by serving the beneficiary as well as the beneficiary's guardian (who must have authority to act in the proceeding). If that beneficiary does not have a guardian but has an attorney for property (who has authority to act in the proceeding), the notice is served on the beneficiary and on her attorney for property. If that beneficiary has neither a guardian nor an attorney, the notice is served on the Public Guardian and Trustee.

Service on unborn beneficiaries is made by serving the Office of the Children's Lawyer.

Accompanying the notice to each residual beneficiary must be a copy of the will. Accompanying the notice to each specific bequest beneficiary must be a copy of the will or the relevant excerpt from the will setting out the particular gift.

The estate trustees do not send notices to themselves if they are beneficiaries because such notices would be redundant. If the estate trustees happen to be the only beneficiaries, it is customary to provide an affidavit to that effect, as in Figure 9.4.

Service is effected, under rule 74.04(7) of the *Rules of Civil Procedure*, by sending the material by regular letter mail to the last known address of the individual or institution being served.

Where there is any question whether a particular person is entitled to share in the distribution of the estate and therefore entitled to be served with notice, the question should always be resolved in favour of service of the notice on that person or entity. It may be that the person's entitlement to share can be decided only through some form of estate litigation, and in that case it is appropriate that she have adequate notice of the application.

Original and Copies of Will and Codicils

The original will and any codicils must be submitted to the court in support of an application for a certificate of appointment of estate trustee with a will. If neither the estate trustee nor the lawyer preparing the application possesses the original will, the lawyer usually obtains it by forwarding a direction signed by all of the estate trustees to the lawyer who does have it. This issue was discussed in Part I, Chapter 1, Wills, from the point of view of the lawyer holding the will.

Requesting a will held by another lawyer poses a problem where the will names as estate trustees certain persons who are not willing to act as such and are uncooperative. Even though a person may be unwilling to assume the role of estate trustee, however, she may be persuaded to sign the direction simply for the purpose of obtaining the original will, although the lawyer and law clerk need to be careful not to inadvertently establish a lawyer–client relationship with such person. If one of the concurrently named estate trustees, or the first-named estate trustee, is deceased, the lawyer holding the will should be given a death certificate as well as the direction from the surviving estate trustees.

FIGURE 9.4   Affidavit of Service of Notice Where the Applicants Are the Only Beneficiaries

ONTARIO

SUPERIOR COURT OF JUSTICE

IN THE ESTATE OF FREDERICK STAINER, deceased.

AFFIDAVIT OF SERVICE OF NOTICE

I, Lana Mattista, of the City of Burlington in the Regional Municipality of Halton, make oath and say/affirm:

1. I am an applicant for a certificate of appointment of estate trustee with a will in the estate.

2. I, along with my sister and co-applicant, Frieda Mattista, represent all of the beneficiaries of the estate and service on others referred to in Rules 74.04(2)–(6) is not applicable.

Sworn/Affirmed before me at the City	)
of Burlington	)
in the Region	)
of Halton	)
this 26th day of October, 2018	)
	)
	)
	)
Monique Tribari	) *Lana Mattista*
	)
A Commissioner for Taking Affidavits	) Signature of applicant
(or as may be)	

The will should not be mailed but instead should be picked up by the estate trustee or someone from the office of the lawyer acting for the estate trustee. The person picking up the will should be prepared to show identification and proper authority by way of direction if it is not the estate trustee herself. The occasion of picking up the will is usually an appropriate time to obtain the affidavit of execution of the will (discussed below). Some lawyers prepare the affidavit of execution themselves and charge a reasonable fee. Unreasonable fees for such preparation should, of course, be resisted. The usual fee is between $100 and $150.

As discussed in Chapter 1, the lawyer holding the will has an ethical duty to keep the document safe and confidential from anyone other than the testator and, after the testator's death, the named estate trustees. If the lawyer or other person holding the will is unreasonably refusing to deliver it to the estate trustee, section 9 of the *Estates Act* provides procedures to compel him to produce it for the court registrar. Again, section 9(2) of the Act deals with the situation where there are reasonable grounds to believe that someone has knowledge of a will or codicil. In such a case, that person can also be compelled to attend court and answer questions relating to the will or codicil.

If the will is on deposit with the court, the procedure for obtaining it is for the estate trustee to submit a written request to the court. The request must state the testator's date of birth and provide a funeral director's proof-of-death certificate.

If only a copy of the original will can be located, the copy must be submitted to the court along with some acceptable form of proof that it is a true copy and the reasons why the original is not being submitted. In this regard, however, section 15 of the *Estates Act* provides that a notarial copy of a notarial will made in Quebec may be admitted to probate in place of an original will.

The original will should be accompanied by two photocopies as part of the application.

Affidavit of Execution

Figure 9.5 is an example of an affidavit of execution (Form 74.8). It is to be completed by one of the witnesses who saw the will signed by the testator. If both of the witnesses are deceased or neither can be located, rule 74.04(1)(c) of the *Rules of Civil Procedure* requires that the applicant provide "such other evidence of due execution as the court may require." In such a case, it may be necessary for the lawyer or law clerk to conduct an investigation of the circumstances surrounding the creation and signing of the will in an attempt to find some evidence that the will was duly executed.

If a will is a holograph (handwritten) will, there will be no affidavit of execution. Instead, an affidavit attesting to the handwriting and signature of a holograph will or codicil is required. This form (Form 74.9), an example of which is reproduced in Figure 9.6, is sworn by someone who is familiar with the testator's handwriting (not necessarily the applicant). An official of the bank the testator frequented is usually a good candidate to sign such an affidavit because the bank would typically have the deceased's signature on file.

If the will is not a holograph but has written markings on it that are not initialled—that is, it contains "an alteration, erasure, obliteration or interlineation that has not been attested" as referred to in rule 74.04(1)(e)—another special affidavit is required, namely, that in Form 74.10. This affidavit is sworn by a witness to the will and proves to the court that the alteration was part of the will when it was signed.

Recall from Chapter 1 that if a beneficiary or a spouse of a beneficiary is a witness to the will, the gift to that beneficiary is void unless it can be proved that there was no improper or undue influence. In such a situation, rule 74.12(5) requires the registrar to draw the applicant's attention to the need for such proof, and it is then up to the applicant to bring a motion under rule 74.15(1)(f) ("Order to Beneficiary Witness") for an order in Form 74.40. The order directs the beneficiary witness to prove no undue influence by a certain date, failing which he or she will not be included in the distribution.

A somewhat similar situation occurs in the case of a gift to a spouse or an appointment of a spouse as estate trustee where the testator and the spouse subsequently divorce. In such a case, the gift or appointment is void unless a contrary intention can be proved. Rule 74.12(6) again requires the court registrar to draw the applicant's attention to this matter, and it is then up to the applicant to bring a motion under rule 74.15(1)(g) for an issuance of the order set out in Form 74.41.

FIGURE 9.5 **Form 74.8: Affidavit of Execution of Will or Codicil**

FORM 74.8

Courts of Justice Act

AFFIDAVIT OF EXECUTION OF WILL OR CODICIL

ONTARIO

SUPERIOR COURT OF JUSTICE

In the matter of the execution of a will or codicil of

JACQUELINE STICK
(insert name)

AFFIDAVIT

I, Darren McDowell   ,
(insert name)

of the City of Toronto in the Province of Ontario   ,
(insert city or town and county or district, metropolitan or regional municipality of residence)

make oath and say/affirm:

1.   On December 15, 2009   , I was present and saw the document marked
(date)

as Exhibit "A" to this affidavit executed by   Jacqueline Stick   .
(insert name)

2.   Jacqueline Stick   executed the document in
(insert name)

the presence of myself and Taline Lusine in the Regional Municipality of Grozda, Ontario

*(insert name of other witness and city or town, county or district, metropolitan or regional municipality
of residence)*

We were both present at the same time, and signed the document in the testator's presence as attesting witnesses.

Sworn/Affirmed before me at the <u>City</u>

of <u>Toronto</u>

in the <u>province</u>

of <u>Ontario</u>   *Darren McDowell*

this <u>10th</u>   day of <u>March</u>   , 20 <u>18</u>

Mary Ross

A Commissioner for Taking Affidavits *(or as may be)*

NOTE: If the testator was blind or signed by making his or her mark, add the following paragraph:

3.   Before its execution, the document was read over to the testator, who (was blind) (signed by making his or her mark). The testator appeared to understand the contents.

WARNING: A beneficiary or the spouse of a beneficiary should not be a witness.

FIGURE 9.6 Form 74.9: Affidavit Attesting to the Handwriting and Signature of a Holograph Will or Codicil

FORM 74.9

Courts of Justice Act

AFFIDAVIT ATTESTING TO THE HANDWRITING AND SIGNATURE
OF A HOLOGRAPH WILL OR CODICIL

ONTARIO

SUPERIOR COURT OF JUSTICE

IN THE ESTATE OF _____ EDWARD MIST _____ , deceased.
(insert name)

**AFFIDAVIT ATTESTING TO THE HANDWRITING AND SIGNATURE
OF A HOLOGRAPH WILL OR CODICIL**

I, Lewis Reno _____ ,
(insert name)

of the City of Hamilton in the Province of Ontario _____ ,
(insert city or town and county or district, metropolitan or regional municipality of residence)

make oath and say/affirm:

1. I was well acquainted with the deceased and have frequently seen the deceased's signature and handwriting.

2. I believe the whole of the document dated _____ November 5, 2004 _____ ,
(insert date)

now shown to me and marked as Exhibit "A" to this affidavit, including the signature, is in the handwriting of the deceased.

Sworn/Affirmed before me at the City _____

of Hamilton _____

in the province _____

of Ontario _____   _____

this 29th   day of April _____ , 20 18

Francis LeCotte

_____
A Commissioner for Taking Affidavits *(or as may be)*

Note that there is no specific form of affidavit of execution in the circumstances (discussed in Chapter 1) where the testator, rather than signing the will, adopts another's signature as her own. In such a case, one of the existing court forms may be altered, or, as it may turn out, a more thorough form of proof may be required by the court, perhaps with a hearing of live witnesses, to prove due execution.

Regarding wills executed by members of the armed forces or mariners at sea in the course of a voyage, if there are no witnesses or the witnesses cannot be found, section 11(2) of the *Estates Act* indicates that the judge of the court "may accept such evidence as he or she considers satisfactory as to the validity and proper execution of such will."

Finally, codicils must be treated in the same way as wills in that they require their own proof of due execution.

Applying for a Certificate of Appointment of Estate Trustee Without a Will

Basic Material to Be Submitted

As in the case of the application for a certificate of appointment of estate trustee with a will, the application without a will is submitted to the court office in the courthouse for the jurisdiction in which the deceased permanently resided at the time of his death. The basic documents to be submitted, in addition to the cheque or bank draft for the estate administration tax payable (and an undertaking to pay the proper amount if the value of the estate is estimated) and proof of death, are as follows:

- completed application for a certificate of appointment of estate trustee without a will (Form 74.14 for an individual applicant or several individuals, or Form 74.15 for a corporate applicant);
- draft certificate of appointment of estate trustee without a will (Form 74.20);
- bond of indemnity from an insurance company (Form 74.32); bond of indemnity from one personal surety who has a net worth of at least double the value of the assets of the estate within Ontario (Form 74.33); or bonds of indemnity from two personal sureties, both of whom have a net worth at least equal to the value of the estate assets within Ontario (Form 74.33); or an application to waive the bond of indemnity;
- affidavit of service of notice of application on appropriate parties (Form 74.6), along with the notice of application (Form 74.17) attached as an exhibit; and
- consents of beneficiaries who (together with the applicant) represent a majority interest in the estate (Form 74.19).

These documents are discussed below.

Application Form

An important preliminary issue in the case of the certificate of appointment of estate trustee without a will is to decide who is going to be the applicant. Apart from the restriction mentioned in Chapter 7, Proof of the Estate Trustee's Status as Estate Trustee, that a non-resident of Ontario cannot be an estate trustee without a will (except through a confirmation by resealing of appointment or a certificate of appointment of foreign estate trustee's nominee as estate trustee without a will), the basic rule on who is entitled is contained in section 29(2) of the *Estates Act*. This section states that in these circumstances, other than circumstances in which the estate is said to be insolvent, the beneficiaries have a right to decide who will be the estate trustee. A case may be made for the major beneficiary of the estate to apply because that beneficiary has the most at stake in the administration of the estate. The *Rules of Civil Procedure* indicate that whoever applies must also submit consents from enough of the other beneficiaries that those who consent (together with the applicant) represent a majority interest in the estate. If there are competing applications for appointment, the applicant who has the support of other beneficiaries who, together with the applicant, have a majority interest will likely succeed in obtaining the appointment. If there is no agreement among the beneficiaries, section 29 of the *Estates Act*, taken as a whole, indicates that the spouse of the deceased (either married or common law and including same-sex spouses) is to be considered first, followed by the various next of kin of the deceased according to the degree of kinship to the deceased.

The situation is different if the estate appears to be insolvent because the parties who are most affected by the actions of an estate trustee are not the beneficiaries but the creditors of the estate. In this connection, section 29(3) of the *Estates Act* states that if the estate is insolvent, or in "other special circumstances," the court may appoint "such person as it thinks fit."

Note as well that under section 29(4) of the *Estates Act*, the court can appoint a trust company as the estate trustee without a will, either alone or jointly with an individual.

Once the issue of who is to apply to be the estate trustee without a will is resolved, the application (Form 74.14 for an individual and Form 74.15 for a corporation) is completed, usually with the help of the lawyer or law clerk. The form, an example of which is shown in Figure 9.7, is similar to the one completed for the certificate of appointment of estate trustee with a will, except that it contains a section entitled "Persons Entitled to Share in the Estate." This information is required by the court so that it knows who, in effect, are the beneficiaries of the estate. It is obviously imperative for the lawyer or law clerk assisting the applicant in completing the form to review with him the rules of intestacy to ensure that no potential beneficiaries are left out.

As in the case of the application for a certificate of appointment of estate trustee with a will, the application for the certificate of appointment without a will is a sworn and signed statement. All statements made on the form are to be confirmed on oath as true, to the best of the applicant's knowledge and belief, in the presence of a notary public or a commissioner for oaths.

FIGURE 9.7 **Form 74.9: Application for Certificate of Appointment of Estate Trustee Without a Will (Individual Applicant)**

FORM 74.14

Courts of Justice Act

APPLICATION FOR CERTIFICATE OF APPOINTMENT OF ESTATE TRUSTEE
WITHOUT A WILL (INDIVIDUAL APPLICANT)

ONTARIO

SUPERIOR COURT OF JUSTICE

APPLICATION FOR CERTIFICATE OF APPOINTMENT OF ESTATE TRUSTEE WITHOUT A WILL (INDIVIDUAL APPLICANT)

(Form 74.14 Under the Rules)

At   Orangeville

This application is filed by *(insert name and address)*
Gwendolyn Grat, Grit, Grat & Groot, Barristers & Solicitors, 15 Cross Street, Toronto, ON, M5A 1Q1, Telephone: 416-555-5555; Facsimile: 416-555-5556

DETAILS ABOUT THE DECEASED PERSON

Complete in full as applicable

First given name	Second given name	Third given name	Surname
Larissa	Connie		Alcala

And if the deceased was known by any other name(s), state below the full name(s) used including surname.

First given name	Second given name	Third given name	Surname
Larissa	Connie		Green

Address of fixed place of abode *(street or postal address) (city or town)*	*(county or district)*
Apt. 23, 212 Bliss Avenue, Orangeville, ON, L9W Q2Q	County of Dufferin

If the deceased person had no fixed place of abode in Ontario, did he or she have property in Ontario? ☐ No ☐ Yes	Last occupation of deceased person store manager

Place of death *(city or town; county or district)*	Date of death *(day, month, year)*
Town of Orangeville, County of Dufferin	31, August, 2018

Marital Status   ☐ Unmarried   ☒ Married   ☐ Widowed   ☐ Divorced

Was the deceased person's marriage terminated by a judgment absolute of divorce, or declared a nullity?   ☒ No   ☐ Yes
If yes, give details in an attached schedule.

Did the deceased person go through a form of marriage with a person where it appears uncertain whether an earlier marriage of the deceased person had been terminated by divorce or declared a nullity?   ☒ No   ☐ Yes
If yes, give the person's name and address, and the names and addresses of any children (including deceased children) of the marriage, in an attached schedule.

Was any earlier marriage of a person with whom the deceased person went through a form of marriage terminated by divorce or declared a nullity?   ☒ No   ☐ Yes
If yes, give details in an attached schedule.

Was the deceased person immediately before his or her death living with a person in a conjugal relationship outside marriage?   ☒ No   ☐ Yes
If yes, give the person's name and address in an attached schedule.

RCP-E 74.14 (November 1, 2005)

FIGURE 9.7 CONTINUED

PERSONS ENTITLED TO SHARE IN THE ESTATE

(Attach a schedule if more space is needed. If a person entitled to share in the estate is not a spouse, child, parent, brother or sister of the deceased person, show how the relationship is traced.)

Name	Address	Relationship to deceased person	Age (if under 18)
Jerry Brown	Apt 23-212 Bliss Avenue Orangeville, ON L9W Q2Q	husband	
Jimmy Brown	35 Railroad Street Orangeville, ON L9W Q4Q	son	

VALUE OF ASSETS OF ESTATE

Do not include in the total amount: insurance payable to a named beneficiary or assigned for value, property held jointly and passing by survivorship, or real estate outside Ontario.

Personal property	Real estate, net of encumbrances	Total
$ 110,346.21	$ 100,000.00	$ 210,346.21

Explain why the applicant is entitled to apply.

AFFIDAVIT(S) OF APPLICANT(S)
(Attach a separate sheet for additional affidavits, if necessary)

I, an applicant named in this application, make oath and say/affirm:

1. I am 18 years of age or older and a resident of Ontario.
2. I have made a careful search and inquiry for a will or other testamentary document of the deceased person, but none has been found. I believe that the person did not leave a will or other testamentary document.
3. I will faithfully administer the deceased person's property according to law and render a complete and true account of my administration when lawfully required.

4. Consents of persons who together have a majority interest in the value of the assets of the estate at the date of death are attached.
5. The information contained in this application and in any attached schedules is true, to the best of my knowledge and belief.

Name *(surname and forename(s))* Brown, Jerry	Occupation retired firefighter

Address *(street or postal address)*	*(city or town)*	*(province)*	*(postal code)*
Apt 23-212 Bliss Avenue	Orangeville	Ontario	L9W Q2Q

Sworn/Affirmed before me at the .... Town ....)

of .... Orangeville ....)

in the .... County ....)

of .... Dufferin ....)

this ...... 29th... day of .... September .... , 20 18 ....)

Jerry Brown

_____
Signature of applicant

Mary Ross

A Commissioner for taking Affidavits *(or as may be)*

Name *(surname and forename(s))*	Occupation

| Address *(street or postal address)* | *(city or town)* | *(province)* | *(postal code)* |

Sworn/Affirmed before me at the ....)

of ....)

in the ....)

of ....)

this .... day of ...., 20........)

Signature of applicant

A Commissioner for taking Affidavits (*or as may be*)

RCP-E 74.14 (November 1, 2005)

Draft Certificate of Appointment

A draft certificate of appointment of estate trustee without a will (Form 74.20) must also be submitted with the application, including the front and back page. As mentioned earlier, some court offices prefer to have an extra copy of the front page for their own records.

Bond of Indemnity

For an application for a certificate of appointment without a will, a bond of indemnity will most likely be required. As explained in Chapter 8, however, if the value of the estate is $200,000 or less and the beneficiary is the spouse of the deceased, the bond will usually be waived on application.

The bond may also be waived or reduced where it can be proved to the satisfaction of the court that the debts of the deceased and of the estate have been satisfied, or that the assets of the deceased are far in excess of the debts. It may also be relevant that the applicants represent all of the beneficiaries of the estate under the laws of intestacy.

Affidavit of Service on Appropriate Parties

In an application for a certificate of appointment without a will, the affidavit of service of the notice of application (Form 74.16) is similar to that for a certificate with a will. In the latter case, the persons to be served are determined by examining the will; in the former case, the persons are determined by consulting the laws of intestacy. In both cases, the affidavit cannot be sworn to by the applicant until the appropriate notices have been served.

The notice of application (Form 74.17) is again served by regular letter-mail to the appropriate parties (and their guardians or attorneys if applicable), including the Children's Lawyer (in the case of underage beneficiaries) or the Public Guardian and Trustee (in the case of mentally incapable beneficiaries who have no guardian or attorney authorized to act for them).

Again, the notice of application must be attached to the affidavit of service of notice, along with a jurat indicating that it is Exhibit "A" to the affidavit.

Although the *Rules of Civil Procedure* do not refer to unborn or unascertained beneficiaries in the context of an application for a certificate of appointment of estate trustee without a will, the possibility of unascertained beneficiaries may nonetheless exist. As may be recalled from Chapter 3, Interpretation of Wills, the *Succession Law Reform Act*[5] defines children as including persons conceived before but born alive after the death of the parent. If there is knowledge of such an unborn child in a case of intestacy, it seems reasonably appropriate to serve the Children's Lawyer with the notice of application.

Consents of Beneficiaries

As indicated above, the consents of the beneficiaries of the estate are required in an application. The form is Form 74.19. Again, a line in the consent form (to be deleted if not applicable) relates to the signatory's consent to an order dispensing with the administration bond. If all persons consenting to the appointment also consent to the order

---

5   RSO 1990, c S.26.

dispensing with the bond, however, it is not automatically the case that the order will be granted. This is because other parties—namely, the creditors of the estate—may be prejudiced if there is no administration bond. The court will consider all of the relevant factors in deciding whether to waive the necessity for the bond.

As already mentioned, the persons consenting to the appointment must, along with the applicant, represent a majority interest in the estate. Despite this rule, as also indicated above, if the estate is insolvent, the creditors of the estate may be able to obtain an appointment of their own choosing.

Applying for the Less Common Certificates of Appointment

Confirmation by Resealing of Appointment of Estate Trustee With or Without a Will

Chapter 7 explained that the confirmation by resealing of appointment applies when the deceased was ordinarily a resident of Canada outside Ontario, or of the United Kingdom or a British possession, and will be required if the deceased owned assets in Ontario that need to be administered by the estate trustee from the outside jurisdiction. As indicated in Chapter 7, it is a necessary precondition to obtaining the resealing that the outside estate trustee has obtained the equivalent of the certificate of appointment in the court of the original jurisdiction. Although it is not clear from the *Estate Administration Tax Act, 1998*[6] that the estate administration tax is payable on the Ontario assets only, the Act defines "value of the estate" in reference to section 32 of the *Estates Act*, which states in section 32(3) that "[w]here the application or grant is limited to part only of the property of the deceased, it is sufficient to set forth in the statement of value only the property and value thereof intended to be affected by such application or grant." Presumably, then, this provision authorizes the inclusion in this application of only the value of the assets within Ontario, and therefore it is only those assets upon which the estate administration tax will be calculated. The court form for the application (Form 74.27) does appear to corroborate this conclusion insofar as it asks for "value of assets located in Ontario." Nevertheless, it is appropriate to bring to the court's attention, in the form of an affidavit, all information that might be relevant in its decision to issue the certificate, including information about assets administered by another will.

Under section 7(2) of the *Estates Act*, the application is to be submitted to the court in the jurisdiction of the area in Ontario in which the deceased had assets. If the deceased had assets in several such jurisdictions, a court from any one of them would be appropriate pursuant to section 7(3) of the Act.

At the time of writing this text it is unknown what form of proof of death would be acceptable to the Ontario court from a jurisdiction outside of Canada. Presumably, an official, government-endorsed certificate would be sufficient. The documents to be submitted,

---

6 SO 1998, c 34.

then, along with the cheque or bank draft payable to the minister of finance for the estate administration tax and proof of death, are as follows:

- completed application for confirmation by resealing of the appointment of estate trustee with or without a will (Form 74.27);
- draft certificate of confirmation by resealing of appointment of estate trustee with or without a will (Form 74.28);
- bond of indemnity from an insurance company (Form 74.32); bond of indemnity from one personal surety with a net worth at least double the value of the assets of the estate within Ontario over which the estate trustee seeks control (rule 74.11(1)(f)); or bonds of indemnity from two personal sureties, each of whom has a net worth at least equal to the value of the estate assets within Ontario over which the estate trustee seeks control (Form 74.33); or an application to waive the bond of indemnity;
- a court-certified copy of the original certificate of appointment; and
- a court certificate from the original court stating that the grant (the equivalent of the certificate of appointment) is still effective.

Certificate of Ancillary Appointment of Estate Trustee With a Will

Chapter 7 explained that the certificate of ancillary appointment applies when the deceased was ordinarily resident in a foreign jurisdiction (outside Canada, the United Kingdom, or a British possession) and when a certificate is needed to administer assets within Ontario. Again, the court forms and the *Estates Act* suggest that the estate administration tax is payable on the Ontario assets only, although the *Estate Administration Tax Act, 1998* is somewhat unclear on this point. As in the case of the confirmation by resealing, the application is to be submitted to the court in the jurisdiction over an area in Ontario in which the deceased had assets.

The documents to be submitted, along with the cheque or bank draft payable to the minister of finance for the estate administration tax and proof of death, are as follows:

- completed application for a certificate of ancillary appointment of estate trustee with a will (Form 74.27);
- draft certificate of ancillary appointment of estate trustee with a will (Form 74.29);
- bond of indemnity from an insurance company (Form 74.32); bond of indemnity from one personal surety with a net worth at least double the value of the assets of the estate within Ontario over which the estate trustee seeks control (rule 74.11(1)(f)); or bonds of indemnity from two personal sureties, each of whom has a net worth at least equal to the value of the estate assets within Ontario over which the estate trustee seeks control (Form 74.33); or an application to waive the bond of indemnity;
- two court-certified copies of the original certificate of appointment; and
- a court certificate stating that the grant (the equivalent of a certificate of appointment of estate trustee with a will) is still effective.

Certificate of Appointment of Foreign Estate Trustee's Nominee as Estate Trustee Without a Will

Chapter 7 explained that the certificate of appointment of foreign estate trustee's nominee as estate trustee without a will applies in a situation in which the deceased died intestate and was resident in a foreign jurisdiction outside Canada, the United Kingdom, or a British possession, and the deceased owned assets in Ontario that require administration. It necessarily follows that, in order to apply for this kind of certificate, there must be an Ontario resident willing to assume the role of nominee, including all of its obligations and liabilities. Again, under section 7(2) of the *Estates Act*, the application is to be brought in the court in Ontario that has jurisdiction over the geographical area in which the deceased's assets are situated.

The documents to be submitted, along with the cheque or bank draft payable to the minister of finance for the estate administration tax and proof of death, are as follows:

- completed application for a certificate of appointment of foreign estate trustee's nominee as estate trustee without a will, signed by the nominee (Form 74.20.1);
- draft certificate of appointment of foreign estate trustee's nominee as estate trustee without a will (Form 74.20.3);
- bond of indemnity from an insurance company (Form 74.32); bond of indemnity from one personal surety with a net worth at least double the value of the assets of the estate (Form 74.33); or bonds of indemnity from two personal sureties, each of whom has a net worth at least equal to the value of the estate (Form 74.33); or an application to waive the bond of indemnity;
- a court-certified copy of the original certificate of appointment from the foreign jurisdiction;
- a certificate from the foreign court that granted the original appointment stating that the foreign appointment remains effective as of the date of the certificate (note that this must be certified by the foreign court within a reasonable amount of time before the certificate is presented to the Ontario court); and
- a nomination form in which the foreign estate trustee nominates the applicant, signed by the original estate trustee or administrator (Form 74.20.2).

As discussed above, rule 74.11(1)(f) states that in the case of a confirmation by resealing of appointment or an ancillary appointment of estate trustee, the administration bond need be based only on the value of the assets of the estate in Ontario over which the applicant seeks control. Because this rule does not mention the certificate of appointment of foreign estate trustee's nominee as estate trustee without a will, the implication is that the bonds to be obtained must be based on the value of the entire estate. The applicant can, however, apply to have the bond reduced.

Certificate of Appointment of Succeeding Estate Trustee With a Will

Chapter 7 explained that the certificate of appointment of succeeding estate trustee applies when the original estate trustee has died intestate or with a will appointing as estate trustee someone who is unable or unwilling to assume the role. The application is submitted to the court that granted the original certificate of appointment of estate trustee with a will. Under the *Estate Administration Tax Act, 1998*, there is no additional estate administration tax payable when obtaining a certificate of appointment of succeeding estate trustee. Instead, pursuant to section 2(1) of O Reg 293/92 (a regulation under the *Administration of Justice Act*) the current fee is set at $125.

The documents to be submitted, along with the cheque or bank draft payable to the minister of finance for the court fee in the amount of $125 and proof of death (of both the original estate trustee and the deceased whose estate is being administered), are as follows:

- completed application for a certificate of appointment of succeeding estate trustee with a will (Form 74.21);
- draft certificate of appointment of succeeding estate trustee with a will (Form 74.23);
- bond of indemnity from an insurance company (Form 74.32); bond of indemnity from one personal surety with a net worth at least double the value of the assets of the estate not yet administered (Form 74.33); or bonds of indemnity from two personal sureties, each of whom has a net worth at least equal to the value of the estate assets within Ontario not yet administered (Form 74.33); or an application to waive the bond of indemnity;
- original certificate of appointment or, if lost, a copy of it certified by the court;
- a renunciation from every living person who is named in the will or codicil as an estate trustee and who has not joined in the application and is entitled to do so (Form 74.11); and
- if the applicant is not named in the will, a consent to the application by persons who are entitled to share in the distribution of the remaining estate and who together have a majority interest in the value of the assets remaining in the estate at the date of the application (Form 74.22).

As indicated above, under rule 74.11(1)(e) of the *Rules of Civil Procedure*, unless the court orders otherwise and assuming there is an administration bond, the amount of the bond is to be calculated on the value of the unadministered assets of the estate only.

Certificate of Appointment of Succeeding Estate Trustee Without a Will

This certificate is similar to that for the succeeding estate trustee with a will except that it relates to the administration of an intestate estate. Again, the application is filed in the court that granted the original certificate of appointment of estate trustee without a will. As in the case of its counterpart, there is no additional estate administration tax payable when obtaining a certificate of appointment of succeeding estate trustee without a will, but there is a fee of $125 (which is set by regulation).

The documents to be submitted, along with the cheque or bank draft payable to the minister of finance for the court fee of $125 and proof of death (of both the original estate trustee and the deceased whose estate is being administered), are as follows:

- completed application for a certificate of appointment of succeeding estate trustee without a will (Form 74.24);

- draft certificate of appointment of succeeding estate trustee without a will (Form 74.26);

- bond of indemnity from an insurance company (Form 74.32); bond of indemnity from one personal surety with a net worth at least double the value of the assets of the estate not yet administered (Form 74.33); or bonds of indemnity from two personal sureties, each of whom has a net worth at least equal to the value of the estate assets within Ontario not yet administered (Form 74.33); or an application to waive the bond of indemnity;

- original certificate of appointment or, if lost, a copy of it certified by the court; and

- a consent to the application by persons who are entitled to share in the distribution of the remaining estate and who together have a majority interest in the value of the assets remaining in the estate at the date of the application (Form 74.25).

Again, pursuant to rule 74.11(1)(e) of the *Rules of Civil Procedure*, unless the court orders otherwise, the administration bond, if any, need cover the value of the unadministered assets only.

Certificate of Appointment of Estate Trustee During Litigation

Chapter 7 explained that the certificate of appointment of estate trustee during litigation applies in a situation where estate litigation is tying up the assets of the estate. Because persons not responsible for bringing the litigation may be prejudiced by the absence of an estate trustee to manage the assets or pay creditors, it is usually ordered (sometimes pursuant to an agreement among the parties to the litigation) that an estate trustee be appointed to manage the estate pending the outcome of the litigation. In such a case, the certificate of appointment must be applied for. The proper court in which to bring the application is the court for the area in which the deceased lived, which is usually the court with jurisdiction over the litigation. As in the case of certificates of appointment of succeeding estate trustee, there is no additional estate administration tax payable at the time of the application to the court for a certificate of appointment of estate trustee during litigation, but there is a fee of $125, also set by section 2(1) of O Reg 293/92.

The documents to be submitted, along with the cheque or bank draft payable to the minister of finance for the court fee of $125 and proof of death (if required by the court), are as follows:

- completed application for a certificate of appointment of estate trustee during litigation (Form 74.30);

- draft certificate of appointment of estate trustee during litigation (Form 74.31);

- bond of indemnity from an insurance company (Form 74.32); bond of indemnity from one personal surety with a net worth at least double the value of the assets of the estate (Form 74.33); or bonds of indemnity from two personal sureties, each of whom has a net worth at least equal to the value of the estate assets within Ontario (Form 74.33); or an application to waive the bond of indemnity; and

- a copy of the order appointing the applicant as estate trustee during litigation.

Although not specifically dealt with in rule 74.11 of the *Rules of Civil Procedure* (the rule dealing with administration bonds), it is suggested that if there is to be a bond in the case of a certificate of appointment of estate trustee during litigation, as in the case of succeeding estate trustees, it is logical to set the amount of the bond of indemnity based on the value of the unadministered assets of the estate in Ontario.

KEY TERM

jurat, 155

REVIEW QUESTIONS

1. Where is an application for a certificate of appointment of estate trustee made?

2. For each of the following certificates, list the standard documentation required to accompany the application, not including the cheque representing the estate administration tax and proof of death of the person whose estate is being administered:

   a. certificate of appointment of estate trustee with a will,

   b. certificate of appointment of estate trustee without a will,

   c. certificate of appointment of succeeding estate trustee with a will,

   d. certificate of appointment of succeeding estate trustee without a will,

   e. confirmation by resealing of appointment of estate trustee with or without a will,

   f. certificate of ancillary appointment of estate trustee with a will,

   g. certificate of appointment of foreign estate trustee's nominee as estate trustee without a will,

   h. certificate of appointment of estate trustee during litigation, and

   i. certificate of appointment of estate trustee with a will limited to the assets referred to in the will.

3. Why is an affidavit of execution required in an application for certificate of appointment of estate trustee with a will?

4. Is a notarial copy of the will sufficient to form part of the application for a certificate of appointment of estate trustee with a will?

5. What is a "jurat" and why is one included on various documents to be submitted to the court?

6. Who signs a renunciation and in what circumstances is one required?

7. When are the consents of persons who have a majority interest in an estate required?

8. Discuss who has the first right to apply for a certificate of appointment when there is no will, or no named estate trustee in the will, or when those named in the will are unable or unwilling to act and the beneficiaries cannot agree among themselves.

9. If an administration bond is required and the surety put forward is a person, what value of net assets is that person required to have?

10. What is the purpose of the "draft" certificate of appointment submitted as part of the application?

11. What individuals or entities must be served with notice of the application and what must accompany the notice?

12. What individual or entity is served in the case of a beneficiary who/that is (a) underage, (b) unascertained, or (c) mentally incapable?

13. How does one prove the execution of a holograph will?

14. What does a witness to a will who is also a beneficiary have to prove in order to sustain his benefit?

15. What preliminary question must be answered where the application to court is made without the deceased having left a will?

16. Discuss the various situations in which estate administration tax is payable on only part of the estate.

Collecting the Assets

10

LEARNING OUTCOMES

After reading this chapter, you should be able to:

- Recount the process for collecting assets of the deceased held by financial institutions
- Understand the procedures involved in collecting assets of the deceased held in publicly traded stocks and other securities
- Know how to collect assets of the estate held in Canada Savings Bonds, including when the Bank of Canada will and will not require a certificate of appointment to release the assets
- Explain how the estate trustee should deal with personal effects and household furniture of the deceased when collecting such assets
- Know the steps to take in collecting and distributing vehicles of the deceased, including the documentation required by the Ministry of Transportation for each possible scenario
- Have an understanding of the process for collecting business assets of the deceased and some of the complications that could arise during this process
- Explain how the estate trustee should collect and/or account for loans and other debts owing to the deceased
- Describe the process to be followed in dealing with real property owned, or partly owned, by the deceased
- Understand the obligations of the estate trustee in situations where the deceased died while pursuing, or in a position to pursue, a legal action
- Know the assets that commonly arise as a result of death, and the estate trustee's obligations in collecting them

Introduction

As is often the case in law, rules can be simple in theory but complex in practice. Such is the case regarding the administration of estates. While the theory is to gather in the assets, pay the creditors, and account to and pay the beneficiaries, in that order, in practice the order of these tasks is not entirely consecutive. Some debts—for example, the funeral account—have to be paid while the estate is being administered, and beneficiaries may be paid before all of the debts. Nevertheless, the procedural steps are followed conceptually. That is, while an estate trustee may transfer an asset before paying all of the debts, she does so only if she is quite certain that there are enough funds in the undistributed portion of the estate to cover such debts.

As already indicated in the introduction to Chapter 7, Proof of the Estate Trustee's Status as Estate Trustee, "gathering together the assets" can mean various things depending on the kinds of assets involved. As you will see, collecting the assets may sometimes be done at virtually the same time as distributing them to the beneficiaries. That is, sometimes an asset that belonged to the deceased immediately before death does not fall into the estate but goes directly to a survivor of the deceased—for example, a bank account with a joint account holder with right of survivorship. The estate trustee, with the help of the lawyer, often assists in transferring such assets even though this is not strictly part of the administration of the estate. This chapter discusses collecting the estate assets and also includes some of the procedures involved in such direct transfers. In all cases the estate trustee must keep in mind the conceptual steps in the administration of the estate because losing sight of the overall process can result in liability.

It should also be kept in mind that the estate trustee is under a legal obligation not only to ensure that all of the assets of the estate are properly valued for the purposes of calculating the estate administration tax, but also to correct any previously reported incorrect values. Sometimes information can come to the estate trustee's attention during the gathering of the assets stage of estate administration—for example, when estate assets are sold for fair market value, which triggers the necessity of filing a revised estate information return with the Ministry of Finance. This topic is discussed in more detail in Chapter 11, Determining, Notifying, and Paying Creditors of the Estate.

Assets Held by Financial Institutions

In this text, third parties holding bank accounts, term deposits, and mutual funds—that is, banks, trust companies, credit unions, and investment brokerages—have been referred to as financial institutions. The deceased's ownership of such assets exists only insofar as the financial institution's records reflect the ownership. It is the job of the estate trustee to instruct the financial institution to change its records to reflect the new ownership in the name of the estate. When it does, the estate trustee has taken control of those assets and is in a position to transfer them directly to beneficiaries of the estate or to liquidate them and transfer the proceeds to beneficiaries or creditors of the estate.

Transfers of Financial Assets to the Estate Trustee With a Certificate of Appointment

If the estate trustee has obtained a certificate of appointment of estate trustee, he will have the financial institution's records altered simply by providing the institution with a notarial copy of the certificate of appointment and a written direction signed by all of the estate trustees (as in Figure 10.1). Occasionally a financial institution requires its own forms to be completed before it will agree to transfer assets into the name of the estate. It is usually best to comply, although any unreasonable requests, such as those for personal information beyond what is relevant to the estate administration or documents that necessitate taking on additional obligations, should normally be resisted.

FIGURE 10.1   **Direction to Transfer Accounts**

AUTHORIZATION AND DIRECTION

TO: Bank of Dundas
      450 Thistle Street
      Toronto, Ontario
      M5A Q8Q

RE: Estate of Jacqueline Stick
      who died January 12, 2018

I, Robert Larise, the estate trustee in the estate of Jacqueline Stick, deceased, hereby authorize and direct you to close out any existing accounts in the name of the deceased or of the estate of the deceased and to forward the cheque or draft for the proceeds payable to my lawyer—namely, Gwendolyn Grat, in trust, to the following address:

      GRIT, GRAT & GROOT
      15 Cross Street
      Toronto, Ontario
      M5A 1Q1

      Attention: Ms. Gwendolyn Grat

This shall be your good and sufficient authority for so doing.

Signed this 2nd day of June, 2018.

Robert Larise
_____
Robert Larise

Transfers of Financial Assets to the Estate Trustee Without a Certificate of Appointment

Testate Estate

As indicated in Chapter 7, if there is no certificate of appointment of estate trustee, it is solely within the discretion of the financial institution whether to transfer the assets held by the deceased alone to the estate. (For the transfer of jointly held assets, see below under "Direct Transfers of Financial Assets to Survivors.") If the deceased died with a will and the financial institution consents (pursuant to the correspondence to the institution discussed in Chapter 7), it will usually have its own set of forms to be completed by the estate trustee.

Such forms usually contain sworn statements by the estate trustee setting out the particulars of the estate, and often the financial institution also requires a personal indemnity to the financial institution (on its own form) from the estate trustee. The personal indemnity usually indicates that in the event that the assets being dealt with actually belong to someone other than those to whom the estate trustee intends to transfer them, the estate trustee will indemnify the financial institution for its liability to the proper recipient. The indemnity typically includes the value of the assets transferred plus any additional damages and costs incurred by the financial institution for the incorrect transfer. Along with the completed forms, the financial institution will request a funeral director's statement of death or some other proof of death and a notarial copy of the will.

Intestate Estate

Chapter 7 explained that, except in rare situations, a financial institution will usually not agree to transfer assets to the estate when the deceased died intestate and no certificate of appointment has been obtained. The reason is that there is then no legally appointed person to instruct the bank on behalf of the estate and, ultimately, no person to be held responsible in the event that the distribution ought not to have been made. As already stated, the authority of an estate trustee in an intestate estate flows solely from a certificate of appointment of estate trustee without a will.

Direct Transfers of Financial Assets to Survivors

The assets so far discussed have been those that the deceased owned alone. In cases where the deceased owned the assets jointly with another person, the circumstances of the creation of the joint holding and the intention of the deceased with respect to its creation must be determined. If the account was originally in the name of the deceased alone and was made into a joint account for convenience only—that is, to give another person access to the funds to assist in paying bills and the like—the estate trustee may have to consider making a claim against the surviving joint account holder for possession of the joint account. On the other hand, if the account was set up with the intention that it pass to the surviving joint account holder, that person will take the account regardless of the claims of any creditors of the estate. In such a case, the account bypasses the estate altogether. The survivor is usually recorded as the sole owner simply by providing the financial institution with proof of death of the deceased, such as a funeral director's statement of death.

Sometimes deceased persons have registered retirement savings plans (RRSPs) and registered retirement income funds (RRIFs) that name a direct beneficiary, usually on file with the financial institution through which the fund is administered. In such cases, the RRSPs or RRIFs pass directly to the named beneficiary and, again, bypass the estate. Such transfers are made after the financial institution is provided with proof of death of the owner of the plan or fund. As will be seen in Chapter 11, however, even if such plans bypass the estate, the tax burden arising from the death of the deceased may attach to the estate itself.

Publicly Traded Stocks and Other Securities

An estate trustee gathers in all investments of money or money's worth held by the deceased, whether shares in a mutual fund, individual stocks and bonds, or other equities, although the manner of collecting each may vary.

Chapter 7 explained that the transfer of publicly traded stocks is handled by a transfer agent, or, in rare instances, by the corporation itself, and the transfer agent determines what documentation is required for the transfer. The discussion below focuses on what is typically required and may not reflect the requirements of any particular transfer agent.

Generally, the transfer agent transfers the shares to the estate trustee, and then the estate trustee either sells the shares or transfers them to the beneficiaries. While it is technically the estate trustee who takes legal ownership of the shares, they are sometimes transferred by the transfer agent into the name of the estate.

As will be seen, it is sometimes possible to transfer the shares directly from the deceased to another person—for example, where the shares are held jointly with right of survivorship (in which case they bypass the estate) or where the estate trustee has the shares transferred directly to the beneficiary of the estate. The latter should be done only where the estate trustee is certain that all of the debts of the deceased and all of the beneficiaries in priority to the recipient (as discussed in Part I, Chapter 3, Interpretation of Wills) have been paid or that funds allocated for them have been set aside or reserved. It can be seen from this that the line between collecting the assets and paying the beneficiaries is sometimes difficult to draw, and where there is any doubt, the lawyer should recommend caution.

Transfers to the Estate Trustee With a Certificate of Appointment

Usually the transfer agent of publicly traded stock needs the following in order to transfer shares owned by the deceased to the estate trustee:

- original stock certificate;
- notarial copy of certificate of appointment;
- declaration of transmission (discussed below);
- stock power of attorney to transfer shares (discussed below); and
- letter of direction from all estate trustees to the transfer agent directing it to transfer the shares.

If the estate trustee has not been able to locate the stock certificate, the transfer agent usually provides procedures to be followed (discussed below), although such procedures can be somewhat onerous for the estate trustee.

An example of a **declaration of transmission** is provided in Figure 10.2. This document is a sworn statement by one or more of the estate trustees that sets out the particulars of the

declaration of transmission
sworn statement by one or more of the estate trustees that sets out the particulars of the deceased and, if necessary, confirms that the deceased is the same person whose name appears on a stock certificate or in a transfer agent's records; used to direct the transfer agent to put the stock directly into the name of the estate or a beneficiary

deceased, such as name, address, and date of death, and, if necessary, confirms that the deceased is the same person whose name appears on the stock certificate or in the transfer agent's records. The declaration of transmission can direct the transfer agent to put the stock directly into a beneficiary's name (although, as mentioned, doing so is risky unless all creditors of the estate and any beneficiaries in priority have been ascertained and paid).

FIGURE 10.2   Declaration of Transmission

DECLARATION OF TRANSMISSION

PROVINCE OF ONTARIO	)	IN THE MATTER OF THE Estate of
in the	)	Jacqueline Stick, late of
City of	)	the City of Toronto,
Toronto	)	Ontario, Deceased.

I, **ROBERT LARISE**, whose current residence address is 345 Needlebrook Avenue, Oakville, Ontario, being the only Estate Trustee of the said Deceased, DO SOLEMNLY DECLARE THAT:

(1) The said Deceased died at 34 Thistle Street, Toronto, Ontario on the 12th day of January 2018 testate and at the date of death was domiciled at 34 Thistle Street, Toronto, Ontario.

(2) Certificate of Appointment of Estate Trustee With a Will of the Deceased was granted to me, ROBERT LARISE, as Estate Trustee on the 25th day of May 2018 by the Ontario Superior Court of Justice at Toronto.

(3) There are registered in the name of the Deceased on the books of Moments Inc., twenty (20) fully paid and non-assessable Shares, of the par value of One Dollar each, of its Capital Stock, represented by certificate numbered 9908872.

(4) The said Jacqueline Stick, Deceased and Jacqueline Stick named in the said certificate was one and the same person.

(5) The aforementioned certificate was physically situate inside the Province of Ontario at the date of the death of the Deceased.

(6) All beneficiaries under the Will are domiciled inside the Province of Ontario.

(7) The said Deceased was not at the time of her death, nor is her estate now, indebted to any person, firm or corporation residing or having its chief place of business in the Province of Ontario.

(8) By virtue of the foregoing the said Shares have devolved upon and become vested in the Estate Trustee as aforesaid, who desires to have the same recorded in the name of the Estate Trustee as aforesaid upon the books of the said Company and immediately thereafter sold, with the proceeds payable to the estate.

And We make this solemn Declaration conscientiously believing it to be true, and knowing that it is of the same force and effect as if made under oath and by virtue of the *Canada Evidence Act*.

SEVERALLY DECLARED before me at	)	
the City of Toronto in the	)	
Province of Ontario	)	*Robert Larise*
this 25th day of May 2018	)	_____
	)	Robert Larise

Mary Ross
_____
A Commissioner etc.

While the declaration of transmission usually requires a statement to be made that all creditors of the estate have been fully paid, this may not in fact be true. (Most notably, the Canada Revenue Agency may not yet have received all taxes due in respect of the estate.) In such a case, the clause pertaining to the creditors should be amended to indicate that estate funds have been at least allocated for the payment of all the creditors.

The **stock power of attorney**, an example of which is provided in Figure 10.3, is a special kind of power of attorney in which the estate trustee is the grantor and the attorney is the transfer agent or an employee of the transfer agent. Usually, the name of the attorney is left blank, to be filled in later by the transfer agent.

Figure 10.4 is an example of a **letter of direction for transfer and sale of shares** from the estate trustee to the transfer agent. It is a standard direction that serves to confirm to the transfer agent that the estate trustee agrees to the sale of the shares.

stock power of attorney
special kind of power of attorney in which the estate trustee is the grantor and the attorney is the transfer agent or an employee of the transfer agent

letter of direction for transfer and sale of shares
standard direction that serves to confirm to the transfer agent that the estate trustee agrees to the sale of the shares

---

FIGURE 10.3   Stock Power of Attorney

IRREVOCABLE STOCK POWER OF ATTORNEY

FOR VALUE RECEIVED the undersigned hereby sells, assigns and transfers unto

the estate of Jacqueline Stick

  (Name of Transferee)

c/o GRIT, GRAT & GROOT, 15 Cross Street, Toronto, ON, M5A 1Q1
  (Address)

Twenty (20) fully paid and non-assessable shares, of the par value of One Dollar each, of the Capital Stock of Moments Inc.

standing in the name of the undersigned on the books of the said corporation represented by certificate No. 9908872

and hereby irrevocably constitutes and appoints

the attorney of the undersigned to transfer the said stock on the books of the said corporation with full power of substitution in the premises.

DATED the 31st day of May, 2018   )
In the presence of   )
)
)
)   *Robert Larise*
)
)   Robert Larise
)

Mary Ross

Signature of Transferor, Robert Larise, is hereby guaranteed.

FIGURE 10.4   Letter of Direction for Transfer and Sale of Shares

AUTHORIZATION AND DIRECTION

TO: Bank of Dundas
       450 Thistle Street
       Toronto, Ontario
       M5A Q8Q

RE: Estate of Jacqueline Stick
       who died January 12, 2018

I, Robert Larise, the estate trustee in the estate of Jacqueline Stick, deceased, hereby authorize and direct you to transfer the shares represented by share certificate No. 9908872 for Twenty (20) fully paid and non-assessable Shares, of the par value of One Dollar each, of the Capital Stock of Moments Inc., to the name of "Robert Larise, estate trustee in the estate of Jacqueline Stick" and to immediately sell such shares and to pay the proceeds to my lawyer—namely, "Gwendolyn Grat," in trust, and to forward such cheque to my said lawyer at the following address:

      GRIT, GRAT & GROOT
      15 Cross Street
      Toronto, Ontario
      M5A 1Q1
      <u>Attention: Ms. Gwendolyn Grat</u>

This shall be your good and sufficient authority for so doing.

Signed this 2nd day of June, 2018.

Robert Larise
Robert Larise

Often one or more of the above documents require that the signatures of the estate trustees be guaranteed by a bank or trust company. This kind of guarantee (sometimes called a **medallion signature guarantee**) can be provided only by a bank or trust company that is in a position to verify the identity of the estate trustees and their respective signatures.

medallion signature guarantee
guarantee of the signatures of estate trustees by a bank or trust company

Upon receiving the required documents, the transfer agent will change the corporation's records of ownership of the shares and reissue and forward a new share certificate in the name of the estate trustee, the estate, or the beneficiary, as requested.

Transfers to the Estate Trustee Without a Certificate of Appointment

Testate Estate

Assuming that the transfer agent has agreed to transfer the shares from the deceased to the estate trustee without a certificate of appointment, the required documents typically include the following:

- original stock certificate;

- notarial copy of will;
- proof of death of the deceased;
- declaration of transmission (changed to indicate that no certificate of appointment was obtained);
- stock power of attorney;
- indemnity to the transfer agent; and
- letter of direction from all estate trustees to the transfer agent directing a transfer of the shares.

The only additional documents typically required when there is a will but no certificate of appointment are the indemnity to the transfer agent and the proof of death. The requirement of proof of death is usually satisfied by providing a funeral director's statement of death.

The form for the indemnity is usually supplied by the transfer agent, but it is similar to the indemnities requested by financial institutions when they are asked to transfer assets on the strength of a will but no certificate of appointment. In signing the indemnity, the estate trustees agree that, if it turns out that for whatever reason another person is entitled to the shares, the estate trustee will indemnify the transfer agent for any of its liability to the person who is actually entitled. The indemnity usually requires that the estate trustee agrees to cover other costs that could be incurred by the transfer agent as a result of a transfer to the incorrect person, including court costs and interest.

Intestate Estate

From a strictly academic point of view, it is questionable whether an estate is an entity capable of owning assets. Despite this theoretical perspective, many institutions, including the governments of Canada and Ontario, purport in some instances to transfer assets "to the estate" of a deceased person. This issue comes to the fore, however, in estates where there is no will and no certificate of appointment of estate trustee. In such cases, a transfer agent will not normally agree to transfer shares to the estate.

It is possible in these circumstances, however, for a transfer agent to agree to transfer shares directly to a beneficiary of the deceased's estate. The typical requirements are discussed below.

Direct Transfers

To Beneficiaries of the Estate Where There Is a Certificate of Appointment of Estate Trustee (With or Without a Will)

A transfer of shares can be made directly to a beneficiary of the estate in a case where there is a certificate of appointment of estate trustee. The transfer is made in the same way as a transfer to the estate trustee, although the declaration of transmission and direction must reflect that the shares are to go into the names of specified persons.

A transfer agent may consent to a direct transfer in a case where there is no certificate of appointment as long as there is a will.

To Beneficiaries of the Estate Where There Is No Certificate of Appointment of Estate Trustee and No Will

It is rare for the transfer agent to agree to transfer shares to a beneficiary of an estate if there is no will and no certificate of appointment, because in those cases the transfer agent has no one with authority—an estate trustee—from whom to take instructions. Nevertheless, in the unlikely event that the transfer agent does agree to make a transfer in such circumstances, the required documentation would likely include the following:

- original stock certificate;
- proof of death of the deceased;
- sworn statement from all of the beneficiaries indicating that they are the only beneficiaries of the deceased's estate and that all the debts of the estate have been paid;
- an indemnity signed by the beneficiaries; and
- letter of direction.

Because the risk to the transfer agent is considerable where there is no will and no certificate of appointment of estate trustee, the transfer agent may require all of the signatures of the beneficiaries to be guaranteed by a bank or trust company, and may also require bonds of indemnity from the beneficiaries.

To Surviving Joint Stock Holders Where There Is a Right of Survivorship

Sometimes the deceased's shares are owned jointly with someone with right of survivorship. In such cases, the stock certificate shows the two names along with the words "as joint owners" or "jointly with right of survivorship." Occasionally only the words "as joint tenants" appear, although such a phrase traditionally applies only to real property.

Joint ownership with right of survivorship means that the asset passes directly to the surviving joint owner and bypasses the estate, including creditors. Assuming that the legality of joint ownership of shares in a corporation would be allowed to stand under the scrutiny of a court resulting from an action brought, say, by a creditor prejudiced by such an arrangement, the transfer from the deceased joint owner to the survivor would normally require the following documents:

- original stock certificate;
- death certificate of the deceased owner; and
- letter of direction from the survivor requesting that the transfer agent reissue the share certificate in the name of the survivor.

As in other cases where assets owned jointly with right of survivorship are transferred to the survivor, transferring shares of a corporation to a survivor is not, strictly speaking, the task of the estate trustee. Nevertheless, estate trustees and their lawyers often agree to assist the survivor in transferring such assets.

Note that it is possible for share certificates to be owned by two or more persons as owners in common (meaning that each owns an undivided portion of the share certificate and each can make a gift of it to his or her respective beneficiaries). In such cases, when one owner dies, a problem may arise for the transfer agent if the number of shares is an odd number and the shares have to be divided evenly. It is likely partly for this reason that ownership of shares in common is rare.

Missing Certificates

Occasionally the estate trustee is aware that the deceased owned shares in a corporation, on the basis of the deceased's tax returns or dividend cheques received, but the share certificates cannot be located. As with all of the procedures outlined above, every transfer agent will have its own requirements for replacing such missing certificates.

Typically the transfer agent requires a declaration of indemnity from the estate trustee and may go so far as to require one or more sureties or bonds of indemnity to protect the transfer agent.

Canada Savings Bonds

Canada savings bonds in the name of the deceased may be transferred to the estate trustee and, eventually, to the creditors or beneficiaries of the estate. As in the case of the other assets discussed above, transfers can be made directly to beneficiaries, but such a course of action should be taken cautiously and only if the estate trustee is certain that all of the creditors of the estate have been or will be paid.

While it may be possible to redeem the bonds at a financial institution and have the cash proceeds deposited to an estate account at that institution, the estate trustee often contacts the Bank of Canada, the issuer of the bonds. The Bank of Canada currently takes the position that estate trustees or beneficiaries needing to redeem the bonds for cash should contact the Bank of Canada and provide particulars of the estate. As discussed in Chapter 7, the Bank of Canada has specific policies as to when it will agree to transfer Canada Savings Bonds without a certificate of appointment. These guidelines can be accessed at <http://www.csb.gc.ca> (search "Bank of Canada Business Rules"). If the Bank of Canada is contacted it will inform the estate trustee or beneficiary as to what documents he must provide. Below is a discussion of what is generally required by the Bank of Canada and the circumstances in which it will transfer or redeem bonds with or without a certificate of appointment.

Transfers to the Estate or to a Beneficiary With a Certificate of Appointment

For bond series issued prior to November 1, 2008, if the transfer to be made is to the estate of the deceased and there is a certificate of appointment, the documents normally required by the Bank of Canada are as follows:

- notarial copy of the certificate of appointment;
- Bank of Canada Estate Transfer Form (2351) completed and signed by the estate trustee;

- bond certificates; and
- letter of direction from the estate trustee.

The signatures of the estate trustees on Estate Transfer Form 2351 must be guaranteed by a chartered bank or other financial institution (such as a trust company) that is acceptable to the Bank of Canada, or the estate trustee's signature must be witnessed by a notary public who must sign the form and affix her notarial seal.

The above requirements also apply to a transfer of any series of bonds to a beneficiary.

It should be noted that bond series issued after November 1, 2008 are no longer eligible to be transferred in the name of the estate. This policy appears to be a reflection of the fact that an estate is not a legal entity in and of itself.

Transfers to the Estate or to a Beneficiary Without a Certificate of Appointment

As discussed in Chapter 7, the Bank of Canada Business Rules set estate value limits and documentation requirements for the transfer or redemption of bonds without a certificate of appointment.

If the bonds are the subject of a specific bequest under the will, there is no bond value limit and the Bank of Canada will require the following documents:

- notarial copy of the will;
- Bank of Canada Estate Transfer Form (2351) completed and signed by the estate trustee;
- bond certificates;
- proof of death; and
- letter of direction from the estate trustee.

Where there is no specific bequest of the bonds under the will, the estate trustee must refer to the Bank of Canada Business Rules for the bond value limits in effect (see the link referred to above). The current limits range from $75,000 if the spouse is the sole beneficiary under the will; $50,000 if children are the sole beneficiaries under the will; and $20,000 if parents, siblings, other family members, or a common law spouse or same-sex partner are the sole beneficiaries under the will. In all cases, the documentation above is required with the signature of the estate trustee on Estate Transfer Form 2351 guaranteed by a financial institution acceptable to the Bank of Canada or witnessed by a notary public under seal.

There are similar rules in place where the deceased died intestate, with the exception that the heirs must consent to any transfer of the bonds.

If the value of the bonds is in excess of $75,000, the Bank of Canada does not normally approve a transfer without a certificate of appointment.

Missing Canada Savings Bond Certificates

If Canada savings bond certificates are missing, the proper procedure is to contact the Bank of Canada and provide it with details about the estate. The first step is usually to replace the missing bonds. The documentation usually requested includes a statutory declaration that the bonds are lost and a bond of indemnity.

Personal Effects and Household Furniture

Any personal property that is given as a gift *in specie*—that is, in the form in which it currently exists—must obviously be retained by the estate trustee until delivery to the beneficiary. Other personal effects and household furniture, furnishings, appliances, and equipment can be either sold or distributed to the beneficiaries.

The proceeds from the sale of such property are not usually large. Normally, then, beneficiaries who want some of the personal effects of the deceased can be accommodated, but unless all residual beneficiaries are in agreement, the estate trustee may find that there are difficulties. Sometimes the smallest item can cause the greatest emotional upset, especially when the deceased is a close member of the family and the emotions of the surviving relatives are high. In such cases, the estate trustee may have to make careful but strong decisions regarding the property. In this connection, as seen in Chapter 2, Will Clauses, the will may provide specific powers to the estate trustee that will help.

If the personal property of the deceased has an unusually high value and is not the subject of a gift *in specie*, the estate trustee must be sure either to sell it individually for fair market value or to obtain a professional valuation and allocate it to a beneficiary who wants to have it as part of his share in exchange for an appropriate setoff, provided that the will allows the estate trustee to do so or the beneficiaries consent.

Vehicles

Where the deceased owned a vehicle, it is the estate trustee's duty to take possession of it and keep it in a safe place until the time comes to transfer it. If the estate trustee is required to move it, she first needs to obtain a temporary trip permit from the Ministry of Transportation to drive it. A temporary trip permit is obtained from the ministry by presenting proof of the estate trustee's status as estate trustee, proof of death, and proof of insurance for the proposed trip.

When it comes time to transfer the vehicle, if the recipient is a beneficiary, the procedure to be followed depends on the beneficiary's relationship to the deceased. If the recipient is one of the following, the procedure is simpler and less costly than it would be otherwise:

- spouse (married or common law);
- parent;
- step-parent;
- grandparent;
- child;
- stepchild;
- grandchild;
- step-grandchild;
- mother-in-law/father-in-law; or
- daughter-in-law/son-in-law.

In these cases, the estate trustee and the recipient both sign a Ministry of Transportation form entitled "Sworn Statement for a Family Gift of a Used Motor Vehicle in the Province of Ontario." The form can be obtained by searching "family gift of used motor vehicle in Ontario" in a search engine or going to <http://www.forms.ssb.gov.on.ca> and searching from that site. As the title of the form suggests, it must be sworn before a notary public or commissioner for oaths by the estate trustee and the recipient. The ministry will also require the following before transferring the ownership:

- in an area where emissions testing is required, a Vehicle Emissions Inspection Report indicating "pass";
- proof of insurance;
- new licence plates and stickers; and
- a safety inspection certificate from a qualified mechanic (unless the recipient is the common law or married spouse of the deceased).

If the recipient beneficiary is not one of those listed above, the following additional documentation is required by the Ministry of Transportation:

- used vehicle information package (which can be purchased from the ministry at a reasonable price); and
- payment of 13 percent harmonized sales tax (HST) on the wholesale value of the vehicle.

Of course, the estate trustee must also prove his status as such. In this regard, a copy of the will and a death certificate are sufficient if the deceased died testate.

If the deceased died intestate, a certificate of appointment may be required, depending on the circumstances. The ministry will usually waive the requirement of a certificate of appointment of estate trustee if the spouse is the sole beneficiary of the estate and is also the recipient of the vehicle. In this case, the ministry must receive evidence of the spouse's inheritance in affidavit form (including a statement that all creditors have been paid) and an indemnity to the ministry in the event that the affidavit is incorrect. If other beneficiaries are entitled to the deceased's estate, all of them must consent in writing, and an affidavit must be provided indicating that they represent all of the beneficiaries and that all of the creditors have been paid. Again, an indemnity must be provided. On receipt of all of the above documentation, the ministry may transfer the vehicle without the certificate of appointment.

Business Assets

As discussed in Chapter 8, Preliminary Steps in Applying for a Certificate of Appointment of Estate Trustee, business assets of the deceased—whether owned as a sole proprietorship, as a share in a partnership, or by way of shares in a private corporation—are assets of the estate. Having reviewed any existing contracts, partnership agreements, and shareholders' agreements to which the deceased was party, the estate trustee is in a position to collect whatever assets or compensation is owing to the estate. Depending on the requirements of the person or institution in charge of the registration of ownership of the business assets, the estate trustee may or may not have to obtain a certificate of appointment of estate trustee.

Loans Owing to the Deceased

Loans owing to the deceased can take many forms with varying degrees of formality, from a registered mortgage secured against real estate to a casual loan to a family member without anything in writing. In all cases, the estate trustee is obligated to the beneficiaries and creditors of the estate to see that the loans are collected.

A mortgage in which the deceased is the mortgagee (the lender) cannot normally be called in simply because she died. In such cases, it may be necessary to assign the mortgage for value or, possibly, to assign it to one or more of the beneficiaries in satisfaction of his gift under the will. In any event, it is important to instruct the mortgagor (the borrower) to make future payments to the estate until further notice. The mortgagor may reasonably ask for proof of death and proof of the estate trustee's appointment.

In the case of an alleged informal loan to a family member, which may be disputed, it is sometimes necessary to determine whether the loan was actually a loan or a gift. If the beneficiaries of the estate do not agree that the transaction was a gift but was instead a loan, and furthermore, that the loan was not intended to be forgiven on the death of the lender, the matter may have to proceed to litigation.

It should be remembered that if the gift was from a parent to a child, the hotch pot rule—the rule against double portions, discussed in Chapter 3—may come into play.

Other Debts Owing to the Deceased

Any other debts owing to the deceased must be collected by the estate trustee. Such a task is ad hoc in the sense that there is no accepted way to collect all debts other than to notify the debtors and take whatever steps are necessary to collect the amounts owing. If the estate trustee does not obtain the cooperation of the debtors, such steps may include taking court action against them. It is important, however, for the estate trustee to weigh the costs of such action against the likelihood of recovery.

Real Property

Collecting the assets in the case of real property involves changing the official records in the land registration system maintained by the government of Ontario. A change of ownership takes place by way of electronic registration of the necessary documentation in the appropriate land registry office (LRO) for that particular piece of real property.

Leaving aside the relatively uncommon situations involving legal and beneficial ownership of real property through various trusts, there are three different ways in which a deceased person can own real property on her death: (1) sole ownership, (2) ownership with another person as a tenant in common, and (3) ownership with another person as a joint tenant. In this chapter, unless otherwise stated, any discussion of ownership by the deceased refers to situations 1 and 2. In such situations, the property—or the undivided part of it that was owned by the deceased as a tenant in common—passes into the estate and is either sold to pay the debts of the estate, sold to distribute the residue of the estate, or transferred outright to a beneficiary according to a **devise**. Where there is no specific devise in the will, the estate trustees and beneficiaries may nevertheless agree to transfer the real property to a beneficiary as part of his share of the residue.

devise
a specific gift of real
property in a will

In the case of jointly held property (situation 3 above), on the death of the joint tenant (joint owner), the property automatically bypasses the estate and becomes vested in the surviving joint tenant. At some point, the land registration records have to be changed to reflect the surviving joint tenant as the sole owner, but such steps need not be taken until the surviving joint tenant wants to deal with the property by either mortgaging it or transferring it to a third party. In cases of joint tenancy, the estate trustee is not officially involved because the property does not form part of the estate. Nevertheless, as has been seen in the case of other kinds of assets, the estate trustee often assists the surviving joint tenant in transferring the property or, in this case, in amending the land registry office records.

The procedure for amending the registration record of ownership or transferring real property varies depending on the following variables:

- whether the property is being sold to a third party or transferred to a beneficiary directly, or whether the records are being changed to show a surviving joint tenant as sole owner;
- whether there is a certificate of appointment of estate trustee; and
- if there is no certificate of appointment of estate trustee, whether the deceased died testate or intestate.

Because it is not the intention of this book to deal with areas that are covered by other courses, such as real estate law, the following discussion only attempts to highlight the relevant issues involved in estate transfers of real property with respect to the above variables. It should be noted as well that, while land is registered in Ontario under one of two separate systems, the older system known as the "registry system" is now mostly phased out (though the government offices maintaining the records are still known as land registry offices or LROs). Accordingly, this text focuses only on the land titles system, which most properties are now registered under.

Before discussion of the procedural issues involved in collecting and selling or distributing real property, some preliminary issues that arise from the unique treatment of real property in our legal system are outlined below.

Preliminary Issues Regarding Real Property and Estates

Selling the Real Property to Pay Debts or With a Power of Sale Clause in the Will

An estate trustee can always sell real property falling into the estate if it is necessary for the purpose of paying debts of the estate. If, on the other hand, the purpose of the sale is to distribute the estate to the beneficiaries, complications in administering the estate may arise if the will does not contain a power of sale clause.

Recall from Chapter 2 that many wills contain a power of sale clause—a clause that expressly authorizes an estate trustee to sell real property and transfer it to a third party without the consent of the beneficiaries.

In some circumstances, the power of sale clause is implied by the terms of the will. If, however, there is no express or implied power of sale clause in the will, the purchaser of the property takes the property subject to the debts of the deceased unless the sale is made with the express consent of a majority of the beneficiaries of the estate who together represent at least a 50 percent interest in the estate. In cases where there are minor beneficiaries or mentally incapable beneficiaries, the consent of the Children's Lawyer on behalf of minor and unascertained beneficiaries, and the consent of the Public Guardian and Trustee on behalf of mentally incapable beneficiaries who are not represented by attorneys or guardians for property, must be obtained in the place of the consent of such beneficiaries. The consent allows a purchaser, acting in good faith, purchasing for value and having no notice of the debts, to take the property free and clear of debt. Note, however, that the estate trustee may in some circumstances still be liable to a beneficiary who did not consent to the transfer. The liability to the beneficiary arises as a result of an automatic vesting of real property in the beneficiaries of an estate. The rule relating to automatic vesting is discussed below.

Automatic Vesting of Real Property After Three Years

When the administration of an estate involves real estate, it is important to know the rule relating to automatic vesting, contained in section 9(1) of the *Estates Administration Act*.[1] This rule holds that real property owned by a deceased that is not transferred within three years of the death of the deceased automatically vests in the persons who are beneficially entitled to it. In other words, upon the expiry of the three-year period, the beneficiaries of the estate automatically become the owners and can convey the property to third parties or put their own names on title to the property. Note that such vesting is subject to the debts of the estate—that is, creditors of the estate can continue to take legal action and satisfy their debts using the real property.

As indicated above, even if real property is transferred to a purchaser free and clear with the concurrence of a majority of beneficiaries representing 50 percent of the value of the estate, a beneficiary not consenting to the transfer would have a claim against the estate trustee for prejudicing her right to have the property vest in her at the expiry of the three-year period. The estate trustee can escape this kind of liability by obtaining consents from all beneficiaries of the estate before transferring the real property or obtaining a court order for sale that effectively eliminates the non-consenting beneficiary's claim. As seen in Chapter 2, if the deceased's will contains a power of sale clause, the estate trustee does not need to obtain the consents of the beneficiaries before selling the real property.

Note that the vesting under section 9(1) of the *Estates Administration Act* can be postponed by filing a caution on title to the property. The caution allows three more years to pass before the property vests. The Act also allows for subsequent cautions to be registered upon expiry of the previous three years, and so on from time to time, thus extending the period for vesting. Rules also come into play when the property is transferred to a beneficiary within the three-year period and the beneficiary subsequently transfers the property to a third party. Discussion of such rules, however, is outside the scope of this text.

---

1   RSO 1990, c E.22.

In this chapter, unless otherwise stated, any situations discussed assume that the transfer is made either for the purpose of paying debts of the estate or pursuant to a power of sale clause in the will. In other words, this chapter does not deal with transfers pursuant to vesting under the *Estates Administration Act*.

Statements About Payments of Debts

As will be seen, transfers of property to third parties must contain evidence in the form of statements by the estate trustee or a lawyer in a document called an acknowledgment and direction to the effect that all creditors have been notified and all debts of the estate have been paid. Such statements serve the purpose of establishing with reasonable certainty that the purchaser has no knowledge of any debts of the deceased. The practice has arisen, however, of making such statements even when some debts are still outstanding so long as funds to pay them have been set aside or allocated within the estate account.

Electronic Registration

Now that Ontario has implemented electronic land registration with respect to properties, a vendor of real property—that is, the estate trustee in the case of an estate—no longer signs a deed or transfer. Instead he signs an acknowledgment and direction authorizing his lawyer to sign the document electronically and effect the electronic registration of the document through Teraview, the software used to access the electronic land registration system. The onus of ensuring that proper documentation supports an electronic registration shifts onto the lawyer effecting the transfer. Whereas before electronic registration, the documentation would be checked by the staff of the land registry office, now the lawyer must ensure that the documentation is sufficient before registering electronically from her office.

Selling Real Property to a Third Party Where There Is a Certificate of Appointment of Estate Trustee

transmission application
application requesting the land registrar to amend the parcel register to show the owner of the property as the estate trustee or the estate

In selling real property to a third party where there is a certificate of appointment of estate trustee, the first step is the creation of a **transmission application** in Teraview, which is to be registered electronically by the lawyer once the estate trustee signs the accompanying acknowledgment and direction. The transmission application is, in effect, an application requesting the land registrar to amend the parcel register to show the owner of the property as the estate trustee. Included in the transmission application are so-called law statements confirming that the estate trustee has authority to act and the particulars of the certificate of appointment. Figure 10.5 is an example of an acknowledgment and direction for a transmission application and the transmission application itself. Once the transmission application is registered in Teraview, the parcel register for the property will reflect the estate trustee as the owner and he will then be in a position to transfer the real property to a third-party purchaser. To transfer the property to a purchaser, the lawyer will generate a **transfer by personal representative** in Teraview, along with another acknowledgment and direction for signing by the estate trustee. The estate trustee signs the acknowledgment and direction prior to the closing of the transaction and, on closing, the lawyer registers the transfer of the property to the purchaser.

transfer by personal representative
a transfer of real property by an estate trustee to a third party

This procedure is identical whether the deceased died testate or intestate, provided that there is a certificate of appointment of estate trustee.

FIGURE 10.5   **Electronic Transmission Application**

ACKNOWLEDGEMENT AND DIRECTION

TO: Gwendolyn Grat

(Insert lawyer's name)

AND TO: Grit, Grat & Groot

(Insert firm name)

RE: McNeil, Joyce - Transmission Application - 30 Country Lane, Burlington   ('the transaction")

(Insert brief description of transaction)

This will confirm that:

● I/We have reviewed the information set out this Acknowledgement and Direction and in the documents described below (the "Documents"), and that this information is accurate;

● You, your agent or employee are authorized and directed to sign, deliver, and/or register electronically, on my/our behalf the Documents in the form attached.

● You are hereby authorized and directed to enter into an escrow closing arrangement substantially in the form attached hereto being a copy of the version of the Document Registration Agreement, which appears on the website of the Law Society of Upper Canada as of the date of the Agreement of Purchase and sale herein. I/We hereby acknowledge the said Agreement has been reviewed by me/us and that I/We shall be bound by its terms;

● The effect of the Documents has been fully explained to me/us, and I/we understand that I/we are parties to and bound by the terms and provisions of the Documents to the same extent as if I/we had signed them; and

● I/We are in fact the parties named in the Documents and I/we have not misrepresented our identities to you.

● I, _____, am the spouse of _____, the (Transferor/Chargor), and hereby consent to the transaction described in the Acknowledgment and Direction. I authorize you to indicate my consent on all the Documents for which it is required.

DESCRIPTION OF ELECTRONIC DOCUMENTS

The Document(s) described in the Acknowledgement and Direction are the document(s) selected below which are attached hereto as "Document in Preparation" and are:

☐   A Transfer of the land described above.

☐   A Charge of the land described above.

☐   Other documents set out in Schedule "B" attached hereto.

Dated at _____ , this _____ day of _____ , 20___ .

WITNESS

(As to all signatures, if required)

_____   _____

                                         _____

                                         _____

                                         _____

FIGURE 10.5 CONTINUED

This document has not been submitted and may be incomplete.

		yyyy mm dd	Page 1 of 1
LRO # 20	**Transmission By Personal Representative-Land**	In preparation on 2018 07 08	at 10:11

Properties

PIN	07208 - 0227 LT
Description	PCL 811-1, SEC M15, LT 811, PL M15; BURLINGTON
Address	30 COUNTRY LANE BURLINGTON

Deceased(s)

Name	MCNEIL, JOYCE Acting as an individual
Address for Service	12 Main Street Burlington, Ontario L7R 2L2

Date of death was 2012/02/15

Applicant(s)

		Capacity	Share
Name	LOVE, MARTIN Acting as an individual	Estate Trustee With A Will	
Address for Service	12 Main Street Burlington, Ontario L7R 2L2		

The applicant is entitled to be the owner by law, as Estate Trustee of the estate of the deceased owner.

This document is not authorized under Power of Attorney by this party.

Statements

The debts of the deceased are paid in full

The applicant is appointed as Estate Trustee with a will by Ontario Superior Court of Justice Court, under file no. 12-1414, dated 2018/08/28 and is still in full force and effect.

Selling Real Property to a Third Party Where There Is No Certificate of Appointment of Estate Trustee

Testate Estate

Only in very limited circumstances can the real property be transferred to a purchaser where there is a will but no certificate of appointment of estate trustee. In the first place, it is in the discretion of the land registrar to permit the transfer. Currently the policy is that real property can be transferred in these circumstances only if the entire estate is worth less than $50,000. In such a case the lawyer must make a law statement to this effect.

Note that if the subject property is a "first dealing"—that is, the first transaction—after conversion of the property from the registry system to the land titles system, no certificate of appointment is necessary. To take advantage of this rule, the lawyer must make a statement as to the date of death, a spousal statement (indicating spousal status of the deceased), a statement that the will is the last will of the deceased and that it was properly executed and witnessed, and a statement that the will was not revoked by marriage or otherwise. The value of the estate must also be stated.

The procedure to transfer the property is to file a transmission application, including the statements discussed above. The estate trustee also has to sign a covenant—a promise—to indemnify the Land Titles Assurance Fund in the event that the transfer turns out to be improper and the fund is forced to compensate a prejudiced party. In such a case, the estate would be responsible for any such claims. Figure 10.6 is an example of a covenant to indemnify.

Again, because of the inherent dangers associated with distributing property without the protection given by a certificate of appointment, it is the author's opinion that even in the rare case that a transfer in land titles without a certificate of appointment of estate trustee with a will is permitted, it is usually advisable to obtain a certificate of appointment nonetheless.

Intestate Estate

As indicated above, real property cannot be transferred directly to a purchaser by an estate trustee where the deceased died without a will and where there is no certificate of appointment of estate trustee.

Transferring Real Property Directly to a Beneficiary Under a Devise or the Laws of Intestacy Where There Is a Certificate of Appointment of Estate Trustee

Again, if real property is to be transferred to a beneficiary of a devise under the will of the deceased or the laws of intestacy, the transfer procedure is the same as it would be if the property were being sold to a third-party purchaser. In addition, the estate trustee or her lawyer will prepare the land transfer tax affidavit for the beneficiary to sign.

FIGURE 10.6   Covenant to Indemnify

Relating to Transmission Application registered as VM99988889

LAND TITLES ACT
COVENANT TO INDEMNIFY THE LAND TITLES ASSURANCE FUND
Section 55 of the Act

This agreement made the 25th day of May, 2018.

Between:

> Nicholas Trip and Vanessa Little
> both of the City of Hamilton, Estate Trustees
> in the Estate of Grant Humlinson, deceased

and

> Her Majesty in right of Ontario

WHEREAS Grant Humlinson and Edith Humlinson were the registered owners as joint tenants of the lands registered as Parts 12 & 13, Plan 999, PIN 9989-9989 (LT);

AND WHEREAS Edith Humlinson died March 20, 1999;

AND WHEREAS a Survivorship Application following the death of Edith Humlinson was not made or registered;

AND WHEREAS Grant Humlinson died February 18, 2018;

AND WHEREAS the said Grant Humlinson left a will executed June 23, 2010 in which he appointed Nicholas Trip and Vanessa Little as estate trustees;

NOW THEREFORE the said Nicholas Trip and Vanessa Little ("the Covenantors"), in consideration of the Director of Land Titles for the Land Division of Wentworth (No. 62) registering the Transmission Application following the death of the said Grant Humlinson for the Covenantors, the Covenantors on behalf of themselves, their administrators, executors, estate trustees and assigns, covenant with Her Majesty the Queen in right of Ontario, her successors and assigns, from and against all loss or diminution of the assurance fund under the Land Titles Act, or established or continued under any other Act of the Province of Ontario, in respect of any valid claim that may hereafter be made on account of the circumstances set out in the recitals hereto and also against all costs in respect thereof and will pay such amount as anyone claiming as aforesaid may be adjudged to be entitled to recover in respect of the premises and costs.

IN WITNESS WHEREOF the said Covenantors have executed this Agreement.

SIGNED, SEALED AND DELIVERED   )
In the presence of:)
)
)
)   _Nicholas Trip_
)   _____
)   _Vanessa Little_
Mary Ross   )   _____
_____

Note Regarding Land Transfer Tax

There are special rules relating to land transfer tax when real property is distributed directly to beneficiaries of an estate. The default situation is that no land transfer tax is payable by the beneficiaries for receiving the real property from the estate. The land transfer tax statements will indicate that nothing of value was paid for the property.

Land transfer tax may be payable, however, if the real property is transferred to more than one beneficiary of the residual assets of an estate. In such a case the Ministry of Finance website indicates that such a transfer of real property "may or may not attract land transfer tax" and invites persons to contact the ministry for advice on the specific situation. The Ministry of Finance website containing this information is <http://www.fin.gov.on.ca/en/tax/ltt/faq.html>.

Note Regarding Mortgages Attached to the Real Property

Under section 32 of the *Succession Law Reform Act*,[2] if a beneficiary receives real property pursuant to a devise in a will, unless the will states otherwise, the beneficiary takes the property subject to any mortgage against it. If the beneficiary takes the real property as part of a gift under the will, the amount deducted from that beneficiary's share of the estate is the value of the real property less the mortgage.

If the beneficiary of a devise of real property that is subject to a mortgage is not a beneficiary of any other gifts under the will, and is not willing or able to assume the mortgage or obtain a new mortgage, the estate trustee will probably be forced to sell the real property in order to pay out the mortgage. The balance of the funds from the transaction would then normally be paid to the beneficiary of the devise.

Section 32 can be overridden by a provision in the will indicating a contrary intention. The standard clause directing the estate trustee to pay the debts of the estate, however, is typically not enough to establish such a contrary intention.

Transferring Real Property Directly to a Beneficiary Under a Devise or the Laws of Intestacy Where There Is No Certificate of Appointment of Estate Trustee

Testate Estate

Where there is a will but no certificate of appointment of estate trustee with a will, the transfer of real property can be made to a beneficiary of the estate provided that the total value of the estate is less than $50,000. In such a case, the transfer can be made by following the same steps as in the case of selling the property to a third-party purchaser.

Intestate Estate

As indicated above, if there is no will and no certificate of appointment of estate trustee, a direct transfer of real property to a beneficiary of the estate cannot be made. Again though, section 9(1) of the *Estates Administration Act* dealing with vesting may come into play.

---

2   RSO 1990, c S.26.

Direct Transfers to Survivors That Bypass the Estate

As indicated in the introduction to this chapter, transferring assets to persons with right of survivorship is not, strictly speaking, estate work. Nevertheless, it often falls to lawyers acting for estate trustees to prepare whatever documents are necessary to effect such transfers.

In the case of real property owned by two or more persons, ownership will automatically pass to the surviving owner or owners upon the death of the deceased owner provided that the land was owned in joint tenancy. The registration record, however, must still be changed. Strictly, such a change only has to be made immediately before the surviving joint tenant either mortgages or sells the property. Nevertheless, most lawyers suggest that the registrations should be made within a reasonable time after the death of the deceased owner because, if the surviving joint tenant dies before the registrations are done, the procedure for transferring the property to the second owner's beneficiaries is slightly more onerous.

The procedure for amending the parcel register to delete the name of the deceased joint tenant and show the surviving joint tenant(s) as the new owner(s) is to prepare and submit a survivorship application.

In the event that the surviving joint owner dies before the first deceased joint tenant's name is deleted from the records, the estate trustee of the second deceased joint tenant must register a transmission application and, in the case of electronic registration, the lawyer must make law statements as to the date of death and the particulars of the certificate of appointment of estate trustee with respect to the estate of the second deceased. The transmission application puts the property into the name of the estate trustee of the second deceased person. Along with the transmission application, the estate trustee must file a covenant to indemnify the Land Titles Assurance Fund.

Legal Actions

Sometimes a person dies while pursuing a legal action against another party (or with a right of action that has not yet been formally pursued). In such a case, the future claim for damages is a form of asset that falls to the estate trustee to manage. It becomes the estate trustee's obligation to assess the likelihood of success of the action combined with the risks associated with continuing to pursue such an action. The fact that the deceased is no longer available to give evidence in the action may certainly be a factor, but such assessment can be properly undertaken only with legal advice. If the conclusion is that the action is worth pursuing, it is the estate trustee's obligation to continue to pursue the action on behalf of the beneficiaries of the estate. In such a case rule 11 of the *Rules of Civil Procedure*[3] is used to officially change the title of the proceedings by replacing the deceased's name with the name of the estate trustee "as estate trustee for estate of [the deceased]."

Note that section 38 of the *Trustee Act*[4] specifically allows an estate trustee to maintain an action for all torts and injuries to the deceased or to the deceased's property. However,

---

3 RRO 1990, reg 194.
4 RSO 1990, c T.23.

section 38 also provides that actions for libel and slander cannot be continued and that the estate trustee cannot maintain an action for the deceased's loss of expectation of life if the tort led to the deceased's death. Loss of expectation of life has been held in case law to include loss of future income.

Assets Arising as a Result of Death

The assets discussed above are those that were owned by the deceased and thereby fall into the estate. This last section of the chapter discusses some of the assets that arise by virtue of the deceased's death. Such assets are also assets of the estate and must be gathered in and distributed by the estate trustee.

Canada Pension Plan and Other Government Benefits

The Canada Pension Plan death benefit is a lump-sum benefit available to estates of deceased persons who paid into the Canada Pension Plan for a minimum of three years. The death benefit is intended to help pay for the funeral of the deceased. If there is no estate trustee, the death benefit can be received by the survivor of the deceased person who was responsible for arranging and paying for the funeral (the order of priority of persons entitled to the benefit in such a case is the married or common law spouse, followed by the "next of kin"). The maximum amount currently available for the death benefit is $2,500. A death benefit application form is often supplied by the funeral director and can also be obtained through Employment and Social Development Canada.

Note in this context that a deceased person who was receiving payments under the Canada Pension Plan or the Old Age Security Plan is entitled to any payments receivable during the month of death. Payments received after that month, whether by cheque or by direct deposit into the deceased's bank account, must be returned to Employment and Social Development Canada. This government department usually appreciates it if the estate trustee also sends proof of death with the returned payments.

If the payments received during the month of death are by cheque payable to the deceased, it may be necessary to send them back to Employment and Social Development Canada with the request that they be reissued in the name of the estate of the deceased. This step has to be taken where a financial institution is unwilling to honour the cheques as payable to the deceased himself.

While it is not within the duties of the estate trustee to do so, estate trustees often help the spouse of the deceased to complete the forms necessary to obtain the available survivor's benefits (ongoing payments) under the deceased's pensions. Such pensions may include the Canada Pension Plan, a teacher's pension, or a private pension (discussed below). Another ongoing public pension that is available to the surviving spouse or common law partner of the deceased, in limited circumstances, is the Canada Pension Plan Survivor Pension. Information about these benefits can be obtained at <http://www.canada.ca/en/services/benefits/publicpensions/cpp/cpp-survivor-pension.html>. This allowance is available to certain low-income persons between the ages of 60 and 64 inclusive.

Death Benefits from Private Pensions

It is the duty of the estate trustee to make inquiries at the place of employment or previous employment of the deceased to determine whether any death benefits are available through a private pension or otherwise. If there are death benefits, and if such death benefits are payable to the estate, the estate trustee must see to it that the proper documentation is submitted in order to receive such benefits. Death benefits from private pensions are usually only available to survivors of the deceased, in which case the estate trustee may assist the payee of the benefits.

Life Insurance

If the deceased had life insurance with no surviving beneficiary, or if the beneficiary is the estate itself, the proceeds belong to the estate. In such a case, it falls on the estate trustee to contact the insurance company to make a claim for the proceeds—that is, to ask what documentation is required and to ensure that the documentation is completed and submitted. Typically, such documentation includes a doctor's certification as to the cause of death.

The estate trustee is advised to seek legal advice as to the advisability of bringing an action against the insurance company, including any applicable limitation period, in the event that there is some difficulty in obtaining the insurance funds.

Again, an estate trustee often assists a beneficiary of life insurance, other than the estate itself, in obtaining the proceeds even though this is not, strictly speaking, estate administration work.

Overpayment of Estate Administration Tax

Any overpayment of estate administration tax submitted with the application for a certificate of appointment must be recovered by the estate trustee as an asset of the estate. Such an overpayment arises when the application for a certificate of appointment included a higher value of the estate than what turned out to be its actual value. The procedure for obtaining a refund is to submit an application under rule 38 of the *Rules of Civil Procedure* to the court from which the certificate of appointment was issued. The application includes an affidavit of the estate trustee setting out the reason for the overpayment, a draft order, a copy of the certificate of appointment of estate trustee and any other documentation that may assist the court. It is also important to note that in the event that the estate trustee obtains a refund of estate administration tax, the estate trustee must file a revised estate information return with the Ministry of Finance within 30 days of receipt of the refund.

KEY TERMS

declaration of transmission, 189
devise, 200
letter of direction for transfer and sale of shares, 191
medallion signature guarantee, 192

stock power of attorney, 191
transfer by personal representative, 202
transmission application, 202

REVIEW QUESTIONS

1. How do you transfer financial institution assets into the estate (a) with a certificate of appointment, and (b) without such certificate?

2. What issue needs to be determined in the case of bank accounts (and other assets held by financial institutions) that are in the name of the deceased and another person?

3. In connection with the transfer of publicly traded stocks and other securities, describe the purpose of the following:

   a. declaration of transmission,

   b. stock power of attorney,

   c. medallion signature guarantee, and

   d. letter of direction.

4. What documentation is required in order to transfer Canada savings bonds to a beneficiary (a) with a certificate of appointment, and (b) without a certificate of appointment?

5. Identify two documents that may be required in order to replace lost stock certificates or bonds.

6. What is a gift *in specie*?

7. Explain how the following assets are transferred to a beneficiary:

   a. personal effects and household furniture

   b. motor vehicles

   c. business assets

   d. loans and debts owing to the deceased

8. What does the *Estates Administration Act* provide with respect to the vesting of real property owned by a deceased?

9. What clause in a will is designed to prevent the vesting of real property owned by a deceased?

10. What is the effect of the registration of a transmission application?

11. What important information must be covered by the law statements in the acknowledgment and direction for a transmission application?

12. When is a covenant to indemnify the Land Titles Assurance Fund required?

13. If a certificate of appointment has not been applied for in an estate, explain how the real property of the deceased can be transferred in the following circumstances:

    a. the deceased died intestate

    b. the deceased died testate

14. In the case of a gift in a will of real property that is subject to a mortgage, is the mortgage paid out by the estate before the property is transferred to the beneficiary?

15. Provide an example of a direct transfer of real property which bypasses the estate.

16. List three possible assets that may arise on death and identify which of those assets form part of the estate.

17. What should an estate trustee do about an overpayment of estate administration tax?

Determining, Notifying, and Paying Creditors of the Estate

LEARNING OUTCOMES

After reading this chapter, you should be able to:

- Explain the circumstances when it is and is not advisable to advertise for creditors of the estate

- Recount some common creditors of an estate, and understand the specifics involved in settling each account

- Describe some of the common issues involved in settling the deceased's account with the Canada Revenue Agency, including outstanding tax returns, terminal tax returns, and voluntary disclosure

- Understand the significance of a Canada Revenue Agency clearance certificate and how to obtain one

- Know the special rules involved in settling insolvent estates

Introduction

Any debts owed by the deceased during his lifetime that are still owed as of the date of death are debts of the estate. The estate itself also incurs debts, such as the funeral account (unless it was prepaid by the deceased), estate income taxes, estate administration tax, and professional fees. The persons or entities to whom these debts are owed are all creditors of the estate. As discussed in Chapter 3, Interpretation of Wills, the creditors of the estate take priority over any beneficiaries. Therefore, the estate trustee must ensure that all the creditors are paid, or at least that sufficient funds in the estate are set aside or allocated to pay them, before distributing the estate to the beneficiaries. It is also the estate trustee's obligation to determine who the creditors are and to ensure that they receive sufficient notification of the death of the deceased so that they may make a claim against the estate before it is distributed.

The mechanism put in place by the law to ensure that estate trustees act responsibly toward the creditors of the estate is to make estate trustees personally liable for the debts of the estate. This personal liability is subject to two qualifications: (1) the estate trustee will be held personally liable for the debts of the estate only to the extent that the estate, properly administered, would be able to pay such debts; and (2) if the estate trustee proceeds properly with respect to her obligation to determine the creditors, she will be absolved of liability for creditors of which she is unaware. It is therefore a very important part of the lawyer's job to ensure that the estate trustee is advised on the proper procedure for notifying and paying creditors. This chapter discusses the procedures for determining who the creditors are, notifying them, and paying them.

Advertising for Creditors

While the estate trustee would probably know about all of the persons or entities to whom the estate became indebted after the estate trustee began to administer the estate, he may not be aware of all of the persons or entities who were owed money by the deceased during her lifetime. Obviously this poses a problem because ultimately the estate trustee has a duty to pay the beneficiaries of the estate. As indicated, if a creditor comes forward after the estate is distributed but before the limitation period for the debt expires, the estate trustee could be held personally liable for the debt. Even if the deceased left a list of assets and liabilities, as discussed in Chapter 1, Wills, in most circumstances it would be too risky for the estate trustee to rely on the list, because the list may be incomplete through inadvertence on the part of the deceased or simply because it is not up to date.

The solution is the advertisement for creditors. If it is done properly, and no creditors come forward in response to the advertisement within the time period specified in it, an estate trustee is absolved of liability to creditors of which he has no knowledge. While this mechanism protects the estate trustee from liability, it is important to note that it will not absolve him from liability from creditors of the estate of which he has actual knowledge or of which he reasonably ought to have knowledge, even if that particular creditor does not come forward in response to the advertisement.

Drafting and Running the Advertisement

An advertisement for creditors does not absolve an estate trustee from liability unless it is done properly—that is, in accordance with the local legal practice. The Toronto legal community, for example, has an accepted practice for drafting and running such advertisements that may vary from the practice in Hamilton, Thunder Bay, or any other jurisdiction in Ontario. The variations may be in the wording of the advertisement, the number of times it should be run, the days of the week on which it should be run, and the local newspaper in which it should be run. If the lawyer is acting for an estate trustee in an area that she is unfamiliar with, the lawyer will usually have the law clerk make inquiries in the local legal community to determine the accepted local practice.

Despite the variations referred to above, there are similarities of practice among the various court jurisdictions within Ontario. The wording of the advertisements is generally the same. Figure 11.1 is an example of an advertisement for creditors. It is, of course, essential that the advertisement not contain any errors. After receiving instructions from the lawyer or law clerk, some newspapers will send a letter to the lawyer or law clerk that sets out a draft of the advertisement. It is then up to the lawyer to check the draft and report back to the newspaper with any changes or to indicate that the draft is acceptable. As a word of caution, however, a lawyer should not rely on receiving such a draft before publication.

FIGURE 11.1   Advertisement for Creditors

Notice to Creditors and Others

IN THE ESTATE OF Susan Mann

ALL CLAIMS against the Estate of Susan Mann, retired lawyer, late of the City of Hamilton, who died on or about the 5th day of February, 2018, must be filed with the undersigned by the 21st day of July, 2018, after which date the Estate will be distributed having regard only to the claims then filed.

DATED AT HAMILTON this 16th day of June, 2018.

GRIT, GRAT & GROOT
Barristers & Solicitors
15 Cross Street
Toronto, Ontario
M5A 1Q1

Solicitors for the estate trustee

Waiving the Advertisement

Sometimes the estate trustee is sufficiently confident of his knowledge of the deceased's affairs that he does not feel the need to advertise for creditors. If the estate trustee has decided not to advertise, it is a good practice for the lawyer acting for the estate trustee to have the estate trustee sign an acknowledgment, as in Figure 11.2, that he has been fully informed about the liabilities and risks associated with not advertising.

FIGURE 11.2 Acknowledgment

Re In the matter of the estate of Clifford Winchester, deceased

THE UNDERSIGNED hereby acknowledges that GWENDOLYN GRAT, the solicitor in the said estate, has advised of the desirability of advertising for creditors and the possible legal consequences of failing to so advertise including the possibility of the estate trustee's becoming personally liable for debts of the deceased and, notwithstanding such advice, has instructed the said solicitor NOT to advertise for creditors in this estate.

Dated at Hamilton, this 16th day of July, 2018.

Carolyn Macartney

Carolyn Macartney

Paying Creditors

Once it is determined who the creditors are and that their claims are valid, paying them simply involves sending cheques written on the estate account and asking that the creditors return acknowledgments of receipt of payment. Such acknowledgments of receipt are called **vouchers**, and they are very important to have on hand when it comes time to account to the beneficiaries (and creditors if need be) when winding up the estate (see Chapter 12, Accounting to the Beneficiaries and Paying the Beneficiaries). Because of the importance of vouchers, the lawyer or estate trustee should send with each payment a stamped, self-addressed envelope along with a letter requesting that the enclosed invoice or bill be receipted and returned or that a separate receipt be returned.

This section describes the particular issues involved in paying some of the more common creditors of an estate.

voucher
acknowledgment of receipt of payment

Funeral Account

If the funeral account is not prepaid, the estate has to pay for the funeral of the deceased. In that event it is, strictly speaking (and perhaps in consultation with members of the immediate family of the deceased), the estate trustee who is responsible for arranging the funeral. This can sometimes pose difficulties in an emotional family situation. Because there can be a great variation in the cost of a funeral, the question will inevitably arise of how much should be spent on the funeral. The answer is that, under the common law, the funeral should be in keeping with the economic and other circumstances of the deceased during her lifetime. A disproportionately expensive funeral for a person whose position in society and financial means were somewhat humble could expose the estate trustee to personal liability to the creditors or beneficiaries of the estate if the amount spent is later deemed to be excessive.

Rented Properties

Under section 91 of the *Residential Tenancies Act, 2006*,[1] where the deceased is the sole tenant in a residential unit, the tenancy is deemed to be terminated 30 days after the death. Thus, if a person dies on June 15, the tenancy is terminated on July 15 regardless of what kind of tenancy or lease governed the relationship between the landlord and the deceased tenant. The deceased's estate trustee would owe the landlord rent to July 15 that, presumably, would be calculated on a daily basis. If, for example, the rent were $750 per month and payable in advance on the first day of the month, the amount owing for July 1 to July 15 would be $750 × 12 divided by 365 (or 366, if a leap year) × 15 (for the number of days in July). The rent owing to the landlord would therefore be $369.86 for July. If it is proved that the deceased tenant was in arrears of rent, the arrears would, of course, also have to be paid. On the other hand, the deceased tenant may be entitled to any prepaid rent (such as a deposit toward the last month's rent) as well as interest on the rent. The Landlord and Tenant Board should be consulted to determine the applicable interest rate for the period in question.

Credit Card Debts

Credit card companies should immediately be notified of the death of the deceased and, at the same time, a balance owing on the account should be requested. If the estate appears to be solvent, the amount owing should then be sent to the company with the usual request for a voucher.

Some credit card companies ask the estate trustee to return the card(s), and this should be done by registered mail. Some lawyers advise that the card(s) be cut up and the pieces mailed. In all other cases, the estate trustee should destroy the card(s).

Utility Bills

Any utility bills—for example, gas, hydro, and water—that are owing on the deceased's residence for the period in which the deceased was responsible for the premises should be paid. If the deceased was the owner of the premises, the utility bills must be paid until the premises are sold or otherwise transferred and the premises are no longer in the control of the estate trustee. When investigating any amounts owing, inquire about any deposits that might be held by the utility company that can be offset against the amounts owing or, in some cases, be paid to the estate to be added to the assets.

---

1 SO 2006, c 17.

Mortgages

If the deceased was a mortgagor (the borrower) and there are arrears owing on the mortgage, the estate trustee must pay not only any arrears but all other mortgage payments as they come due. If funds are not immediately available, it is important for the estate trustee to contact the mortgagee (the lender, usually a bank or other financial institution), because any default in payment of a mortgage typically gives the mortgagee the right to call in the loan. Financial institutions usually allow a tolerance for default until the estate trustee organizes the estate accounts, although this should not be assumed.

A provision in section 8 of the *Estates Administration Act*[2] addresses the enforcement of mortgages against deceased persons. In an action to enforce the terms of the mortgage, if there is no estate trustee in an estate, the mortgagee can name the persons beneficially entitled to the property as the defendants.

Outstanding Loans

If the deceased owed any money in the form of loans, even to private persons, such loans constitute debts of the estate and must be paid. As with all other creditors, the estate trustee must be satisfied that there is sufficient proof of the loan and the balance owing before making any payments.

Overpayments of Government Benefits

Many government bodies make automatic payments to people during their lifetime. Examples of such government bodies are Veterans Affairs Canada, Employment and Social Development Canada (Canada Pension Plan, Old Age Security, and Employment Insurance), and the Ministry of Community and Social Services (Ontario Disability Support Program). In most cases, the government payments cease upon death, although, as in the case of Canada Pension Plan and Old Age Security, the estate is entitled to the payments received for the month of death.

As explained in Chapter 10, Collecting the Assets, it is important to notify the government body making the payments that the person has died. This is usually done by sending a death certificate or a notarial copy of the certificate, along with a letter providing the deceased's account number and other relevant particulars.

Also, as explained in Chapter 10, if the estate trustee has cheques payable to the deceased for the month of death, they should be returned to the government body with a request that they be reissued in the name of the estate. Cheques for later months must be returned. If such payments were made by direct deposit into a bank account, it is the estate trustee's obligation to see that those amounts are refunded because, until they are, they constitute debts of the estate.

Professional and Expert Fees

Fees to professionals or experts hired to perform work or provide advice in administering the estate usually constitute debts of the estate. Such professionals and experts include the

---

2 RSO 1990, c E.22.

lawyer acting for the estate trustee, an accountant who is hired to provide income tax advice or prepare tax returns, and appraisers of personal and real property.

The estate trustee should, however, be cautious in retaining such outside help because when it comes time for the estate trustee to account to the beneficiaries (discussed in detail in Chapter 12), it may be decided that certain of the fees charged by professionals constitute debts of the estate trustee rather than debts of the estate. In other words, payment of such professionals would come out of the estate trustee's compensation rather than the estate. Such a finding could be made on the basis that the jobs performed by such professionals would normally be work performed by the estate trustee.

Claims Against the Estate by Persons Other Than Creditors

Various claims can be made against an estate by persons who are not, strictly speaking, creditors. Such claims include a surviving spouse's right to claim part of the estate under the *Family Law Act*[3] election and a dependant's claim for support (both dealt with in Chapter 16, Statutory Forms of Estate Litigation). In addition, the deceased may have been party to a contract, either under the *Family Law Act* or otherwise, which requires him to have drafted the will in a certain way.

If such claims are made, it may be that the estate trustee has good reason to defend them, in which case the matter may have to proceed to litigation. On the other hand, if the claims are valid, the claimants must be treated in the same way as creditors of the estate. As in the case of creditors, if the estate is distributed and a claim is then successfully made against the estate, the estate trustee can be held liable for the amount of the claim that would have been covered by the estate but for the actions of the estate trustee. In this regard, the six-month limitation period for making a *Family Law Act* election or bringing a dependant's relief application under the *Succession Law Reform Act*[4] must be noted by the estate trustee.

As in the case of legal actions of the deceased that can be continued by the estate trustee (discussed in Chapter 10), it is possible that the deceased was defending a legal action brought by another party at the time of the deceased's death. In such a case, the other party is not technically a creditor because the deceased's liability has yet to be established. The other party is, however, able to make use of rule 11 of the *Rules of Civil Procedure*[5] to continue the action. The action would then be continued against the estate trustee in her capacity as estate trustee, and any judgment obtained is paid from the estate as are other creditors (if there is no estate trustee, the other party is able to use rule 11 to appoint a person to represent the estate for the purpose of the litigation). When faced with a legal action against the deceased, it is incumbent on the estate trustee to obtain legal advice about whether to continue to defend or to negotiate a settlement. The decision in this regard must be based on what is in the best interests of the estate (that is, the creditors and the beneficiaries).

---

3 RSO 1990, c F.3.

4 RSO 1990, c S.26.

5 RRO 1990, reg 194.

Estate Administration Tax (Ministry of Finance)

As indicated in Chapter 8, Preliminary Steps in Applying for a Certificate of Appointment of Estate Trustee, when applying for a certificate of appointment, the prospective estate trustee must pay a deposit to the court representing the estate administration tax owing. The amount owing is based on the value of all of the assets of the estate, including assets that arise as a result of the death of the deceased—for example, life insurance payable to the estate. The tax is payable to the minister of finance. While in some cases the deposit will cover the full amount payable to this important creditor, the estate trustee has continuing obligations with respect to estate administration tax. These continuing obligations are discussed below.

Estate Information Return

Under the regulation to the *Estate Administration Tax Act, 1998,*[6] the estate trustee must file an estate information return with the minister of finance within 90 days of obtaining the certificate of appointment. Figure 11.3 is a reproduction of the estate information return. As can be seen, all information relevant to the deceased, the assets of the estate, and the amount of estate administration tax must be reported on the return. The estate information return is filed with the minister by mailing it to 33 King Street West, PO Box 625, Oshawa, Ontario, L1H 8H9. Note that section 2 of the regulation under the Act states that an estate information return is deemed to be given to the minister on the day on which it is received by the minister. This means that an estate trustee should mail the return at least a week before the end of the 90-day period.

In a situation of urgency and hardship, where the payment of the deposit is not made at the time of applying for the certificate of appointment, the estate information return must contain a copy of the order allowing delayed payment and details about the security provided to the court.

As will be seen below, there are circumstances where it will be necessary for the estate trustee to file a revised estate information return.

Underpayment of Estate Administration Tax

As seen in Chapter 10, the estate trustee must apply for a refund of any overpayment of estate administration tax because such overpayment is an asset of the estate. Conversely, the estate trustee must ensure that any underpayment of estate administration tax is paid because it is a debt of the estate. Underpayments of estate administration tax can arise in a number of different ways, such as where a previously given estimate of the value of one or more assets was too low or where new property is discovered. In whatever manner it arises, if the value of the estate turns out to be more than initially reported, any underpayment will have to be corrected.

The procedure for paying the additional estate administration tax is to submit to the court an affidavit setting out the circumstances, as shown in Figure 11.4, along with a cheque or bank draft payable to the minister of finance representing the amount of the underpayment.

It will then be incumbent upon the estate trustee to file a revised estate information return showing the new information.

---

6 SO 1998, c 34, Sched.

FIGURE 11.3   Affidavit Regarding Corrected Value of the Estate

Ontario

Ministry of Finance
33 King St W
PO Box 625
Oshawa ON L1H 8H9

Enquiries: 1 866 ONT-TAXS (1 866 668-8297)
1 800 263-7776 Teletypewriter (TTY)
1 866 888-3850 (Fax)

Estate Information Return
Estate Administration Tax Act, 1998

Page 1 of 7

Ministry Use Only - Date Received

If you received a certificate of appointment of estate trustee from the Ontario Superior Court of Justice, this return **must** be completed and **received by the Ministry of Finance within 90 calendar days** after the certificate of appointment of estate trustee is issued. It will be used by the Ministry of Finance to administer the *Estate Administration Tax Act, 1998*.

If after submitting this return, you discover information was incorrect or incomplete, an amended return must be received by the Ministry of Finance **within 30 calendar days** from when the error or additional information about the property of the estate is known. See guide for additional information.

Is this an Amended Return?
(if yes, check ✓ box) . . . . ☐   Please explain below why this return is being amended ▼

Reason: (Note: If the return is amended due to a fulfillment of an undertaking, include particulars and amounts of additional tax paid.)

A **Information about the Certificate of Appointment of Estate Trustee**

Indicate which type of certificate of appointment of estate trustee was granted by the Court (please choose one)

Form No.

☑ 74.13 Certificate of Appointment of Estate Trustee with a Will

☐ 74.13.1 Certificate of Appointment of Estate Trustee with a Will Limited to the Assets Referred to in the Will

☐ 74.20 Certificate of Appointment of Estate Trustee without a Will

☐ 74.20.3 Certificate of Appointment of Foreign Estate Trustee's Nominee as Estate Trustee without a Will

☐ 74.28 Confirmation by Resealing of Appointment of Estate Trustee

☐ 74.29 Certificate of Ancillary Appointment of Estate Trustee with a Will

Date (yyyy/mm/dd)

Enter the date above Certificate/Confirmation was issued . . . . . . | 2017/02/15 |

Enter the Court File No. assigned . . . . | 1 | 2 | 3 | 4 | 5 | 6 | | | | | | | |

Which Superior Court of Justice in Ontario was used to file your application? (please specify location)

| Ostcliff |

	Yes	No	Date of Undertaking (yyyy/mm/dd)
Was the deposit amount submitted based on an estimated value of the estate? If yes, please attach a copy of the undertaking submitted to the court.	☑	☐	2016/12/12

	Yes	No
Was the certificate of appointment of estate trustee issued without payment of deposit equal to tax?	☐	☑

(subsections 4(1) and (2) of the *Estate Administration Tax Act, 1998*)

If yes, please attach a copy of the court order and details about the security provided to the court.

9955E (2016/08)   © Queen's Printer for Ontario, 2016   Disponible en français

FIGURE 11.3 CONTINUED

Court File No.

| 1 | 2 | 3 | 4 | 5 | 6 | | | | | | | | | |

B **Deceased Person Information**

First Name

Neno

Middle Name (s)

Jurica

Last Name

Josko

If the deceased was known by any other name(s), please enter

Date of Birth (yyyy/mm/dd)

1940/11/23

Date of Death (yyyy/mm/dd)

2016/10/11

Address - Last Place of Residence (do NOT use post office box)

Unit/Apt/Suite   Street Number and Name (Postal Stn/Rural Route)

34 Shadelake Lane

City/Town

Finnville

Province/State ▼   Postal/Zip Code

ON   L2C 3V5

Country

Canada

C **Estate Representative Information** (For additional representatives, attach a separate list.)

First Name

Iva

Middle Name

Jelka

Last Name

Josko

Business Name (if applicable)

Title

Telephone Number

905 555-5555

Extension   Fax Number   Email Address

Mailing Address

Unit/Apt/Suite   Street Number and Name (Postal Stn/Rural Route)

107   376 Swynport Avenue North

City/Town

Finnville

Province/State ▼   Postal/Zip Code

ON   L2C 4N8

Country

Canada

9955E (2015/08)

Details of Estate Assets

Page 3 of 7

Court File No.
1 2 3 4 5 6

List the fair market value of **all** assets and the balance of all bank accounts of the deceased at the date of death. If the court issued a Certificate of Appointment of Estate Trustee with a Will Limited to the Assets Referred to in the Will, only those assets included in such will are to be listed. If the court issued a Confirmation by Resealing of Appointment of Estate Trustee, a Certificate of Ancillary Appointment of an Estate Trustee with a Will, or a Certificate of Appointment of Foreign Estate Trustee's Nominee as Estate Trustee without a Will, only those assets located in Ontario are to be included. Only the value of encumbrances that are registered against real estate should be subtracted. Enter dollar amounts only (no cents).

D Real Estate in Ontario

Please also include assets/properties in which the deceased had an equitable interest, even though legal title was held by a person other than the deceased. (refer to guide)

Property 1 - Assessment Roll No. 23-98-34-4-359-00387-0012-01	Property Identifier No. (PIN) 457987	$ Fair Market Value (at date of death) 425,000
Address - Unit/Apt/Suite, Street Number and Name, Postal Stn/Rural Route 34 Shadelake Lane		Percentage of Ownership X 100 %
		Value of Percentage Owned 425,000
		Subtract: Encumbrances (see guide) 91,243
City/Town Finnville	Province Postal Code ON L2C 3V5	$ **Net Value** 333,757

Property 2 - Assessment Roll No.	Property Identifier No. (PIN)	$ Fair Market Value (at date of death)
Address - Unit/Apt/Suite, Street Number and Name, Postal Stn/Rural Route		Percentage of Ownership X %
		Value of Percentage Owned
		Subtract: Encumbrances (see guide)
City/Town	Province Postal Code ON	$ **Net Value**

Property 3 - Assessment Roll No.	Property Identifier No. (PIN)	$ Fair Market Value (at date of death)
Address - Unit/Apt/Suite, Street Number and Name, Postal Stn/Rural Route		Percentage of Ownership X %
		Value of Percentage Owned
		Subtract: Encumbrances (see guide)
City/Town	Province Postal Code ON	$ **Net Value**

Attach separate list(s) if required.

Total Net Value of all Ontario Real Estate
- for percentage owned by the deceased at date of death
Include amounts from separate list(s).   ▶ [1] $ 333,757

9955E (2015/08)

FIGURE 11.3 CONTINUED

Court File No.

Page 4 of 7 | 1 | 2 | 3 | 4 | 5 | 6 | | | | | | | | |

Details of Estate Assets continued

E Bank Accounts (list details from all financial institutions in Canadian Funds - include credit unions and caisses populaires)

Bank Account 1 - Name of Financial Institution			Account Number
DFG First Mortgage Trust			345-346378
Address - Unit/Apt/Suite, Street Number and Name, Postal Stn/Rural Route			$ Balance (at date of death)
45 Main Street			23,457
City/Town			Percentage of Ownership
Finnville			X 100 %
Province/State	Postal/Zip Code	Country	$ Value of Percentage Owned
ON	L2C 4T7	Canada	23,457

Bank Account 2 - Name of Financial Institution			Account Number
DFG First Mortgage Trust			345-346462
Address - Unit/Apt/Suite, Street Number and Name, Postal Stn/Rural Route			$ Balance (at date of death)
45 Main Street South			4,526
City/Town			Percentage of Ownership
Finnville			X 100 %
Province/State	Postal/Zip Code	Country	$ Value of Percentage Owned
ON	L2C 4T7	Canada	4,526

Bank Account 3 - Name of Financial Institution			Account Number
Address - Unit/Apt/Suite, Street Number and Name, Postal Stn/Rural Route			$ Balance (at date of death)
City/Town			Percentage of Ownership
			X %
Province/State	Postal/Zip Code	Country	$ Value of Percentage Owned

Bank Account 4 - Name of Financial Institution			Account Number
Address - Unit/Apt/Suite, Street Number and Name, Postal Stn/Rural Route			$ Balance (at date of death)
City/Town			Percentage of Ownership
			X %
Province/State	Postal/Zip Code	Country	$ Value of Percentage Owned

Attach separate list(s) if required.

Total Value of all Bank Accounts
- for percentage owned by the deceased at date of death
Include amounts from separate list(s).   ▶ | 2 | $ 27,983

9955E (2015/08)

Details of Estate Assets continued   Page 5 of 7

Court File No.

| 1 | 2 | 3 | 4 | 5 | 6 | | | | | | | |

F **Investments** (list type and details of all shares, stocks, bonds, other investments, etc.)

Investment 1 - Name of Issuer	Number of Units
Foretest Mutual Investment Group	350

Type and Details of Instrument or Account No.	
Mutual Fund 28549-3452	

Name of Broker/Agent	Telephone No.
Sabina Dianal	905 555-5533

Address of Broker/Agent - Unit/Apt/Suite, Street Number and Name, Postal Stn/Rural Route	$ Fair Market Value (at date of death)
10 Main Street South	12,479

City/Town	Percentage of Ownership
Finnville	X 100 %

Province/State	Postal/Zip Code	Country	$ Value of Percentage Owned
ON	L2C 4R9	Canada	12,479

Investment 2 - Name of Issuer	Number of Units

Type and Details of Instrument or Account No.	

Name of Broker/Agent	Telephone No.

Address of Broker/Agent - Unit/Apt/Suite, Street Number and Name, Postal Stn/Rural Route	$ Fair Market Value (at date of death)

City/Town	Percentage of Ownership
	X %

Province/State	Postal/Zip Code	Country	$ Value of Percentage Owned

Investment 3 - Name of Issuer	Number of Units

Type and Details of Instrument or Account No.	

Name of Broker/Agent	Telephone No.

Address of Broker/Agent - Unit/Apt/Suite, Street Number and Name, Postal Stn/Rural Route	$ Fair Market Value (at date of death)

City/Town	Percentage of Ownership
	X %

Province/State	Postal/Zip Code	Country	$ Value of Percentage Owned

Attach separate list(s) if required.

Total Value of all Investments
- for percentage owned by the deceased at date of death
Include amounts from separate list(s).   ▶ $ 12,479   [3]

9955E (2015/08)

FIGURE 11.3 CONTINUED

Details of Estate Assets continued   Page 6 of 7

Court File No.
| 1 | 2 | 3 | 4 | 5 | 6 | | | | | | | | | |

G Vehicles and Vessels (include motorcycles, boats, all-terrain vehicles, bicycles, snowmobiles, etc.)

Vehicle/Vessel 1 - Vehicle Identification No. (VIN) or Hull Serial No. (HIN)	$ Fair Market Value (at date of death)
JN4EU2VH9M9672787	5,000

Make	Percentage of Ownership
Venerex	x 100 %

Model	Year	$ Value of Percentage Owned
Ex-88	2014	5,000

Vehicle/Vessel 2 - Vehicle Identification No. (VIN) or Hull Serial No. (HIN)	$ Fair Market Value (at date of death)

Make	Percentage of Ownership
	x %

Model	Year	$ Value of Percentage Owned

Vehicle/Vessel 3 - Vehicle Identification No. (VIN) or Hull Serial No. (HIN)	$ Fair Market Value (at date of death)

Make	Percentage of Ownership
	x %

Model	Year	$ Value of Percentage Owned

Attach separate list(s) if required.

Total Value of all Vehicles and Vessels
- for percentage owned by the deceased at date of death
Include amounts from separate list(s). [4]   ▶ $ 5,000

H Other Assets (include all other assets not listed in previous sections, e.g., business interests, copyrights, patents, trademarks, household contents, art, jewelry, loans receivable, etc.)

Item 1 - Description	$ Fair Market Value (at date of death)
Listerlock watch	1,900
	Percentage of Ownership
	x 100 %
	$ Value of Percentage Owned
	1,900

Item 2 - Description	$ Fair Market Value (at date of death)
Personal effects	200
	Percentage of Ownership
	x 100 %
	$ Value of Percentage Owned
	200

Attach separate list(s) if required.

Total Value of all Other Assets
- for percentage owned by the deceased at date of death
Include amounts from separate list(s). [5]   ▶ $ 2,100

9955E (2015/08)

Court File No.

| 1 | 2 | 3 | 4 | 5 | 6 | | | | | | | | |

I Summary of All Estate Assets (includes any amounts shown on separate lists)

Enter Dollars only

Total Net Value of all Real Estate in Ontario.............................		1	333,757
Total Value of all: Bank Accounts......................................	+	2	27,983
Investment	+	3	12,479
Vehicles and Vessels	+	4	5,000
Other Assets	+	5	2,100
Total Value of all Estate Assets - owned by the deceased at date of death (sum of Lines [1] to [5])	=	6	381,319

Total Amount of Estate Administration Tax Payable

Enter Total Estate Assets from Line [6] ▶ (round up this amount to the nearest $1,000)	7	382,000	

The calculation should be:

a) $5 for each $1,000 of estate assets up to $50,000, **plus**	8	250		
b) $15 for each $1,000 of estate assets over $50,000 + ...	9	4,980	▶ =	10	5,230
Subtract: **Total Amount of Deposit Paid with the Application for Estate Certificate**	−	11	4,855
Net Amount of Tax Owing (or Refund)...........................	=	12	375

Make your cheque or money order in Canadian funds payable to the **Minister of Finance**.
Submit your payment to the Courthouse where the **certificate for appointment of estate trustee** was issued together with an affidavit attesting to the new total value of the estate.

J Certification

I certify that the information I have given in this return, and in the documents I have provided, is true, correct and complete. Attach additional page(s) to include the signature of any other estate representative(s).

First Name	Middle Name
Iva	Jelka

Last Name
Josko

Business Name (if applicable)	Title

Signature of Estate Representative	Date (yyyy/mm/dd)
X	2017/02/19

It is an offence to make a false or misleading statement in a return as required under the *Estate Administration Tax Act, 1998* and its Regulation.

The personal information on the Estate Information Return is collected under the authority of the *Estate Administration Tax Act, 1998* and will be used to determine the value of estates and the amount of estate administration tax payable. This information may be used to develop and/ or evaluate tax or benefit policy. It may also be used in the administration or enforcement of an Act that imposes a tax or confers a benefit. Questions about the collection of this information should be directed to the Senior Manager-Audit, Compliance Branch, 33 King Street West, PO Box 625, Oshawa ON L1H 8H9, 1 866 668-8297

9955E (2015/08)

FIGURE 11.4 **Affidavit Regarding Corrected Value of the Estate**

Court File No. 5545/18

ONTARIO

SUPERIOR COURT OF JUSTICE

IN THE ESTATE OF **JACQUELINE STICK**, deceased.

IN THE MATTER OF an application for a certificate of appointment of estate trustee

AFFIDAVIT

I, ROBERT LARISE, estate trustee in the estate of Jacqueline Stick, deceased, MAKE OATH AND SAY,

1. I am the estate trustee named in the certificate of appointment of estate trustee with a will in the estate of the deceased, Jacqueline Stick, who died on the 12th day of January 2018.

2. In March of 2018, I made an application to the Ontario Superior Court of Justice at 393 University Avenue, Toronto, Ontario for a certificate of appointment of estate trustee with a will.

3. In the application for a certificate of appointment of estate trustee with a will, I declared the value of the deceased's property (real property and personal property combined) to be $214,007.12. Attached to this affidavit as Exhibit "A" is a copy of my application for a certificate of appointment of estate trustee with a will.

4. The amount paid on account of estate administration tax was $2,725.00.

5. A certificate of appointment of estate trustee with a will was granted to me on May 25, 2018. Attached to this affidavit as Exhibit "B" is a copy of the certificate of appointment of estate trustee with a will.

6. Subsequent to receiving the certificate of appointment I learned that the deceased owned an additional asset in the form of a term deposit valued at $9,974.21 as of the date of death.

7. In light of this discovery, I now realize that the estate administration tax should have been $2,860.00.

8. I swear this affidavit to accompany my supplementary payment of $135.00 in estate administration tax.

SWORN BEFORE ME at the City	)
of Toronto, in the	)
Province of Ontario	)
this 31st day of May, 2018	)

Robert Larise
Robert Larise

Raymond Braxton

A Commissioner, etc.

Deadlines Respecting Underpayments of Estate Administration Tax

There may be some confusion under the Act and the regulation with respect to deadlines for paying additional estate administration tax. The Act apparently contemplates that the value of the estate assets disclosed on an application for a certificate of appointment is based on either (1) an estimated value of the estate, or (2) the actual value of the estate. Pursuant to the Act and the regulation, if it is an estimated value, the deadline to pay any additional tax is six months from the date of the application (pursuant to the undertaking required if the value is estimated). In such a case the regulation specifies that a revised estate information return will be due 30 days from the date of payment. If, on the other hand, the estate trustee purported to provide the actual value of the estate on the application form but that value turned out to be incorrect, there is no deadline specified in the legislation for payment of the additional tax owing (though there is a deadline to file a revised estate information return, which is 30 days from learning of the error). Common sense suggests that the deadline for payment is sometime within the 30-day period.

Additional complications arise where the legislation contemplates the expiration of the estate trustee's obligation to report previously given incorrect or incomplete information pertaining to the amount of estate administration tax owing. Section 4(3) of the regulation provides that, if the estate trustee becomes aware of such incorrect or incomplete information, a revised estate information return is not required if four years have passed since the date the tax would have been payable. This implies (though the legislation does not specifically state it) that tax is not owing for value mistakes found after four years.

Section 4(4) of the regulation does, however, provide an exception to the rule in section 4(3) (an exception within an exception). Section 4(4) provides that where newly discovered property belongs to the estate, the estate trustee must file a revised return (and presumably pay the tax owing) even if it is after the passage of four years. This rule is in keeping with section 32(2) of the *Estates Act*[7] which requires that the estate trustee deliver a sworn statement as to the value of the newly discovered property to the registrar of the court within six months of discovering it. Section 4(4) of the regulation requires that in such a situation the revised estate information return be filed within 30 days of delivering the statement to the court. In summary, the legislation draws a distinction between incorrect information as to the value of known estate assets (for which the obligation to report expires after four years) and incorrect information as to the existence of estate assets (for which the obligation to report continues after four years).

Finally, note that the estate trustee also has a duty to report to the minister of finance any incorrect information in the estate information return that does not pertain to the amount of estate administration tax payable. Such reporting, however, does not require a revised return but merely a letter. Information of this nature would include a corrected spelling of the deceased's name or corrected particulars regarding the estate trustees.

Canada Revenue Agency

The Canada Revenue Agency (CRA) (formerly called the Canada Customs and Revenue Agency, and Revenue Canada) is probably one of the most important creditors in any

---

7 RSO 1990, c E.21.

estate. For that reason, this chapter devotes a special section to it. The importance of the CRA derives from the fact that, as the government of Canada's biggest revenue generator, it has many special powers to collect debts and to impose liability on an estate and on the estate trustee. The CRA is a creditor that will appear in most estates. It is also usually the last creditor to be dealt with in any particular estate because it takes time for all income tax liabilities to come due and to be paid. When the CRA is finally dealt with, the winding up of the estate follows shortly thereafter.

Income tax law is a highly technical and specialized field, and this is no less true as it applies to estates. It is an area in which accountants are often retained even though a lawyer is already involved in advising the estate trustee. The section that follows is not meant to be a thorough analysis of the topic of income tax as it relates to estates but rather an introduction. It is a discussion of some of the more common issues and is designed to allow such issues to be recognized when they arise.

For the purposes of this section, it is assumed that the deceased taxpayer was ordinarily a resident of Canada. Under Canadian income tax law, a Canadian resident's income tax is calculated on the basis of her income from all sources, including those outside Canada.

Outstanding Tax Returns from Previous Years

Usually the first CRA issue to be dealt with in an estate is determining whether the deceased filed all past tax returns that were supposed to be filed during his lifetime. A tax return must be filed if the taxpayer had taxable income during the year. Any tax owing on returns that were not filed but were supposed to have been filed becomes a liability of the estate. It is therefore the obligation of the estate trustee to file all past due returns and pay all taxes, interest, and penalties accruing under those returns.

An inquiry to the CRA will help to determine which, if any, past years' returns are due. However, some experts advise caution in making inquiries to the CRA about overdue tax returns too soon because making such inquiries could possibly end up nullifying the valuable advantage of making voluntary disclosure as discussed below. If the CRA is approached for information, it will have to be provided with a completed CRA Form T1013 (entitled "Authorizing or Cancelling a Representative") an example of which is in Figure 11.5. This form (which can be obtained by going to <http://www.cra-arc.gc.ca/E/pbg/tf/t1013/README.html>) must be signed by all of the estate trustees of the estate. The answer from the CRA is usually in the form of a printout indicating which year's taxes have been filed. If one or more years are missing, it is up to the estate trustee to make reasonable inquiries into the deceased's financial affairs—employment, business, investment, and other financial records—to determine whether the deceased earned enough income during those years that filing a return is required.

When filing past returns, there is no deadline as such because they are already past due and likely incurring ongoing penalties. In such a case, a letter explaining the situation should be sent along with the returns and the payment. In some cases, voluntary disclosure of overdue returns and amounts owing can result in reduction of liability to the estate. In order to qualify for forgiveness under the voluntary disclosure policies of the CRA, the disclosure cannot be made after a demand for payment has been made by the CRA. Estate trustees who have reasonable grounds to believe that past taxes may be owing are well advised to seek expert advice and guidance from an accountant before taking any steps.

FIGURE 11.5   Authorizing or Cancelling a Representative Form

Canada Revenue Agency / Agence du revenu du Canada

Authorizing or Cancelling a Representative

Protected B when completed

Important – If you moved recently, update your address and contact information with the Canada Revenue Agency (CRA) online if you are registered with MyAccount at **www.cra-arc.gc.ca/myaccount**, by telephone at **1-800-959-8281**, or in writing.

Complete this form to authorize the CRA to deal with another person who would act as your representative for income tax matters or to cancel any existing representatives on your account. Only forms received with a valid account number will be processed.

By registering with MyAccount at **www.cra.gc.ca/myaccount**, you will be able to provide immediate access to your representative and cancel and manage your representatives through "Authorize my representative." You can also authorize or cancel a representative by completing this form and mailing it to your tax centre. We aim to process this paper form in 20 business days or less from the date it is received at the tax centre. To **immediately cancel** a representative, call us at **1-800-959-8281**.

Part 1 – Taxpayer information

You will need to complete a **separate Form T1013** for each account and representative. Complete the line that applies.

SIN, TTN or ITN

First name: _____   Last name: _____

Trust account number

T _____   Trust name: _____

T5 filer identification number

H A _____   Filer name: _____

Part 2 – Representative information and authorization

Name of your representative (individual or business): _____

Mailing address: _____

Do not complete a new form every year if there are no changes. Complete section A **or** B, as applicable.

A. Authorize online access (includes access by telephone, in person, and in writing)

To grant online access to your representative, your representative must register online through "**Represent a Client**" at **www.cra.gc.ca/representatives** and obtain a RepID or GroupID or register their business number (BN). Our online services do not have a year-specific option. Therefore, your representative will have access to **all** tax years.
By completing this section to authorize a representative for a trust account, the representative will have access to **all** tax years with **no** online access.

RepID
_____   First name: _____   Last name: _____

GroupID
G _____   Name of group: _____

Business number (BN)
_____   Name of business: _____

Enter the **level of authorization** (level 1 or 2): _____   If you **do not specify** a level of authorization, we will **assign a level 1**.

If you authorize your representative for **online** access and have a **"care of"** address, you will receive a letter to confirm the authorization.

or

B. Authorize access by telephone, in person, and in writing (no online access)

Enter the full name of the individual or business you are authorizing. If you do not identify a specific representative from that business, you will be authorizing the CRA to deal with any representative from that business.

Individual: First name: _____   Last name: _____

Name of business: _____

Telephone: _____   Ext: _____   Fax: _____

Tick the appropriate box and indicate the level of authorization:

☐ All tax years (past, present, and future)   **Level of authorization** (level 1 or 2) _____   If you **do not specify** a level of authorization, we will **assign a level 1**.
or

☐ Enter the applicable tax year or years (past and/or present), and specify the level of authorization (level 1 or 2) for **each** tax year.

Tax year(s)								
Level of authorization								

T1013 E (15)   (Vous pouvez obtenir ce formulaire en français à **www.arc.gc.ca/formulaires** ou en composant le **1-800-959-7383**.)

Canada

FIGURE 11.5 CONTINUED

Protected B when completed

Part 3 – Authorization expiry date

Enter an expiry date, if applicable, otherwise the authorization will stay in effect until **you** or **your representative** cancels it or we are notified of your death.

Year	Month	Day

Part 4 – Cancel one or more existing authorizations

Complete this section **only** to cancel an existing authorization. Tick the appropriate box.

☐ Cancel **all** authorizations

or

☐ Cancel the authorizations given for the individual, group, or business identified below:

RepID

First name: _____   Last name: _____

GroupID

G _____   Name of group: _____

Business number (BN)

Name of business: _____

Part 5 – Signature and date

If you are the **taxpayer**, you must **sign** and **date** this form. If you are the **legal representative**, you must **tick** the box below, and **sign** and **date** this form.

☐ **I am the legal representative for this taxpayer or estate/trust** (executor/administrator, power of attorney, the legal guardian or the trustee or custodian of this trust account).

Important: You must send a **complete** copy of the **legal document** giving you the authority to act in this capacity to the taxpayer's tax centre. Read the attached information sheet for tax centre addresses.

If **two or more** legal representatives are acting **jointly** on the taxpayer's behalf, **each** legal representative must sign below.

_____
Print name of taxpayer or each legal representative

X _____
Signature of taxpayer or each legal representative,
a parent if taxpayer is under the age of 16,
a witness when signed with a mark

Year	Month	Day

Date of signature

If your representative has not electronically submitted this form on your behalf then it must be submitted **within six months** of the date of signature. If not, it will not be processed.

Privacy Act, personal information bank number CRA PPU 175

When a person dies between January 1 and April 30, and the tax return for the last calendar year has not yet been filed, it is the estate trustee's obligation to ensure that the return is filed. In such a case, however, the deadline for filing is extended to six months following the date of death.

Note that, in this regard, unfiled past tax returns can sometimes lead to additional assets of the estate if, for example, the deceased would have been entitled to tax refunds or HST rebates. In such a case it is imperative to file past tax returns as quickly as possible because interest income on the refunds will be lost to the estate and the ability to collect past rebates will disappear altogether after ten years have passed.

Terminal T1 Tax Return

The next CRA issue to be dealt with by the estate trustee is filing the final T1 tax return. This important return covers the period from January 1 in the year of death to the date of death. For example, if the deceased died on June 30, 2017, the final T1 return would cover any income she earned between January 1, 2017 and June 30, 2017. This tax return is called the Terminal T1 Tax Return but is also referred to as the terminal T1, terminal return, final T1 tax return, final T1, or final return. The terminal T1 is completed using an ordinary T1 tax return form and is signed by the estate trustee.

Filing the terminal T1 is often the most important step with respect to estate income taxes because it involves special rules for calculating income. It usually means that the deceased's entire circumstances as they relate to income tax must be examined. All property owned by the deceased in the year of death (or even before that) and all tax-reduction mechanisms used by the deceased during his lifetime must be thoroughly examined.

The deadline to file the final T1 return is the deadline that would have applied if the deceased had lived the full year—that is, April 30 of the following year. For the above example, the deadline to file the terminal T1 would be April 30, 2018. As with any other tax deadline, if it is missed, the estate may incur interest and penalties. If it is missed due to the fault of the estate trustee, he or she may have to reimburse the estate for the amount of the interest and penalties.

If a deceased person died in November or December of any year, the CRA has determined that forcing the estate trustee to file the terminal T1 by April 30 of the following year may be too onerous. The rule, then, for estates in which the person died in November or December is that the terminal T1 must be filed within six months of the date of death. For example, if a person dies on November 17, 2017, his estate trustee has until May 16, 2018 to file the return.

Subject to the rules discussed below that may provide tax relief, the income to be included in the terminal T1 tax return is any unreported income from any source that has accrued to the date of death.

Income "accrued to the date of death" means income earned, whether received or not. For example, if a person is paid $500 on Friday for the week's work, on Tuesday of the week she has earned $200 even though she will not receive it until Friday. Income is conceptualized in this way when using the accrual basis of accounting. The opposite form of accounting is the cash basis. Using the example already provided, under the cash basis of accounting, the person is not considered to have earned the $200 for Monday and Tuesday until she has actually received it. The CRA will sometimes permit the reporting of income on a cash basis (even though, strictly, it should be done on the accrual basis). When a person dies, however, the strict accrual method of accounting must be used.

Income from Employment, Business, or Office

Subject to the discussion below, any income from employment or from a person's business that has accrued in the last year of the person's life is reported on the terminal T1 tax return. As will be seen, a special tax advantage is available for income, such as salary and wages, that should have been paid to the deceased during her lifetime but has not been paid. Also, there are particular rules for a situation where the deceased owned a business either as a sole proprietor or as a partner. Some of these rules are discussed below.

Income from Property

Income Earned by Property

Income from property is also to be reported on the terminal T1 tax return. Such income includes any rents, royalties, and interest. Income from property also includes capital gains, which are discussed below and in Chapter 13, Administering Testamentary and Inter Vivos Trusts and Powers of Attorney.

Capital Gains from Property Disposed of During the Last Year

It is important for the estate trustee to determine whether the deceased disposed of any capital property during the last year of his life. Capital property is basically any property that is not normally used up in a year (in the way that, for example, gasoline and food are). If the deceased disposed of capital property, the estate trustee has to declare any capital gain on the deceased's terminal T1. A capital gain occurs when there is an increase in value—that is, when the property is sold for a higher amount than the purchase price. Currently, the *Income Tax Act*[8] generally requires that 50 percent of the increase in value be reported as income on the taxpayer's tax return, subject to certain exceptions.

For example, if the deceased died on November 15 and had disposed of an antique table on February 15 of the same year, the terminal T1 would have to report 50 percent of any increase in the value of the table between the time it was purchased (the "adjusted cost base") and the time it was sold. If the table was originally purchased in 1980 for $1,000, and its fair market value at the time of selling it—regardless of what price was eventually obtained for it (although a sale on the open market is usually very good evidence of its true value)—was $7,000, 50 percent of $6,000 (the increase in value), or $3,000, would have to be reported as capital gains income on the deceased's terminal T1.

Because capital gains tax came into force on January 1, 1972, any increase in value of a capital asset before that date is tax-free. Furthermore, many individuals have made capital gains elections for certain capital properties—that is, a filing with the CRA that had the effect of counting the increase in value only from the date of the election. Such elections were allowed in response to the then-upcoming elimination of a capital gains exemption tax benefit that had previously existed for a number of years, and it was deemed fair to

---

8 RSC 1985, c 1 (5th Supp).

allow taxpayers to use up this capital gains exemption on, for example, the family cottage. Making such an election (which was made on the 1994 tax return) had the effect of setting the adjusted cost base of the property at the value as of the date of the election instead of at the date of acquisition.

Deemed Disposition of Capital Property Owned on the Date of Death

As explained above, any capital gain earned in the last year of the deceased's life must be reported on the terminal T1. Using the accrual method of accounting that must be used on the terminal T1, any capital gains that would have been earned by the deceased if he had disposed of all of the capital property in the last year of his life must also be reported on the terminal T1 tax return. This rule is called the **deemed disposition rule**. In other words, the *Income Tax Act* deems a person to have disposed of all of his capital property, whether he has disposed of it or not, at fair market value as of the day before his date of death. The effect of the deemed disposition rule is that all unreported capital gains accrued throughout the deceased's life or, more accurately, from January 1, 1972 (the date the capital gains rule came into force) are brought into the deceased's income.

deemed disposition rule
rule that states that any capital gains that would have been earned by the deceased if he or she had disposed of all of the capital property in the last year of life must also be reported on the terminal T1 tax return

Exemption for Capital Gains Earned with Respect to Principal Residence

An important exemption from capital gains tax is any gain earned on a person's principal residence. This means that, no matter how much increase in value has occurred during the time that a property was the person's principal residence, the gain does not have to be reported on a tax return.

Capital Property Depreciated by an Unincorporated Business

If the deceased was involved in a business, either as a sole proprietor or a partner, a factor to consider in the context of deemed dispositions of capital property is whether there are any business assets for which the deceased claimed depreciation in past tax returns. Depreciation is the loss in value of an asset—that is, capital property. This factor is important because it has a bearing on the value of the business assets for the deemed disposition at death.

If a person owns capital property that is used for the business, she is allowed to deduct from her income each year certain amounts representing the depreciation of the capital property in the year. The amounts that can be deducted are called **capital cost allowance**, and the *Income Tax Act* specifies a certain percentage per year that can be deducted for each kind of capital asset. Not all assets used in a business are depreciable. The categories or classes of depreciable capital assets, and the corresponding percentages allowed for the capital cost allowance, are listed in the Regulations under the Act.

In any given year, a certain percentage of the value of a depreciable asset has not yet been depreciated. This value is called the **undepreciated capital cost** of the asset.

A person in business may have several capital assets in several classes of depreciable capital assets. If, at the deceased's death, the undepreciated capital cost of the assets in any particular class is lower than their actual fair market value, the estate trustee must take the difference between the assets' undepreciated capital cost and their fair market value and report the difference as income on the terminal T1 tax return. This is called a

capital cost allowance
amount that can be deducted from income each year by a business for depreciation of its capital property

undepreciated capital cost
percentage of the value of a depreciable asset that has not yet been depreciated by a business

recapture of income. In contrast, if the undepreciated capital cost of the assets is higher than their actual fair market value, the estate trustee is allowed to take the difference and deduct it from the income reported on the terminal T1 tax return. This is called a **terminal loss**.

This simplified discussion of depreciable capital assets applies only to unincorporated businesses because a corporation is a taxpayer in and of itself. Any depreciation claimed by a corporation is not claimed by a taxpayer personally and therefore does not directly affect the deceased's terminal T1 tax return.

Rollovers

In certain situations, capital property can be transferred to a beneficiary of the estate upon the taxpayer's death without immediate tax consequences. Such a transfer has the effect of deferring income tax until the recipient of the property becomes liable for the capital gain. Such situations are called **rollovers**. The asset is "rolled over" to the recipient without immediate tax consequences for either the estate or the recipient. Only certain circumstances allow for a rollover to take place. One circumstance is where the asset is transferred to the deceased's spouse. No capital gains tax is payable until the spouse sells (or otherwise disposes of the asset) or dies. At that time, the spouse's estate must pay capital gains tax on the asset as if the estate had purchased it at the time the original deceased spouse purchased it and at that value (or at whatever value the asset had as of January 1, 1972).

This rollover applies only if the following conditions are met:

- The deceased and his spouse were both Canadian residents immediately before the deceased's death.
- The spouse ended up with the capital asset as a consequence of the deceased's death (for example, through the deceased's will).
- The spouse ended up owning the capital asset within 36 months of the deceased's death.

The spousal rollover also applies if the capital asset went to a spousal trust rather than to the spouse outright. While it should be noted that the 2016 amendments to the *Income Tax Act* affecting tax rates payable by spousal trusts may render spousal trusts less common, spousal trusts will likely still exist in limited circumstances. In such cases, a rollover will apply to a spousal trust if the following conditions are met:

- the deceased was a Canadian resident immediately before her death;
- the spousal trust received the capital asset as a consequence of the deceased's death;
- the spousal trust is a testamentary trust set up by the deceased's will;
- the spouse is entitled to all of the income from the trust; and
- no other person has a right to the income or capital of the trust while the spouse is alive.

Under the *Income Tax Act*, the definition of "spouse" includes common law couples and married couples. If any questions arise in this regard, the current CRA policies and law should be consulted.

A rollover also exists in the case of a transfer of a family farm (or farm property) from a deceased parent to a son or daughter. Where normally capital gains tax may be payable on farm property under the deemed disposition rule, the transfer from the estate of the deceased to the recipient is without immediate tax consequences if the following requirements are met:

- the recipient child was a Canadian resident immediately before the deceased's death;
- the farm property was used principally as farm property by the deceased or the deceased's child immediately before the deceased's death;
- the child ends up owning the farm within 36 months of the deceased's death; and
- the farm is in Canada.

Income from Other Sources

Section 56 of the *Income Tax Act* discusses income from other sources that must be included in the deceased's income. Some of these sources are pension benefits, employment insurance benefits, maintenance payments, spousal support, social assistance, and general taxable benefits. The Canada Pension Plan death benefit is not included in income on the terminal T1 but rather in the trust return discussed below and in Chapter 13.

RRSPs and RRIFs

Many individuals contribute to registered retirement savings plans and registered retirement income funds during their lives. Up to certain limits, the amount contributed during the year (or within 60 days of the end of the year) can be deducted from income for income tax purposes. When funds from the RRSP are withdrawn, income tax is payable. If at that time the taxpayer is in a lower tax bracket than at the time the deductible contributions were made, a tax benefit is obtained. The usual case is for the taxpayer to build up RRSPs during his working life and then to transfer them to a RRIF at retirement or when required by legislation; the RRIF is then paid out periodically. As the money filters out of the RRIF, the taxpayer must declare the payouts as income. A person must either redeem her RRSPs or transfer them to a RRIF in the year in which she attains age 71. If the RRSPs are not redeemed or transferred into a RRIF during that year, the whole amount is deemed to be brought into income.

If a deceased person did not have a spouse or a financially dependent child or grandchild at the time of his death, the fair market value of the RRSPs must be declared as income in her terminal T1 tax return. If, on the other hand, the deceased had a surviving spouse, or no surviving spouse but a financially dependent child or grandchild who is named as a direct beneficiary of the RRSPs, there is a mechanism whereby the RRSP can be transferred to that beneficiary without tax being payable by the estate or by the beneficiary. Furthermore, if the surviving spouse or financially dependent child or grandchild is entitled to the RRSP by virtue of the will or the laws of intestacy, an election can be filed to avoid the paying of tax by the estate and by the recipient spouse, child, or grandchild. If no direct beneficiary is named in the RRSP, the spouse does not have to be predeceased before the benefit can accrue to the financially dependent child or grandchild. The mechanism in the *Income Tax Act* allowing this deferral of tax is similar to the rollover, discussed above, although it is implemented differently.

If the tax advantage is to be gained with respect to the transfer of RRSPs from the deceased to her spouse or financially dependent child or grandchild, all requirements of the *Income Tax Act* must be complied with. For example, the recipient spouse, child, or grandchild must, within 60 days of the end of the year in which the RRSPs are received, place them in his or her own name as RRSPs or in a life annuity (or, in the case of a financially dependent child or grandchild, an annuity that pays out until the child turns 18, unless that child or grandchild is financially dependent owing to a physical or mental disability, in which case the annuity can be a life annuity).

The above-noted rules relate to unmatured RRSPs. Special rules come into play when a person dies while owning RRSPs during the year in which he attains age 71. RRIFs are dealt with in a way that is similar to unmatured RRSPs.

In the case of RRSPs or RRIFs that designate a specific beneficiary who is not the spouse or financially dependent child or grandchild of the deceased, the tax consequences to the estate must be heeded with particular care. Such RRSPs and RRIFs may often represent a large tax burden to an estate. If a large RRSP or RRIF is given directly to a named beneficiary in the plan itself for whom the tax advantages discussed above are unavailable, an estate can easily become insolvent simply by having to pay the income tax on the RRSP or RRIF. It is a similar, although more equitable, situation if RRSPs or RRIFs are left to a person as a demonstrative gift in a will. In such a case, the estate must still pay the tax owing from the estate, and according to the rules of will interpretation discussed in Chapter 3, the demonstrative gift takes precedence over most other gifts in the will. As a result, the recipient of the RRSPs or RRIFs can often be the only beneficiary to receive anything from the estate. Lawyers and law clerks should be aware of such results when drafting wills.

Reductions of Income Tax on the Terminal T1

Deductions for Medical Expenses

Medical expenses paid by a taxpayer during the taxation year can normally be claimed as a tax credit in calculating the taxpayer's tax. In the case of a terminal T1, the estate trustee is allowed to claim medical expenses paid in any two-year period in which the deceased died provided they have not been claimed in a previous year.

Deductions for Charitable Donations

The *Income Tax Act* provides tax incentives for making charitable donations, and there are many rules pertaining to charitable donations by a deceased person. The primary rule for the purposes of filing the terminal T1, however, is that gifts made to charities in the deceased's will can be designated as having been made while the deceased was alive, thus giving the estate the tax benefit at the time of filing the terminal T1. The *Income Tax Act* also allows for the charitable gift to be given in a year following the date of death if it is advantageous from a tax point of view to do so. In this regard, for deaths after 2015, there is flexibility in claiming the donation either on the terminal T1 or on the estate tax return. Estate tax returns are discussed in Chapter 13 under the topic of "Special Rules for Income Taxation of Trusts."

Elective Tax Returns

Advantages to Filing Elective Returns

In certain specified situations, discussed below, it is possible to file separate tax returns (called **elective tax returns**) that cover the same taxation period as the terminal T1 return. Filing elective returns is generally considered advantageous from a taxpayer's point of view because each return can claim its own set of available tax credits—such as the personal tax credit, the spousal tax credit, the equivalent to spouse tax credit, the dependant tax credit, and the age tax credit—that are normally available only once a year. Also, because filing multiple tax returns has the effect of splitting the income into smaller amounts, the result can be lower tax brackets for one or more of the returns (and therefore less overall tax payable).

Not all such tax credits and deductions may be claimed or allowed for each individual elective tax return. Similarly, the capital gains deduction and the Northern residents deduction cannot be claimed on each return. Some of the deductions discussed above, and others (including deductions for employee stock option benefits included in income and deductions for certain amounts received under the *Workplace Safety and Insurance Act*[9]), can be claimed on each of the individual elective tax returns, but the total amount claimed on all returns cannot exceed what would be claimed if there were only one return.

elective tax returns separate tax returns that cover the same taxation period as the terminal T1 return; allowed in certain specified situations

Rights and Things Return

If the deceased earned income falling within the category of a "right or thing" under the *Income Tax Act*, the deceased is entitled to report the income from such sources on a separate tax return (an ordinary T1 tax return referred to as a "rights and things" return because of the kind of income reported). Rights and things include accounts receivable, certain work in progress of professionals, dividends that are declared but not paid, remuneration owing from employment for a period ending before the date of death, and payments for grain to be received from the Canadian Wheat Board. If it is decided that a rights and things return should be filed, all of the deceased taxpayer's rights and things must be reported on that tax return.

Rights and things can also be taxed in the hands of some or all of the individual beneficiaries of the estate. The concept of taxing income in the hands of beneficiaries is similar to what occurs in certain trust situations, which will be discussed in Chapter 13.

Stub Period Return for Certain Income from an Unincorporated Business

If the deceased taxpayer was a partner in business at the time of her death and the death caused the partnership to end, it is possible that an elective return can be filed. The possibility of filing the elective return hinges on whether the death was in the same calendar year as the end of the last taxation year for the partnership. If the two dates do occur in the same calendar year, a separate tax return for the "stub" period between the end of the last taxation year for the business and the date of death can be filed. If the two dates do not

---

9   SO 1997, c 16, Sch A.

occur in the same calendar year, the income from the last year must be reported on the deceased's terminal T1 tax return.

If the death of the taxpayer did not cause the partnership to end, the income can usually be reported in a rights or things tax return.

If the taxpayer was the sole proprietor of an unincorporated business and her death created a stub period, again the income from the stub period can be claimed on a separate return.

Stub Period T3 Trust Income Tax and Information Return (Trust Return) for Certain Income from a Testamentary Trust

Another situation in which an elective stub return can be filed is where the deceased is an income beneficiary of a testamentary trust and the date of his death is in the same calendar year as the end of the taxation year of the trust. As in the situation outlined above, this results in a stub period for which a separate tax return can be filed.

Corporate Issues

If the deceased operated a business by way of owning shares of a private corporation, in addition to there being a whole separate set of tax issues owing to the fact that the corporation is a taxable entity, it is important for the estate trustee to examine the articles of incorporation, corporate minute books, and any shareholders' agreements to find out what measures, if any, were put in place or agreed to among the shareholders in preparation for the eventuality of the death of a shareholder. As stated earlier, often shareholders of private corporations enter into agreements whereby the shareholders are not allowed to make the shares in the corporation the subject of gifts under their wills, but require the estate of the deceased shareholder to sell the shares to the surviving shareholders at fair market value or as set out in the agreement. It should be noted in this context that any shares owned by a deceased person on the date of death will be subject to the capital gains tax under the deemed disposition rule.

T3 Trust Income Tax and Information Return

As explained above, the terminal T1 covers income and deductions up to the date of death. Any income earned or deductions taken by the estate between the date of death and the final distribution of the estate are to be reported on a tax return called a T3 Trust Income Tax and Information Return or T3 trust return. In addition to reporting any income earned in this period through investments made by the deceased during her lifetime and investments made by the estate trustee after the deceased's death, the T3 trust return reports any interest earned on the estate account as well as the Canada Pension Plan death benefit. In contrast to T1 tax returns, including the terminal T1, no personal tax credits are available; as a result, tax is usually paid on every dollar of income earned by the estate.

As its name suggests, the T3 trust return is the same kind of tax return as is filed for trusts. In fact, the CRA treats the estate as if it were a testamentary trust for the purposes of the T3 trust return. The rules for filing T3 trust returns are dealt with in Chapter 13 under "Special Rules for Income Taxation of Trusts." An immediately distributable estate usually files only one T3 trust return. If the estate is complex and remains open for two or more years, the estate trustee will file a T3 trust return for several years in a row—that is, as long as the trust remains active.

The deadline for filing the T3 trust return is 90 days following the end of the trust's taxation year, which is also the calendar year. For the purposes of the T3 trust return, the year commences on the day following the date of death and ends on December 31, unless the estate is a "graduated rate estate." If the estate is a graduated rate estate, the year-end can be any date. The term "graduated rate estate" is discussed in more detail in Chapter 13. If the estate does remain open—that is, continues to earn income—after the first year-end, an additional T3 trust return has to be filed for every 12-month period thereafter.

Income Tax Holdback

Where there is no testamentary trust for which T3 trust returns need to be filed on an ongoing basis, the estate is usually wound up after the terminal T1 and the first and only T3 trust return have been filed and notices of assessment have been received from the CRA indicating that no further taxes are owing. However, because it takes weeks to receive such notices of assessment, often an interim distribution representing most of the estate is made to the beneficiaries before the notices of assessment are received. The interim distribution is, of course, made only when the estate trustee is quite certain that all of the debts either have been paid or can eventually be paid from the estate account.

While it is certainly safer for the estate trustee not to distribute any of the estate until the notice of assessment has been received, she must also keep in mind her fiduciary duty to distribute the estate to the beneficiaries in a reasonably timely manner.

Before making the interim distribution, the estate trustee must decide on an amount to hold back from distribution in case the terminal T1 and the T3 trust return are assessed at a greater amount of tax owing than was calculated by the estate trustee or her accountant. The holdback amount is usually arrived at with the advice of the accountant, and it is always better to play it safe and be liberal because once the interim distribution is made, the funds will usually not be recoverable from the beneficiaries if more funds are needed to pay the tax or other debts.

Once the holdback amount has been determined and before making the interim distribution, it is normal practice for the estate account to be changed into a non-interest-bearing account. This step prevents further income from accruing to the estate for which further T3 tax returns would have to be filed. The estate account can be changed from interest-bearing to non-interest-bearing by instructing the bank accordingly, usually by way of letter. Alternatively, the estate trustee can close the estate account and deliver the holdback amount to the lawyer to hold in his mixed trust account, which is a non-interest-bearing account.

The holdback amount is held in the non-interest-bearing account until the notice of assessment for the last T3 tax return and a clearance certificate from the CRA are received. The clearance certificate is discussed below.

Clearance Certificate

The **clearance certificate** is confirmation from the CRA that all income taxes have been paid and the estate trustee is discharged from further responsibility for the estate with respect to such taxes. As in the case of other debts of the estate, if the estate trustee

clearance certificate
Canada Revenue Agency document that confirms that all income taxes on an estate have been paid and the estate trustee is discharged from further responsibility for the estate with respect to such taxes

distributes property to beneficiaries before the clearance certificate is received and there is further tax owing, the estate trustee will be held personally liable for the amounts owing.

A clearance certificate is obtained by filling out Form TX19, "Asking for a Clearance Certificate." This form is reproduced in Figure 11.6. Certain documentation must be submitted along with the form, including:

- a copy of the will, if there is one, including any codicils, and any renunciations by persons appointed in priority to the estate trustee or, if there is a certificate of appointment of estate trustee, a copy of the certificate;
- if the deceased died intestate, the names, addresses, and social insurance numbers of each beneficiary and a statement indicating each beneficiary's relationship to the deceased; and
- a statement of the assets in the estate and, for each piece of capital property, the adjusted cost base, the date of distribution, and the fair market value at distribution.

In addition, if it is intended that the CRA communicate with someone other than the estate trustee with respect to the clearance certificate, such as the lawyer or accountant, a T1013 form, signed by all of the estate trustees should be included with the TX19 form. If all the proper documentation is submitted and all necessary tax is paid, the clearance certificate will arrive by mail anywhere from a few weeks to a few months after the application is submitted. Usually receiving it is the second-last step in the administration of the estate, the final step being the distribution of the holdback amount to the beneficiaries of the estate.

Special Rules on Insolvent Estates

There are many legal risks for an estate trustee in acting for an insolvent estate. An insolvent estate is one in which the debts are greater than the assets. If this appears to be the case, the person appointed as estate trustee is usually well advised not to assume the role. The estate trustee can refuse as long as he has not taken any steps as estate trustee. If, however, he has already taken steps toward administering the estate, he may be obligated to continue either until the estate is fully wound up or until some other person assumes the role.

How much a person can do before crossing the line and automatically assuming liability for the role of estate trustee is based on the facts of the individual case. It is likely that taking control of the deceased's assets, unless they are of negligible value, would be crossing the line. It is also possible that presenting oneself to a financial institution as "the estate trustee" or "executor" and proceeding to instruct the institution to transfer assets would also be crossing the line. Because of this, it is essential for a lawyer who is first contacted by a client who is a designated estate trustee of an estate that might be insolvent to advise the client accordingly.

FIGURE 11.6   Asking for a Clearance Certificate

Clear Data   Help

Canada Revenue Agency / Agence du revenu du Canada

ASKING FOR A CLEARANCE CERTIFICATE
Instructions

Who can request a Clearance Certificate?

Use this form if you are the legal representative for an estate, business, or property and you are asking for a clearance certificate before distributing the assets of the estate, business, or trust. A legal representative includes an executor, administrator, liquidator, trustee, or like person other than a trustee in bankruptcy. The TX19 form should be signed by all legal representatives.

Important – Do not send us this form until:

- you have filed the required tax return(s) and have received the related notice(s) of assessment (attach a copy of the notice(s) of assessment);
- you have received the notice(s) of reassessment if you sent a request(s) for reassessment (attach a copy of the notice(s) of reassessment); and
- you have paid or secured all income taxes (including the provincial or territorial taxes we administer), Canada Pension Plan contributions, employment insurance premiums, and any related interest and penalties.

Do **not** attach this form to the tax return.

For more information, refer to Information Circular IC82-6, *Clearance Certificate*, visit **www.cra.gc.ca**, or call **1-800-959-8281**.

Required Documents

Important – If the following required documents are not provided, your request will not be processed.

For T1 Deceased and T3 Trust, we require:

- a complete and signed copy of the taxpayer's will, including any codicils, renunciations, disclaimers, and all probate documents if applicable. If the taxpayer died intestate (without a will), attach a copy of the document appointing an administrator (for example, the Letters of Administration or Letters of Verification issued by a provincial court);
- a copy of the trust agreement or document for inter vivos trusts;
- any other documents that are necessary to prove that you are the legal representative;
- a detailed list of the assets that were owned by the deceased at the date of death, including all assets that were held jointly and all registered retirement savings plans and registered retirement income funds (including those with a named or designated beneficiary), their adjusted cost base (ACB) and fair market value (FMV) at the date of distribution by the estate;
- a list, description, and the ACB of all assets transferred to a trust as well as the FMV at the date of distribution;
- a detailed statement of distribution of the assets of the trust or the deceased's estate to date;
- a statement of proposed distribution of any holdback or residual amount or property;
- the names, addresses, and social insurance numbers or account numbers of any beneficiaries of property other than cash; and
- a completed Form T1013, *Authorizing or Cancelling a Representative*, signed by all legal representatives, authorizing a representative such as an accountant, notary, or lawyer if you want us to communicate with any other person or firm, or you want the clearance certificate sent to any address other than your own.

For T2 (Corporation), we require:

- a copy of the director's or shareholder's resolution confirming the intention to dissolve the corporation and the date of dissolution;
- a copy of the notice of assessment for the final T2 filed;
- a completed Form RC59, *Business Consent*, signed by all legal representatives, authorizing a representative such as an accountant or lawyer if you want us to communicate with any other person or firm, or if you want the clearance certificate sent to any address other than your own; and
- a statement of distribution of the company assets to date as well as the scheme of the distribution of company assets at the date of wind-up.

Additional documents or information may be requested to support this application.

Where to send this form

Send this form to your regional tax services office.

Atlantic Region:

Nova Scotia Tax Services Office
Estates and Trusts Audit
47 Dorchester Street
Sydney NS B1P 6K3

Quebec Region:

Western Quebec Tax Services Office
Audit – Clearance Certificates
44 du Lac Avenue
Rouyn-Noranda QC J9X 6Z9

Ontario Region and Nunavut:

Sudbury Tax Services Office
Audit – Clearance Certificates
1050 Notre Dame Avenue
Sudbury ON P3A 5C1

Prairies Region and the Northwest Territories:

Winnipeg Tax Services Office
Audit – Clearance Certificates
5th Floor, 360 Main Street
Winnipeg MB R3C 2W2

Pacific Region:

For Vancouver, Fraser Valley, and Northern BC/ Yukon tax services offices, send it to:

Vancouver Tax Services Office
Estates and Trusts Audit
9755 King George Boulevard
Surrey BC V3T 5E1

For Victoria and Southern Interior BC tax services offices, send it to:

Vancouver Island Tax Services Office
Estates and Trusts Audit
9755 King George Boulevard
Surrey BC V3T 5E1

TX19 E (15)   (Vous pouvez obtenir ce formulaire en français à **www.arc.gc.ca/formulaires** ou en composant le **1-800-959-7383**.)   Canada

FIGURE 11.6 CONTINUED

| Clear Data | Help |

Protected B
when completed

|✦| Canada Revenue   Agence du revenu
Agency   du Canada

ASKING FOR A CLEARANCE CERTIFICATE

Identification area

Name of deceased, corporation, or trust, whichever applies

Elaine Taylor

Address

33 Brunswick Lane, Burlington, ON L7R 1Q1

| Social insurance number | Trust account number | Business number |
| 9 9 9 0 1 0 0 9 0 | T – – | |

DO NOT USE THIS AREA

Legal representative's name (if there is more than one, please provide the details on a separate sheet)

Raymond Braxton

Legal representative's address (we will send the clearance certificate to this address)

14 Cat Drive, Burlington, ON L8R 1Q1

| Legal representative's capacity (for example, executor, administrator, liquidator, or trustee) | Telephone number |
| Estate Trustee | 905-555-6312 |

Type of clearance certificate requested

Indicate what type of tax return(s) you filed. For more information, see guides T4011, *Preparing Returns for Deceased Persons*, T4012, *T2 Corporation – Income Tax Guide*, or T4013, *T3 Trust Guide*, whichever applies.

[✔] T1 final return   Date of death: 2017-01-02

[ ] T1 return for rights or things

[ ] T1 return for income from a testamentary trust

[ ] T1 return for partner or proprietor

[ ] T3 Trust Income Tax and Information Return – Partial Distribution*   Last fiscal period ending filed: _____

[✔] T3 Trust Income Tax and Information Return – Final Distribution   Wind-up date: 2018-04-02

[ ] T2 Corporation Income Tax Return   Fiscal period end date of the final T2: _____

*T3 Partial distribution is only considered when there is an actual partial distribution of property of the estate or trust.

Certification and undertaking

I am asking for a clearance certificate from the Minister of National Revenue. The certificate will certify that all taxes (including provincial or territorial taxes administered by the Canada Revenue Agency), Canada Pension Plan contributions, employment insurance premiums, and any related interest and penalties for which the deceased, corporation, or trust named above is liable (or can reasonably be expected to become liable) have been paid or that the Minister has accepted security for the amounts. The certificate will apply to the tax year in which the distribution is made and any previous year for which I am liable (or can reasonably be expected to become liable) as the legal representative of the deceased, corporation, or trust identified. I will complete the distribution of all of the property as soon as possible after I receive the clearance certificate.

| 2017-12-07 | estate trustee | |
| Date | Capacity (for example, executor, administrator, liquidator, or trustee) | Signature |

| | | |
| Date | Capacity (for example, executor, administrator, liquidator, or trustee) | Signature |

Personal information is collected under the *Income Tax Act* to administer tax, benefits, and related programs. It may also be used for any purpose related to the administration or enforcement of the Act such as audit, compliance, and the payment of debts owed to the Crown. It may be shared or verified with other federal, provincial, and territorial government institutions to the extent authorized by law. Failure to provide this information may result in penalties, interest payable, or other actions. Under the *Privacy Act*, individuals have the right to access their personal information and request corrections if there are errors or omissions. Refer to Info Source at **www.cra.gc.ca/gncy/tp/nfsrc-eng.html**, Personal Information Bank CRA PPU 015.

TX19 E (15)   (Vous pouvez obtenir ce formulaire en français à **www.arc.gc.ca/formulaires** ou en composant le **1-800-959-7383**.)

Canadä

If an estate trustee has already assumed the role of estate trustee and it appears that the estate may be insolvent, she would be advised to call a meeting of the creditors in accordance with section 59 of the *Trustee Act*.[10] The meeting is designed to assist the creditors and the estate trustee in seeing to it that the estate is administered properly. As a general rule, if one creditor is more fully paid than another one, the payer runs the risk of running afoul of section 50 of the *Trustee Act*, which requires proportionality of unsecured debt payments from an estate with a deficiency of assets. This is similar to what is found in the *Assignments and Preferences Act*,[11] which applies to any situation (not just estates) in which a debtor with deficient assets prefers one unsecured creditor over another.

It is worth noting in this context, as indicated in Chapter 9, Applying for a Certificate of Appointment of Estate Trustee, that section 29(3) of the *Estates Act* provides that where a person dies intestate or dies with a will not appointing someone as estate trustee, and the estate is insolvent, the court may appoint "such person as it thinks fit" to act as estate trustee.

---

10   RSO 1990, c T.23.
11   RSO 1990, c A.33.

KEY TERMS

capital cost allowance, 235
clearance certificate, 241
deemed disposition rule, 235
elective tax returns, 239
recapture of income, 236

rollover, 236
terminal loss, 236
undepreciated capital cost, 235
voucher, 216

REVIEW QUESTIONS

1. Who or what is liable for the debts of the deceased?

2. How are creditors determined?

3. In connection with debts of an estate, what are vouchers and why are they important?

4. What does the law provide with respect to rent and the residential tenancy of a deceased?

5. Explain how an estate trustee should deal with the following debts of a deceased:

   a. credit card debts

   b. utility bills

   c. mortgage payments

   d. overpayment of government benefits

6. In addition to creditors, who can make claims against the estate?

7. What tax returns must be filed for a deceased?

8. What is the "deemed disposition rule" under the *Income Tax Act* as it relates to deceased persons?

9. What income is reported on the terminal T1 tax return?

10. Explain a situation where a "recapture of income" must be reported on a terminal T1 tax return.

11. How does a "rollover" of capital assets benefit an estate?

12. What is the filing deadline for a terminal T1 tax return?

13. What income is reported on the T3 Trust Income Tax and Information Return?

14. What are the advantages of filing elective income tax returns?

15. Identify five items considered "rights or things" pursuant to the *Income Tax Act*.

16. What is a "clearance certificate" and why is it important?

17. What are the implications for an estate trustee of an insolvent estate?

Accounting to the Beneficiaries and Paying the Beneficiaries

12

LEARNING OUTCOMES

After completing this chapter, you should be able to:

- Understand the reasons for making interim distributions, when they are appropriate, and why estate trustees need to be mindful when making them

- Recognize the importance of estate accounting, understanding the difference between formal and informal accounting and when each is called for

- Understand the proper way for an estate trustee to present a release to a beneficiary

- Recount the specific elements of formal estate accounts

- Understand the procedure involved in making interim and final distributions

Introduction

It has been said in previous chapters that an estate trustee should only make a distribution to the beneficiaries of an estate if all of the creditors have been paid or if sufficient funds have been set aside to pay the creditors. Making sure that there are enough funds to pay the creditors, however, is not the estate trustee's only concern. The estate trustee must also make sure that the beneficiaries of the estate are made aware of her actions and decisions with respect to the administration of the estate. This task is accomplished by accounting to the beneficiaries. As will be seen, while it is advisable for the estate trustee to account to the beneficiaries and to seek their approval prior to a distribution, it is sometimes necessary to bypass the objections of the beneficiaries and obtain the approval of the court instead. The approval ultimately protects the estate trustee from liability up to that point in time. This chapter deals with the subject of accounting to the beneficiaries, obtaining approval for the accounting, and distributing the estate to the beneficiaries.

Final and Interim Distributions

An estate trustee often makes interim distributions to the residual beneficiaries that represent partial or even major shares of the estate owing to each beneficiary. While it may seem safest for the estate trustee not to make interim distributions at all, failing to do so would not be in keeping with the estate trustee's fiduciary duty to the beneficiaries, including the duty to deliver their share of the estate within a reasonable period of time. The beneficiaries, after all, have a vested interest in the estate.

Whether each distribution is interim or final, however, it is essential that the estate trustee first account to the residual beneficiaries for the part of the estate being distributed.

Usually an estate trustee will at least pay all of the debts that arose during the lifetime of the deceased, such as credit card debts and other loans, and those that arise as a result of the death of the deceased, such as the funeral expenses and taxes owing under the terminal T1 tax return, before making an interim distribution. Debts of the estate arising during the course of administration, such as professional fees and taxes to be paid under the trust tax returns, as long as they are known with reasonable certainty, are often left unpaid at the time of an interim distribution.

If an estate trustee has advertised for creditors because of uncertainty about the deceased's financial affairs, he should not consider distributing until the advertisement has been placed and the time limit for creditors to assert their claims has expired. As stated several times previously, an estate trustee may be personally liable to the creditors of an estate of whom she has notice or knowledge if the estate has been distributed without regard to them.

Accounting

Estate accounting is the process of communicating to the residual beneficiaries of the estate how the amount representing their share of the estate was arrived at. It includes a disclosure of the assets owned by the deceased at his death. It shows

- the amounts expended during the administration of the estate and the amounts, if any, earned by the estate after the deceased's death;
- the amount claimed by the estate trustee by way of compensation; and
- on an interim distribution, the amounts held back from the beneficiaries pending the final payment of all of the creditors.

An accounting is not normally given to beneficiaries of specific bequests or creditors because the amounts owing to these people are **sums certain**—that is, the amounts do not depend on the decisions made by the estate trustee in administering the estate. If, however, the estate's assets are insufficient to pay the creditors or the specific bequest beneficiaries in full, it is likely that the creditors or the specific bequest beneficiaries would insist on an accounting.

The accounting protects the beneficiaries of the estate, or the creditors if the estate is insolvent, in that it provides them with a means to confirm that the estate trustee has acted properly and that they are getting their fair share of the estate. The accounting also protects the estate trustee because it provides a finality to her obligations as estate trustee. If the accounting is a **final accounting**, the estate trustee can wind up the estate after it is done and the beneficiaries are fully paid. If it is an **interim accounting**, the estate trustee will be able to concentrate her efforts on the remaining unadministered part of the estate after paying the beneficiaries the amounts set out in the interim accounting.

As will be seen, there are two ways for an estate trustee to account to the beneficiaries: informal and formal. Informal accounting is the faster, simpler, and least-expensive form of accounting and is usually therefore the preferable method. What usually determines whether the accounting will be informal or formal is the preference of the beneficiaries or—in the case of beneficiaries represented by other persons or institutions, including the Children's Lawyer—the beneficiaries' respective representatives. On the other hand, it could be the estate trustee herself who decides that there will be a formal accounting. In other words, an informal accounting should be provided only when all beneficiaries, beneficiaries' representatives, and the estate trustee agree that such accounting is sufficient.

Informal Accounting

Informal accounting is usually done by way of letter to the beneficiaries or their representatives setting out the assets as of the date of death, the debts of the deceased and of the estate, and the amounts "brought in" or earned by the estate subsequent to the deceased's death. The letter then indicates the number of residual beneficiaries, their respective shares of the estate, any compensation being claimed by the estate trustee, and any proposed holdback. Figure 12.1 is an example of a letter showing an informal accounting.

estate accounting
process of communicating to the residual beneficiaries of the estate how the amount representing their share of the estate was arrived at

sums certain
specific bequests; amounts that do not depend on the decisions made by the estate trustee in administering the estate

final accounting
accounting after which the estate trustee can wind up the estate

interim accounting
accounting made during the course of estate administration that allows the estate trustee to pay the beneficiaries and concentrate on the remaining unadministered part of the estate

informal accounting
accounting made by letter to the beneficiaries or their representatives that requires obtaining releases from them

FIGURE 12.1 Letter Showing Informal Accounting

My File: B8-9989
September 30, 2018

Mr. Sidney Coulter
45 Hindley Drive
Owen Sound, Ontario
N4K 9Q9

Ms. Nancy Vida
356 Nister Boulevard
London, Ontario
N6K Q7Q

Dear Mr. Coulter and Ms. Vida,

Re: Estate of Mia Borden
      who died February 28, 2017

Sandra Blundell, as estate trustee for your aunt's estate, has completed as much of the work in connection with the administration of this estate as is possible for her to do at this time. This letter forms her and my report to you thereon and I would urge you to seek your own legal advice on these matters.

In many estates, a formal set of "Estate Trustee's Estate Accounts" is drawn to serve as a summary of how the estate was administered. However, if you are satisfied with this informal accounting, it will not be necessary to prepare such a formal set of accounts.

This letter forms a summary of the estate administration. It can also serve as a useful reference should any question come up about the estate administration at some future date.

THE LAST WILL

Your aunt's will, dated March 1, 1995, appointed Ms. Blundell as the sole estate trustee. The will specifies that the *Human Fund* receive a gift of $25,000, *the balance of the estate to be divided equally between the two of you.*

CERTIFICATE OF APPOINTMENT OF ESTATE TRUSTEE WITH A WILL

This document, formerly called "Letters Probate," is simply a court document proving that the will filed in court is indeed the authentic and last will of the deceased. Production of a notarial copy of the certificate of appointment of estate trustee is usually required by financial institutions, or other legal entities holding assets of the deceased, before such assets will be released. Obtaining a certificate of appointment of estate trustee requires the payment of "estate administration tax."

After determining that a certificate of appointment of estate trustee was necessary in this case, this office made an application to court and obtained the certificate in question.

DUTIES OF ESTATE TRUSTEE

In brief, the estate trustee must protect the assets; collect or gather them in; pay the debts of the deceased or the estate; pay the cash bequests, if any; and distribute the residue, if any, in accordance with the will. Included in the obligation to pay the debts is the obligation to pay all taxes owing by the deceased or her estate and I will refer to this later in connection with income tax returns. For this reason, it was necessary to hold back a portion of the funds in the said bank account to cover possible liabilities that exceed the small amount of residue in the estate.

ESTATE DEBTS

The estate trustee and this office attended to cancellation of all charge accounts and payment of the known debts from the estate account. Details are set out in the list of estate expenditures, which follows. Unless the estate trustee places a "Notice to Creditors and Others" in a newspaper with a general circulation in the place of residence of the deceased informing the public that the estate will be distributed having regard only to those debts of which the estate trustee then has notice, the estate trustee is personally liable for any debts of the deceased or her estate which may come to light after distribution.

On the instructions of Ms. Blundell, this office placed the appropriate advertisement for creditors.

INCOME TAX RETURNS

As stated above, the obligation of the estate trustee to pay the debts of the deceased includes, of course, the liability for taxes. This requires the filing of the following returns or applications:

(a) The Final T1 or Personal Return

The period of the final T1 or personal return to be filed for your aunt ran from January 1 to February 28, 2017. Filing time was April 30, 2018. There must be taken into account in this return not only all capital gains or losses not hitherto reported, but there also must be included in income the proceeds from all registered retirement income funds and annuities held by the deceased at her death. In due course the Canada Revenue Agency will confirm or recalculate the return by a Notice of Assessment.

(b) The T3 or Trust Return

All income earned by the estate after the date of death and before the estate is distributed falls into this return. The trust year cannot be greater than 12 months and the return is due within 90 days of such year-end. I am hoping that only one trust return need be filed in this case.

(c) Final Clearance Certificate

Once the final trust return has been filed, the estate trustee may apply for a "Clearance Certificate." I normally advise that such an application be made, because the certificate normally absolves the estate trustee from personal liability should it turn out that additional taxes are claimed to be owing.

Pending the receipt of the Clearance Certificate, I have advised Ms. Blundell to make a holdback of $10,000.00 to cover tax liabilities upon the returns being assessed, as well as any other liabilities.

FIGURE 12.1 CONTINUED

You should also be aware that in order to permit the final trust return to be filed, no further income should accrue to the estate and therefore the holdback will not bear interest.

ESTATE LEGAL ACCOUNT

My legal account for work done on behalf of the estate trustee has been rendered to the estate trustee and is listed with the disbursements.

COMPENSATION OF THE ESTATE TRUSTEE

Estate trustees (formerly called executors or administrators) are entitled by law to receive compensation for, as the statute puts it, their "care, trouble, out-of-pocket expenses and responsibility," which they incur in acting in that capacity. The amount usually allowed in an estate of normal complexity, such as this one, is 2.5 percent of receipts and 2.5 percent of disbursements. If the estate administration extends beyond the first year, an allowance can also be made for an annual administration fee of two-fifths of 1 percent of the average value of the estate.

In this case, it is my opinion that a court would allow approximately $8,300 in compensation to Ms. Blundell.

PROPOSED DISTRIBUTION

The proposed distribution of this estate can be calculated based on the actual assets received and disbursements made in the estate, as set out in the following figures:

Receipts

Contents of Bank of London account	$24,784.34	
Interest after date of death	17.81	
Natural gas credit account	81.86	
Canada Pension Plan death benefit	2,500.00	
University of Ontario pension	465.05	
Art collection	125,000.00	
Antique table	15,000.00	$167,849.06

Disbursements

Estate administration tax	$ 2,020.00	
Funeral account	6,534.21	
Legal account	2,499.06	
Bank of London credit card	341.65	
Gift to the Human Fund	25,000.00	
Canada Revenue Agency (T1)	19,764.96	
Canada Revenue Agency (T3)	890.32	$ 57,050.20
		$110,798.86
Income tax holdback	$10,000.00	
Estate trustee's compensation	8,300.00	
Remainder		$ 92,498.86

The remainder of $92,498.86 is to be divided between the two of you as your residual gift. Thus, if the two of you should find this informal accounting acceptable, you will each be mailed a cheque in the amount of $46,249.43.

PASSING OF ACCOUNTS

Estate trustees are sometimes required to have their accounts audited. This proceeding is called a "passing of the accounts," whereby a judge, in effect, referees a questioning of the accounts in a formal proceeding in which interested parties may appear or be represented by counsel. If you accept this informal accounting, there is no point in going through this proceeding or in having a formal set of accounts prepared, as would then be required.

If you accept this accounting, please complete the enclosed "release" and have your signature witnessed by an adult person other than your spouse. Particulars of the witness should also be provided as set out on the form. The release should then be returned to me in the enclosed stamped and self-addressed envelope.

If you do not accept this informal accounting, please let me know (or have your lawyer let me know) as soon as possible, because in that case, an appointment for a court date will have to be obtained, notices served, and a formal set of accounts prepared.

CONCLUSION

This review of the estate has been sometimes in general terms, and other matters or questions that I have not touched upon may have arisen in your minds. Do not hesitate, however, to get in touch with Ms. Blundell if you have any questions or concerns and, again, I urge you to seek your own legal advice with respect to the above.

Yours truly,
GRIT, GRAT & GROOT

Gwendolyn Grat

Gwendolyn Grat
cc. client

An important aspect of informal accounting is the necessity of obtaining releases signed by the beneficiaries or their respective representatives before any distribution is made. Figure 12.2 is an example of such a release. The release is the beneficiary's written agreement with the accounts as well as his agreement not to bring an action against the estate trustee with respect to anything that is covered by the accounts or that is by implication included in the accounts—for example, assets with no value that have been disposed of by the estate trustee and therefore do not appear in the accounts. It is important to note that courts have been critical of estate trustees who are seen as coercing a beneficiary to sign a release. In other words, if the estate trustee takes the position that he has a right to a release, he may be faced with disapproval and a cost award from a court if the beneficiary is ultimately vindicated with respect to her objections to an accounting. To be safe, an estate trustee should always point out to the beneficiary that she has a right to seek more information, a formal accounting, or a hearing before a judge if she objects to anything in the formal accounts. It is also good practice to urge a beneficiary to seek independent legal advice.

FIGURE 12.2 Release

RELEASE

FROM: Sidney Coulter
45 Hindley Drive
Owen Sound, Ontario
N4K 9Q9

TO: Ms. Sandra Blundell
AND TO: The estate of Mia Borden

Re: Estate of Mia Borden

This release is given to you, Sandra Blundell, estate trustee, to release you from all claims that I might have against you arising out of your administration of the estate of the above named deceased who died on February 28, 2017. For your protection I confirm to you that I am one of the residuary beneficiaries of the estate and that I am entitled to a one half share of the residue of the estate which to this point in time amounts to $46,249.43.

I have reviewed the letter dated September 30, 2018 from Ms. Gwendolyn Grat, Grit, Grat & Groot, Barristers and Solicitors, 15 Cross Street, Toronto, Ontario, M5A 1Q1, and enclosures, if any, therein mentioned. I am satisfied that such letter and enclosures, if any, are accurate, I require no further proofs than those already given to me, and I am satisfied with your actions as estate trustee.

On condition that I receive a final accounting with respect to my share of the holdback when the clearance certificate under the *Income Tax Act* is issued, I agree that I will not question any statement contained in the said letter and enclosures, if any, and if I do, this release may be pleaded as an estoppel to such questioning.

On this condition I hereby remise, release, quit claim, and forever discharge you and your heirs, executors, administrators, and assigns of and from any further payment of my share as residuary beneficiary of the estate and of and from all types of action, causes of action, suits, account bonds, debts, covenants, contracts, claims, and demands whatsoever that against you I now have or may have in the future arising out of the administration of the estate.

In addition to the above, I remise, release, quit claim, and forever discharge the estate of Mia Borden and Ms. Sandra Blundell from any claims that I may have with respect to the will of Mia Borden dated March 1, 1995 ("the will"). Without limiting the generality of the foregoing, I specifically accept the will, including all of its provisions, and I agree not to make any claims as to the validity of the will, including but not limited to such claims relating to the testamentary capacity of Mia Borden at the time of executing the will or at the time of giving instructions for the drafting of the will; claims relating to undue influence on Mia Borden at the time of executing the will or at the time of giving instructions for the drafting of the will; claims relating to trusts, other than those specifically set up in the will; and claims as to suspicious circumstances at the time of executing the will, or at the time of giving instructions for the drafting of the will.

Signed and dated this   day of   , 2018

)
)
)

_____   )   _____
Witness   )   Sidney Coulter

Particulars of witness to Release signed by Sidney Coulter:

_____
Signature of Witness

_____
Printed Form of Signature

_____
Number and Street

_____
City, Town, etc. Postal Code

_____
Telephone

_____
Occupation

If any one beneficiary or his representative fails to respond by returning his signed release, signifies that he is not satisfied, or wants a formal accounting, it is inadvisable for the estate trustee to distribute the funds to any of the beneficiaries. Instead, the proper course of action is to seek a passing of accounts. This, as will be seen in Chapter 14, Challenging the Conduct of the Estate Trustee, does not require the signatures, or even the agreement, of the beneficiaries.

If any beneficiary is under the age of 18 or legally incapacitated, it is advisable for the beneficiary's legal guardian to sign the release on that person's behalf. Note, however, that even if the guardian has consented, the estate trustee should obtain a letter from the Children's Lawyer or the Public Guardian and Trustee indicating agreement with the accounting before distribution is made to any beneficiary. The Children's Lawyer or the Public Guardian and Trustee will usually accept an informal accounting provided that there are no unusual issues with respect to the administration of the estate and that the informal accounting is complete and accurate.

It may be that some of the beneficiaries are willing to sign the releases on the condition that they review certain documents confirming the amounts provided in the accounts. The beneficiaries may, for example, want to see bank statements or statements from financial planners confirming the values of certain assets set out in the informal accounting letter. Such requests are reasonable and should be honoured by the estate trustee. If, on the other hand, such requests become frivolous and unreasonably burdensome, it may be appropriate for the estate trustee to seek a passing of accounts as discussed below.

Formal Accounting

When a Passing of Accounts Is Necessary or Advisable

A **passing of accounts** is a process whereby a **formal accounting** is provided to all parties and the court in the hopes that the court will approve—that is "pass"—the accounts. The passing of accounts can occur at a hearing before a judge or without a hearing, depending on whether a beneficiary continues to object. If there is no hearing and the accounts are proper, a judge will sign a judgment passing the accounts. The formal accounting, required for a passing of accounts, is dictated by the *Rules of Civil Procedure*.[1]

As indicated above, one circumstance that dictates the necessity of a passing of accounts is when the beneficiaries of the estate either refuse to sign the releases that accompany an informal accounting or ignore them. A formal accounting is then prepared with the object of obtaining a judgment of the court (a passing of accounts), whether the beneficiaries agree with such accounts or not. If the judge is in agreement with the accounts—if he believes that there has been a sufficient disclosure and proper conduct by the estate trustee and that the estate trustee's claim for compensation is in order—he will render a judgment approving the accounts as presented. Alternatively, he may order a change in the expenses claimed or a more thorough accounting, or he may reduce the amount claimed in compensation.

Requesting a passing of accounts is a right of any residual beneficiary, and any such beneficiary may insist on such formality even if all the other beneficiaries are willing to sign releases. Similarly, as indicated above, the estate trustee can insist on passing the accounts formally for his own protection.

The procedure for passing of accounts is covered under the estate litigation section of this text, specifically in Chapter 14, because it is a process that directly involves the court. The process begins, however, with the compilation of formal estate accounts. The remainder of this chapter deals with that task.

Form of Formal Estate Accounts

The form that formal estate accounts take is dictated by rule 74.17 of the *Rules of Civil Procedure*. The accounting is always done for a specified period, which could be from the date of death to a recent date or from the date of the last accounting (whether formal or informal) to a recent date. According to the rules, formal estate accounts must include the following:

1. a statement of the deceased's assets owned as of the date of death (or a statement of the assets of the estate as of the last accounting);

2. a statement of all moneys received by the estate, excluding any returns from investments made by the estate trustee on behalf of the estate;

3. a statement of all moneys disbursed from the estate, including money already paid out for the estate trustee's compensation but excluding any money invested by the estate trustee on behalf of the estate;

4. if the estate trustee invested money on behalf of the estate, an account showing all of the money paid by the estate trustee toward such investments, all money received on behalf of the estate from such investments, and all money remaining in such investments;

---

1 RRO 1990, reg 194.

5. a statement showing all of the unrealized assets as of the end of the accounting period;

6. a statement of all money and investments in the estate as of the end of the accounting period; and

7. a statement of compensation claimed by the estate trustee and, if the estate trustee is also claiming a management fee (compensation for ongoing estate matters), a statement setting out the method used for determining the value of the assets for the calculation of the management fee (discussed below under "Estate Trustee's Compensation").

If the will of the deceased specifies that principal amounts (capital) and income amounts (revenue) are to be dealt with separately—as, for example, in a testamentary trust where the income is to be distributed in one set of circumstances and the capital in another—the accounts described in 2 and 3 above must each be divided into capital and revenue accounts. The result would be the following four categories: capital receipts, revenue receipts, capital disbursements, and revenue disbursements (which terms are discussed below). In practice, estate accounts are almost always divided into capital and revenue receipts and disbursements whether the will differentiates between the two or not. The items entered into each of these four accounts are discussed below.

The estate accounts are usually made up of several pages or sections, as follows:

- a cover page showing the deceased's name, the period for which the accounts are prepared, and the estate trustee's name (Figure 12.3);

- a table of contents (Figure 12.4);

- a summary showing capital receipts, capital disbursements, revenue receipts, revenue disbursements, and the balance remaining in the estate (Figure 12.5);

- a statement of original assets (with cross-references to the rest of the accounts explaining how such assets were dealt with) (Figure 12.6);

- a statement of capital receipts to the estate showing the particulars of each separate capital item received and the date on which it was received by the estate (Figure 12.7);

- a statement of revenue receipts to the estate showing the particulars of each separate revenue receipt and the date on which it was received by the estate (Figure 12.8);

- a statement of capital disbursements from the estate showing the particulars of each separate capital disbursement and the date on which it was disbursed (Figure 12.9);

- a statement of revenue disbursements showing the particulars of each separate revenue disbursement and the date on which it was disbursed (Figure 12.10);

- a statement showing investments made by the estate trustee on behalf of the estate (Figure 12.11);

- a statement of unrealized assets;

- a statement of the estate trustee's proposed compensation and, if the estate trustee is claiming a management fee, a statement indicating how the fee was calculated (Figure 12.12); and

- a statement of proposed distribution (Figure 12.13).

Figures 12.3 to 12.13, when put together, are one set of estate accounts. As can be seen, each item is numbered for ease of reference and to relate each capital and revenue receipt to the statement of original assets.

FIGURE 12.3   Estate Accounts: Cover Page

STATEMENT OF ACCOUNTS
FOR THE ESTATE OF JACQUELINE STICK
WHO DIED JANUARY 12, 2018
FOR THE PERIOD
FROM
JANUARY 12, 2018
TO
DECEMBER 31, 2018

ESTATE TRUSTEE:
ROBERT LARISE

FIGURE 12.4   Estate Accounts: Table of Contents

ESTATE OF JACQUELINE STICK

Table of Contents

FIGURE 12.5   Estate Accounts: Summary

ESTATE OF JACQUELINE STICK

SUMMARY

CAPITAL ACCOUNT

RECEIPTS	$214,007.12	
DISBURSEMENTS	46,205.76	$167,801.36

REVENUE ACCOUNT

RECEIPTS	$ 3,587.62	
DISBURSEMENTS	90.00	3,497.62
NET CASH CREDIT BALANCE		$171,298.98

FIGURE 12.6 Estate Accounts: Statement of Original Assets

ESTATE OF JACQUELINE STICK

STATEMENT OF ASSETS AT JANUARY 12, 2018

		HOW DISPOSED OF
		Page – Item

Real Estate

| 34 Thistle Street . . . . | $160,000.00 | 3 – 4 |

Cash

Bank of Dundas
450 Thistle Street
Toronto, Ontario
M5A Q8Q

| chequing account no. 34836276 . . . | 7,621.63 | 3 – 1 |

Bank of Dundas
450 Thistle Street
Toronto, Ontario
M5A Q8Q

| term deposit no. 34874451 . . . . | 30,000.00 | 3 – 2 |

Unpaid interest on
Bank of Dundas
450 Thistle Street
Toronto, Ontario
M5A Q8Q

| term deposit no. 34874451 . . . . | 133.29 | 3 – 3 |

Equities
20 shares of

| Moments Inc. @ $812.61 . . . . | 16,252.20 | 3 – 5 |

| TOTAL ASSETS . . . . | $214,007.12 | |

FIGURE 12.7   Estate Accounts: Capital Account Receipts

ESTATE OF JACQUELINE STICK

CAPITAL ACCOUNT RECEIPTS

Jan. 12	chequing account no. 34836276 Bank of Dundas, 450 Thistle St. Toronto, Ontario, M5A Q8Q	$ 7,621.63	1
Jan. 12	term deposit no. 34874451 Bank of Dundas, 450 Thistle St. Toronto, Ontario, M5A Q8Q	30,000.00	2
Jan. 31	unpaid interest on term deposit Bank of Dundas, 450 Thistle St. Toronto, Ontario, M5A Q8Q no. 34874451	133.29	3
June 5	proceeds from the sale of 34 Thistle Street	160,000.00	4
June 20	proceeds from the sale of 20 shares of Moments Inc. @$812.61	16,252.20	5
TOTAL CAPITAL ACCOUNT RECEIPTS........................		$214,007.12	

FIGURE 12.8 **Estate Accounts: Revenue Account Receipts**

ESTATE OF JACQUELINE STICK

REVENUE ACCOUNT RECEIPTS

Jan. 31   interest
chequing account no. 34836276
Bank of Dundas, 450 Thistle St.
Toronto, Ontario, M5A Q8Q . . . . $ 15.88   1

Jan. 31   interest
term deposit no. 34874451
Bank of Dundas, 450 Thistle St.
Toronto, Ontario, M5A Q8Q 137.50   2

Feb. 29   interest
chequing account no. 34836276
Bank of Dundas, 450 Thistle St.
Toronto, Ontario, M5A Q8Q 15.80   3

Feb. 29   interest
term deposit no. 34874451
Bank of Dundas, 450 Thistle St.
Toronto, Ontario, M5A Q8Q 137.50   4

Mar. 31   interest
chequing account no. 34836276
Bank of Dundas, 450 Thistle St.
Toronto, Ontario, M5A Q8Q 14.67   5

Mar. 31   interest
term deposit no. 34874451
Bank of Dundas, 450 Thistle St.
Toronto, Ontario, M5A Q8Q 137.50   6

Apr. 30   interest
chequing account no. 34836276
Bank of Dundas, 450 Thistle St.
Toronto, Ontario, M5A Q8Q 14.50   7

Apr. 30   interest
term deposit no. 34874451
Bank of Dundas, 450 Thistle St.
Toronto, Ontario, M5A Q8Q 137.50   8

May 31   interest
chequing account no. 34836276
Bank of Dundas, 450 Thistle St.
Toronto, Ontario, M5A Q8Q 14.61   9

May 31   interest
term deposit no. 34874451
Bank of Dundas, 450 Thistle St.
Toronto, Ontario, M5A Q8Q 137.50   10

June 30   interest
chequing account no. 34836276
Bank of Dundas, 450 Thistle St.
Toronto, Ontario, M5A Q8Q 5.91   11

June 30   interest
term deposit no. 34874451
Bank of Dundas, 450 Thistle St.
Toronto, Ontario, M5A Q8Q 68.75   12

Dec. 15   proceeds from investment in
term deposit no. 34887544
Bank of Dundas, 450 Thistle St.
Toronto, Ontario, M5A Q8Q
(see investment account
page 8, item 3) 2,750.00   13

TOTAL REVENUE ACCOUNT RECEIPTS $3,587.62

FIGURE 12.9 Estate Accounts: Capital Account Disbursements

ESTATE OF JACQUELINE STICK

CAPITAL ACCOUNT DISBURSEMENTS

Mar. 17	Estate Administration Tax.........................	$ 2,725.00	1
May 10	The Human Fund		
	re specific bequest	25,000.00	2
May 10	Raoul Thurgood		
	re specific bequest	5,000.00	3
May 15	Canada Revenue Agency		
	re terminal T1 tax return.........................	2,543.26	4
June 5	Hexer Realty Ltd.		
	re sale of 34 Thistle St...........................	10,272.00	5
June 15	Canada Revenue Agency		
	re T3 trust tax return.............................	248.20	6
June 30	Hertzman Accountants preparation		
	re income tax returns............................	417.30	7
TOTAL CAPITAL ACCOUNT DISBURSEMENTS		$46,205.76	

FIGURE 12.10   Estate Accounts: Revenue Account Disbursements

ESTATE OF JACQUELINE STICK

REVENUE ACCOUNT DISBURSEMENTS

Jan. 31   service charges
            chequing account no. 34836276
            Bank of Dundas, 450 Thistle St.
            Toronto, Ontario, M5A Q8Q $15.00   1

Feb. 29   service charges
            chequing account no. 34836276
            Bank of Dundas, 450 Thistle St.
            Toronto, Ontario, M5A Q8Q 15.00   2

Mar. 31   service charges
            chequing account no. 34836276
            Bank of Dundas, 450 Thistle St.
            Toronto, Ontario, M5A Q8Q 15.00   3

Apr. 30   service charges
            chequing account no. 34836276
            Bank of Dundas, 450 Thistle St.
            Toronto, Ontario, M5A Q8Q 15.00   4

May 31   service charges
            chequing account no. 34836276
            Bank of Dundas, 450 Thistle St.
            Toronto, Ontario, M5A Q8Q 15.00   5

June 30   service charges
            chequing account no. 34836276
            Bank of Dundas, 450 Thistle St.
            Toronto, Ontario, M5A Q8Q 15.00   6

TOTAL REVENUE ACCOUNT DISBURSEMENTS $90.00

FIGURE 12.11 Estate Accounts: Investment Account

ESTATE OF JACQUELINE STICK

INVESTMENT ACCOUNT

July 1	investment in term deposit			
	Bank of Dundas			
	450 Thistle St.			
	Toronto, Ontario			
	M5A Q8Q			
	no. 34887544	$150,000.00		1
Dec. 1	cashed term deposit			
	Bank of Dundas			
	450 Thistle St.			
	Toronto, Ontario			
	M5A Q8Q			
	no. 34887544		$152,750.00	2
Dec. 1	profit on term deposit			
	(see revenue receipts			
	page 5, item 13)	2,750.00		3
TOTAL INVESTMENT ACCOUNT.	$152,750.00	$152,750.00	

FIGURE 12.12 Estate Accounts: Statement of Estate Trustee's Proposed Compensation

ESTATE OF JACQUELINE STICK

STATEMENT OF ESTATE TRUSTEE'S COMPENSATION

(Subject to Judgment on Passing of Accounts)

Capital Account Receipts

2.5% of $214,007.12 = ... $5,350.18

Capital Account Disbursements
  (not including distribution)

2.5% of $46,205.76 = ... 1,155.14

Revenue Account Receipts

2.5% of $3,497.62 = ... 87.44

Revenue Account Disbursements

2.5% of $90.00 = ... 2.25

Available for Distribution

Net cash credit balance from page 1 .... $171,298.98

Less:

Grit, Grat & Groot legal account..	$ 1,342.87	
Income tax holdback	4,000.00	
Estate trustee compensation ..	10,481.86	15,825.73

2.5% of amount to be distributed = $155,474.25 = 3,886.85

Total compensation claimed...................................... $10,481.86

No management fee is being claimed

FIGURE 12.13 **Estate Accounts: Statement of Proposed Distribution**

ESTATE OF JACQUELINE STICK

STATEMENT OF DISTRIBUTION

(Subject to Judgment on Passing of Accounts)

Net cash credit balance from page 1		$171,298.98
Less:		
Grit, Grat & Groot legal account	$ 1,342.87	
Income tax holdback	4,000.00	
Estate trustee compensation	10,481.86	15,824.73
Balance for distribution to Gordon Ponner Trust		$155,474.25

Capital Receipts

capital receipts
money coming
into the estate
in lump sums

Capital receipts include all money coming into the estate in lump sums. Some assets, such as bank accounts, are capital receipts of the estate as of the date of death because on that date their liquidated value automatically passed into the estate. Other assets, such as real estate solely owned by the deceased or owned by the deceased as a tenant in common, become a capital receipt of the estate upon their sale.

If the deceased owned stocks for which dividends were declared but not paid at the time of death, the dividends are considered capital receipts. This is based on the principle of accrual accounting, which specifies that income accrued is income earned. If any income is earned before the date of death and not spent by the deceased, it is a capital receipt to the estate even though, for income tax purposes, it will be declared as income.

In this connection, bank account interest that has accrued but has not been paid as of the date of death is at least partially a capital receipt. That is, the part of the interest that has accrued as of the date of death is a capital receipt to the estate. In contrast, the part of the interest that accrued from the date of death to the date of payment is a revenue receipt. It is sometimes necessary for an estate trustee or the lawyer acting for her to make her own calculation as to what part of an interest payment belongs properly to the capital receipts account and what belongs to the revenue receipts account. This calculation is done on a *per diem*—day-by-day—basis. The number of days for which the interest is payable are added up. The amount of the interest payment is then divided by the number of days (taking it to three or four decimal places for accuracy), and the resulting number is multiplied by the number of days during which the deceased was alive during that period. The result is the amount that should be added to the capital receipts account. The balance of the interest should be added to the revenue receipts account.

Another kind of capital receipt occurs when the deceased held a mortgage on a property for which he was receiving payments at the time of his death. Any payments coming due but not paid as of the date of death are capital receipts. Payments received after the date of death are usually capital and revenue receipts combined, because most mortgages require that the payments are part principal (capital) and part interest (revenue). The capital portion of each payment received is included as a separate entry in the capital receipts account (and the revenue portion in the revenue receipts account). Note that mortgage payments are usually a set amount, but the interest portion decreases with every payment while the capital portion increases. To determine what portion of each payment received after the date of death is principal and to be added to the capital receipts account, and what portion is interest and therefore added to the revenue receipts account, the lawyer should run off an amortization schedule of the entire loan. Each payment is usually added to the estate accounts as a separate entry.

Revenue Receipts

Revenue receipts are moneys or payments earned by the estate during the accounting period. If it is a first accounting, the revenue receipts account will include all such receipts from the day after the date of death to the end of the accounting period. Revenue receipts include such things as bank interest, dividends on stocks coming due during the accounting period, rents received, and (as indicated above) the interest portion of any mortgage payments coming due and received after the deceased's death.

> **revenue receipts**
> money or payments earned by the estate during the accounting period

Capital Disbursements

Capital disbursements generally include any lump-sum payments made out of the estate other than those that are revenue disbursements (discussed below). Examples of capital disbursements are funeral expenses; professional fees; payments to creditors, including taxes to the Canada Revenue Agency (CRA); estate administration taxes; and payments to specific bequest beneficiaries. In most cases, real estate commissions paid to sell real estate owned by the estate are considered capital disbursements.

> **capital disbursements**
> lump-sum payments made out of the estate other than those that are revenue disbursements

Revenue Disbursements

Revenue disbursements include money spent for the purpose of maintaining an asset that earns income. Legal fees incurred by the estate in establishing the estate's right to collect revenue from an asset, such as a share of a corporation, would likely qualify as a revenue disbursement. If money is paid toward maintaining a rental property, for example heating and electricity charges, they would generally be considered revenue disbursements. Most lawyers consider bank account service charges to be revenue disbursements.

> **revenue disbursements**
> money spent for the purpose of maintaining an asset that earns income

Estate Trustee's Compensation

Compensation paid to the estate trustee is still commonly called **executor's compensation**. Executor's compensation is set out in the estate accounts and should be taken only after a

> **executor's compensation**
> compensation paid to the estate trustee for administering the estate

passing of accounts or upon making an informal accounting to and obtaining releases from all of the residual beneficiaries. It is not advisable for an estate trustee to take compensation before the accounts are passed or a report is provided because the court may not agree with the amount claimed. If the compensation has already been taken, the estate trustee may be asked to reimburse the estate and possibly compensate it for any damages incurred, such as lost interest, as a result of the pre-taking.

The amount of compensation is based on the value of the estate (or the portion of the estate) that has been administered by the estate trustee. As a starting point, executor's compensation is calculated as an amount equal to 2.5 percent of the receipts to the estate, including capital and revenue, and 2.5 percent of the disbursements from the estate, including capital and revenue.

Some alterations are made to this basic calculation. The first is mathematical and is based on the principle that, generally, an estate trustee is not entitled to collect executor's compensation for the portion of the estate that is paid to herself for compensation. This rule makes the calculation of executor's compensation a form of "chicken and egg" problem: the amount to be distributed to beneficiaries is reduced by the amount of executor's compensation; the executor's compensation is again reduced because the amount to be distributed to beneficiaries is less, and so on. Figure 12.12 shows the final result of a calculation of executor's compensation that, on its face, may appear to be somewhat circular. This, however, is how such circular calculations are often shown.

Similarly, where the estate trustee is a beneficiary of the estate, the calculation of executor's compensation must indicate that compensation is not being taken on the part of the estate going to the estate trustee as a gift. Figure 12.14 gives an example of such a calculation. These kinds of calculations are more complicated where the estate trustee is a residual beneficiary because, again, they become somewhat circular: the more compensation that is taken, the less that will be distributed to the residual beneficiaries, including the estate trustee. In such cases, the usual practice is to make an estimate rather than an exact calculation.

The next alteration that may apply is laid out in the case of *Logan v Laing Estate*,[2] in which the Ontario Court of Appeal confirmed that the appropriate way to determine executor's compensation is to take the basic calculation and then look at five different factors to determine whether the result should be adjusted up or down. The five factors are as follows:

1. the size of the estate;
2. the care and responsibility arising from the estate;
3. the time spent administering the estate;
4. the skill and ability displayed by the estate trustee; and
5. the success of the estate trustee in the estate administration.

A thorough analysis of all the different ways in which these five factors can affect the executor's compensation is beyond the scope of this book. What should be understood in this context is that the mathematical calculation for determining estate trustee compensation is a starting point only.

---

2 (1998), 11 ETR (2d) 268 (Ont CA).

FIGURE 12.14   Calculation of Estate Trustee's Compensation

The estate trustee is a beneficiary of a specific bequest of $100,000.

Estate Trustee Compensation

Capital Receipts:

   2.5% of $445,875.37 = ... $11,146.88

Capital Disbursements:

   $112,334.55

   2.5% of ($112,334.55 less $100,000.00) = ... 308.36

Revenue Receipts:

   2.5% of $979.15 = ... 24.48

Revenue Disbursements:

   2.5% of $45.87 = ... 1.15

Net cash credit balance for distribution $334,474.10

Less:

   Grit, Grat & Groot legal account... $ 1,834.30

   Income tax holdback 8,000.00

   Estate trustee compensation...... 11,480.87   21,315.17

   2.5% of amount to be distributed = ... $313,158.93 = 7,828.97

Total estate trustee compensation claimed......... $19,309.84

If the estate is ongoing, which means generally that it will take longer than a year to administer, the estate trustee may also be able to claim a **care and management fee**. This fee is calculated as two-fifths of 1 percent per annum of the value of the estate being administered on an ongoing basis. One-third of this fee is usually taken from revenue earned by the estate, and two-thirds is usually taken from capital of the estate. The care and management fee is also subject to the five factors listed above. Note that if it is through the fault or neglect of the estate trustee that the estate takes longer than a year to administer, he will not likely be allowed the care and management fee.

care and management fee compensation paid to the estate trustee for administering an ongoing estate

If the estate trustee is normally in the business of acting as estate trustee, such as a trust company or a lawyer or other professional, harmonized sales tax (HST) must be charged on the executor's compensation. The person or company that is acting as estate trustee should be made aware of this. If, on the other hand, a question arises about the applicability of the HST, the minister of revenue should be consulted prior to the completion of the accounts.

The estate trustee should also be informed that executor's compensation is income for tax purposes and must be included in the estate trustee's income tax return for the year in which the compensation is collected. This can be a factor in deciding whether the estate trustee claims executor's compensation at all. If, for example, the estate trustee is the major residual beneficiary of the estate, in taking executor's compensation she may be converting part of a non-taxable receipt (the residual gift under the will) into taxable income (the amount of the executor's compensation).

Investment Account

investment account
account that sets out the principal amount that was paid out by the estate trustee to invest funds for the estate and the principal amount that was received back from the investment

The **investment account** sets out the principal amount that was paid out by the estate trustee to invest funds for the estate and the principal amount that was received back from the investment. Such amounts are not included in the receipts and disbursements of the estate for the purposes of calculating executor's compensation on the grounds that doing so would artificially augment those accounts and thereby artificially augment the amount of compensation. As seen in Figure 12.11, the investment account lists all the particulars of the investments, including where the funds are invested, when they were invested, and what returns they have earned. The returns on the investments are included in revenue receipts.

Vouchers

All expenditures made by an estate trustee should be confirmed in writing by receipts—called vouchers, as mentioned in Chapter 11, Determining, Notifying, and Paying Creditors of the Estate—obtained from the payees. Upon the passing of accounts, the vouchers must be made available for inspection by any interested party (beneficiary, creditor, or representative), usually in advance of the hearing. They should be neatly organized and numbered, with the numbers corresponding to those in the disbursement part of the estate accounts. For every item in the statements of capital and revenue disbursements, there should be a corresponding voucher. The time for inspecting the vouchers is usually arranged by telephone on an informal basis.

Passing of Accounts

over-the-counter passing of accounts
uncontested passing of accounts (without a hearing)

As indicated above, the procedure for actually passing the accounts is covered in Chapter 14. As will be seen, an application to pass estate accounts ultimately ends in some form of court order, whether that be an **over-the-counter** order or an order following a hearing. "Over the counter" is a term used to describe a court procedure that does not involve a formal hearing before a judge. In either case, the process is commenced the same way.

Paying the Beneficiaries

After the assets are secured, the creditors are ascertained and paid, the beneficiaries have received an accounting and have released the estate trustee, or a judgment has been rendered upon a passing of accounts (discussed in more detail in Chapter 14), the payment of the beneficiaries is somewhat of an anticlimax. Once the releases have been signed and delivered to the estate trustee, or judgment has been entered in the court records, cheques to the beneficiaries for their respective shares of the estate are simply delivered to the beneficiaries.

KEY TERMS

REVIEW QUESTIONS

1. Define the following terms or concepts:

    a. interim distribution;

    b. payment of a "sum certain";

    c. interim accounting;

    d. informal accounting;

    e. passing of accounts.

2. What course of action is advisable when not all of the beneficiaries are willing to sign a release on an informal accounting?

3. What statements must be included in a formal estate accounting?

4. What are the usual starting rates for calculating the compensation of estate trustees?

5. What five factors can increase or decrease these rates?

6. What is the care and management fee and how is it usually calculated?

7. Explain the purpose of the investment account.

8. Why are vouchers required, how are they arranged, and for what purpose are they so organized?

9. What is the alternative to a passing of accounts?

10. Why is an estate accounting not normally provided to a creditor or a beneficiary of a sum certain?

11. Explain the importance of obtaining releases from all beneficiaries if a formal passing of accounts is not being carried out.

12. At what point in the administration of an estate is it acceptable for an estate trustee to take his compensation?

Administering Testamentary and Inter Vivos Trusts and Powers of Attorney

13

LEARNING OUTCOMES

After studying this chapter, you should be able to:

- Recount the obligations of trustees in the administration of testamentary and *inter vivos* trusts

- Explain the duties of attorneys or guardians of property in the administration of properties

- List the expectations for attorneys for personal care and guardians of the person

Introduction

We have seen that the administration of an estate consists of performing certain tasks, all of which are intended to lead to the result that the assets of the estate are completely distributed to the parties entitled to them, whether such parties are beneficiaries or creditors. This chapter introduces other kinds of administration: administration of trusts (both testamentary and *inter vivos*) and administration of powers of attorney or court-appointed guardianships.

It will be seen that the kinds of administration dealt with in this chapter are similar to estate administration in that the person charged with the duty—the trustee, attorney, or guardian—has a fiduciary obligation to make decisions for the benefit of another person and on that person's behalf. Furthermore, as in the case of the administration of an estate, it often falls to the lawyer to advise the person administering a trust, power of attorney, or guardianship with respect to his obligations.

Administration of Inter Vivos and Testamentary Trusts

As explained in Chapter 6, Trusts, the rules of a trust are set out in the trust document, whether it is a will or a deed of trust. Such rules are the starting point in administering a trust. As long as the rules make logical sense and are not contrary to law, they must be followed by the trustee.

Chapter 6 explained, however, that the rules of a trust are often quite open-ended and subject to a considerable amount of discretion on the part of the trustee. When grey areas appear, the law of fiduciary obligation, some of which is encoded in the *Trustee Act*,[1] must be adhered to. Some of those codified obligations are discussed below.

At the outset, two fundamental points about fiduciary obligations in trusts should be kept in mind. The first is that a trustee's actions taken with respect to the trust must always be in the best interests of the beneficiaries of the trust. It almost goes without saying that a trustee cannot have ulterior motives when taking actions with respect to a trust because doing so constitutes a breach of trust in both the civil and the criminal sense. This fiduciary principle of acting in the best interests of the beneficiaries, however, also extends to what is often called the **even hand principle**. According to this principle, the trustee must not act in the best interests of one beneficiary to the prejudice of another beneficiary, even if that other beneficiary is unborn or unascertained. Note, however, that the even hand rule may be modified by the trust document, which may state explicitly, for example, that the unborn or unascertained beneficiaries need be considered only in the event that the main beneficiary dies.

The second fundamental point with respect to a trustee's fiduciary obligations is that the trustee may delegate certain tasks in the administration of a trust, but she may never delegate responsibility or escape liability through such delegation. This is not to say that

even hand principle
principle according to which a trustee must not act in the best interests of one beneficiary to the prejudice of another beneficiary, even if that other beneficiary is unborn or unascertained; this principle can be modified by the terms of the trust document

---

1   RSO 1990, c T.23.

trustees are not allowed to seek advice—on the contrary, seeking professional advice in appropriate circumstances is the proper course of action.

Section 35 of the *Trustee Act* holds that some technical breaches of trust may be forgiven from the point of view of liability if the trustee "has acted honestly and reasonably, and ought fairly to be excused for the breach of trust, and for omitting to obtain the directions of the court in the matter in which the trustee committed the breach." This provision, while not providing an open-ended forgiveness of any breach of trust, may be called upon in the event that a breach of trust has occurred in the past, provided that the trustee acted honestly and reasonably in the circumstances.

Investment Obligations

One common duty of a trustee is to invest the funds of the trust to produce income for the beneficiaries or to increase the overall trust fund over time. The trust document often specifies certain kinds of investments that can and cannot be made. In the past there was a default scheme in the *Trustee Act* pertaining to the kinds of investments that could and could not be made by a trustee. In very general terms, investments in mutual funds and other kinds of equity were prohibited because of their inherent financial instability and because mutual funds are, by their nature, a delegation of decision-making authority to the financial institution in charge of the fund. This default rule could be overridden by the trust document, and many existing trusts and wills contain those kinds of overriding provisions.

The *Red Tape Reduction Act, 1998* (now *Red Tape Reduction Act, 2000*[2]) removed such restrictions. Now the rule is that a "trustee may invest trust property in any form of property in which a prudent investor might invest" (*Trustee Act*, section 27(2)). To give further guidance to trustees, the *Trustee Act* now sets out seven criteria to be considered when deciding whether to make a particular investment. The criteria, contained in section 27(5) of the Act, are as follows:

1. the general economic conditions;
2. the possible effect of inflation or deflation;
3. the expected tax consequences of investment decisions or strategies;
4. the role that each investment or course of action plays within the overall trust portfolio;
5. the expected total return from income and appreciation of capital;
6. the need for liquidity, regularity of income, and preservation or appreciation of capital; and
7. an asset's special relationship or special value, if any, to the purposes of the trust or to one or more of the beneficiaries.

The lawyer acting for the trustee should review this list of criteria with the trustee client to ensure that it is understood.

Another rule to be considered by a trustee client is that of diversification of investments. Section 27(6) of the *Trustee Act* states that a "trustee must diversify the investment of trust

---

2 SO 2000, c 26.

property to an extent that is appropriate to (a) the requirements of the trust, and (b) general economic and investment market conditions." With regard to diversification, and any other investment advice, section 27(8) of the Act provides that a trustee may obtain and act on advice from an expert (for example, a financial planner) as long as a prudent investor would rely on such advice in comparable circumstances. The reason for this rule is that, under common law, following such advice may in some circumstances be seen as an improper delegation of decision-making power over the trust. Nothing in section 27 allows a trustee to act in a way that is inconsistent with the terms or rules of the trust.

If the trustee relies on investment advice from an expert and a loss to the trust results, section 28 of the *Trustee Act* provides that the trustee is not liable for the loss "if the conduct of the trustee that led to the loss conformed to a plan or strategy for the investment of trust property, comprising reasonable assessments of risk and return, that a prudent investor could adopt under comparable circumstances." If a trust incurs a loss and it is questionable whether the trustee's assessment of the situation or her actions upon that assessment were reasonable, the matter may have to be referred to a court for a decision.

Accounting Obligations

A trustee, as a fiduciary, is obligated to account to the beneficiaries of the trust. Rule 74.16 of the *Rules of Civil Procedure*[3] states that the rules pertaining to estate accounts and passing of estate accounts "apply to accounts of estate trustees and, with necessary modifications, to accounts of trustees other than estate trustees, persons acting under a power of attorney, guardians of the property of mentally incapable persons, guardians of the property of a minor and persons having similar duties who are directed by the court to prepare accounts relating to their management of assets or money." Thus, the procedures to be followed as discussed in Chapter 12, Accounting to the Beneficiaries and Paying the Beneficiaries, apply with respect to the accounting by a trustee to beneficiaries of a testamentary or *inter vivos* trust.

As in the case of estate trustees, trustees proper are allowed payment for their services, which can be deducted from the trust fund usually after approval is obtained from the court. While in the case of estate trustees this remuneration is called executor's compensation, the payment to trustees is usually called **trustee's allowance**. The trustee's allowance may be fixed by the trust document itself, but if it is not, the allowance can be decided by a judge of the Superior Court upon a passing of accounts. Generally, the trustee's allowance is calculated in the same way as executor's compensation—that is, on the basis of the value of the trust property combined with the five factors outlined in the case of *Logan v Laing Estate*[4] (as discussed in Chapter 12).

allowance compensation paid to the trustee for administering the trust

Special Rules for Income Taxation of Trusts

The Relationship Between Estates and Testamentary Trusts

As discussed in Chapter 11, Determining, Notifying, and Paying Creditors of the Estate, an estate trustee must file tax returns for the deceased, including unfiled tax returns for past years and the terminal T1 tax return, as well as for the estate. The Canada Revenue

3 RRO 1990, reg 194.
4 (1998), 11 ETR (2d) 268 (Ont CA).

Agency (CRA) treats the estate as a testamentary trust, and for that reason the estate files a T3 trust income tax and information return. This section on filing tax returns for trusts should therefore also be borne in mind when approaching the filing of a tax return for the estate itself. Again, income tax is a highly technical area with ever-changing rules. What follows is a discussion of some issues that are commonly encountered in the administration of estates and is not meant as a complete treatment of the subject.

An estate is generally expected to be settled within 12 months of the date of death of the deceased. This period of time is referred to in the common law as "the executor's year." It is generally the case that during the executor's year the beneficiaries of the estate are not entitled to compel the estate trustee to make payment of their respective gifts. Where the estate trustee is also the trustee of a testamentary trust that was set up in the will of the deceased, it is during the executor's year that his dual role as estate trustee and trustee proper begins to diverge into two distinct roles.

Strictly speaking, from the date when a testamentary trust is set up, the income must be reported on a separate T3 trust return, which will eventually be filed according to the deadlines discussed below. A T3 trust return will also be filed for the estate itself covering the period from the date of death until the estate year end. The estate can select a year end that is any time before the anniversary of the date of death (where the estate is not wound up by that time). In addition, if the will created more than one testamentary trust—one with different beneficiaries—there can be separate T3 tax returns for each trust. Sometimes, where the estate trustee and the trustee proper are the same person, the estate account is used as the trust account for the testamentary trust, in which case single T3 trust returns are filed for each year during which the testamentary trust and the estate are active (although, see the discussion below regarding graduated rate estates). In such situations, the distinction between the role of estate trustee and trustee proper can get murky, and it may be necessary to scrutinize the trust provisions of the will to ensure that the testamentary trust is being administered in accordance with its rules. As a general guiding principle, the estate trustee should be able to account separately, and to the penny, for both the estate funds and the testamentary trust funds.

As indicated in Chapter 11, the estate trustee must file additional T3 trust returns for estates that extend beyond a year.

Graduated Rate Estates and Qualified Disability Trusts

Before January 1, 2016, all testamentary trusts had beneficial tax treatment. Now only certain kinds of testamentary trusts have such treatment—namely, "graduated rate estates" and qualified disability trusts. A graduated rate estate (referred to herein as a "graduated rate estate trust") is a testamentary trust that has been designated by the estate trustee as such. Only one such designation is allowed per estate or per person and the trust exists as a graduated rate estate trust only for the first 36 months following the death of the deceased.

A qualified disability trust is a testamentary trust in which one of the beneficiaries is eligible for the disability tax credit under the *Income Tax Act*.[5]

---

5 RSC 1985, c 1 (5th Supp).

Special Tax Treatment of Graduated Rate Estates and Qualified Disability Trusts

T3 trust returns are filed for all testamentary trusts and *inter vivos* trusts. There are, however, differences in how a trust is treated by the CRA depending on whether the trust is a graduated rate estate trust or a qualified disability trust on the one hand or any other kind of trust on the other hand. The most significant difference is the fact that graduated rate estate trusts and qualified disability trusts pay tax in accordance with the various tax brackets that are available to individuals while all other trusts (including spousal trusts) are taxed at the highest tax bracket.

It should be noted as well that all trusts, except the graduated rate estate trust, will have a calendar year end. A graduated rate estate trust can have a non-calendar year end until the expiration of the 36-month period, at which time it becomes an ordinary testamentary trust with a calendar year-end.

Neither testamentary trusts nor *inter vivos* trusts are entitled to the personal exemptions that are available to individuals. In other words, while individuals need not file tax returns if their income is below the personal tax credit of approximately $11,000, a trustee must file a T3 tax return if any income at all is earned by the trust. This rule requiring the filing of a T3 trust return for any income applies to estates as well, except in the limited circumstances where a T3 trust return need not be filed, as discussed below.

Waiving the Need for Filing the T3 Trust Return in Certain Circumstances

In the event that the total annual income of the trust (or the estate, as the case may be) is less than $500, no more than $100 is allocated to each beneficiary of the trust or estate, and none of the beneficiaries are non-residents of Canada, the T3 trust return need not be filed. In such cases, however, the beneficiaries must be notified by the trustee or estate trustee that they must report their share of any income of the trust or estate on their own personal tax returns for the year.

Filing Dates for the T3 Trust Return

For both testamentary trusts and *inter vivos* trusts, the deadline to file the T3 trust return is 90 days from the end of the taxation year. In most cases this is 90 days from the end of the last year.

Reporting the Tax on a Beneficiary's Return

Income Paid or Payable

The determination of whether the income can be taxed in the trust or taxed to the beneficiaries depends on the wording of the will. If the will requires all income to be paid to the beneficiaries it must be taxed to the beneficiaries unless an election is filed to tax it in the estate. This election has several restrictions. If the will does not require the payment of income to the beneficiaries, in order to tax it to the beneficiaries the income must be paid or payable to the beneficiary during the taxation year. Income is payable if the beneficiary is entitled by virtue of the rules of the trust to force the trustee to pay the income for the year to the beneficiary. In this connection, note that in normal circumstances, the beneficiary is not entitled to force payment of her share during the executor's year.

Income Spent on Trust Property

Income can also be reported on a beneficiary's tax return where the income from the trust is spent on trust property being used by the beneficiary. If, for example, some of the income from the trust is paid toward repairing the furnace of a house that the beneficiary occupies according to the terms of the trust, the amount spent can be reported on the beneficiary's individual tax return. Similarly, if the money is spent on municipal property taxes for the house, that amount can be reported on the beneficiary's individual tax return.

Preferred Beneficiary Election

Another situation in which the income from a trust can be reported on the beneficiary's tax return relates to what is called the **preferred beneficiary election**. If a beneficiary is disabled—that is, entitled to the disability tax credit—and related to the settlor of the trust, an election can be filed to report any income that is accumulating in the trust to the benefit of the disabled beneficiary. The income that can be reported on a beneficiary's individual tax return under this election is not just income that is paid or payable but any income accruing to the trust to the benefit of the disabled beneficiary. The deadline to file the preferred beneficiary election is 90 days from the end of the taxation year of the trust.

preferred beneficiary election
election that can be filed by a disabled beneficiary to report any income that is accumulating in the trust to the benefit of the beneficiary

Trust as a Conduit of Income

Under the *Income Tax Act*, benefits are available for income from certain sources. One example is income from capital gains. Besides the concession that only 50 percent of the capital gain be included in the taxpayer's income, it is possible to reduce a capital gain by the amount of certain capital losses. Other sources of income for which there are special beneficial tax treatment provisions are dividends from taxable Canadian corporations, for which there is a dividend tax credit, and foreign source income, for which there is often an available reduction based on tax treaties with other countries.

When the income of a trust is taken to be income of the beneficiary (for example, when the income is paid or payable to the beneficiary, or when the beneficiary and the trustee make a preferred beneficiary election), the beneficiary may not be able to take advantage of any benefit that would otherwise have been available had he received the income from the specified source directly. In other words, the trust is a conduit of the income itself but is not a conduit of the source of the income. There are, however, some exceptions for certain specific sources of income, in respect of which the trust is a conduit of both the income and the source.

Some of these exceptions are income from taxable Canadian corporations (for which there is a dividend tax credit), capital gains income from the sale of qualified farm property or qualified small business corporation shares (for which there is capital gains exemption), ordinary capital gains (which can be reduced by capital losses), deferred profit-sharing plan benefits, and certain death benefits. For such specific exceptions, the benefit arising from the source of the income flows through to the beneficiary.

Withholding Tax for Non-Resident Beneficiaries

If the beneficiary who is to report the income is a non-resident of Canada, 25 percent of the income (the percentage may vary depending on the country of residence in question) must be held back and remitted to the CRA. As in the case of any other kind of withholding tax, if no withholding is made, the party charged with the responsibility of withholding and remitting—in this case, the trustee—is personally liable for the amount.

Income Tax Consequences on Distribution of Capital from the Trust

If capital, as opposed to income, is being distributed from a trust to a beneficiary, it will be disposed of by the trust without capital gain consequences to the trust. In other words, if the capital is non-depreciable property, the *Income Tax Act* deems the value of the capital property on the date of disposition to be the adjusted cost base of the property, and the beneficiary is deemed to have received the property at its adjusted cost base. When the beneficiary of the property finally disposes of it, the capital gains are calculated using the original adjusted cost base at which the trust acquired the property. If the capital being distributed is depreciable capital property, the trust is deemed to have disposed of it at its undepreciated capital cost, and the beneficiary is deemed to have acquired it at that value.

Notwithstanding this rule, if the capital is being distributed from a spousal trust while the spouse is still alive but to a beneficiary who is not the spouse, the *Income Tax Act* deems the transaction to be made at fair market value (meaning that capital gains tax may be payable by the estate). If, on the other hand, the spouse dies before there is a capital distribution from the spousal trust, there is a deemed disposition at fair market value of the capital property held by the spousal trust. This special rule relating to the capital distribution from a spousal trust somewhat counteracts the special treatment afforded spousal trusts under the Act. It should be noted, in this context, that much of the usefulness of spousal trusts has now been eliminated insofar as they are now taxed at the highest tax bracket.

Twenty-One-Year Deemed Disposition

The basic rule for trusts is that they are not allowed to accumulate capital value over long periods of time without paying tax. Under the *Income Tax Act*, every 21 years a trust is deemed to have disposed of all of its capital property at fair market value. The rule, known as the **21-year deemed disposition rule of trusts**, does not apply to spousal trusts. Such a trust can accumulate capital without tax consequences as long as the spouse is alive and the spousal trust remains active.

21-year deemed disposition rule of trusts rule that every 21 years a trust is deemed to have disposed of all of its capital property at fair market value

Clearance Certificate for Trusts

Clearance certificates from the CRA were discussed in Chapter 11 in the context of the administration of an estate. In that chapter, it was stated that the estate trustee should obtain a clearance certificate before winding up the estate as confirmation that she has paid all necessary tax and can consider the estate wound up. Clearance certificates are also available for trusts upon the final winding up of a trust. Because trusts often remain in existence for long periods of time, however, trustees sometimes obtain interim clearance certificates periodically as assurance that all necessary taxes have been paid up to that point in time. The procedure for obtaining a final or interim clearance certificate for a trust is similar to that for obtaining a final clearance certificate for an estate.

As in the case of estates, the form to be used is Form TX19, "Asking for a Clearance Certificate." Instead of providing the will or the particulars of the family of the deceased (as in the case of intestacy), the trustee provides the trust document (the will of the deceased if it is a testamentary trust, or the deed of trust if it is an *inter vivos* trust). In addition, the trustee must provide particulars of any distributions made during the period for which the clearance certificate is being sought. The particulars should include any instances in which the income was taxed in the hands of beneficiaries and the details of any capital distributions, including the adjusted cost base or undepreciated capital cost of the property and its fair market value.

If the trustee is requesting a final clearance certificate, he must also provide a distribution plan for any income or capital of the estate to be distributed, including the particulars outlined above.

As in the case of requests for clearance certificates in estates, if the trustee wants the CRA to communicate with the trustee's lawyer, law clerk, or anyone else, she should provide the CRA with a Form T1013 which must be signed by all of the estate trustees. As in the case of estates, as long as all the proper documentation is submitted and all necessary tax is paid, the clearance certificate will arrive by mail in due course.

Powers of Attorney for Property and Guardianships of Property

Powers of attorney for property were discussed in Chapter 5, Powers of Attorney. Guardianships of property occur when a person who is not acting as attorney for property applies to a court to be made a guardian of an incapable person's property. Obtaining such guardianships is dealt with in Part III, Estate Litigation, Chapter 16, Statutory Forms of Estate Litigation, because it involves a court procedure.

The attorney or guardian of property has a duty to see that the property is looked after (administered) in an appropriate manner. The duty is similar to that of a trustee in that it is fiduciary in nature.

Powers of the Attorney for Property and the Guardian of Property

As indicated in Chapter 5, subject to any restrictions contained in the power of attorney document, the attorney for property is able to do anything with respect to property that the grantor of the power of attorney could have done, if capable, except make a will. The powers of a guardian of property are the same.

Duties of the Attorney for Property and the Guardian of Property

The duties of an attorney for property and a guardian of property are fiduciary in nature. That is, the attorney for property and the guardian of property have a duty to act in the best interests of the incapable person at all times with respect to administering her property. As indicated in Chapter 5, the attorney has a duty to always be in a position to account for his actions taken as attorney. This requires that the attorney maintain accounts at all times.

The duties and powers of a court-appointed guardian of property are set out in sections 32 to 42 of the *Substitute Decisions Act, 1992*.[6] These include, for example, the duty to consult from time to time with supportive family and friends of the subject person—that is, the person whose property is being managed—and with the persons from whom the subject person receives personal care, as well as the duty to encourage the subject person to participate, to the best of her abilities, in decisions made on her behalf.

A guardian of property also has a duty to maintain accounts. Under the *Substitute Decisions Act, 1992*, O Reg 100/96 gives particulars of the accounts that are to be maintained by attorneys and guardians. They are similar to those required to be kept by an estate trustee in the administration of an estate. As indicated above, the procedure for a formal passing of accounts relating to a power of attorney for property or a guardianship of property are similar to the procedure for a formal passing of accounts in estates under rule 74.16 of the *Rules of Civil Procedure*. The lawyer preparing the documentation for the passing of accounts would make whatever modifications are required in view of the fact that the accounting is for the administration of a guardianship or a power of attorney rather than an estate.

It should be noted that O Reg 26/95 (under the *Substitute Decisions Act, 1992*) indicates that the default amount of compensation allowed to attorneys for property and guardians of property is 3 percent of capital and income receipts, 3 percent of capital and income disbursements, and a care and management fee of three-fifths of 1 percent.

Attorneys for Personal Care and Guardians of the Person

Powers of attorney for personal care were also discussed in Chapter 5. Like guardianships of property, guardianships of the person occur when a person who is not acting as attorney for personal care applies to a court to be made a guardian of an incapable person and thereby be in a position to make decisions regarding that person's health care, nutrition, shelter, clothing, hygiene, or safety. Again, obtaining such a guardianship is dealt with in Part III, Chapter 16.

---

6 SO 1992, c 30.

Powers of the Attorney for Personal Care and the Guardian of the Person

An attorney for personal care or a guardian of the person has the power to make whatever decisions the incapable person could have made with respect to his personal care if he were mentally capable. The administration of such a power or guardianship takes place through decisions concerning the personal care of the incapable person, including the giving of health care instructions to professionals and other people assisting the incapable person. As explained in Chapter 5, a power of attorney for personal care can contain specific restrictions, which would apply to limit the power of the attorney for personal care. The power of attorney for personal care should, of course, be carefully reviewed.

Duties of the Attorney for Personal Care and the Guardian of the Person

The duties of a court-appointed guardian of the person are set out in sections 66 to 68 of the *Substitute Decisions Act, 1992*. These include the duty to keep records of personal care decisions made on the subject person's behalf, the duty to encourage the subject person to participate as best as she can in personal care decisions, and the duty to choose the least restrictive and intrusive course of action that is available in the circumstances with respect to the subject person. It is also a requirement of the Act for the guardian of the person to attempt to foster regular personal contact between the subject person and her supportive family members and friends, and to consult with them from time to time regarding personal care decisions to be made on behalf of the subject person.

KEY TERMS

21-year deemed disposition rule of trusts, 282
allowance, 278

even hand principle, 276
preferred beneficiary election, 281

REVIEW QUESTIONS

1. Identify two types of trust documents that set out the rules of a trust.

2. What are the fiduciary obligations of the trustee to the beneficiaries?

3. What are the investment obligations of the trustee?

4. What criteria must be considered when a trustee makes investment decisions?

5. What are the accounting obligations of the trustee?

6. How is the allowance to the trustee determined?

7. What is a graduated rate estate trust?

8. What other kind of trust can use the various tax brackets available to individuals, besides the graduated rate estate trust?

9. When must the T3 trust return be filed for (a) a testamentary trust and (b) an *inter vivos* trust?

10. Under what circumstances might a "preferred beneficiary election" be filed?

11. Why is it desirable to report income from a trust on a beneficiary's income tax return?

12. Explain how a trust can be a conduit of income but not the source of the income for its beneficiaries.

13. When is a trustee not required to file a T3 trust return?

14. What is required with respect to the payment of income to a non-resident beneficiary of a trust?

15. Why is there a "21-year deemed disposition of capital rule" in trust tax law? What is the exception to this rule?

16. What is the importance of applying for a final clearance certificate?

17. What is the difference between an attorney for property and a guardian of property?

18. What are the powers and duties of both an attorney for property and a guardian of property?

19. What are the powers and duties of both an attorney for personal care and a guardian of the person?

PART III

Estate Litigation

Challenging the Conduct of the Estate Trustee and Passing of Accounts

14

LEARNING OUTCOMES

After completing this chapter, you should be able to:

- Understand the basic differences among actions, applications, and motions

- Have a working knowledge of the possible orders for assistance under rule 74 of the *Rules of Civil Procedure* and how they can assist in challenging the conduct of an estate trustee

- Know the procedures to be used to obtain an order for assistance

- Know the procedures for commencing a passing of accounts

- Know the procedures for obtaining an uncontested passing of accounts

- Know the procedures for obtaining a contested passing of accounts, including requests for costs and requests for increased costs

- Understand the use of and procedures associated with a request for further notice in a passing of accounts

Introduction

Part I of this text covered the topic of estate planning and Part II covered estate administration. This final part covers estate litigation, which is a term that is commonly used by lawyers and yet is perhaps not well understood by the general public. In its widest definition, the term "estate litigation" encapsulates any dispute involving an estate (or a trust or a power of attorney) that cannot be resolved without a decision from a judge or a negotiated settlement. Perhaps somewhat confusing to people is the fact that the courts are involved in estates even where there is no dispute or litigation. This is because certificates of appointment of estate trustee are granted by the court and applications for them are made to the court in accordance with the *Rules of Civil Procedure*.[1] The drafters of the *Rules of Civil Procedure* appear to have acknowledged that it would be useful to draw a distinction between estate litigation matters and estate administration matters when, in 1995, they enacted rules 74 and 75. From that time forward, rule 74, and all of its subrules, were grouped under the heading "Rule 74—Estates—Non-Contentious Proceedings" and rule 75 with its subrules were grouped under the heading "Rule 75—Estates—Contentious Proceedings." In broad strokes, rule 74 covers the procedures for obtaining certificates of appointment and passing accounts and rule 75 covers the procedures for contesting wills, trusts, and powers of attorney. As we will see, however, many procedures outlined in rule 74 arise in contentious proceedings and require a judicial decision or negotiation. Accordingly, rather than looking at rule 74 as applying to non-contentious proceedings and rule 75 as applying to contentious proceedings, it is perhaps more useful to view rule 74 as the rule directed at challenges to the conduct of the estate trustee (or the trustee or attorney as the case may be) and to view rule 75 as the rule directed at challenges to the validity of the will (or trust or power of attorney). This chapter, which deals with challenges to the conduct of the estate trustee, focuses on the procedures set down in rule 74 of the *Rules of Civil Procedure*.

We have seen in Part II, Estate Administration, that the estate trustee has several tasks to perform when administering an estate—securing and collecting the assets, ascertaining and paying the creditors, rendering accounts, and paying the beneficiaries. Sometimes during the course of the administration of an estate, a person with an interest in the estate takes the position that the estate trustee has failed in one or more of her duties. The person may allege, for example, that the estate trustee failed to properly value the assets or is claiming too much in compensation or that the estate is taking too long to administer. In all cases of this nature, it is open to the person wishing to challenge the conduct of the estate trustee to seek the court's assistance using the *Rules of Civil Procedure*. If the court finds that the conduct is deficient in some way, it may order the estate trustee to do something or to refrain from doing something or it may remove the estate trustee altogether. On the other hand, the court may find that the estate trustee's conduct was appropriate in the circumstances and approve her actions. Indeed, an estate trustee may herself decide that her own accounts should be passed by the court so that she can safely wind up the estate.

This chapter also covers the procedures for seeking the court's assistance where a person is named as estate trustee in the will but has declined to accept the role. While such actions are brought against the person named as estate trustee, it is not necessarily on the basis of

---

1   RRO 1990, reg 194.

an allegation that he has done something wrong, but rather that the issue of who is to act as estate trustee must be resolved so that the estate can be properly administered.

Note in relation to estate litigation in general (including the matters covered in this chapter as well as in Chapters 15, Challenging the Validity of the Will, and 16, Statutory Forms of Estate Litigation) that many disputes or challenges can be resolved through mediation, which is an out-of-court process overseen by an independent third party—a mediator—who facilitates negotiation among the parties. In some jurisdictions in Ontario, mediation is mandatory in estate litigation matters, meaning that the parties are obligated to attempt to settle the issues in dispute with a mediator. In all other jurisdictions, mediation is an option for the parties to consider and can be ordered by the court. The final chapter of this book, Chapter 17, Mediation in Estate Litigation, deals with the subject of mediations, both voluntary and court-ordered.

Organization of the Rules of Civil Procedure

Each rule in the *Rules of Civil Procedure* covers a specific area of operation of the Superior Court of Justice of Ontario. Each rule is like a chapter insofar as it has its own set of sub-rules and covers its own topic. Rule 3, for example, is entitled "Time" and contains all rules needed for interpreting any reference to time as it occurs in the *Rules of Civil Procedure*. For example, rule 3.01(1)(a) states that where the rules indicate that there must be a certain number of days between two events, the number of days is counted by excluding the first day on which the first event happens and counting the day on which the second event happens. Also under the subject of time is rule 3.02(1), which states that notwithstanding any other rule, the court may extend or abridge any deadline set out in the rules "on such terms as are just." In general discourse between lawyers and law clerks, it may be confusing when someone says, for example, "the answer is in rule 74" or "I am relying on rule 74.16." Nevertheless, the context of each statement should make it clear whether the statement is referring to a chapter (rule 74) or a particular rule in the chapter (rule 74.16).

The forms prescribed by each rule of the *Rules of Civil Procedure* are set out in an appendix to the rules and follow the number system of the rule or chapter prescribing the form. For example, rule 49 deals with offers to settle litigation and prescribes a special form, Form 49C, in which an offer to settle should be made. In this way, any form referred to in a rule will be identified by a whole number (the number of the rule or chapter in which the form is mentioned) and a letter or a decimal (to differentiate the form from any other form mentioned in the same rule or chapter). All forms in the *Rules of Civil Procedure* are available in PDF or MS Word format on the following website: <www.ontariocourtforms. on.ca/en/rules-of-civil-procedure-forms/>. It may be noted that all of the forms mentioned in Chapter 9, Applying for a Certificate of Appointment of Estate Trustee, refer to forms that start with the number 74, which means that these forms are prescribed in specific rules under Rule 74—Estates—Non-Contentious Proceedings in the *Rules of Civil Procedure*.

Finally, it should be mentioned that the *Rules of Civil Procedure* are constantly being amended to accommodate new situations and growing difficulties in the administration of the courts. You will see that several rules, as they currently stand, do create quandaries and even confusion for lawyers and law clerks in the area of estate litigation. This text points out some of these areas of difficulty, not to be critical of the drafters of the rules, but to highlight areas in which a lawyer or law clerk must think especially carefully about how to proceed in order to best serve the client.

Orders for Assistance

Rule 74.15 of the *Rules of Civil Procedure* provides for parties in estate matters to obtain what the rules call "orders for assistance." This rule sets out a number of possible orders a person can request from the court, some of which are useful when challenging the conduct of the estate trustee or moving an estate beyond an impasse arising from the inaction of a person appointed as estate trustee. What follows is a discussion of some of the possible orders specifically outlined in that rule.

Types of Orders for Assistance

Order to Accept or Refuse Appointment of Estate Trustee With a Will

As outlined in Part II, if a person has been named as estate trustee in a will but does not wish to accept that role, the job will normally fall to the next-named estate trustee. If there is no alternate estate trustee named, then it is open to any person to apply for an appointment (although some have interpreted section 29(1) of the *Estates Act*[2] as giving priority to spouses or next of kin). Regardless of who is next in line, before that person can apply, the court needs to be sure that the first named does not accept the job. This is normally communicated to the court by way of a document called a "renunciation," signed by the first-named estate trustee, or with a death certificate of that person. If, however, the first-named estate trustee declines to sign a renunciation, the estate administration process can be frustrated. In that situation, the court can be asked pursuant to rule 74.15(1)(a) to issue an order to accept or refuse an appointment in Form 74.36 (see Figure 14.1). Such an order gives the named estate trustee a specified period of time in which to apply for a certificate of appointment and also specifies that if he has not done so by a certain date, he is deemed to have renounced.

Order to Accept or Refuse Appointment of Estate Trustee Without a Will

If a person dies without a will, section 29(1) of the *Estates Act* suggests that first the spouse of the deceased and then the next of kin take priority over other persons regarding who is entitled to apply as the estate trustee without a will. If someone has such apparent priority but is taking no steps, another person who wishes to act can obtain an order that is similar to the one discussed above insofar as it gives the person with priority a specified period of time to apply for a certificate of appointment, failing which someone else can then apply. The rule providing for such an order in an intestate estate is rule 74.15(1)(b), which states that a person can apply for an order "requiring any person to accept or refuse an appointment as an estate trustee without a will." The form provided for this kind of order is Form 74.37.

---

2   RSO 1990, c E.21.

FIGURE 14.1 **Order to Accept or Refuse Appointment as Estate Trustee With a Will (Form 74.36)**

Court File No. 19-784RT45

ONTARIO
SUPERIOR COURT OF JUSTICE

The Honourable Madam)
Sung) the 10th day of February, 2018
)

IN THE ESTATE OF Musa Yavuz, deceased

B E T W E E N:

ENGIN KEMAL

Applicant
(Moving Party)

- and -

HASIP PEDRINHO

Respondent
(Responding Party)

**ORDER TO ACCEPT OR REFUSE APPOINTMENT
AS ESTATE TRUSTEE WITH A WILL**

A motion for this order has been made by Engin Kemal. From an affidavit made by Engin Kemal that has been filed it appears that you are named as estate trustee in a will or codicil of the deceased dated June 2, 2015.

1. THIS COURT ORDERS THAT you file an application for a certificate of appointment of estate trustee with a will in the court office within 20 days after this order is served on you.

2. THIS COURT ORDERS THAT if you do not do so within that time, you shall be deemed to have renounced your right to be appointed.

_____D.A. Sung_____
Signature of Judge

Address of court office:

10 Weather Road
Weatherston, ON
Y7X 2H3

TO: Hasip Pedrinho
32 Highpond Road
Swynham, ON
H8T 3C9

RCP-E 74.36 (November 1, 2005)

Order to Consent or Object to Proposed Appointment

As indicated in Chapter 9, a person seeking a certificate of appointment of estate trustee without a will may need to file consents from the beneficiaries before being appointed. Recall that the applicant and the beneficiaries consenting must represent a majority interest in the estate. If a person is seeking an appointment of estate trustee without a will and needs a consent from a beneficiary who is not providing it, an order to consent or object to a proposed appointment under rule 74.15(1)(c) can assist. The order, in Form 74.38, provides a certain amount of time to object to the proposed appointment, beyond which time the beneficiary is deemed to consent. The order requires that a Notice of Objection to Appointment of Estate Trustee form be attached as Schedule "A," presumably to make it easier for a beneficiary to signify his objection if he has one.

Order to File a Statement of Assets

Another order that can be useful to a person who believes she is not being provided sufficient information about the estate from the estate trustee is an order to the estate trustee that he file a statement of assets pursuant to rule 74.15(1)(d). This order, in Form 74.39 as shown in Figure 14.2, requires the estate trustee to file a statement of each asset owned by the deceased on the date of death and its value at that time. This kind of order is particularly useful early in the estate administration process when it is too early to expect a full accounting but some sense of the value of the estate is being sought and the estate trustee is not cooperating.

Order for Further Particulars of Assets

If an order to file a statement of assets is obtained and the resulting information is vague or wanting of useful details, an order for further particulars can be obtained. The *Rules of Civil Procedure* do not provide a special form for this kind of order (unlike the other orders for assistance) but an example of such an order is reproduced in Figure 14.3.

Order to Pass Accounts

If the estate trustee has been given sufficient time to administer the estate and is failing to account to the beneficiaries, an order can be obtained pursuant to rule 74.15(1)(h) forcing the estate trustee to pass the accounts. In this context, it is worth recalling the discussion in Chapter 2, Will Clauses, that an estate trustee is generally considered to have an "executor's year" to wind up an estate. This would suggest in the normal course that within approximately 10 to 16 months it would be reasonable to expect some form of accounting. The order to pass accounts is in Form 74.42 and an example is reproduced in Figure 14.4. It provides for the estate trustee and the beneficiaries to take part in a particular process that is discussed in detail below under "Passing of Accounts."

FIGURE 14.2   Order to File Statement of Assets (Form 74.39)

Court File No. 18-4549P8

ONTARIO
SUPERIOR COURT OF JUSTICE

The Honourable Madam   )
Sung   )   the 17th   day of   September, 2018
)

IN THE ESTATE OF Kristina Nataliya, deceased

B E T W E E N:

MARYA NONNA

Applicant
(Moving Party)

- and -

INNOKENTY NONNA

Respondent
(Responding Party)

ORDER TO FILE A STATEMENT OF ASSETS OF THE ESTATE

A motion for this order has been made by Marya Nonna. From an affidavit made by Marya Nonna that has been filed it appears that you are an estate trustee of the estate and that you should provide further information about the assets of the estate.

THIS COURT ORDERS THAT you file a statement of the nature of each asset of the estate and its value at the date of death in the court office within 30 days after this order is served on you.

_____
D.A. Sung
Signature of Judge

Address of court office:

10 Weather Road
Weatherston, ON
Y7X 2H3

TO: Innokenty Nonna
       13-879 Mooremead Cres
       Lochport, ON
       R84 3L3

RCP-E 74.36 (November 1, 2005)

FIGURE 14.3 **Order for Further Particulars of Assets**

Court File No. 18-4549P8

ONTARIO
SUPERIOR COURT OF JUSTICE

The Honourable Madam	)	
Sung	)	the 10th day of December, 2018
	)	

IN THE ESTATE OF Kristina Nataliya, deceased

B E T W E E N:

MARYA NONNA

Applicant
(Moving Party)

- and -

INNOKENTY NONNA

Respondent
(Responding Party)

ORDER

THIS MOTION made by the moving parties for an order for further particulars was heard this day at Weatherston, Ontario, in the presence of the lawyers for the moving parties, the responding parties.

ON READING the motion record of the moving parties dated November 25, 2018, the motion record of the responding parties dated December 10, 2018, filed, and on hearing submissions made,

1.   **THIS COURT ORDERS** that within 10 days of the date of this order, the responding party, Innokenty Nonna, shall provide the moving party, Marya Nonna, with copies of the 2016 to 2018 statements from the Anchor Savings Credit Union bank accounts bearing account numbers 004-784963 and 004-478398.

_____D.A. Sung_____
Signature of Judge

Address of court office:

10 Weather Road
Weatherston, ON
Y7X 2H3

FIGURE 14.4   Order to Pass Accounts (Form 74.42)

Court File No. 18-34AA89

ONTARIO
SUPERIOR COURT OF JUSTICE

The Honourable Madam)
Sung   )   the 10th day of February, 2018
)

IN THE ESTATE OF Saleem Doka, deceased

B E T W E E N:

JABAAR ALI

Applicant
(Moving Party)

- and -

NABEEL HABACHI

Respondent
(Responding Party)

ORDER TO PASS ACCOUNTS

A motion for this order has been made by *Jabaar Ali*. From an affidavit made by Jabaar Ali that has been filed it appears that you are an estate trustee of the estate and that you have made no accounting to the court of your dealings with the estate during the period from *November 24, 2017* to *the present*.

THIS COURT ORDERS THAT you file accounts of the estate and an application to pass accounts, in accordance with rules 74.17 and 74.18 of the Rules of Civil Procedure, in the court office within 30 days after this order is served on you.

_____
Signature of Judge

Address of court office:

10 Weather Road
Weatherston, ON
Y7X 2H3

TO: Nabeel Habachi
        34 Madison Road
        Fairmont, ON
        Y9M 3D3

RCP-E 74.42 (November 1, 2005)

Order to Deliver Will or Codicil to the Registrar or to Provide Information

The preamble to rule 74.15(1) makes reference to section 9(1) of the *Estates Act*, which provides that an order can be obtained on a motion or application requiring a person with possession of a will or codicil of a deceased person to bring it to the registrar of the court. Section 9(2) provides that if there are reasonable grounds to believe that a person has knowledge of a will or codicil of a deceased person, that person can be ordered to attend before the court, or anywhere else that the court directs, for questioning regarding the will or codicil. The preamble to rule 74.15(1) is worded in such a way as to suggest that these orders under the *Estates Act* are to be considered orders for assistance under the rule and can be obtained in the same way as the other possible orders outlined in the rule.

Order for Other Matters

Rule 74.15(1)(i) allows for "an order providing for any other matter that the court directs." This catch-all language makes it clear that creative requests, provided they are reasonable and justifiable in the circumstances, will be entertained by the court.

Procedures for Obtaining Orders for Assistance

Who Can Challenge the Conduct of the Estate Trustee

It is not open to anybody to challenge the conduct of the estate trustee or to obtain an order for assistance. In order to have standing to do so, one must be able to show that she is a **person who appears to have a financial interest in the estate**. This term, which appears in rules 74 and 75 of the *Rules of Civil Procedure*, is not specifically defined, but is clearly open-ended so as to include not just beneficiaries but also potential beneficiaries and creditors who may be prejudiced by the estate trustee's actions.

By natural extension, those representing persons appearing to have a financial interest in the estate such as attorneys, litigation guardians, and government officials (the office of the Children's Lawyer and the Public Guardian and Trustee), have standing if the person represented has standing.

person who appears to have a financial interest in the estate person who can demonstrate that she is likely to have a personal stake in the estate

Motions, Applications, and Actions

Although this text is not intended to be about civil procedure, one fundamental point should be mentioned in order to make the following discussion meaningful. It concerns the difference between actions that are commenced by a statement of claim and applications that are commenced by a notice of application. Both *actions* and *applications* are proceedings used by litigants to bring a matter before the court for a decision. In actions, the court's decision is intended to be based, at least in part, on *viva voce* evidence—the testimony of live witnesses. In applications, the court's decision is intended to be based on affidavit evidence.

From this fundamental difference arise other differences, such as the length of time for the hearing. Actions are typically heard over the course of several days or weeks, while applications are typically heard over the course of hours. Not surprisingly then, the cost of actions is usually many times more than that of applications. Actions often take months, if not years, to prepare for hearing, whereas applications can usually be prepared in a matter of days, weeks, or months.

The *Rules of Civil Procedure* identify the situations in which an estate matter should be brought by way of action or by way of application (for example, rule 14.05(3) sets out estate matters to be brought by way of application), but such rules are often intended only as guidelines. The real determining factor is whether factual issues are in dispute—that is, differing versions of the facts and events that are relevant to a final determination of the matter. If two or more parties are in disagreement and they claim that conflicting facts exist that are relevant to determining the legal issues, the matter can usually only proceed by way of action. The reason for this is that the evidence must be weighed and decided "first hand" by the trier of fact—the judge, or judge and jury, as the case may be—through the testimony of witnesses who are subject to cross-examination.

Applications are often compared with motions. Motions, like applications, are brought on the basis of affidavit evidence, are brought quickly and comparatively inexpensively before the court, and are usually dealt with in a matter of hours. The difference between motions and applications is that (except in very rare circumstances outside the scope of this text) motions are brought only within the confines of an overall action or ongoing application. Motions are usually brought to deal with a matter, often procedural, that has come up during the course of pursuing the action or application. Because of the foregoing, rule 74.15(1) can create a quandary insofar as it provides that the orders for assistance can be obtained by way of motion where there is no overriding procedure in which to bring the motion. What many lawyers do to accommodate this quandary is commence an application for all matters being pursued with respect to the estate. This would then be followed by a motion for an order for assistance within that application. An alternative would be simply to bring an "application" for an order for assistance rather than a "motion." In general, the procedures for bringing motions are contained in rule 37 of the *Rules of Civil Procedure*, and the procedures for bringing applications are contained in rule 38.

The sample draft orders provided in Figures 14.1 to 14.4 are based on the assumption that the orders are being sought by way of motion within an overall application. Note that the various orders for assistance laid out in rule 74.15 are always within the discretion of the court. If a judge is of the view that a requested order is not reasonable or necessary in the circumstances, she will of course decline to sign the order or she may make changes to the order before signing it.

Notice Requirements

All orders for assistance, except an order for further particulars in accordance with rule 74.15(1)(e), can be obtained without notice to the estate trustee (or to any other affected party). This provision, contained in rule 74.15(2), is extraordinary insofar as it departs from the policy underlying much of the *Rules of Civil Procedure* that notice of a step in a proceeding is akin to a right of the person affected by such a step. What should be taken from this fact is the absolute necessity for the party seeking the order to be candid and complete with the information provided to the court. It should also be noted that notwithstanding rule 74.15(2), it is within a judge's inherent jurisdiction to adjourn a motion brought without notice under Rule 74.15 and order that the affected party—in this case the estate trustee—receive notice of the motion so that she can make representations.

Examinations Out of Court

Here, mention should be made of rule 74.15(4), which specifically allows for an order requiring any person to be examined under oath for the purpose of deciding a motion for an order for assistance. This rule would be invoked in a situation where more information is needed by a party seeking an order for assistance, or a party resisting one, prior to the hearing of that motion. A preliminary motion would be brought for an order requiring a person to be examined on matters relevant to the main motion. Assuming the court orders the examination to take place, the person would attend on an agreed date at an official examiner's office and answer questions under oath posed by the lawyer for the other party on matters related to the main motion. A written transcript would then be generated and, at the hearing of the main motion, portions from the transcript could be read into evidence at the hearing. Typically, the order allowing an examination out of court will set the parameters as to what areas the person to be examined can be asked about in order that the examination will not go too far afield.

Passing of Accounts

One of the orders for assistance that a person appearing to have a financial interest in an estate can obtain is an order requiring the estate trustee to pass her accounts. Such an order can be sought when an estate trustee appears reluctant to provide accounts. However, an estate trustee may decide herself to pass the accounts because a passing of accounts provides protection to an estate trustee who feels that the beneficiaries have unreasonable expectations. If the estate trustee decides to pass the accounts, it is not necessary for her to obtain an order requiring her to do it. She simply follows the procedures set out in the *Rules of Civil Procedure* for passing accounts. Whether she decides on her own to pass the accounts or she is ordered to pass the accounts, the procedure is the same. What follows is a discussion of those procedures.

Starting the Process

The passing of accounts starts with the preparation of a set of formal estate accounts as discussed in Chapter 12, Accounting to the Beneficiaries and Paying the Beneficiaries. The estate trustee then follows the process laid down in rule 74.18 as outlined below. Note that during the process, the estate trustee or her lawyer should have on hand a compilation of the vouchers representing the disbursements from the estate. Such documentation may provide an answer to an objection to the accounts that is delivered pursuant to the rules.

Once the estate trustee has prepared the formal accounts, the lawyer or law clerk for the estate trustee then prepares a notice of application to pass accounts (Form 74.44 of the *Rules of Civil Procedure*), along with an affidavit sworn by the estate trustee and verifying the estate accounts, which are attached as Exhibit "A."

The estate trustee then files the following with the court:

- the affidavit;
- a copy of the certificate of appointment of estate trustee;
- a copy of the latest judgment (if any) pertaining to the passing of accounts; and
- a cheque for the filing fee payable to the minister of finance ($390).

The court registrar issues the notice of application setting a date for the hearing, which is usually in about 9 to 12 weeks.

In addition to filing the documents outlined above, the estate trustee or her lawyer and law clerk also prepare a draft judgment in Form 74.50, which is a judgment contemplating that there will be no objection to the accounts.

Service of Documents

The next step in the process is designed to give all persons with a contingent or vested interest in the estate, or their representatives, the opportunity to review the estate accounts and the draft judgment being sought. The *Rules of Civil Procedure* provide that if the Office of the Public Guardian and Trustee or the Children's Lawyer is representing a party with a vested or contingent interest in the estate, the estate accounts (and all other documents filed with the court as outlined above) are to be served on those offices along with the draft judgment. Similarly, if a person with an interest in the estate is represented by a guardian of property or an attorney under a power of attorney for property, the guardian or attorney is to be served with all documents. Curiously, the rules do not provide that all parties be served with all documents, though such documents are available for review in the court because they form part of the public record. Notwithstanding the rules, all documents mentioned above are typically supplied to all parties with a vested or contingent interest in the estate. Such documents are supplied in the form of a brief (called an application record), which includes all of the documents described above in separate tabs as outlined in rule 38.09(2) and a light blue back cover as outlined in rule 4.07(1) of the *Rules of Civil Procedure*.

The documents must be served at least 45 days before the hearing date set in the notice of application. If the person with the vested or contingent interest in the estate is outside Ontario, the notice must be served at least 60 days before the hearing date. In all cases, the service can be made by regular letter mail. Rule 16.06(2) of the *Rules of Civil Procedure* states that service is deemed to be made on the fifth day after the document is mailed.

Note that rule 74.18(6) specifically allows the court to appoint someone to represent a person with a vested or contingent interest in the estate where the person is unknown or under a disability and is not represented by the Office of the Public Guardian and Trustee or the Office of the Children's Lawyer or a litigation guardian. Presumably, this rule is in place to accommodate a situation where the estate has an unascertained, underage, or mentally incapable beneficiary who has no connection with Ontario or Canada.

Following a Review of the Accounts

Following a review of the accounts, a person with a vested or contingent interest in the estate may have objections to the accounts. If so, he or his representative may serve a notice of objection to accounts (Form 74.45, Figure 14.5) on the estate trustee and file it with the court. The notice must state the nature of the objection and must be served at least 35 days before the date set for the hearing in the notice of application, failing which the court will not normally deal with the objection. The fee for filing a notice of objection is $85, which is payable to the minister of finance. As outlined below, a notice of objection may later be withdrawn by serving a notice of withdrawal of objection (Form 74.48) at least 15 days before the date set for the hearing in the notice of application.

FIGURE 14.5   **Notice of Objection to Accounts (Form 74.45)**

ONTARIO
SUPERIOR COURT OF JUSTICE

IN THE ESTATE OF Emil Karlsson, deceased.

NOTICE OF OBJECTION TO ACCOUNTS

1. I, Malin Halvorsen, object to the amount of compensation claimed by the estate trustee on the following grounds:

> The amount claimed for compensation is excessive in the circumstances insofar as (1) the estate trustee took over 3 years to account for his actions as estate trustee (2) the estate was relatively simple to administer and (3) the estate trustee is claiming estate trustee compensation on the value of the entire estate which is inappropriate insofar as he is a 40% beneficiary of the residue

2. I, Malin Halvorsen, object to the accounts of the estate trustee on the following grounds:

> The estate trustee has claimed excessive amounts in expenses to the estate for which expenses there is insufficient documentation, namely, items 3-10 on page 4 of the estate accounts.

DATE: April 2, 2018

> Ivanov Gebrezghi
> Lawyers
> 35 Catalpa Street North
> Roslyn, ON
> E9X 3M9
>
> Fatima Gebrezghi
> Tel: 705-555-5555
> Fax: 705-555-5556
>
> Lawyer for the objecting person
> Malin Halvorsen

TO: Nailea M. Ortiz
       Lawyer
       345-45 Fairmont Blvd.
       Roslyn, ON
       E8C 2D5

       Tel: 705-555-5566
       Fax: 705-555-5577

       Lawyer for the estate trustee,
       Pablo Schroeder

RCP-E 74.45 (July 1, 2007)

The Children's Lawyer or the Public Guardian and Trustee can file a notice of objection to accounts. These parties also have the option of filing a notice of no objection to accounts (Form 74.46) or a notice of non-participation in a passing of accounts (Form 74.46.1). Or, instead of serving any of these documents, the Children's Lawyer or the Public Guardian and Trustee may simply approve the draft judgment's form and content.

Uncontested Passing of Accounts

If no notices of objection are served and filed 35 days before the date set for the hearing, or if all notices of objection are subsequently withdrawn 15 days before the hearing, the estate trustee may obtain a judgment without a hearing—sometimes called an over-the-counter passing of accounts. To obtain the judgment, the estate trustee must file with the court, at least five days before the date set for the hearing, an application record containing the following:

- an affidavit of service of all the documents required to be served;
- the notices of no objection to accounts or notices of non-participation in a passing of accounts of the Children's Lawyer or the Public Guardian and Trustee, or a copy of the draft judgment approved by the Children's Lawyer or the Public Guardian and Trustee as to form and content;
- an affidavit from the estate trustee or his lawyer stating that a copy of the accounts was provided to each person who requested a copy, that the time for filing the notices of objection to accounts has expired and no notices of objection were received from any person served, or the notices of objection were received but were subsequently withdrawn by a notice of withdrawal of objection, a copy of which is attached to the affidavit;
- any requests for costs or increased costs, any answers thereto that were served, and any costs outlines supporting the requests;
- a certificate from a lawyer stating that all of the above-noted documents (set out in rule 74.18(9)(a)) are included in the application record; and
- a draft of the judgment sought in duplicate (Form 74.50).

The application record should also contain all the other documents required by rule 38.09 to be included in any application record, although **factums** are not normally required for a passing of accounts. On submission of the above documents, unless the judge reviewing the application record believes that there should be a hearing, the accounts will be passed—that is, the judgment will be signed without a hearing.

Even though the record to be filed for an uncontested passing of accounts requires inclusion of any requests for costs or requests for increased costs, the *Rules of Civil Procedure* allow the court to separate the issue of costs from the issue of the passing of accounts when the accounts themselves are not contested. In other words, where there are no outstanding notices of objection to accounts, the court may pass the accounts even though there are outstanding issues of costs among the parties. Costs for uncontested passing of accounts applications are discussed below.

factum
formalized statement of the facts, issues, and law in a case composed by a lawyer and submitted to the court to aid in the proper disposition of a matter in issue

Costs in Uncontested Passing of Accounts

In the normal course, the court will allow costs to an estate trustee, payable from the estate, to assist the estate trustee in paying the lawyer for the task of passing the accounts. Similarly, if a person with a financial interest in the estate retains a lawyer to review the estate accounts and does not object to the accounts (or withdraws an objection), that person is also entitled to costs in order to pay his lawyer. Finally, if the Children's Lawyer or the Public Guardian and Trustee reviews the estate accounts and makes no objection (or withdraws an objection), it is entitled to costs as well. The court costs allowed to estate trustees, persons with an interest in the estate, or to the Children's Lawyer or the Public Guardian and Trustee are set out in Tariff C of the *Rules of Civil Procedure*, which is reproduced in Figure 14.6.

FIGURE 14.6   Tariff C from the Rules of Civil Procedure

(1)   ESTATE TRUSTEE

Amount of receipts	Amount of costs
Less than $300,000	$2,500
$300,000 or more, but less than $500,000	3,000
$500,000 or more, but less than $1,000,000	3,500
$1,000,000 or more, but less than $3,000,000	5,000
$3,000,000 or more	7,500

(2)   PERSON WITH FINANCIAL INTEREST IN ESTATE

If a person with a financial interest in an estate retains a **lawyer** to review the accounts, makes no objection to the accounts (or makes an objection and later withdraws it) and serves and files a request for costs, the person is entitled to one-half of the amount payable to the estate trustee.

(3)   CHILDREN'S LAWYER OR PUBLIC GUARDIAN AND TRUSTEE

If the Children's Lawyer or the Public Guardian and Trustee makes no objection to the accounts (or makes an objection and later withdraws it) and serves and files a request for costs, he or she is entitled to three-quarters of the amount payable to the estate trustee.

Request for Costs

The estate trustee's entitlement to costs in an uncontested passing of accounts in accordance with Tariff C is automatic. For a person with a financial interest in the estate or the office of the Children's Lawyer or Public Guardian and Trustee, the entitlement arises upon service on the applicant and filing (at least ten days before the hearing date) a request for costs. An individual would file the request in Form 74.49 and the Children's Lawyer or the Public Guardian and Trustee would file Form 74.49.1.

Request for Increased Costs

In the event that the estate trustee or any other person or office considers the amounts set out in Tariff C to be insufficient in the circumstances, such person or office must do the following within 15 days of the date set for the hearing:

- prepare a Request for Increased Costs in Form 74.49.2 (for estate trustees) or Form 74.49.3 (for any other person) as in Figure 14.7;
- prepare a costs outline in Form 57B;
- serve the above documents on every person who has filed a notice of objection to accounts (even if she has withdrawn the objection) or a request for further notice (discussed below); and
- serve the above documents on the Children's Lawyer or the Public Guardian and Trustee if the latter were served with the application to pass accounts (unless a non-participation in passing of accounts was then served).

As seen in Figure 14.7, the party receiving a request for increased costs may then signify his objection or consent to the increased costs by completing or returning the form accordingly. The person receiving the request for increased costs (be it the estate trustee or a person with a financial interest in the estate) is directed to return the form to the party requesting increased costs ten days before the hearing. The person or office requesting increased costs must then prepare and file a supplementary record (a bound brief entitled "Supplementary Record for Increased Costs under Rule 74.18(11.3)"), at least five days before the hearing. The supplementary record would contain the following:

- the documents referred to above along with an affidavit of service; and
- an affidavit containing a summary of the responses to the request for increased costs and a list of persons who did not respond and the factors that underpin the alleged entitlement to the increased costs.

On receipt of the supplementary record, the court may grant judgment relating to costs without a hearing or may direct the person making the request to provide additional information or documentation.

Request for Further Notice

Another option now available under the *Rules of Civil Procedure* to a person with an interest in the estate is to serve on the applicant and file a request for further notice (Form 74.45.1) as in Figure 14.8. This document, which must be served and filed within 35 days before the date set for the hearing in the notice of application, signals to the estate trustee and the court that, while that individual is not contesting the estate accounts, she reserves the right to take part in any hearing that deals with the issue of costs for the passing of accounts. As the name would suggest, a **request for further notice** also entitles the person filing it to receive notice of any further step in the proceeding and receive any documents served and filed.

request for further notice
a request made by a beneficiary of an estate who is not objecting to the estate accounts, but who wants notice of any further step or document in the application to pass accounts, including any requests for costs or requests for increased costs, and which gives the person requesting further notice the right to take part in a hearing on the issue of increased costs

FIGURE 14.7 **Request for Increased Costs (Person other than Estate Trustee)**

ONTARIO
SUPERIOR COURT OF JUSTICE

IN THE ESTATE OF Roni Ben-David, deceased.

REQUEST FOR INCREASED COSTS (PERSON OTHER THAN ESTATE TRUSTEE)

1. I, Sarah Levin, have retained Hadeel Afnan as my lawyer to review the estate accounts. I have no objection to the estate accounts or to the claim for compensation by the estate trustee.

2. I request that I be awarded costs payable out of the estate in the amount of $5,500.00, in addition to the cost of attendance at a hearing, if required, which is greater than $2,500.00, being one-half the amount payable to the estate trustee under Tariff C. I understand that this request may require a hearing on the date specified in the notice of application, in the discretion of the presiding Judge.

DATE June 15, 2018

Afnan Maro
Lawyers
232 Colville Blvd
Cornish, ON
T9C 3D9

Hadeel Afnan
Tel: 613-555-5555
Fax: 613-555-5556

Lawyer for the beneficiary
Sarah Levin

TO: Tamar Levin
34 Albermarle Lane
Cornish, ON
T6E 3E5
Beneficiary

AND TO: Alexsandr Lebedev
Weir Road
Salisbury, ON
H9K 3R5
Beneficiary

AND TO: Daniil Zaytesev
Barrister & Solicitor
3 Oakland Acres
Cornish, ON
T9C 4R6

613-555-5555
613-555-5556

Lawyer for the estate trustee
Katerina Racz

Response by Estate Trustee or person with a financial interest in the estate:

(A) I object to this request for increased costs, for the following reasons:

-

-

OR:

(B) I consent to this request for increased costs.

Date:

Signature of person listed above

Any person with a financial interest in the estate who wishes to object or consent to a request for increased costs shall do so by returning the completed form 74.49.3 to the person making the request so that such person receives it at least 12 days before the date fixed for the hearing in the Notice of Application to Pass Accounts.

The person making the request for increased costs shall, at least 10 days before the date fixed for the hearing, file with the court a supplementary record described in subrule 74.18 (11.3) containing (i) the documents served under subrule 74.18 (11.1), together with an affidavit of service of those documents, (ii) an affidavit containing a summary of the responses to the request for increased costs and a list of persons who failed to respond, and (iii) the factors that contributed to the increased costs.

RCP-E 74.49.3 (April 11, 2012)

FIGURE 14.8   Request for Further Notice in Passing of Accounts (Form 74.45.1)

ONTARIO
SUPERIOR COURT OF JUSTICE

IN THE ESTATE OF Toku Hirohata, deceased.

REQUEST FOR FURTHER NOTICE IN PASSING OF ACCOUNTS

I, Ami Uehara, have been served with a notice of application to pass accounts. By serving this request for further notice, I acknowledge that:

I do not object to the accounts but wish to receive notice of any further step in the application, including a request for costs or a request for increased costs, and

I shall, at least 35 days before the hearing date specified in the notice of application, serve on the applicant, and file with proof of service, this request for further notice.

I further acknowledge that, unless the court orders otherwise, I am entitled to,

(a)   receive notice of any further step in the application to pass accounts;

(b)   receive any further document in the application;

(c)   file material relating to a request for increased costs on the application at least 10 days before the hearing date of the application; and

(d)   in the event of a hearing, be heard at the hearing, examine a witness and cross-examine on an affidavit, but with respect only to a request for increased costs.

DATE   SIGNATURE

August 20, 2018   **A. Uehara**

Ami Uehara
34 Tancred Road West
Harwickburg, ON
B7Y 9P7

Telephone: 905-555-5555

RCP-E 74.45.1 (February 1, 2015)

Formal Passing of Accounts Hearing (Contested)

A hearing for the passing of accounts will take place if notices of objection are filed and not withdrawn at least ten days before the hearing. In such a case, Rule 74.18(11.5) requires the applicant to consolidate all the remaining notices of objection to accounts, prepare a reply in Form 74.49.4, and serve the notices of objection and the reply on the following persons:

- every person who has served and filed a notice of objection to accounts and not withdrawn it;
- every person who has served and filed a request for further notice; and
- the Children's Lawyer or the Public Guardian and Trustee if the latter were served with the application to pass accounts (unless a non-participation in passing of accounts was then served).

Then, within five days of the date set for the hearing, the applicant must compile a brief containing the following:

- the application to pass accounts;
- consolidation of all the remaining notices of objection to accounts not withdrawn and the estate trustee's reply;
- any responses to the reply received by the estate trustee;
- if any notices of objection were withdrawn since receiving the above-noted reply, a copy of such notices of withdrawal of objection;
- any notices of non-participation in the passing of accounts received from the Public Guardian and Trustee or the Children's Lawyer;
- any requests for further notice in passing of accounts;
- any requests for costs;
- any requests for increased costs, cost outlines, and responses to requests for increased costs; and
- any draft order for directions or of the judgment sought by the court.

The rules specify that the above-noted brief be filed with the court and, while the rules do not specify, it is considered to be good practice to serve the brief on all parties expected to be involved in the hearing. Rule 74.18(11.9) provides for a party other than the estate trustee applicant to file an alternative draft order with the court so long as she does this within three days before the hearing date.

If a hearing is to proceed, the estate trustee and any objecting parties, including lawyers representing the Children's Lawyer or the Public Guardian and Trustee, attend at the court for a hearing before a judge. Estate trustees and beneficiaries are often represented at the hearing by their respective lawyers. At the hearing, the judge hears submissions from the estate trustee's lawyer as well as from the objecting parties and may ask questions of the parties, particularly the estate trustee.

Under the *Rules of Civil Procedure*, only those objections set out in a notice of objection to accounts served within the proper time can be raised at the hearing. The estate trustee should attend the hearing with the estate accounts and vouchers. As a general rule, the entire file relating to the estate should also be brought to court.

Upon hearing the submissions of the parties, the judge may pass the accounts as presented or may pass the accounts with alterations, or make a ruling that more information or documentation is necessary. In some circumstances, a judge may order a more formal hearing or a trial of a factual matter in dispute. For example, where there are insufficient funds in the estate to fully pay out all of the bequests in the will (as discussed in Chapter 3, Interpretation of Wills), a more detailed hearing with factums may be ordered.

If requests for increased costs have been served, the presiding judge will normally ask to hear arguments on that issue and make an order accordingly.

KEY TERMS

factum, 303

person who appears to have a financial interest in the estate, 298

request for further notice, 305

REVIEW QUESTIONS

1. Identify the various situations where an order for assistance may be required.

2. Explain the difference between an "action" and an "application" in an Ontario court.

3. When might an examination out of court arise?

4. Under what circumstances is an application for an order brought to accept or refuse a certificate of appointment of estate trustee with or without a will?

5. What would the procedure be if the estate trustee refuses to disclose particulars of the assets?

6. What is the "catch-all rule" when the estate trustee is being uncooperative?

7. Explain the procedure to be followed for an uncontested passing of accounts.

8. Why are vouchers required, how are they arranged, and for what purpose are they so organized?

9. Under what circumstances will a hearing for a passing of accounts be required?

10. What objections can be raised at the hearing of a passing of accounts?

11. What possible judgments may be made on a formal passing of accounts?

12. Who must be served with a notice of application to pass accounts?

13. Within what time frame must a non-resident of Ontario be served with a notice of application to pass accounts?

Challenging the Validity of the Will

LEARNING OUTCOMES

After completing this chapter, you should be able to:

- Have a basic knowledge of the substantive law used in will challenges including claims of a lack of testamentary capacity, lack of knowledge, and approval of the contents of the will and claims of undue influence

- Have a basic knowledge of the shifting of the onus of proof as it relates to the due execution of a will and suspicious circumstances

- Have a basic understanding of unjust enrichment and constructive trust claims

- Know the limitation period applicable to will challenges

- Understand the significance of costs in will challenges

- Know the forms and procedures set up in the *Rules of Civil Procedure* for challenging a will including the notice of objection, notice to objector, notice of appearance, and the motion for directions

- Understand the importance of a motion for directions in will challenges

- Understand the situations involving a submission of rights to the court and the rights that a person submitting his rights to the court has and does not have

- Have an understanding of some situations in which part of a will may be held to be invalid and the obligations of an estate trustee upon learning that part of the will might be invalid

Introduction

Will challenges are the most commonly recognizable form of estate litigation, perhaps even its public face. Notwithstanding this widespread recognition, however, successful will challenges are not common. This is owing in no small part to the inherent evidentiary problems of proving something that occurred years in the past where the main person involved is now deceased. This chapter discusses will challenges from the lawyer and law clerk's point of view. As will be seen, such challenges typically involve allegations that the will is invalid on account of (1) a lack of the necessary mental capacity on the part of the testator (2) lack of knowledge and approval of the contents of the will, or (3) the presence of undue influence or fraud perpetrated on the testator. If such allegations are proven, the will is set aside as if it never existed. In such a case, the previous will of the deceased or the laws of intestacy, as the case may be, will govern the distribution of the estate. A will challenge can also involve allegations which, if proven, do not invalidate the will but do change the distribution. An example of this kind of will challenge is where a person alleges unjust enrichment in respect of the distribution of the estate as set out in the deceased's will. If such allegations are proven to the satisfaction of the court, the usual result is a court-imposed trust, known as a constructive trust, on part of the assets of the estate or in the alternative, damages. In such a case, the estate will be distributed in accordance with the will after taking into account the constructive trust or the damages as the case may be. In either case, the procedures used by the lawyer or law clerk are those outlined in this chapter.

Substantive Law of Will Challenges

It is not the intention for this text to provide an analysis of the substantive law in this field, but a basic understanding of the law of will challenges is relevant for the purposes of identifying some of the more common issues when they arise. Also, while this discussion appears in Part III of this text, it should not be considered as relevant only in the context of estate litigation. On the contrary, estate litigation often clarifies the practical issues of estate planning and administration. The present discussion, for example, should be kept in mind when considering how will instructions should be obtained, how the client should be approached about the draft of the will, and how the will should be executed.

Note, in the context of a discussion of the substantive law of will challenges that the party in the litigation who is seeking to set aside the will is often called the **party impugning the will**, and the party seeking to uphold the will is often called the **party propounding the will** or the *propounder of the will*. The will being challenged is usually referred to as "the impugned will."

Testamentary Capacity

As explained in Chapter 1, Wills, in order to make a valid will, the testator must have a sufficient level of mental capacity or testamentary capacity. Testamentary capacity is often described as the state of mind in which a person has a disposing mind and memory. If it is proven that a person lacks testamentary capacity at the time of giving instructions for the will and at the time of signing it, the will is not valid.

party impugning the will
party in litigation who is seeking to set aside the will

party propounding the will
party in litigation who is seeking to uphold the will

Generally, testamentary capacity is understood with reference to the 1870 British case of *Banks v Goodfellow*,[1] in which four touchstones of testamentary capacity were identified. Using these four points, the testator is said to have testamentary capacity if he

1. understands what it means to make a will;
2. understands the extent of his own property;
3. understands the relationships he has with those persons who might be expected to receive a portion of his estate; and
4. understands the claims of the persons whom he is leaving out of his will.

While the first two points are easy to grasp, the third and fourth are perhaps more elusive. Taken together, points three and four are sometimes referred to as a person's appreciation of "the true objects of his bounty." While at first blush it is tempting to interpret this principle as indicating that a person must gift her estate to those closest to her, such an interpretation misses the true point, which is that a testator must at least appreciate the fact that someone close to her may reasonably expect to receive a share of her estate. Theoretically, the claims of all persons with whom the testator had close personal relationships have to be considered by the testator at the time of making her will in order to prove that she had testamentary capacity. This principle is sometimes articulated in terms of "moral obligation." That is, if it can be proven that the testator did not appreciate the moral claims of the persons he is leaving out of his will, the will may be set aside on the grounds of lack of testamentary capacity.

At the time of taking instructions for the will, it is considered appropriate for the lawyer to ask the client, the prospective testator, questions about her assets and relationships with other people, particularly family members. If a client intends to disinherit a family member, the lawyer should take careful notes as to the client's reasons for doing so in order to be able to defend an allegation down the road that the testator did so as a result of a lack of testamentary capacity. It is also appropriate at the time of signing the will to engage the client in conversation and make notes if the lawyer is at all concerned that there may be an allegation of a lack of testamentary capacity at a later date. In such circumstances, it is important that the lawyer's notes be made contemporaneously with the discussion with the client, so that the notes may stand up as evidence at a later date.

If the lawyer has any reason to believe that the client lacks testamentary capacity at the time of giving instructions, the lawyer may need to send the client to a physician for an opinion as to the client's testamentary capacity. In such cases, the instructions can be taken and, while the will is being drafted, the client can be asked to obtain a letter from her family doctor, a psychologist, or other competent professional. Notwithstanding the foregoing, the case law is clear that, at a hearing to determine the testamentary capacity of a deceased testator, the evidence of professional witnesses is not necessarily to be preferred over that of lay witnesses who had an opportunity to observe the deceased testator around the time that she made and signed the will.

---

1 (1870), LR 5 QB 549.

Knowledge and Approval

Sometimes testamentary capacity is described in case law and legal literature as being equated with knowledge and approval of the contents of the will. The correct view, however, appears to be that knowledge and approval on the part of the testator is a requirement for a valid will that is separate from the requirement of testamentary capacity (although see below under "Overlap"). In other words, it could be said that a person may have testamentary capacity and yet not know and approve of the document he is signing or what is contained in it.

While the client need not understand the wording of all of the clauses of a will (examples of which were provided in Chapter 2, Will Clauses), it is essential that he know what is in the disposition section of the will and that he approve of it. From the point of view of the lawyer who is retained to prepare the will, establishing that the testator has knowledge and approval of the contents of the will is usually done by sending a draft of the will to the client with a letter asking that he read it over carefully to ensure that it meets with his approval. If, on the other hand, the instructions are to make up a will "on the spot," the lawyer must be prepared to insist that the client read the will over carefully or have it read to him, and then obtain confirmation that he is satisfied with the contents before the client signs the will. Similarly, if the lawyer has any reason to believe that the client did not read the will as sent in the mail, the will should be read to the client before its execution. Again, notes made by the lawyer or law clerk contemporaneously with such a discussion will likely be valid evidence of the testator's knowledge and approval of the contents of the will.

Due Execution of the Will

While it is possible to successfully challenge the validity of a will based on an allegation that it was not properly signed or witnessed, such a challenge is normally easily rebuffed with an affidavit of execution from a witness to the signing of the will. The affidavit of execution, however, does more than defend an allegation that the will was not duly executed. It also provides the court with a presumption that the testator had knowledge and approval of the contents of the will and the necessary mental capacity to execute the will. In other words, if a party is challenging the will based on an allegation of a lack of knowledge and approval or a lack of testamentary capacity, an affidavit of execution will shift the burden to the party impugning the will to prove her claim. As discussed below, evidence of suspicious circumstances will again shift the burden of proving testamentary capacity and knowledge and approval back to the party propounding the will. It is important to note in this context, again as discussed below, that the law treats allegations of undue influence differently from allegations of a lack of testamentary capacity and knowledge and approval when it comes to burden of proof.

Suspicious Circumstances

The law of testamentary capacity, knowledge and approval, and undue influence (discussed below), and how it relates to suspicious circumstances, is complex and somewhat inconsistent. Fortunately, the 1995 Supreme Court of Canada case of *Vout v Hay*[2] has clarified

---

2 (1995), 7 ETR (2d) 209 (SCC).

the law a great deal in this area. The basic rule arising out of *Vout v Hay* is that evidence of suspicious circumstances has the effect of forcing the party propounding the will to produce more evidence of the testator's testamentary capacity or knowledge and approval of the contents of the will (depending on what kind of case is made out) than that provided by an affidavit of execution.

It appears that "suspicious circumstances" is an open-ended category of circumstances that should generally excite the suspicion of the court with respect to the testator's lack of testamentary capacity or the testator's lack of knowledge and approval of the contents of his will. For example, the party impugning a will might cite evidence that the testator did not remember a certain family member around the time he signed his will as a suspicious circumstance tending to suggest that the testator lacked testamentary capacity. Similarly, the party impugning a will might cite evidence that the testator did not read the will and did not pay attention when the will was read to him as a suspicious circumstance tending to suggest that the testator lacked knowledge and approval of its contents.

Once the burden of proof is shifted back to the propounder, it is up to the propounder to present evidence that, despite the suspicious circumstances, the testator did indeed have testamentary capacity or knowledge and approval of the contents of the will. Using the examples above, the propounder of the will may provide evidence that the testator had a detailed conversation with someone immediately after signing the will in which the testator discussed his assets, friends, and relatives. Similarly, the propounder of the will may provide evidence that the will was made according to the testator's specific instructions. If, in the opinion of the court, the circumstances cited by the party impugning the will are supported by evidence and are suspicious (relating to either lack of testamentary capacity or lack of knowledge and approval), and if the propounder of the will does not provide additional evidence sufficient to discharge the burden, the court will set the will aside. If, in the opinion of the court, the propounder of the will satisfies the burden, it will uphold the will.

In reaching its conclusion as to whether the circumstances are suspicious and whether the burden is satisfied, the court uses the civil standard of proof, which is a balance of probabilities. As indicated in *Vout v Hay* (at 226), however, "[t]he evidence must ... be scrutinized in accordance with the gravity of the suspicion." In other words, if the alleged suspicious circumstance would create a great deal of doubt about the testator's testamentary capacity, for example, then the evidence tendered in support of it must be examined by the court more carefully than otherwise.

Undue Influence and Fraud

Case law indicates that if it can be proved to the satisfaction of a court that a testator was influenced unduly to make and execute a will, the court will set aside the will. Undue influence, however, should not be confused with mere influence. **Undue influence** occurs when the testator, as a result of coercion or pressure exerted by those around her, is going against her own wishes in signing the will. The kind of influence contemplated by this legal rule is influence of a physical or an emotional nature. The question whether the influence crossed the line from mere influence to undue influence is one to be determined by a court after considering all the facts in evidence. The lawyer and the law clerk should be sensitive to any signs of undue influence both at the time of receiving instructions for the will and

undue influence
improper pressure exerted on the testator

at the time of signing the will. A typical warning sign may be where a proposed beneficiary under the will insists on being present while the instructions for the will are given to the lawyer. Depending on the situation, the lawyer may have to refuse to act.

Although undue influence and fraud are separate allegations, the case law generally treats them as a single category. In this connection, it should be noted that the law of suspicious circumstances, insofar as it relates to the shifting of legal burdens, does not pertain to allegations of undue influence and fraud. According to the decision in *Vout v Hay*, suspicious circumstances tending to suggest undue influence or fraud (as opposed to lack of testamentary capacity or knowledge and approval) does not shift the burden of proof to the person accused of such acts to disprove that they occurred. In other words, allegations of undue influence and fraud upon the testator have to be proven outright.

Overlap

It is sometimes difficult to conceptualize the difference between claims that a testator lacked knowledge and approval of the contents of a will on the one hand and claims that the testator was unduly influenced on the other hand. In this regard, the following passage from *Vout v Hay* (at 228) may help:

> It may be thought that proof of knowledge and approval will go a long way in disproving undue influence. Unquestionably there is an overlap. If it is established that the testator knew and appreciated what he was doing, in many cases there is little room for a finding that the testator was coerced. None the less, there is a distinction. … A person may well appreciate what he or she is doing but be doing it as a result of coercion or fraud.

Similarly, a claim that the testator lacked testamentary capacity and a claim that he lacked knowledge and approval of the contents of his will may both be present at the same time. While the distinction is important to bear in mind, a court will expect that there may be an overlap and, if the case warrants it, the two areas can be treated as a single claim (though if there are different onuses of proof applicable to the two claims they will have to be treated separately).

Unjust Enrichment and Constructive Trust

As indicated in the introduction to this chapter, some so-called will challenges involve an allegation of unjust enrichment. It is impossible to describe all situations in which unjust enrichment occurs but the typical case is where a person puts time, money, and effort into the acquisition or preservation of real property that is owned by someone else, on the understanding that she will acquire an interest in it in the future, but does not ultimately acquire the property. To prove unjust enrichment, the claimant must establish each of the following elements to the satisfaction of the court:

1. that there was an enrichment (that is, that the will of the deceased gifted the property to someone other than the claimant);
2. that there was a corresponding deprivation (that is, that the claimant put money or effort into the acquisition or preservation of the property);

3. that there was no jurisdic reason for the enrichment (that is, that there was no other legally justifiable reason for the enrichment—for example, that the property was gifted to a dependant of the deceased for his support or that the property was gifted to another person pursuant to a valid domestic contract).

If the court is satisfied that all of the necessary elements of unjust enrichment exist, the judge will typically impose a constructive trust (a trust constructed by the court) naming the real property as the trust property and the claimant as the beneficiary. A constructive trust can have any terms that a court considers appropriate in the circumstances although constructive trusts are typically not ongoing concerns requiring a trustee to file trust returns and report to the beneficiary. Rather, constructive trusts are usually considered to be wound up—with the trust property provided to the beneficiary outright—when the decision is made by the court. As indicated above, a claim for unjust enrichment is a will challenge only in the sense that the person alleging it is essentially taking the position that the will does not contain a gift clause that it should contain. Once a constructive trust is imposed by a court, the remaining property in the estate would normally be distributed in accordance with the will.

It is worth bearing in mind, particularly in the context of unjust enrichment, that section 13 of the *Evidence Act*[3] of Ontario specifies that in an action against the estate, a person cannot obtain a judgment based on her own evidence, unless that evidence is corroborated by other material evidence. In other words, a person alleging unjust enrichment based on a promise made by the deceased would need to supply additional corroborative evidence of the promise in order to be successful in the case. The rule in section 13 would also apply to creditors, and any other person making a claim against the estate. In all such cases, corroboration of the claim against the estate is required.

Preliminary Issues Regarding Will Challenges

Limitation Periods

Prior to commencing proceedings to challenge a will, it is necessary to consider any legal deadlines that might be applicable. Although a full discussion of the law of limitation periods as it applies to estate litigation is beyond the scope of this text, a brief discussion is appropriate. Until fairly recently, many people in the legal community held the view that there was no limitation period applicable to will challenges. In 2014, however, the decision in *Leibel v Leibel*[4] was released, which made it clear that the *Limitations Act, 2002*[5] does indeed apply to will challenges. Noting that a will speaks from the date of death, Madame Justice Greer found that a person seeking to challenge a will has two years from the date of death to do so. Likely the discoverability principle applies to this rule to extend the limitation period in cases where the material facts forming the basis of the claim are not or cannot be reasonably discovered until a date later than the two-year anniversary of the

---

3   RSO 1990, c E.21.
4   2014 ONSC 4516.
5   SO 2002, c 24, Sched B.

date of death. In cases of discoverability, it must be kept in mind that the *Limitations Act, 2002* has an ultimate limitation period of 15 years, beyond which the discoverability principle will no longer apply.

Notwithstanding the two-year limitation period in the *Limitations Act*, it should also be noted that the *Real Property Limitations Act*[6] provides a ten-year limitation period for claims respecting an interest in real property. The Ontario Court of Appeal decision of *McConnell v Huxtable*[7] makes it clear that this longer limitation period will apply to cases alleging unjust enrichment in which a constructive trust is being claimed as a remedy where real property is the subject matter.

It might well be asked in the context of a will challenge what constitutes compliance with a limitation period. Normally a limitation period has been complied with when a statement of claim (or a notice of action) has been issued but, as discussed below, sometimes a will challenge proceeds as a trial of issues with no statement of claim ever being filed. Common sense suggests that the filing of a notice of objection would constitute the commencement of a proceeding to challenge a will (and therefore compliance with the limitation period) but other interpretations of the law might well be argued. These are issues that still have to be worked out by the courts; in the meantime they are worth bearing in mind by the lawyer and law clerk venturing into the area of will challenges.

Costs

In any litigation, the risk of costs is a factor that must be considered at every stage. If a person challenges a will and is ultimately unsuccessful, he will likely be ordered by the court to pay something toward the costs incurred by the successful party or parties in the litigation. While costs ordered are at the discretion of the court, they will usually be reflective of the cost incurred by the winning party for all of the procedures involved in the will challenge including responding to the notice of objection, preparing and arguing a motion for directions, exchanging affidavits of documents, examining witnesses, arguing interlocutory motions, and attending the trial. Costs will also likely be ordered against a party who defends a will and is ultimately unsuccessful.

Procedures for Challenging the Validity of a Will

This section discusses the procedures to be resorted to by a person seeking to set aside a will. Note that the person impugning the will can simply issue a statement of claim alleging that the will is invalid and proceed through the steps laid out in the *Rules of Civil Procedure*[8] for what might be called "standard" legal actions. The only requirement under the rules in this regard is set out in rule 9.01(2)(a), which provides that the beneficiaries under a will are to be made parties to any litigation challenging the validity of the will. Though will challenges are sometimes pursued as if they were ordinary actions, it is not the best practice in the normal course to challenge the validity of a will without making use of the

---

6   RSO 1990, c L.15.

7   2014 ONCA 86.

8   RRO 1990, reg. 194.

special procedures laid out in rule 75 of the *Rules of Civil Procedure*. The special procedures discussed below, though not mandatory, address the particular difficulties that arise in estate litigation. For example, estate litigation often involves persons who may or may not benefit directly from the estate depending on the outcome of the litigation. Also court actions can take many months to resolve and, during this time, someone needs to manage the estate (secure assets, pay creditors, etc.) while the litigation proceeds. Furthermore, if the validity of the will is in question, the appointment of the estate trustee in the will may also be in question and yet that person may already have started the process of administering the estate. The special rules under rule 75, discussed below, are designed to address these unique problems by providing a means to ensure that all persons with a financial interest in the estate have an opportunity to take part in the litigation, to ensure that the administration of the estate does not proceed in accordance with the impugned will during the litigation, and to ensure that someone is appointed to manage the estate in the meantime.

As discussed below, which of the procedures laid out in rule 75 are to be used will vary depending on what, if anything, has taken place in the administration of the estate under the impugned will at the time the will challenge is commenced. The first question to be asked is whether a certificate of appointment of estate trustee with a will has been issued or even applied for. The objecting party can confirm this by checking with the court registrar's office for the jurisdiction in which the deceased normally resided immediately before death. If little information is known as to where the deceased resided, the estate registrar for Ontario could be consulted. If there is already a certificate of appointment in the estate, the procedures to be followed are outlined below under "Where the Certificate of Appointment Has Already Been Issued." If there is no certificate of appointment, the procedures to be followed are outlined in the section immediately below.

Where No Certificate of Appointment of Estate Trustee With a Will Has Been Issued

Notice of Objection

If a certificate of appointment of estate trustee with a will with respect to the impugned will has not been issued, a person seeking to challenge the will usually commences the challenge by filing a notice of objection in the court pursuant to rule 75.03(1). The notice of objection is filed in the court representing the jurisdiction in which the deceased lived. If the objector is not certain of the correct jurisdiction, the notice of objection may be filed with the estate registrar for Ontario instead of a local court. The purpose of the notice of objection is to stop the issuance of a certificate of appointment under the impugned will. As seen in Figure 15.1, the **notice of objection**, in Form 75.1 from the *Rules of Civil Procedure*, briefly sets out the basis of the objection and the objector's interest in the estate.

It should be noted that under rule 75.03(1), only a person who appears to have a financial interest in the estate is allowed to file a notice of objection. In practical terms, the court will not reject the filing so long as it states that the objector appears to have a financial interest in the estate. There is case law, however, suggesting that a notice of objection can be struck on a motion to the court if the objector cannot establish, with affidavit evidence, the very low threshold of a reasonable possibility of a personal stake in the will challenge.

notice of objection
form that is filed setting out the basis of an objection to the issuing of the certificate of appointment of estate trustee with a will and the objector's interest in the estate

FIGURE 15.1   Notice of Objection

ONTARIO
SUPERIOR COURT OF JUSTICE

In the Estate of the deceased person described below:

Details about the Deceased Person

First given name	Second given name	Third given name	Surname
Monique	Blaine		Lastman

IN THE MATTER OF an application for a certificate of
appointment of estate trustee

NOTICE OF OBJECTION

I, Alvin Stanger, object to the issuing of a certificate of appointment of estate trustee to Mary Gliddy without notice to me because:

There is reason to believe that the deceased lacked testamentary capacity at the time she executed her will appointing the applicant as the estate trustee.

The nature of my interest in the estate is:

I was a friend of the deceased.

I was a beneficiary of the deceased's estate under her previous will.

DATE: July 28, 2018

Grit, Grat & Groot
Barristers & Solicitors
15 Cross Street
Toronto, Ontario
M5A 1Q1

Telephone: 416-555-5555
Facsimile: 416-555-5556

Notice of Filing of Objection

If the Application for a Certificate of Appointment Is in Process

If, at the time of receiving the notice of objection, an application for a certificate of appointment has been applied for but not issued, the court registrar will cease processing the application and will send a notice of the filing of the objection to the applicant for the certificate of appointment. The notice to the applicant, called "notice that objection has been filed" is in Form 75.2 and is sent along with a copy of the notice of objection to the applicant by regular mail. This notice states that no further action will be taken by the court regarding the application for the certificate of appointment until the applicant takes the next step (serving the notice to objector form), discussed below.

If the Application for a Certificate of Appointment Has Not Been Made

If the application for the certificate of appointment has not been made, the notice of objection remains on file to the attention of the registrar for three years (or for additional three-year periods if it is re-filed by the objector) to be acted on by the registrar if and when the application is made to the court. If the estate trustee named in the impugned will has no intention of applying for a certificate of appointment, the discussion below is germane.

If the Estate Trustee Does Not Intend to Apply for a Certificate of Appointment

As was seen in Chapter 7, Proof of the Estate Trustee's Status as Estate Trustee, in some circumstances it is possible to administer an estate without a certificate of appointment. This situation can create a problem for a person seeking to challenge a will because, notwithstanding the filing of the notice of objection, it may be that the estate trustee appointed in the impugned will is continuing to administer the estate pursuant to the provisions of that will.

One way around this problem is to use rule 75.01, which allows a person appearing to have a financial interest in the estate to bring an application (under rule 75.06) for an order directing the estate trustee to "prove the will" or to formally apply for a certificate of appointment of estate trustee.

One of the provisions of the order could be the return of the original will and, if necessary, an order that the estate trustee take no further steps as estate trustee. If it is warranted, a court may also order that security—that is, an administration bond—be filed by the estate trustee.

Upon the application for the certificate of appointment pursuant to the order that the estate trustee prove the will, the registrar sends the notice that objection has been filed (Form 75.2) to the applicant, and the matter proceeds according to the process set out above.

The remaining discussion in this section assumes that the person named as the estate trustee in the will has applied for a certificate of appointment and, accordingly, has received the "notice that objection has been filed" from the court registrar.

Notice to Objector

The rules specify that, when the applicant receives the notice in Form 75.2 that someone has objected to the issuance of a certificate of appointment, she must serve the objecting party with a notice to objector in Form 75.3 and file it with the court along with an affidavit of service. The notice to objector, an example of which is provided in Figure 15.2, tells the objector that he has 20 days in which to file a notice of appearance, failing which the application process for a certificate of appointment will proceed as if there were no objection.

If the objecting party receives no such notice to objector, it may mean one of three things: (1) the applicant for the certificate of appointment has received the notice of objection and has chosen to take no further action; (2) nobody has yet applied for a certificate of appointment; or (3) the certificate of appointment had already been issued at the time of filing the notice of objection.

FIGURE 15.2 **Notice to Objector**

ONTARIO

SUPERIOR COURT OF JUSTICE

IN THE ESTATE OF Monique Blaine Lastman, deceased.

IN THE MATTER OF an application for a certificate of appointment of estate trustee

NOTICE TO OBJECTOR

AN APPLICATION for a certificate of appointment of estate trustee in the estate has been made by Mary Gliddy.

IF YOU WISH TO OPPOSE this application, you or an Ontario lawyer acting for you must within 20 days of service on you of this notice to objector prepare a notice of appearance in Form 75.4 of the Rules of Civil Procedure, serve it on the applicant's lawyer, or where the applicant does not have a lawyer serve it on the applicant, and file it with proof of service in the court office at 10 Weather Road, Weatherston, ON, Y7X 2H3.

IF YOU FAIL to serve and file a notice of appearance, the application for certificate of appointment of estate trustee shall proceed as if your notice of objection had not been filed.

DATE August 7, 2018

Adnan, Ivar
Lawyers
30 Weather Road
Weatherston, ON
Y75 4I8

Ulvi Adnan
Tel: 519-555-5555
Fax: 519-555-5556

Lawyer for the estate trustee
Mary Gliddy

TO: Grit, Grat & Groot
        Barristers & Solicitors
        15 Cross Street
        Toronto, ON
        M5A 1Q1
        Tel: 416-555-5555
        Fax: 416-555-5556

        Lawyers for the Objector

RCP-E 75.3 (July 1, 2007)

If no notice to objector form is received by the objecting party, and it is confirmed that no certificate of appointment has been issued, she can bring a motion for directions, as outlined below, to set up the process for challenging the will.

Notice of Appearance

As indicated above, if the objecting party receives a notice to objector she will have 20 days in which to file a notice of appearance with the court, failing which the application for a certificate of appointment will proceed. The notice of appearance, in Form 75.4, states, albeit redundantly, "I desire to oppose the issuance of a certificate of appointment of estate trustee for the reasons set out in the notice of objection filed" and has the effect, once filed with proof of service, of suspending the issuance of a certificate of appointment.

Upon receiving the notice of appearance, the applicant has 30 days in which to bring a motion for directions as discussed below. If the applicant does not bring such a motion within 30 days, the objecting party herself can bring such a motion.

Motion for Directions

The **motion for directions** is a motion to the court under rule 75.06 for guidance on how to proceed with a determination of any matter arising with respect to an estate. As discussed above, a motion for directions will normally be brought by the applicant in response to a notice of appearance filed by a person objecting to the certificate of appointment of estate trustee with a will. Alternatively, the notice of motion can be brought by the objecting party in the event that the applicant has not responded to a notice that objection has been filed with a notice to objector within a reasonable time, or in the event that the applicant has not brought a motion within 30 days of being served with the objector's notice of appearance.

motion for directions
motion to the court for guidance on how to proceed with a determination of the matters in issue

Again rule 75.06, on its face, is available only to persons "who appear to have a financial interest in the estate" although by context this term clearly includes the estate trustee whether or not he has a personal financial interest in the estate.

Order Pursuant to the Motion for Directions

The order granted pursuant to the motion for directions directs one or more of the following (as quoted from rule 75.06(3)):

> (a) the issues to be decided;
> (b) who are parties, who is the plaintiff and defendant and who is submitting rights to the court;
> (c) who shall be served with the order for directions, and the method and times of service;
> (d) procedures for bringing the matter before the court in a summary fashion, where appropriate;
> (e) that the plaintiff file and serve a statement of claim (Form 75.7);
> (f) that an estate trustee be appointed during litigation, and file such security as the court directs;
> (g) such other procedures as are just.

An example of an order pursuant to a motion for directions is in Figure 15.3. As seen from the above list and the example provided, the order on the motion for directions determines the manner in which the litigation will proceed. If, for example, the court is of the opinion that it is appropriate for the matter to be dealt with in a summary (simple and relatively quick) manner, the order will indicate which steps that would otherwise be taken may be bypassed.

Rule 75.06(4) states that the order granted pursuant to a motion for directions will be in Form 75.8 or 75.9. The difference between these two forms is that the latter is ordered where the court believes that a statement of claim is not necessary (that is, the issues are clear and agreed upon), and the former is ordered where a statement of claim is deemed necessary. The example provided is of the former.

It should also be noted that when a motion or application for directions is brought, the court may order that the parties take part in mediation. This topic is discussed in more detail in Chapter 17, Mediation in Estate Litigation.

Submission of Rights to the Court

If a person has a financial interest in the estate but does not want to be involved in the litigation, he can submit his rights to the court pursuant to rule 75.07.1 by filing a statement of submission of rights to the court. A person submitting his rights to the court is not considered a party to the proceedings, will not be entitled to costs, and will not be liable for costs (except indirectly, where costs are ordered to be paid out of the estate). By submitting one's rights to the court, however, the person does acquire some limited rights related to the proceeding, namely:

- he is entitled to written notice of the time and place of trial;
- he is entitled to receive a copy of a judgment disposing of the matter; and
- he is to be given ten days' notice of a proposed settlement of the issues in dispute, during which time he can reject the settlement by serving a rejection of settlement in Form 75.12.

In the event of a proposed settlement of the issues in dispute, a notice of settlement in Form 75.11 must be sent to the person submitting his rights to the court. The court will not approve the settlement without an affidavit from one of the lawyers of record in the dispute attaching the notice of settlement as an exhibit and attesting to the fact that ten days have gone by without receiving a rejection of settlement.

In this regard, while the topic is beyond the scope of this text, it is worth noting that technically, a settlement of a will challenge cannot occur without the involvement of the court. This is because a will, unlike a contract for example, is the legal expression of the wishes of the deceased testator who can no longer speak for himself. In such circumstances, the court assumes the role of *parens patriae* or "parent of the country" to act as a kind of guardian over the will. That being said, any reasonable settlement of a dispute involving the validity of a will, which takes into account the law and public policy, is normally approved by the court.

FIGURE 15.3   Order Giving Directions Where Pleadings Directed

Court File No. 18-456bb45

ONTARIO

SUPERIOR COURT OF JUSTICE

The Honourable Madam	)	
Sung	)	the 31st day of March, 2018
	)	

IN THE ESTATE OF Marjan Jankovic, deceased

B E T W E E N:

BRIGIT DRESNER and UTE DRESNER

Applicants

(Moving Parties)

- and -

YVONNE EICHMANN and LUCA EICHMANN

Respondents

(Responding Parties)

-and –

FIGURE 15.3 CONTINUED

GRAYCE EICHMANN

Persons Submitting

Rights to the Court

(Responding Party)

- and -

RODRICK LAWYERSON

Non-Party to the Application

(Responding Party)

ORDER GIVING DIRECTIONS

THIS MOTION made by the moving parties for directions was heard this day at Weatherston, Ontario, in the presence of the lawyers for the moving parties, the responding parties and the non-party lawyer, Roderick Lawyerson, and Grayce Eichmann appearing in person.

ON READING the motion record of the applicants (moving parties) dated January 15, 2018, the motion record of the respondents (responding parties) dated February 10, 2018, filed, and on hearing submissions made,

1.   **THIS COURT ORDERS** that the applicants, Brigit Dresner and Ute Dresner, shall be plaintiffs and the respondents, Yvonne Eichmann and Luca Eichmann, shall be defendants, and that the respondent, Grayce Eichmann, is submitting her rights to the court.

2.   **THIS COURT ORDERS** that the plaintiffs shall serve upon the defendants and file with the court a statement of claim in Form 75.7 within 20 days after this order is entered, after which pleadings shall be served and filed under rule 75.07 of the *Rules of Civil Procedure*.

3.   **THIS COURT ORDERS** that the applicants and the respondents shall serve and file affidavits of documents and attend and submit to examinations for discovery in accordance with the *Rules of Civil Procedure*.

4.   **THIS COURT ORDERS** that on filing the appropriate documents with the court, Brigit Dresner and Yvonne Eichmann, shall be appointed as estate trustees during litigation, acting together, without the need for security.

5.   **THIS COURT ORDERS** that the plaintiffs and the defendants are hereby granted leave to examine for discovery the non-party, Blake Lawyerson, on matters within the latter's knowledge, information and belief respecting the preparation and execution of the will of the deceased, Marjan Jankovic, dated July 10, 2010

FIGURE 15.3 CONTINUED

6. **THIS COURT ORDERS** that the applicants and the respondents herein are each hereby authorized to compel production of any paper or electronic files, information, documents, notes, records or copies thereof, relating to the deceased, Marjan Jankovic, or the estate of the deceased, in the same manner and to the same extent as the deceased would have been able to if she were alive and had the necessary legal capacity, such productions to include, but not be limited to

   (a) any clinical notes and records of any physician, institution, assisted living facility, healthcare facility, healthcare provider or person who provided care to, or an assessment of the deceased during her lifetime or afterwards (including any predecessors or successors in interest in possession of such documents or information) whether in Canada, the United States of America or elsewhere;

   (b) any records of any financial or banking institution or person that held or dealt with the assets or liabilities of the deceased during her lifetime or afterwards (including any predecessors or successors in interest in possession of such documents or information) whether in Canada, the United States of America or elsewhere, including the records of any assets or liabilities which were held jointly by the deceased and another person or persons;

   (b) any records held by the Canada Revenue Agency or any other government agency (federal, provincial or municipal whether in Canada, the United States of America or elsewhere) pertaining to the deceased during her lifetime or afterwards;

(c) any records held by any lawyer, paralegal or other legal advisor who acted for or was consulted by the deceased (including any predecessors or successors in interest in possession of such documents or information) whether in Canada, the United States of America or elsewhere;

and copies of such productions so obtained shall be produced to the other parties in the action as part of the ongoing duty of disclosure.

7. **THIS COURT ORDERS** that the charges for the production of all records and files in accordance with the foregoing shall be paid from the estate with the final determination as to payment of such costs and expenses to be reserved to the trial judge.

8. **THIS COURT ORDERS** that all property belonging to the estate of the deceased shall be turned over to the estate trustees during litigation to be held by them and not to be distributed, sold or otherwise disposed of without agreement among all parties or further order of this court.

9. **THIS COURT ORDERS** that the parties are hereby granted leave to move for further directions or amendments to this order, as may appear to the moving party to be necessary or advisable.

10. **THIS COURT ORDERS** that the parties shall mediate the issues in dispute on a date to be agreed upon by the parties but no later than April 2, 2020 and with a mediator to be agreed upon by the parties or, failing such agreement, on a mediator to be appointed by the court.

FIGURE 15.3 CONTINUED

11.   **THIS COURT ORDERS** that, if it is not settled or otherwise disposed of, the action shall be tried by a judge without a jury at Weatherston, Ontario on a date to be fixed by the registrar following the filing of a trial record.

D.A. Sung
_____
Signature of Judge

Address of court office:

10 Weather Road

Weatherston, ON

Y7X 2H3

Further Procedures in the Order for Directions

The procedures that follow the order from the motion for directions will be based on the order made by the court. Except for the specific differences between estate litigation and "standard" civil litigation (such as the statement of claim being made on Form 75.7 and the fact that there might be a person who has submitted his rights to the court), the matter proceeds according to the rules of civil litigation applicable to all actions. For example, the parties will normally be directed to exchange affidavits of documents in accordance with rule 30 of the *Rules of Civil Procedure* and submit to examinations for discovery in accordance with rule 31.

As seen in the example provided in Figure 15.3, the order for directions often includes provisions allowing the parties to obtain copies of relevant records pertaining to the deceased and his assets. Without such provisions, the third parties holding such records would be prevented by privacy legislation from allowing access to anyone other than the estate trustee.

Also, the order for directions often includes a provision allowing the parties to examine the lawyer who drafted the will as a non-party witness in accordance with rule 31. If such a provision is being sought, the non-party lawyer will need to be served with the motion materials for the motion for directions. In such cases, even where the lawyer is not likely at fault, it is customary for the lawyer to notify her professional insurer who may wish to make representations at the motion.

Note as well that if the estate has unascertained beneficiaries, it is appropriate to ask the court to include a representation provision in the order for directions pursuant to rule 10 of the *Rules of Civil Procedure*. Rule 10.01 allows the court to appoint a person to represent beneficiaries of an estate or trust who are unborn or unascertained and who have a present, future, contingent, or unascertained interest in the outcome of the litigation and cannot be determined or served. If there are such unascertained beneficiaries, the lawyer or law clerk should anticipate that the judge will want to put a representative's name in the order and make inquires ahead of time. Most jurisdictions have a senior lawyer in private practice who agrees to take on such work in exchange for reasonable fees, which can be specified in the order.

Finally, note that the example provided in Figure 15.3 indicates that the trial of the issue is to be in front of a judge as opposed to a judge and jury. This is because section 108(2) of the *Courts of Justice Act*[9] provides that matters relating to the "[r]ectification, setting aside or cancellation of a deed or other written instrument" or the "execution of a trust" are not to be tried by a jury. These provisions effectively remove juries from most, if not all, estate litigation.

Where the Certificate of Appointment Has Already Been Issued

If it has come to the knowledge of the party impugning the will that a certificate of appointment has already been issued, the party must bring a motion under rule 75.05 for an order directing the estate trustee to return the certificate of appointment to the court. As in the case of an order directing the estate trustee to prove the will, discussed above, the

---

9   RSO 1990, c C.43.

order can contain any provisions that, in the opinion of the court, are warranted in the circumstances.

A party who has successfully obtained an order directing the estate trustee to return the certificate must, within 30 days of obtaining the order, bring a motion for directions under rule 75.06 (discussed above). If no such motion is brought within 30 days, the estate trustee may bring a motion without notice for release of the certificate. Rule 75.05(3) specifies that until one of these motions is brought, the certificate of appointment will have no legal effect and cannot legally be acted upon. During the 30-day period following the order under rule 75.05, the estate trustee may herself bring a motion for directions.

If a motion for directions is brought pursuant to the order directing that the certificate be returned, it will be as discussed above, and the procedures to be followed thereafter will be dictated by the order according to the requirements of the particular situation.

Challenges to Part of a Will

The foregoing discussion pertains to challenges to the validity of the will which, if successful, will result in the entire will being set aside. In such cases, it will be a previous will of the deceased or the laws of intestacy that will govern the estate. Nevertheless, it is possible for there to be other challenges in relation to the will which, if successful, do not result in a finding of invalidity of the will. For example, a person might allege that the will ought to have contained a gift pursuant to a contract with a third party. In such a case the party challenging the will is, in effect, saying that the will does not contain a provision that it ought to have contained. If such a challenge is successful, the gift will be imposed upon the estate and the remainder of the estate administered in accordance with the will. A discussion of will challenges that do not necessarily involve allegations of invalidity of the will itself follows.

Invalid Gifts

Gifts to Witnesses of the Will

It might be recalled from Chapter 1 that neither of the witnesses to a will can be a beneficiary named in the will or the spouse of a beneficiary. This rule is provided in section 12(1) of the *Succession Law Reform Act*,[10] which also provides that, if it does occur, the gift to the witness or her spouse is void. Section 12(3) goes on to provide, however, that where the court is satisfied that the witness did not unduly influence the testator, the gift will not be void. Picking up from this provision in the Act is rule 74.15(1)(f) of the *Rules of Civil Procedure*, which comes under the orders for assistance discussed in the previous chapter. This rule provides an estate trustee with the means to deal with the issue in the event that she becomes aware that a beneficiary or a spouse of a beneficiary witnessed the will. The order in Form 74.40 will allow a period of time for the beneficiary to bring a motion to provide evidence (presumably by way of affidavit) that he or his spouse did not unduly influence the testator. If the circumstances of the case are such that the absence of undue influence cannot be proven by way of affidavit evidence, it is open to the witness to seek directions

10 RSO 1990, c S.26.

from the court under rule 75.06 for a trial of the issue. The order also provides that if the witness does not come forward within the specified time, the gift will be void.

Gifts or Appointments of Estate Trustee to a Former Spouse

It may be recalled from Chapter 3, Interpretation of Wills, that a divorce voids a gift to the former spouse of the testator and also voids the appointment of the former spouse as estate trustee. In such cases, the will is read as if the former spouse predeceased the testator. This rule is contained in section 17(2) of the *Succession Law Reform Act*, which also provides that these consequences do not occur if a contrary intention appears in the will. Again, picking up from this provision in the Act is rule 74.15(1)(g), which provides a mechanism for an actual or prospective estate trustee to deal with the situation where there is a former spouse named as a beneficiary or estate trustee. This order for assistance is contained in Form 74.41 and, like the other orders for assistance, gives the former spouse a specified period of time in which to signify that he wishes to take part in the court's determination of whether a contrary intention appears in the will with respect to the gift or appointment as estate trustee. If the former spouse wishes to take part, he must file a notice of appearance within the time specified. Otherwise, the determination will be made in his absence and he will be bound by the result.

Ambiguous Gift Clauses

Some wills, particularly homemade wills, have gifts that are ambiguous on their face. If the testator's intention cannot be determined based on a plain reading of the will, it may be the case that the parties are forced to seek an interpretation from the court. In such cases, all evidence of the testator's intentions must be put before the court for a decision and declaration as to how the will ought to be interpreted.

Wills or Gifts Void for Public Policy

In very rare cases, the court may strike a gift set out in an otherwise valid will if the gift contravenes public policy. An example of this kind of decision occurred in the 2014 New Brunswick decision in *McCorkill v Streed*.[11] In *McCorkill*, the testator's will provided a gift of approximately $250,000 to a white supremacist organization based in the United States called the National Alliance. The deceased had no spouse or children but did have siblings, one of whom brought an application to the court seeking a declaration that the gift to the National Alliance should be voided as being illegal or contrary to public policy. In a carefully written decision, Justice Grant, speaking for the New Brunswick Court of Queen's Bench, struck the gift as being contrary to public policy. The New Brunswick Court of Appeal upheld the decision in 2015 and in 2016 the Supreme Court of Canada refused to hear the appeal. This decision was cited in the 2015 Ontario decision of *Spence v BMO Trust Company*[12] in which the court set aside the entire will of a testator who had disinherited his daughter because she had married and had a child with a person of different ethnicity than himself. The *Spence* decision was overturned on appeal.

11   2014 NBQB 148.
12   2015 ONSC 615; 2016 ONCA 196.

Duties of the Estate Trustee Having Information Suggesting That the Will Is Invalid

There may be cases in which an estate trustee has information suggesting that the will in which he is appointed estate trustee is invalid or contains an invalid gift. In such a case, particularly where there are underage, mentally incapable, or unascertained beneficiaries, the appropriate course of action for the estate trustee to take is to seek the advice of the court by way of an application for directions.

In such a case, a procedure may be designed to notify the persons who have a financial interest under the previous will, or under the laws of intestacy, and to have them come forward if they wish to take steps respecting the validity of the will or the gift.

If the estate trustee ignores information suggesting that the will in which he is appointed estate trustee is invalid and proceeds to administer the estate to the prejudice of persons who would otherwise be beneficiaries, those persons may have a right of action against the estate trustee.

KEY TERMS

motion for directions, 325
notice of objection, 321
party impugning the will, 314

party propounding the will, 314
undue influence, 317

REVIEW QUESTIONS

1. What are four typical challenges to a will?

2. What terminology is used for the party seeking to (a) set aside the will, and (b) uphold the will?

3. What are the four touchstones of testamentary capacity?

4. What steps should a lawyer take to establish testamentary capacity when taking instructions for a will?

5. How can a lawyer establish that the testator has knowledge and approval of the will's contents before its signing?

6. How can undue influence be determined and avoided when the client is giving instructions for and signing the will?

7. Why is proper execution of the will important when the will is being impugned?

8. What is the effect of evidence of "suspicious circumstances" on the party propounding a will?

9. What is the result of a successful will challenge?

10. Identify the form used to commence a challenge of the validity of a will or the appointment of an estate trustee.

11. Who is entitled to file a notice of objection?

12. What is the limitation period applicable to a will challenge?

13. What is a motion for directions?

14. What does the order given upon a motion for directions include?

15. What recourse does someone have who wishes to impugn a will and objects to an estate being administered even where a certificate of appointment has been issued?

16. What step should be taken by an estate trustee who has information that suggests that a will may be invalid?

Statutory Forms of Estate Litigation

16

LEARNING OUTCOMES

After completing this chapter, you should be able to:

- Know when the possibility of the *Family Law Act* election will affect the administration of an estate and how it affects the estate trustee's obligations

- Know how to determine whether a *Family Law Act* election is advisable to a surviving spouse and how to make the election

- Know the procedure for claiming dependant's relief under the *Succession Law Reform Act*

- Know how a court determines entitlement and quantum of dependant's relief under the *Succession Law Reform Act*

- Understand the significance of section 72 of the *Succession Law Reform Act* in defining the estate for the purposes of determining dependant's relief

- Understand the role played by moral obligations in the court's determination of dependant's relief

- Know the procedure for applying to the court for guardianships of property and for termination of guardianships of property

- Know the procedure for applying to the court for guardianships of a person and for termination of guardianships of a person

Introduction

In addition to claims against the estate trustee and claims that the will of the deceased is invalid, there are other forms of litigation that some people categorize as estate litigation. This chapter discusses estate litigation that arises from specific statutes. As will be seen, estate litigation of this type sometimes deals with estates of deceased persons and sometimes, as in the case of litigation under the *Substitute Decisions Act, 1992*,[1] with the property of living persons or the living persons themselves.

Family Law Act Election

The *Family Law Act*[2] was discussed in Chapter 2, Will Clauses, in the context of the will clause "Exclusion of Benefits from Community of Property," which relates to the scheme contained in Part I of the Act for equalization of net family property between spouses upon the breakdown of a marriage. The scheme for equalization of net family property is also relevant in a situation where one spouse survives the other provided they were married when the death occurred. To deal with the possible inequities that might fall upon a surviving spouse in situations where the deceased spouse's will or the laws of intestacy do not adequately provide for him, section 5(2) of the *Family Law Act* entitles the surviving spouse to an equalization of net family property from the deceased spouse's estate. Essentially, a surviving spouse has a choice whether he wants to take what he is entitled to under the deceased's will (or the laws of intestacy as the case may be) or under the equalization scheme contained in Part I of the Act. The mechanism for choosing one or the other is contained in section 6, which gives the surviving spouse six months to elect to choose entitlement under Part I of the Act. The election is made by filing an election form, entitled Form 1 under the *Family Law Act*, in the office of the Estate Registrar for Ontario. Figure 16.1 is an example of such an election. Section 6(11) stipulates that if the election form is not filed within six months, the surviving spouse is deemed to have elected to receive under the deceased spouse's will or the laws of intestacy as the case may be. In the case of a partial intestacy (where the will does not deal with all of the assets), the deemed election will be to receive entitlement under the will and the rules of partial intestacy combined.

A lawyer retained by a surviving spouse who was not left the entire estate in the deceased spouse's will must be aware of the possibility of a *Family Law Act* election and must determine in fairly short order whether the surviving spouse would be better off electing rather than taking under the will. Similarly, if there was no will and the spouse must share the estate with the children of the deceased under the laws of intestacy, the lawyer must determine quickly whether the spouse would be better off taking an equalization of net family property or taking under the laws of intestacy. Determining this requires a working knowledge of the property distribution scheme set out in Part I of the *Family Law Act*.

---

1 SO 1992, c 30.
2 RSO 1990, c F.3.

FIGURE 16.1 Family Law Act Election With Will (Form 1)

Election Under *The Family Law Act*

Family Law Act, R.R.O. 1990, Reg. 368

Form 1

Court File No.
93412

This election is filed by *(solicitors)*

Grit, Grat & Groot, Barristers & Solicitors, 15 Cross Street, Toronto, ON M5A 1Q1

Name of Deceased *Surname*	Given Name(s)
Kreiberg	Mona

Last Address of Deceased   *Street or Postal Address   City, Town, Etc.   Postal Code*

16 Lincoln Blvd., Hamilton, ON L8S 1Q2

Date of Death   *Day, Month, Year*

12 February 2018

Surviving Spouse *Surname*	Given Name(s)
Kreiberg	William

Address of Spouse   *Street or Postal Address   City, Town, Etc.   Postal Code*

16 Lincoln Blvd., Hamilton, ON L8S 1Q2

I,...............................William Kreiberg...................................... the surviving spouse, elect:

(Please print)

[X] to receive the entitlement under section 5 of the *Family Law Act;*

OR (check one box only)

[ ] to receive the entitlement under the will, or under Part II of the *Succession Law Reform Act*, if there is an intestacy, or both, if there is a partial intestacy.

William Kreiberg   May 16, 2018

....

Signature of Surviving Spouse   Date

NOTE: THIS ELECTION HAS IMPORTANT EFFECTS ON YOUR RIGHTS. YOU SHOULD HAVE LEGAL ADVICE BEFORE SIGNING IT.

The Scheme Set Out in Part I of the Family Law Act

The basic scheme under the Act is based on the premise that spouses share debts and assets (although only with respect to each other and not with respect to third parties) from the date of marriage until the day before the date of death or the date of separation. The day before the date of death or the date of separation, as the case may be, is called the **valuation date**. It is relevant to know what each spouse owned and owed as of the date of marriage and as of the valuation date. A spouse gets credit for the assets she has at the time of the marriage and will, in a sense, be penalized—that is, have deductions made—for whatever debts she has at the time of the marriage. In contrast, a spouse has to share what she acquired during the marriage in the way of assets and debts. A spouse's financial position at the valuation date, less her financial position as of the date of marriage, is her net family property (subject to the rules discussed below). Figure 16.2 gives an example of an analysis of net family property and a resulting election to set aside a spouse's will.

In the calculation of net family property, a spouse can come into a marriage with a negative value, which will be factored into the calculation (as in Figure 16.3). In contrast, a spouse whose financial position as of the valuation date is in the negative is deemed to be zero (as in Figure 16.4). In other words, one spouse cannot get credit against the other spouse for spending more than his own financial worth during the marriage. Again, while the scheme under section 5 of the Act is designed to have the spouses share assets and debts, this sharing does not extend to the outside world. In other words, a husband's creditors are not able to collect against the wife unless, of course, there is some agreement on the part of the wife to indemnify the husband.

As seen from the examples, in calculating net family property it is not relevant that the assets brought into the marriage no longer exist or are no longer owned by the spouse who originally owned them.

Special Rule for the Matrimonial Home

A unique rule relates to calculating net family property when it comes to the **matrimonial home** of the spouses. "Matrimonial home" is defined in section 18(1) of the *Family Law Act* as "[e]very property in which a person has an interest and that is ... ordinarily occupied by the person and his or her spouse as their family residence." Here the rule is that a party who owns a house on the date of marriage does not get credit for such ownership at the time of calculating the net family property if the house was occupied as the matrimonial home on the valuation date.

Figures 16.5 and 16.6 illustrate this principle. In the former case, the home is occupied at the date of death; in the latter, the home ceases to be the matrimonial home before the date of death. The reason for this rule is rooted in the fact that the matrimonial home is considered a special kind of asset that deserves special treatment in family matters. Note that this discussion is only an outline; a full treatment of the rules on division of property and the matrimonial home is beyond the scope of this text. Many legal issues can arise regarding the matrimonial home, such as the qualification of the home as such or the existence of more than one home. In such cases, the rules and common law in the field of family law must be consulted.

valuation date
day before the date of death or the date on which the spouses separated with no reasonable prospect of reconciliation

matrimonial home
a residence in which a person has an interest and which is normally occupied by him and his spouse

FIGURE 16.2   Calculation: Net Family Property

Deceased: Steve

Family circumstances:
Steve and Jane married on May 1, 1994. Steve died on January 1, 2018.

	Steve		*Jane*	
Assets owned on the date of marriage:				
car	$4,000	car	$9,000	
bank account	1,000	cash	1,000	

Debts owed on the date of marriage:
nil

Assets owned on the date of death:

	Steve		*Jane*	
car	$20,000	car	$15,000	
bank account	50,000	cash	15,000	

Debts owed on the date of death:
credit card .... ($10,000)
owed by Steve

Relevant clause of Steve's will:
$15,000 to my brother Joe
$15,000 to my brother William
$15,000 to my sister, Sally
$5,000 to my nephew
Residue to my wife, Jane

Other facts:
Steve had no life insurance
Steve's bank account is solely owned (with no right of survivorship)

Question:
Should Jane elect to set aside the will under the *Family Law Act*?

Answer (assuming no pertinent facts missing):
Steve's net family property is $55,000
Jane's net family property is $20,000
Under a *Family Law Act* election Jane would receive ½ of the difference, or $17,500

Under the will Jane would receive $10,000
Therefore, yes

FIGURE 16.3   Calculation: Negative Value on Date of Marriage

Deceased: Julie

Family circumstances:
    Julie and Jim married on October 1, 1987. Julie died on January 1, 2018.

	Julie		*Jim*
Assets owned on the date of marriage:			
car	$4,000	car	$9,000
bank account	1,000	cash	1,000

Debts owed on the date of marriage:
    student loan ($50,000) owed by Jim

Assets owned on the date of death:			
car	$20,000	car	$15,000
bank account	80,000	cash	15,000
½ 4 Tead St.	60,000	½ 4 Tead St.	60,000

Debts owed on the date of death: ½
    nil

Relevant clause of Julie's will:
    $25,000 to my husband, Jim
    Residue to my brother, Albert

Other facts:
    Julie had no life insurance
    4 Tead Street is owned by Julie and Jim as tenants in common
    Julie's bank account is solely owned (with no right of survivorship)

Question:
    Should Jim elect to set aside the will under the *Family Law Act*?

    Answer (assuming no pertinent facts missing):
    Julie's net family property is $155,000
    Jim's net family property is $130,000
    Under a *Family Law Act* election Jim would receive ½ of the difference, or $12,500
    Under the will Jim would receive $25,000
    Therefore, no

FIGURE 16.4   Calculation: Negative Value on Valuation Date (Deemed to Be Zero)

Deceased: Jeff

Family circumstances:
    Jeff and Kelly married on July 20, 1994. Jeff died on January 1, 2018.

Jeff		*Kelly*	
Assets owned on the date of marriage:			
car	$4,000	car	$9,000
bank account	1,000	cash	1,000

Debts owed on the date of marriage:
    nil

Assets owned on the date of death:

car	$20,000	car	$15,000
bank account	85,000	cash	15,000

Debts owed on the date of death:
    line of credit .... ($80,000)
    owed by Kelly

Relevant clause of Jeff's will:
    $60,000 to Kelly
    Residue to my friend Rashid

Other facts:
    Jeff had no life insurance
    Jeff's bank account is solely owned (with no right of survivorship)

Question:
    Should Kelly elect to set aside the will under the *Family Law Act*?

Answer (assuming no pertinent facts missing):
    Jeff's net family property is $100,000
    Kelly's net family property is $0
    Under a *Family Law Act* election Kelly would receive ½ of the difference, or $50,000
    Under the will Kelly would receive $60,000
    Therefore, no

FIGURE 16.5   Calculation: Matrimonial Home Occupied on Valuation Date

Deceased: Tanya

Family circumstances:
   Tanya and Bill married on April 15, 1995. Tanya died on January 1, 2018.

	Tanya		Bill

Assets owned on the date of marriage:

car	$ 5,000	car	$ 5,000
66 Home Ave.	100,000	cash	100,000

Debts owed on the date of marriage:
   nil

Assets owned on the date of death:

car	$ 20,000	car	$ 15,000
bank account	10,000	cash	15,000
66 Home Ave.	150,000	bonds	150,000

Debts owed on the date of death:
   nil

Relevant clause of Tanya's will:
   $40,000 to my husband, Bill
   Residue to the Person Fund Charity

Other facts:
   Tanya had no life insurance
   Tanya's bank account is solely owned (with no right of survivorship)
   66 Home Ave. was occupied by Tanya and Bill as the matrimonial home on the evaluation date

Question:
   Should Bill elect to set aside the will under the *Family Law Act*?

Answer (assuming no pertinent facts missing):
   Tanya's net family property is $175,000
   Bill's net family property is $75,000
   Under a *Family Law Act* election Bill would receive ½ of the difference, or $50,000
   Under the will Bill would receive $40,000
   Therefore, yes

FIGURE 16.6   Calculation: Former Matrimonial Home

Deceased: Sharon

Family circumstances:
  Sharon and Arnold married on June 28, 1994. Sharon died on May 1, 2018.

	Sharon		*Arnold*

Assets owned on the date of marriage:

car	$ 5,000	car	$ 5,000
34 Mortgage Ave.	100,000	cash	100,000

Debts owed on the date of marriage:
  nil

Assets owned on the date of death:

car	$ 20,000	car	$ 15,000
bank account.	10,000	cash	15,000
34 Mortgage Ave.	150,000	bonds	150,000

Debts owed on the date of death:
  nil

Relevant clause of Sharon's will:
  $40,000 to my husband, Arnold
  Residue to the Person Fund Charity

Other facts:
  Sharon had no life insurance
  Sharon's bank account is solely owned (with no right of survivorship)
  34 Mortgage Ave. was the matrimonial home until one year before she died, when they moved from the house into an apartment

Question:
  Should Arnold elect to set aside the will under the *Family Law Act*?

Answer (assuming no pertinent facts missing):
  Sharon's net family property is $75,000
  Arnold's net family property is $75,000
  Under a *Family Law Act* election Arnold would receive ½ of the difference, or $0
  Under the will Arnold would receive $40,000
  Therefore, no

Excluded Property

Under Part I of the Act, section 4(2) lists certain categories of property that are to be excluded from the calculation of net family property. For this reason, when a lawyer is calculating net family property for a surviving spouse, it is important to ask the appropriate questions to determine whether either spouse has (or had, in the case of the deceased spouse) any assets that qualify as **excluded property** under section 5 of the *Family Law Act*. Such exclusions give a benefit to the spouse claiming the exclusion because such

excluded property property which, under the *Family Law Act*, is not included in the calculation of net family property on the breakdown of a marriage or upon the filing of an election by a surviving spouse

assets, in effect, do not need to be shared. Any excluded property of either spouse affects the calculation of net family property and is therefore relevant to the surviving spouse's decision whether to elect to set aside the will or the rules of intestacy.

The first exclusion referred to in the Act is property acquired by way of gift or inheritance. In other words, if one spouse received a gift or a bequest during the marriage, that spouse is entitled to exclude or deduct the amount of the gift from her net family property, subject to the comments below on traceability. Figure 16.7 illustrates this kind of exclusion.

FIGURE 16.7   Calculation: Exclusion of Gift

Deceased: Jason

Family circumstances:
  Jason and Debbie married on May 29, 1995. Jason died on January 1, 2018.

Jason		Debbie	
Assets owned on the date of marriage:			
car	$5,000	car	$9,000
		cash	1,000

Debts owed on the date of marriage:
  nil

Jason		Debbie	
Assets owned on the date of death:			
car	$20,000	car	$15,000
bank account	85,000	cash	15,000
½ 3 Red Ave.	50,000	½ 3 Red Ave.	50,000

Debts owed on the date of death:
  nil

Relevant clause of Jason's will:
  Everything to my brother, Randy

Other facts:
  Jason had no life insurance
  3 Red Avenue is owned by Jason and Debbie as tenants in common
  Jason's bank account is solely owned (with no right of survivorship)
  During the marriage Jason received an inheritance of $85,000, which he put into his bank account, and the interest on the bank account was spent

Question:
  Should Debbie elect to set aside the will under the *Family Law Act*?

Answer (assuming no pertinent facts missing):
  Jason's net family property is $65,000
  Debbie's net family property is $70,000
  Under a *Family Law Act* election Debbie would receive ½ of the difference, or *negative* $5,000
  Under the will Debbie would receive nothing
  Therefore, no

Similarly, any income from a gift or inheritance received during the marriage can be excluded from the recipient spouse's net family property if it is expressed by the giver of the gift or bequest that the income be excluded. Figure 16.8 illustrates this kind of exclusion. A statement that the income from the gift is to be excluded is often contained in a testator's will, as in the sample will discussed in Chapter 2.

FIGURE 16.8   Calculation: Exclusion of Income from Gift

Deceased: John

Family circumstances:
   John and Sandy married on March 24, 1998. John died on January 1, 2018.

John	Sandy
Assets owned on the date of marriage:	
car...................... $5,000	car...................... $10,000
cash..................... 5,000	

Debts owed on the date of marriage:
   nil

Assets owned on the date of death:	
car...................... $ 25,000	car...................... $20,000
investments.............. 100,000	cash 5,000

Debts owed on the date of death:
   nil

Relevant clause of John's will:
   Everything to my sister, Alison

Other facts:
   John had no life insurance
   John's investments are solely owned (with no right of survivorship)
   During the marriage John received an inheritance of $80,000, which he put into investments.
       The gift specified that the income was not to be included in net family property.
       The investments earned $20,000, which was also invested.

Question:
   Should Sandy elect to set aside the will under the *Family Law Act*?

Answer (assuming no pertinent facts missing):
       John's net family property is $15,000
       Sandy's net family property is $15,000
       Under a *Family Law Act* election Sandy would receive ½ of the difference, or $0
       Under the will Sandy would receive nothing
   Therefore, no

Also qualifying as excluded property are damages or settlement funds for personal injury, including nervous shock, mental distress, and loss of guidance or care and companionship received during the marriage. Figure 16.9 illustrates this kind of exclusion.

FIGURE 16.9 Calculation: Exclusion of Damages

Deceased: Sarah

Family circumstances:
Sarah and Jack married on April 1, 2001. Sarah died on January 1, 2018.

Sarah		Jack	
Assets owned on the date of marriage:			
car	$5,000	car	$10,000
cash	5,000		

Debts owed on the date of marriage:
nil

Assets owned on the date of death:			
car	$11,000	car	$ 10,000
bank account	19,000	bank account	199,000

Debts owed on the date of death:
nil

Relevant clause of Sarah's will:
$6,000 to my husband, Jack
Residue to my sister, Louise

Other facts:
Sarah had no life insurance
Sarah's bank account is solely owned (with no right of survivorship)
During the marriage Jack received personal injury damages in the amount of $199,000, which he deposited into his bank account

Question:
Should Jack elect to set aside the will under the *Family Law Act*?

Answer (assuming no pertinent facts missing):
Sarah's net family property is $20,000
Jack's net family property is $0
Under a *Family Law Act* election Jack would receive ½ of the difference, or $10,000
Under the will Jack would receive $6,000
Therefore, yes

Life insurance proceeds received during the marriage also qualify as excluded property. This is not to be confused with life insurance payable on the death of the deceased spouse, which is dealt with below.

An important principle with respect to excluded property is that the ownership of the excluded property must be traceable from the time of acquisition by the spouse until the valuation date. The simplest way for an asset to be traceable is for it to be continuously owned separately by the spouse from the date of acquisition to the valuation date. If, on the other hand, the spouse gives up ownership of the asset before the valuation date, it is important to determine how the ownership ceased. If the asset is given away during the marriage, it is considered lost as excluded property. If the excluded asset is sold during the marriage, and the sale proceeds are kept separate from any bank accounts owned jointly by the spouses and are not otherwise mixed with jointly owned property, the sale proceeds can qualify as excluded property. Similarly, if the sale proceeds are used to purchase an asset that is again solely owned by the spouse, the second asset can qualify as excluded property. Figure 16.10 gives an example in which the concept of traceability is relevant.

FIGURE 16.10   Calculation: Traceability

Deceased: Marcel

Family circumstances:
   Marcel and Amanda married on August 24, 1995. Marcel died on May 3, 2018.

Marcel		*Amanda*	

Assets owned on the date of marriage:

car	$4,000	car	$10,000
cash	1,000		

Debts owed on the date of marriage:
   nil

Assets owned on the date of death:

car	$25,000	car	$ 10,000
bank account	75,000	investment property	150,000

Debts owed on the date of death:
   nil

Relevant clause of Marcel's will:
   $30,000 to my wife, Amanda
   Residue to my brother, Jean-Paul

Other facts:
   Marcel had no life insurance
   Marcel's bank account is solely owned (with no right of survivorship)
   During the marriage Amanda received personal injury damages in the amount of $150,000, which she used to purchase her investment property.

Question:
   Should Amanda elect to set aside the will under the *Family Law Act*?

Answer (assuming no pertinent facts missing):
   Marcel's net family property is $95,000
   Amanda's net family property is $0
   Under a *Family Law Act* election Amanda would receive ½ of the difference, or $47,500
   Under the will Amanda would receive $30,000
   Therefore, yes

Again, an exhaustive discussion of all the permutations of the laws of net family property is outside the scope of this text. In addition, many factual issues can arise out of the rules in section 5 of the Act, some of which can be negotiated and others of which may require the decision of a court. In this regard, section 7 of the Act provides for an application to be brought to a court to "determine any matter respecting the spouse's entitlement under section 5."

Property Falling Outside the Estate

Property falling outside the estate, such as jointly owned property with right of survivorship, can be received by the spouse in addition to what the spouse is entitled to under section 5 of the *Family Law Act*.

Domestic Contracts

A domestic contract, such as a prenuptial agreement, that is made in accordance with Part IV of the *Family Law Act* and sets out an agreement between spouses that is inconsistent with a spouse's right of election will override the spouse's right of election. There are very stringent requirements for a domestic contract to be valid. In brief, it must be in writing, witnessed, and signed by the spouses. It must also have been made with full financial disclosure between the spouses, and will likely not be valid if both spouses did not have independent legal advice, or at least the opportunity to obtain it, before entering into the agreement.

Effect of Election

If a spouse elects to exercise her entitlement under section 5(2) of the *Family Law Act*, the deceased spouse's will is treated as if the surviving spouse had predeceased. Thus, after the surviving spouse has received her entitlement, the estate will be administered in the normal course except that the gifts in the will to the spouse will be ignored. An exception to this rule applies if the deceased spouse's will specifically indicates that the surviving spouse is entitled to the gifts in the will in addition to the entitlement under the election.

If the spouse is the appointed estate trustee in the deceased spouse's will and she chooses to make the election, she cannot act as estate trustee. A spouse who is considering whether to elect should not take any steps as estate trustee because doing so would create a conflict of interest.

Similarly, if a spouse elects under section 6 and there is no will, the spouse is deemed to have waived any rights of entitlement under the laws of intestacy.

Under section 6(12), the spouse's right of entitlement has priority over anyone else's interest under laws of intestacy and over dependants' claims (discussed below), except for claims of dependent children of the deceased.

Deductions from the Surviving Spouse's Entitlement under the Family Law Act

There are important deductions from a spouse's entitlement under section 5(2) of the Act that apply unless a contrary intention is set out in the will. These provisions, set out in section 6(7) apply in the case of (1) life insurance payable to the surviving spouse on the life of the deceased spouse, (2) a lump-sum payment under a pension plan (or similar plan) payable to the surviving spouse on the death of the deceased spouse, or (3) property passing to the surviving spouse from the deceased spouse by right of survivorship. Section 6(7) of the Act indicates that if the surviving spouse receives such payments or property and has also elected to receive an equalization payment under section 5(2) of the Act, the estate is entitled to a credit against the spouse's entitlement under section 5(2) for the amount of the payment or property (less any tax liability in respect of such payment or property). Perhaps more important from the lawyer or law clerk's point of view is the fact that in the event of an election, the estate trustee is also entitled to recover from the surviving spouse any amount the surviving spouse received from the lump-sum payment in excess of her entitlement under the Act. An illustration of this principle at work is shown in Figure 16.11.

FIGURE 16.11   Calculation: Deductions from Surviving Spouse's Entitlement

Deceased: Emanuel

Family Circumstances:
  Emanuel and Nada married on June 1, 1990. Emanuel died October 20, 2018.

	Emanuel		Nada

Assets owned on the date of marriage:
  car . . . . $ 5,000   car . . . . $ 5,000

Assets owned on the date of death:
  investment account . . . . $405,000   cottage $155,000
  ½ of 48 Silvermaple Drive . . .   500,000   ½ of 48 Silvermaple Drive. . .   500,000

Relevant clause in Emanuel's will:
  $100,000 to my wife, Nada
  Residue to my son, Silvio

Other facts:
  48 Silvermaple Drive is owned by Emanuel and Nada as joint tenants*

Question:
  Should Nada elect to set aside the will under the *Family Law Act*?

Answer (assuming no pertinent facts missing):
    Emanuel's net family property is $900,000
    Nada's net family property is $650,000
    Under a *Family Law Act* election, Nada would receive ½ of the difference, or $125,000, but from this would be deducted $500,000 pursuant to section 6(7) of the *Family Law Act*, rendering her liable to the estate trustee for the amount of $375,000
    Under the will Nada would receive $100,000 plus the other half of 48 Silvermaple Drive pursuant to the joint tenancy, for a total of $600,000.
    Therefore, no

*If Emanuel and Nada owned 48 Silvermaple Drive as tenants in common, Nada would be advised to elect to take her entitlement under the *Family Law Act*.

While it may be assumed, section 6(4) of the Act makes it clear that if a spouse elects to take under the will or to receive his entitlement pursuant to the laws of intestacy, any property held jointly by the deceased spouse and the surviving spouse will pass to the surviving spouse in addition to whatever entitlements exist under the will.

Implications of the Family Law Act for Estate Lawyers and Law Clerks

The spousal election takes precedence over any other gifts in the will; therefore, no distribution can be made by the estate trustee after the deceased's spouse makes an election and before the spouse receives his entitlement. Similarly, the lawyer assisting the estate trustee must be sure that the latter is made aware that he must not distribute the estate before the six-month limitation period has expired if the deceased was survived by a spouse. This rule is contained in section 6(14) of the *Family Law Act*, which prohibits such distributions without the consent of the spouse or the court, and section 6(19), which states that the estate trustee will be held personally liable to the surviving spouse for the amount that the spouse is unable to collect from the estate owing to such distribution. Notwithstanding these sanctions, however, it should be noted that section 6(17) of the Act provides that the estate trustee is entitled to make "reasonable advances to dependants of the deceased spouse for their support" during this six-month period.

An extension of the six-month limitation period to elect can be requested under section 6(16) of the Act and an order suspending the administration of the estate can be requested under section 6(20). If an extension under section 6(16) is granted by the court after the expiry of this period, the estate trustee will not be held liable for any distribution made after the original expiry date, if he did not have notice of the application to extend the time, and the assets will be lost by the electing spouse if there is a shortage.

A lawyer acting for the surviving spouse must consider all relevant factors and have full financial disclosure before deciding whether the client should or should not elect under section 5 of the *Family Law Act*. The election is, in most circumstances, irreversible. It is possible for a spouse to make an election only to find that she would have been in a better financial position to take under the will.

Finally, note that under a partial intestacy, the election would be considered in light of the surviving spouse's overall entitlement to the estate—that is, under the rules discussed in Chapter 4, Intestacy, on the one hand, and under the *Family Law Act* on the other.

Dependant's Relief Claims Under the Succession Law Reform Act

Part V of the *Succession Law Reform Act*[3] sets out rules allowing dependants of a deceased person to apply to a court for an order for provision of support from the deceased's estate regardless of the deceased's will or the laws of intestacy. To qualify as a dependant under the Act, a person must be a spouse or same-sex partner, parent, child, grandchild, or sibling of the deceased. In the context of dependant's relief claims, "spouse" has the expanded

---

3 RSO 1990, c S.26.

definition that includes common law spouses provided the claimant for dependant's relief and the deceased had cohabited continuously for at least three years or were in a relationship of "some permanence" and the parents of a child.

Procedure

Dependant's relief claims are brought by way of notice of application, the form and supporting documents for which are set out in rule 38.09 of the *Rules of Civil Procedure*.[4] The applicant—that is, the person who actually brings the application before the court—can be any of the following persons:

1. the dependant;
2. the dependant's parent;
3. the Ministry of Community and Social Services in the name of the minister;
4. a municipal corporation (metropolitan, district, or regional but not including an area municipality);
5. a district social services administration board;
6. an approved native band; or
7. a delivery agent under the *Ontario Works Act, 1997*.[5]

The agencies listed under 3 to 7 above can be parties if the agency is providing or has provided benefits under the *Family Benefits Act*,[6] the *Ontario Works Act, 1997*, or the *Ontario Disability Support Program Act, 1997*,[7] or if an application on behalf of the dependant has been made to such agencies under such acts.

A dependant seeking support from the deceased's estate has six months from the date of issuance of the certificate of appointment of estate trustee with a will or without a will in which to apply for dependant's relief. Under section 60(2) of the *Succession Law Reform Act*, however, as long as one of the dependants has brought an application within the six-month period, all dependants will be deemed to have complied with the limitation period. Similarly, if an application is brought on behalf of one dependant, the court will consider all the dependants of the deceased when making its decision. In this regard, under section 63(5) of the Act, the court is not to make the order until it is satisfied that all persons who may have an interest in the proceeding, or who may be affected by the order, have been served with the notice of application.

Where an application for dependant's relief is made, the estate trustee is prohibited from distributing the estate until the court has issued a ruling on the application. If she nevertheless makes the distribution, she may be held personally liable to the dependants to the extent that they are prejudiced by the distribution.

dependant's relief
financial support ordered to be paid by an estate to a dependant of the deceased pursuant to Part V of the *Succession Law Reform Act*

---

4 RRO 1990, reg. 194
5 SO 1997, c 25 (Sched A).
6 RSO 1990, c F.2.
7 SO 1997, c 25 (Sched B).

Financial Statements

It is customary for the party seeking dependant's relief to supply sworn financial statements to the estate trustee in Form 13.1 from the *Family Court Rules* which would be included in the application record. This form, called "Financial Statement (Property and Support Claims)" can be obtained online at <http://www.ontariocourtforms.on.ca/en/family-law-rules-forms>. If a financial statement is not supplied by the person seeking dependant's relief, the court will likely order him to supply one as the information on the form is necessary for the court to make a determination of entitlement or quantum of dependant's relief.

Orders Pursuant to Applications for Dependant's Relief

The criteria to be weighed by a judge in determining whether to order support and the amount to be ordered are set out in sections 62(1)(a)-(s) of the *Succession Law Reform Act*. They include, for example, the dependant's current assets and means, physical or mental health, and prospects. If the dependant is a spouse or same-sex partner of the deceased, there is a special list of criteria contained in sections 62(1)(r)(i)-(viii). These criteria include such considerations as the length of time that the spouse or partner and the deceased cohabited, the extent to which the spouse or partner may have forgone career opportunities for the benefit of the family, and whether there was a course of conduct by the person claiming dependant's relief during the deceased's life that was "so unconscionable as to constitute an obvious and gross repudiation of the relationship."

The kinds of orders that will be made by a judge on an application for dependant's relief are set out in section 63(2) of the Act. There is a great deal of flexibility in such orders in that the support can be ordered by way of payment out of the income or capital of the estate or out of both income and capital. The payment can be ordered to be made directly to the dependant or to a trust, the beneficiary of which is the dependant. The payment can also be ordered to be made directly to an agency in reimbursement for the agency's payment to the dependant. The payment may be by way of a single lump-sum payment or by periodic payments for a specified or indefinite period of time.

Section 71 of the *Succession Law Reform Act* states that if the deceased entered into a contract in good faith and for valuable consideration to make a gift of certain assets in his will to the other contracting party, such contracts supersede the dependant's relief provisions. An exception to this rule occurs where, in the opinion of the court, the value of the property is greater than the consideration paid to the deceased under the contract. In such a case, the value of the gift made by way of contract that is in excess of the value of the original consideration will be made available to dependants on an application for dependant's relief.

An important provision in Part V of the Act is section 72, which provides that, for the purposes of calculating dependant's relief, the value of certain transactions are deemed to be part of the deceased's estate notwithstanding that they would normally fall outside of the estate. The transactions listed include the following:

- money owned by the deceased that passed to a surviving bank account holder on the deceased's death;

- real property owned by the deceased that passed to a surviving joint tenant on the deceased's death;
- life insurance payable on the death of the deceased; and
- gifts *mortis causa* (certain gifts made by the deceased during his life but in contemplation of his death).

The provisions of section 72 are sometimes referred to as **claw back provisions** because they allow the court to claw certain assets back into the estate for the purpose of quantifying and satisfying an order for dependant's relief. One qualification to bear in mind with respect to the above-noted provisions is that section 72 of the Act is subject to section 71, which means that a valid contract between the deceased and a third party will not be affected by the operation of section 72.

Finally, note that under the current state of the case law, when determining the entitlement or amount of dependant's relief, the court is not only directed to consider the means and needs of the applicant but also the deceased's moral obligations toward his beneficiaries who may not be asserting a claim for dependant's relief. This kind of consideration can be particularly important where the person claiming dependant's relief has a legitimate claim to the entire estate of the deceased (including those assets that would normally pass outside of the estate but which are caught by section 72) but where there are other persons who may be dependants of the deceased as well.

> **claw back provisions** (in the context of dependant's relief claims) statutory provisions allowing the court to order that certain assets, normally falling outside the estate, be paid to a dependant

Substitute Decisions Act Applications

The *Substitute Decisions Act, 1992* provides for three schemes under which substitute decision-making for an incapable person is possible. The first scheme is through a power of attorney, which may be a continuing power of attorney for property or a power of attorney for personal care. The second scheme, called statutory guardianship, is through the Public Guardian and Trustee (or a person allowed under the Act to take over such statutory guardianship). The third scheme through which substitute decision-making of an incapable person is possible is the subject of this part of the text: **court-appointed guardianship**.

As the name suggests, court-appointed guardianship can be obtained through the court with respect to guardianship of a person's property or of a person. Any other kind of guardianship, including other court-appointed guardianships, can be reviewed and changed by a court.

> **court-appointed guardianship** scheme under which substitute decision-making for an incapable person is possible

In the following discussion regarding the rules and procedures relating to court-appointed guardianships, the person who is the subject of the application (the person who is alleged to be incapable) will be referred to as "the subject person." This terminology is adopted in this chapter because in such court applications the subject person's mental incapability is not presumed. The person applying for guardianship will be referred to as "the applicant" or "moving party" (depending on whether the process is an application or a motion).

Guardianships of Property

Application to Replace Public Guardian and Trustee

Section 17 of the *Substitute Decisions Act, 1992* allows an applicant to apply directly to the Public Guardian and Trustee to be allowed to assume control of the subject person's property. This provision would be invoked in the event that the Public Guardian and Trustee had assumed control of the subject person's property and the applicant wants to take on that role. The kinds of applications considered in this chapter do not include applications to the Public Guardian and Trustee but only applications to a court.

Application to Appoint Guardian of Property

The Act provides that any person may apply to the court for an appointment as the subject person's guardian of property as long as there is evidence that the subject person is incapable of managing his affairs and it is necessary for someone to make decisions on his behalf. The court makes its decision whether to grant guardianship on the basis of written material and argument. The court is, however, directed by section 22(3) of the Act not to appoint a guardian if another course of action is less restrictive of the subject person's decision-making rights and does not require that the subject person be found incapable of managing his affairs.

As will be seen below regarding the persons to be served with the application, it is possible for someone to make an application to the court for guardianship of the subject person's property despite the fact that the subject person already has an attorney under a continuing power of attorney for property. If the court finds that the applicant is better suited for the task of guardian for property, it will order that the applicant be the guardian and that the continuing power of attorney be void.

The documents required for the application are as follows:

1. an application record (containing notice of application, affidavit material, and other material as set out in rule 38.09 of the *Rules of Civil Procedure*);
2. the proposed guardian's consent (s 70(1)(a));
3. a plan of management for the property in the form prescribed by the regulations (Form 2 in O Reg 26/95) unless the applicant is the Public Guardian and Trustee, in which case Form 2 is not required; and
4. a statement signed by the applicant indicating that the subject person has been informed of the nature of the application and her right to oppose the application, and describing the manner in which the subject person was informed. Alternatively, if it was not possible to give the subject person this information, the statement must explain why it was not possible.

All the documents set out above must be filed in court along with an affidavit of service and be served on the following persons:

1. the subject person;
2. if known, the subject person's attorney under a continuing power of attorney for property;

3. if known, the subject person's guardian of the person;

4. if known, the subject person's attorney under a power of attorney for personal care;

5. the Public Guardian and Trustee;

6. the proposed guardian of property (who is typically the applicant);

7. the subject person's spouse or partner;

8. the subject person's children who are at least 18 years old;

9. the subject person's parents; and

10. the subject person's brothers and sisters who are at least 18 years old.

The Act specifies that the persons listed in 7 to 10 may be served by ordinary mail to their last known address. Presumably the other persons are to be served by personal service or an alternative to personal service in accordance with rule 16 of the *Rules of Civil Procedure*. Under section 69(7) of the Act, the persons set out in 7 to 10 above need not be served if they are not known to the applicant and if their existence or address cannot be determined through reasonable diligence.

The notice of application is to name, as parties, the persons set out in numbers 1 to 6 above (although the persons listed in numbers 2 to 4 will obviously be parties only if they exist and if they are known to the applicant). Normally, the proposed guardian is the applicant himself. The Act specifies, in section 69(9), that any of the persons set out in numbers 7 to 10, if not served with the notice of application, are entitled to be made parties to the proceeding. The Act does not address the possibility, but it must be assumed, that the persons set out in numbers 7 to 10 can be made parties whether they are served or not. The benefits of being made a party include the right to file written materials responding to the applicant's materials, the right to notice of the steps of the proceedings, and the right to make argument in court.

The procedure for parties who are served with the application and who wish to take part in the process is to file a notice of appearance (Form 38A in the *Rules of Civil Procedure*), which indicates that the person will be taking part in the application process. If the person feels it is warranted, she may also file affidavit evidence responding to those filed with the application record.

The Act provides for a summary procedure for applications to appoint a guardian of a person's property in certain situations. The advantage of the summary procedure is that it can be done "over the counter," which is generally faster and less expensive for the applicant. The summary procedure, set out in section 77 of the Act, is available only in the event that no person served with the notice of application files a notice of appearance with the court.

In a summary application to appoint a guardian of property, the applicant must file, along with all the other material listed above, two statements in Form A prescribed by O Reg 460/05. Both statements, at least one of which must be made by a qualified assessor, must state that the person making the statement is of the opinion that the subject person is incapable of managing property and must set out the facts upon which the opinion is based. A list of qualified assessors, as defined in section 2 of O Reg 460/05, can be obtained by sending a request by fax to (416) 327-6724 or mail to the following address: Capacity Assessment Office, Suite 800, 595 Bay Street, Toronto, ON, M5G 2M6.

The person making the statement must also indicate that he has no monetary conflict of interest in making the statement—that is, he cannot expect any direct or indirect monetary benefit as a result of the appointment of guardian of property. The statement may also indicate that the person is of the opinion that it is necessary for decisions to be made on the subject person's behalf, and if that is the case, the statement sets out the facts upon which this opinion is based. A statement by an assessor will be valid only if it indicates that the assessor performed an assessment of the person's capacity and indicates the date on which the assessment was performed. The date of the assessment cannot be earlier than six months before the issuance of the notice of application.

If the second statement is not made by a qualified assessor, it must be made by a person who knows the subject person and who has been in personal contact with her during the 12 months before the notice of application was issued. In the event that the person making the statement is not a qualified assessor, the statement is to be made on Form 8 in O Reg 26/95.

In addition to the above, the summary procedure is available only if the applicant certifies to the court in writing that (1) no person has delivered a notice of appearance, (2) the documents described above are included with the application, and (3) at least one of the statements described above expresses an opinion that the subject person needs another person to be authorized to make decisions on the subject person's behalf.

If the application is brought by way of summary procedure, the judge may grant the relief, require additional evidence, or order a hearing of the application by way of formal application with argument or, if need be, a trial.

Motion to Terminate Guardianship of Property

A similar procedure is available under the *Substitute Decisions Act, 1992* in the event that a termination of guardianship of property is desired. Such a proceeding is described in the Act as a motion, rather than an application, presumably because there already is an ongoing proceeding—that is, the original application to appoint the guardian. As discussed briefly in Chapter 14, Challenging the Conduct of the Estate Trustee and Passing of Accounts, when an action is already underway with respect to the same matter, instead of a notice of application, as above, the process is carried out by way of notice of motion. Rather than an applicant, the party seeking the change is the moving party. Typically, in the case of a motion to terminate guardianship of property, the moving party is the subject person herself or someone acting under her direction.

The only documents that appear to be required under the Act for a motion to terminate a guardianship of property are those that are contained in the motion record (including notice of motion, affidavit material, and other material as set out in rule 37.10 of the *Rules of Civil Procedure*). The motion record must be filed in court along with an affidavit of service and be served on the following persons:

1. the subject person;
2. if known, the subject person's guardian of the person;
3. if known, the subject person's attorney under a power of attorney for personal care;
4. the Public Guardian and Trustee;
5. the guardian of property;
6. the subject person's spouse or partner;

7. the subject person's children who are at least 18 years old;

8. the subject person's parents; and

9. the subject person's brothers and sisters who are at least 18 years old.

As in the case of an application to appoint a guardian, section 69(7) of the Act provides that the persons representing family of the subject person (set out in 6 to 9 above) need not be served if they are not known to the applicant and if their existence or address cannot be determined through reasonable diligence. In addition, such persons need be served only by regular mail sent to their last known address. It is assumed that the other persons named above are to be served in accordance with rule 16 of the *Rules of Civil Procedure*— that is, by personal service or an alternative to personal service.

As in the case of an application to appoint a guardian, the summary procedure is available for a motion to terminate a guardianship of property in the event that (1) the moving party is able to certify in writing to the court that the two statements described in section 73 of the Act accompany the motion materials; (2) all persons entitled to be served with the notice of motion have been served; and (3) all such persons have filed with the court a statement indicating that they do not intend to take part in the proceedings. If such statements are not filed by everyone entitled to be served with the motion materials, the motion cannot proceed by way of summary procedure.

Section 73 of the Act states that at least one of the two statements must be by an assessor (as described above). If a person making a statement is not an assessor, he must know the subject person and have been in personal contact with him during the 12 months preceding the notice of motion. The statements must indicate that the subject person is capable of managing property and set out the facts upon which the opinion is based. The statements must also indicate that the person making the statement can expect no monetary benefit as a result of the termination of guardianship.

Application to Terminate Statutory Guardianship of Property

If a person is seeking an order from the court terminating the guardianship of the Public Guardian and Trustee ("statutory guardianship"), the procedure to be used is called an **application to terminate statutory guardianship of property**. This procedure is outlined in section 69(0.1) of the *Substitute Decisions Act, 1992*. The procedure is not brought by way of motion because, as far as the court is concerned, it is an originating process.

The documents required for an application to terminate a statutory guardianship of property are those that are contained in the application record (including notice of application, affidavit material, and other material as set out in rule 38.09 of the *Rules of Civil Procedure*). According to the Act, the application record must be filed in court along with an affidavit of service and be served on the following persons:

1. the statutory guardian of property (usually this will be the Public Guardian and Trustee but, under section 17(1) of the Act, it could be the subject person's spouse or partner, a relative of the subject person, the subject person's attorney under a continuing power of attorney that did not give authority over the subject person's entire assets, or a trust company if the subject person's spouse has consented);

2. the applicant's guardian of the person;

application to terminate statutory guardianship of property application to end the guardianship of the Public Guardian and Trustee

3. the applicant's attorney for personal care, if known;

4. the Public Guardian and Trustee, in the event that the Public Guardian and Trustee is not the statutory guardian;

5. the subject person's spouse or partner;

6. the subject person's children who are at least 18 years old;

7. the subject person's parents; and

8. the subject person's brothers and sisters who are at least 18 years old.

Somewhat mysteriously, numbers 2 and 3 above require that the applicant's guardian of the person or attorney under a personal care power of attorney be served with the notice of application, rather than the subject person's guardian or attorney. This requirement suggests that it is contemplated that the application will be brought only by the applicant herself and not by a person under her direction.

As in the case of the other applications, those of the subject person's family to be served (listed in 5 to 8 above) need only be served by ordinary mail sent to their last known address. The others, presumably, must be served by personal service or by an alternative to personal service (as set out in rule 16 of the *Rules of Civil Procedure*).

No summary procedure is available for an application to terminate statutory guardianship of property.

Court-Appointed Guardian of the Person

Application to Appoint Guardian of the Person

An applicant can also apply to be appointed guardian of a person. The documents required for the application are as follows:

1. an application record (containing notice of application, affidavit material, and other material as set out in rule 38.09 of the *Rules of Civil Procedure*);

2. the proposed guardian's consent pursuant to section 70(2)(a);

3. a guardianship plan in the form prescribed by the regulations (Form 3 in O Reg 26/95), unless the proposed guardian is the Public Guardian and Trustee, in which case Form 3 is not required; and

4. a statement signed by the applicant indicating that the subject person has been informed of the nature of the application and his right to oppose the application, and describing the manner in which the person was informed. Alternatively, if it was not possible to give the subject person this information, the statement must explain why it was not possible.

Section 71(1) of the Act also specifies that the following documents may be submitted with the application:

5. one or more statements in the prescribed form by a person who knows the subject person and has been in personal contact with him during the 12 months preceding the application.

The procedure in the case of applications for guardianship of the person is almost identical to that of applications for guardianship of property. The persons to be served with the application material are as follows:

1. the subject person;
2. if known, the subject person's attorney under a continuing power of attorney for property;
3. if known, the subject person's guardian of property;
4. if known, the subject person's attorney under a power of attorney for personal care;
5. the Public Guardian and Trustee;
6. the proposed guardian of the person (who is typically the applicant);
7. the subject person's spouse or partner;
8. the subject person's children who are at least 18 years old;
9. the subject person's parents; and
10. the subject person's brothers and sisters who are at least 18 years old.

The rules pertaining to service of the application materials and the rights of persons to be made parties are identical to the procedures outlined above in the discussion on applications for guardianship of property.

A summary procedure is also available for applications for guardianship of the person. Again, the summary procedure is generally faster and less expensive. The summary material includes the applicant's certification to the court in writing that no person delivered a notice of appearance in response to the notice of motion and the two statements (at least one of which must be from an assessor) discussed above under applications for guardianship of property. The contents of the statements in the case of applications for guardianship of the person are outlined in section 74 of the *Substitute Decisions Act, 1992*. Such statements must indicate that the person is incapable with respect to her own health care, nutrition, shelter, clothing, hygiene, or safety.

Motion to Terminate Guardianship of the Person

If a termination of guardianship of the person is desired, the procedure to be followed is a motion to terminate the guardianship. This procedure is carried out by serving the same persons as in the case of the application to appoint a guardian of the person. The documents to be served are the same, except that the official notice is brought by way of notice of motion rather than notice of application and the record to be submitted is a motion record.

Again, a summary procedure is available in the event that the moving party is able to certify to the court in writing that every person entitled to be served with the notice of motion has been served and that all such persons have filed with the court a statement indicating that they do not intend to take part in the hearing. If the summary procedure is to be used, the moving party must also certify to the court that the two statements, discussed in section 75 of the Act, accompany the motion materials.

Section 75 of the Act indicates that both of the statements must be made by assessors in the prescribed form, and both must indicate that the author of the statement is of the opinion that the subject person is capable of personal care. The prescribed form is Form B from O Reg 460/05. Each statement is to set out the facts upon which the assessor's opinion is based. It is a requirement that the assessment has been performed within the six months preceding the notice of motion.

KEY TERMS

application to terminate statutory guardianship
of property, 361
claw back provisions, 357
court-appointed guardianship, 357

dependant's relief, 355
excluded property, 347
matrimonial home, 342
valuation date, 342

REVIEW QUESTIONS

1. Describe the spouse's right to elect under the *Family Law Act*.

2. What is the "valuation date" for a spouse's election?

3. How is "net family property" calculated?

4 What is the rule relating to the matrimonial home in calculating net family property?

5. What property can be excluded from the calculation of net family property under the *Family Law Act*?

6. What is important to establish with respect to excluded property under the *Family Law Act*?

7. What is the status of jointly owned property with right of survivorship in relation to net family property?

8. What are the essential requirements of a domestic contract?

9. Within what time frame must a surviving spouse make an election under the *Family Law Act*?

10. If the spouse does elect under the *Family Law Act*, what is the effect on the will?

11. If the spouse elects under the *Family Law Act*, what deductions can be made from the entitlement?

12. When can the estate be distributed if (a) the spouse has made an election, and (b) the spouse has not yet made an election?

13. Who can apply for dependant's relief under the *Succession Law Reform Act*?

14. How does the court decide whether a person is entitled to dependant's relief?

15. If the deceased's assets fall outside of the estate by virtue of joint ownership with a person other than the spouse, will the spouse be unable to get any dependant's relief? Why?

16. In a dependant's relief application, does the court only have to consider the dependant's claims?

17. Under what three schemes is substitute decision-making possible for an incapable person?

18. What procedure must be followed to terminate the statutory guardianship of a person's property?

Mediation in Estate Litigation

17

LEARNING OUTCOMES

After completing this chapter, you should be able to:

- Understand what a mediation is

- Understand the role of a mediator

- Have a working knowledge of the rules pertaining to mandatory estate mediations (in jurisdictions where mediation is mandatory)

- Have a working knowledge of the rules pertaining to court-ordered estate mediations

Introduction

Mediation is often referred to as "alternative dispute resolution" or "ADR." The word "alternative" denotes the fact that mediation provides a different route toward resolution of the issues in a civil dispute than that provided by the courts. Where the court process is intended to end with a decision from a judge or jury, mediation is intended to end with a negotiated settlement between the parties. Although there are actually several different forms of alternative dispute resolution, including arbitration (where the parties hire a person to make a binding decision) and one-on-one negotiation, this chapter deals with mediation, which is probably the most commonly recognized form of ADR.

Traditionally, mediation was always arranged cooperatively and privately among the parties and their lawyers when it was collectively determined that the presence of a neutral facilitator during the negotiation would be helpful in bringing the issues in dispute to a conclusion. Many people in the profession were of the view that such mediations enjoyed a high success rate because the entire process was voluntary. Then, on September 1, 1999, two important new rules were added to the *Rules of Civil Procedure*[1] making it mandatory for parties in civil litigation disputes, in certain jurisdictions of Ontario, to submit to the process of mediation. The new rules, rule 24.1 and rule 75.1, represented a pilot project by the government to determine whether forcing parties to mediate would result in more cases settling. The jurisdictions used for the pilot project were Toronto, Ottawa, and eventually, the County of Essex (Windsor). Rule 24.1 was created to apply to general civil disputes and rule 75.1 was created to apply to disputes in estate litigation. Both rules 24.1 and 75.1 were scheduled to expire on July 4, 2001 but it soon became clear that the project was a success and, accordingly, amendments were brought in to make mandatory mediation permanent in the named jurisdictions. Then, on January 1, 2016, rule 75.2, which applies only to estate litigation, was introduced. Rule 75.2, entitled "Court-Ordered Estates Mediation," allows a judge in any jurisdiction of Ontario to order the parties in an estate dispute to take part in mediation.

This chapter covers the topic of mediation of estate disputes. It will start with a general discussion of the elements of private mediation and will then cover the areas that are unique to mandatory mediation and court-ordered mediation.

What Is a Mediation

Overview

mediator
a neutral third party whose role is to facilitate a negotiation among the parties in a dispute with a view to reaching a settlement of some or all of the issues

Mediation is a process in which a neutral third party, called the **mediator**, attempts to facilitate a negotiated settlement between the parties in a dispute. The word "mediation" refers to a general way of handling disputes, like the word "litigation"; but unlike the latter term, mediation is also used to describe a singular session where mediation is taking place. For example, one often hears sentences like "We are having a mediation next week," but not "We are having a litigation next week." While the term mediation is used interchangeably in this way, many mediators use the term "mediation session" or "mediation

1   RRO 1990, reg 194.

conference" to describe the event in which mediation takes place. This text will follow this practice in the discussion below.

Essentially, a mediation session is a formalized meeting between the parties in a litigation matter, usually with their respective lawyers, the form and process of which they have agreed beforehand to allow the mediator to control. While the process is controlled by the mediator, it is voluntary in the sense that any party can leave a mediation session at any time. A mediation session only continues if all parties agree that it should continue. Another important characteristic common to all mediation sessions is that the communications taking place at the session or connected with the session are confidential. In other words, statements made at the mediation session cannot be relied on later by the other parties in the litigation. This core characteristic of mediation is for the purpose of encouraging the parties to be candid with each other and creative in coming up with solutions regarding the issues in dispute. Under the protection of confidentiality, a party can suggest a compromise without fear that it will affect the overall litigation if the compromise does not result in settlement. What follows from this is the fact that any offers made at a mediation session that are not accepted cannot be accepted later unless the offers are specifically extended again.

Mediation sessions can take many forms, but a popular form starts with the parties and their lawyers sitting around a table taking turns to explain their respective positions. The mediator encourages such explanations be made in non-provocative language and then invites the various parties to make offers of settlement to each other. Usually starting offers are not accepted, but this process continues, sometimes all day or even for several days, until an offer is eventually accepted or until it is clear that all avenues of possible settlement have been explored. The mediator usually arranges for food and refreshments to be provided during the mediation session to prevent the lack thereof from becoming a distraction to the parties.

Mediators often prefer to put each of the parties with their lawyers into separate rooms before offers are made. This practice, known as **caucussing**, is done so that as much as possible, emotions do not become attached to communications among the parties. In the event that a settlement is reached, a memorandum of the settlement, called a "minutes of settlement," is drafted at the mediation session and signed by the parties. Naturally, the rule of confidentiality does not apply to any signed minutes of settlement arising out of a mediation. It should also be noted that the courts have allowed parties to reveal confidential communications made in a mediation session where a legitimate question arises as to the existence or the terms of a settlement agreement.

caucussing
separating parties in a dispute, along with their legal representatives, into separate rooms

Advantages of Mediation Over Litigation

Most lawyers and law clerks hold the view that mediation is a much preferable path toward resolution of the issues in dispute than that provided by litigation. The reasons are numerous and include the fact that mediation is quicker and less expensive than litigation. It is also the case that a mediated solution allows the parties to retain some control over the outcome and is more likely to preserve the pre-existing relationships between the parties.

Note that viewing mediation in the context of litigation sometimes causes lawyers, law clerks, and parties to think of mediation sessions in terms of "success" or "failure." In reality, however, this view is somewhat simplistic insofar as mediation sessions not resulting in settlement often still bring the parties closer to a resolution of the issues and can assist greatly in narrowing the issues in dispute going forward. This in itself saves the parties time and money.

The Mediator

Prior to the day of a mediation session, the parties agree on and book a mediator. For privately arranged mediations, there are no legal requirements as to who can conduct a mediation, but a sensible choice for an estate litigation matter is a senior member of the legal profession who has an appreciation of the emotions and complex legal issues that arise in such disputes. The mediator is usually given a retainer from the various parties to the dispute and makes the arrangements to book a time and place for the session in consultation with the parties' lawyers. The mediator also forwards a draft mediation agreement to the parties' lawyers with the requirement that it be signed by all parties and their lawyers prior to the commencement of the mediation session. The mediation agreement, which is discussed below, sets out the rules of the mediation to which all parties must agree in order for the mediation session to take place. The mediator also receives and reviews mediation briefs from each of the lawyers for the various parties so that she is aware of the parties in the dispute and the issues and positions of the parties with respect to the issues. The mediation briefs set out a short summary of the case from each party's perspective, and include copies of any documents the party feels is important to the case.

It is sometimes better to understand the mediator's role in terms of what it is not. The mediator's role is not to decide a case or in any way to adjudicate the issues, and her role is not to provide advice and legal guidance to the parties with respect to their positions in the lawsuit. That being said, it is sometimes the case that a mediator is asked by the lawyers to provide the parties with a sense of context to the dispute—that is, how their case may appear with respect to other cases the court has dealt with. In such situations, mediators will often provide generalized information that may be useful to the parties in assessing the strengths and weaknesses of their respective cases.

Mediation Agreement

An example of a mediation agreement is provided in Figure 17.1. The various provisions that are usually found in a mediation agreement in one form or another are discussed below.

Role of the Parties

In the example provided, the role of the parties in the mediation session is set out as a term of the agreement. The agreement specifies that the parties' role is to attend and participate in the mediation process in good faith. This means that the parties are obligated to show up at the mediation session with an attitude toward trying to settle the issues. While it is probably impossible to enforce a contractual provision of this nature, most mediation agreements set it out as a term in order to start the parties on the path toward resolving the issues by having them signify, at least in principle, that they are trying to reach an agreement.

FIGURE 17.1   Mediation Agreement

MEDIATION AGREEMENT

B E T W E E N:

NADEELA MARSAL

Party

- and –

TUNC MANSUR

Party

- and –

NIMAL MAITI

Mediator

1.   INTRODUCTION

The parties to this agreement are Nadeela Marsal and Tunc Mansur. The mediator is Nimal Maiti.

The parties agree to seek a mediated resolution of the issues between/among them arising out of the Marsal estate, through a mediation conference ("mediation") to be conducted on April 13, 2018 at Unit 3302, 16 Laison Street South, Barmwich, Ontario. The following are the terms and conditions agreed to by the parties.

The signing of this agreement is evidence of the intention of the parties, their counsel and the mediator to conduct the mediation in a bona fide and forthright manner and to attempt, in good faith, to resolve the issues arising out of or relating to the matters in dispute.

2.   SETTLEMENT TO BE IN WRITING

The parties agree that, to be effective, any settlement must be in writing and be signed by the parties.

FIGURE 17.1 CONTINUED

3.   **ROLE OF THE PARTIES**

The parties acknowledge and agree:

    (a)   that the mediation process is entered into and will be carried on voluntarily;

    (b)   that they will participate in the mediation in good faith;

    (c)   to make full disclosure of all relevant information in order for discussion to proceed in an open and constructive manner;

    (d)   to assist in generating options for settlement;

    (e)   to attempt to find mutually acceptable solutions to the issues between/ among them.

4.   **ROLE OF THE MEDIATOR**

The parties and their counsel acknowledge and agree that the mediator:

    (a)   is an impartial neutral facilitator whose role is to assist the parties to reach their own negotiated resolution to the issues in the conflict;

    (b)   shall be given authority and control over the process of the mediation session so long as the mediation continues;

    (c)   is not an adjudicator;

    (d)   is not a representative of any party in the mediation;

    (e)   will not offer legal advice and will not assist or protect the legal rights of any party or non-party participant;

    (f)   is not under an obligation to raise any issue not raised by the parties themselves;

    (g)   is not under an obligation to determine which persons need to participate in the mediation in order for there to be a valid or complete resolution of the issues in dispute;

    (h)   has no duty to ensure the enforceability or validity of any agreement reached.

5.   TERMINATION OF THE MEDIATION

It is agreed that the mediation may be terminated at any time by any party, his or her counsel, or the mediator for any reason.

6.   AUTHORITY TO SETTLE

It is agreed that in order to have an effective mediation, the parties will attend with their counsel and have full authority to settle the issues in dispute at the mediation. It is also agreed that all persons whose approval is necessary to finalize a settlement of the issues are taking part in the mediation session and are signors to this agreement.

7.   CONFIDENTIALITY OF THE MEDIATION TO OUTSIDE PERSONS

For the purposes of this agreement, "mediation communication" shall include all statements, promises, offers, views, opinions, admissions and communications between/among the parties, their lawyers, other participants and/or the mediator for the purposes of considering, initiating, continuing, or participating in a mediation, together with the content of any documents pertaining to the mediation that are delivered or exchanged in the course of or prior to the mediation.

The parties agree that:

(a)   the mediation is a settlement negotiation conducted on a without prejudice and non-binding basis in pursuit of a settlement of the issues;

(b)   the mediation is confidential and no stenographic, visual, or audio recordings shall be made;

(c)   no mediation communication shall be discoverable or admissible for any purpose, including impeachment, in the action or in any other proceeding involving the parties, and no mediation communication shall be discussed with anyone except insofar as a party may confer with his or her own representative, agent, expert witness or spouse;

(d)   the mediator has the privilege to refuse to disclose and to prevent any other person from disclosing a mediation communication in any proceeding. The mediator may also refuse to provide evidence of a mediation communication in such a proceeding;

(e)   the parties will not subpoena, or otherwise require the mediator to testify or produce his records or notes in the action or in any other proceeding and in this respect the mediator will have the same immunity from liability as a judge;

FIGURE 17.1 CONTINUED

    (f)   the mediator may not disclose a mediation communication unless all the parties agree in writing or the mediator reasonably believes that disclosure is required by law, or by a specific public policy established by statute, regulation or court decision, or by professional reporting requirements;

    (g)   notwithstanding the foregoing, there is no privilege or prohibition against disclosure of a mediation communication where the communication:

        (i)   appears in a record or memorandum of an agreement between/among the parties or where the parties have specifically agreed in writing that they may disclose the communication;

        (ii)   amounts to a threat to inflict bodily harm or unlawful property damage or where a person uses or attempts to use the mediation to plan or commit a crime;

        (iii)   is introduced to establish or disprove a claim or complaint of professional misconduct or malpractice filed against the mediator, by a party, a non-party participant, or a representative of a party based on conduct occurring during the mediation;

        (iv)   is sought to be introduced in a proceeding in which fraud, duress or incapacity pertaining to a party is an issue regarding the validity or enforceability of an agreement evidenced by a memorandum of agreement and reached by the parties as a result of the mediation, but only if such mediation communication is provided by a person other than the mediator of the dispute at issue.

8.   CONFIDENTIALITY WITHIN THE MEDIATION

It is further agreed that, during the mediation, the mediator may disclose to any party or to the party's counsel or to other participants any information provided by a party, his or her counsel or by a non-party participant which the mediator believes to be relevant to the issues being mediated unless a party or her/his counsel specifically requests that the mediator keep that particular information confidential from the other party.

9.   OTHER PARTICIPANTS IN THE MEDIATION

In the event that the parties wish to have other persons ("non-party participants") present at the mediation, the parties agree that such presence requires the acquiescence of the other party.

In the event that a non-party participant is to be present at the mediation, she/he must signify her/his agreement to the terms of the mediation by signing this agreement.

Notwithstanding the foregoing, the mediator reserves the right to require any non-party participant(s) to leave the mediation conference, either temporarily or permanently.

10.   FEES AND EXPENSES

The parties agree that the fees and expenses of the mediation shall be paid by the parties in equal shares, unless otherwise agreed to in writing between/among the parties. The parties shall be jointly and severally liable to pay all fees and disbursements associated with the mediation, unless otherwise ordered by the court, or unless otherwise agreed between/among the parties.

The fees for the mediation are as follows:

     (a) $1,500.00 for a half day mediation (3 hours) which fee includes preparation time by the mediator and travel time;

     (b) $350.00 per hour for any time beyond a half day mediation or as otherwise agreed to between/among the mediator and the parties or their respective lawyers.

plus any applicable disbursements and HST.

11.   INDEMNITY

The parties hereby jointly and severally covenant and agree to indemnify and save the mediator harmless for any and all liability, cost, claims, demands, proceedings, and causes of action howsoever arising under this agreement, or as a result of the mediation and its consequences, provided that the mediator has carried out his duties in good faith.

12.   EXECUTION OF THIS AGREEMENT

This agreement may be executed in separate counterpart copies, each of which when so executed and delivered shall be an original, and all such counterpart copies shall together constitute one and the same instrument.

This agreement shall enure to the benefit of and be binding upon the parties and the mediator and their respective heirs, estate trustees, administrators, successors and assigns.

FIGURE 17.1 CONTINUED

DATED at Barmwich, Ontario this   30th   day of   March, 2018

SIGNED by each of the parties, their lawyers and the mediator:

NIMAL MAITI

Per: __Nimal Maiti_____
Nimal Maiti

100 Laison Street North
Barmwich, ON Y4R 2N3
Tel: 705-555-5555
Fax: 705-555-5554

Parties:

__Tunc Mansur_____   __Nadeela Marsal_____

Counsel:

__Hector Seals_____   __Youn Se-ri_____

SIGNED by each of the non-party Participants:

__Elena Mansur_____   __Florian Marsal_____

_____   _____

Role of the Mediator

A mediation agreement typically sets out the role of the mediator as impartial neutral fa-cilitator and contains a provision where the parties signify their agreement that, as long as the mediation session continues, they are relinquishing authority over the form and pro-cess of the mediation to the mediator. The mediation agreement may also go on to describe the mediator's role in terms of what it is not, as we did above. That is, the mediator's role is not to be an adjudicator, not to provide legal advice to the parties, not to protect the par-ties' legal rights, not to raise any legal issues that the parties themselves do not raise, not to determine which parties must take part in the mediation in order for there to be a valid or complete resolution of the issues, or to ensure the enforceability or validity of any agree-ment reached.

Termination of the Mediation

The termination clause of a mediation agreement underscores the fact that the process is voluntary and that, as long as the mediation session continues, all of the parties are in agreement that a settlement of the issues is the common goal. This clause also provides that the mediator herself has the right to end the mediation session, which provision may be invoked by the mediator where she reasonably comes to the conclusion that one or more of the parties in the mediation session is not negotiating in good faith.

Authority to Settle

This provision of the mediation agreement ensures that a settlement can be reached during the mediation session itself. In other words, if a settlement cannot be finalized without the approval of a particular person, that person should be a party to the mediation session. This provision does not address the situation that sometimes occurs in estate mediations whereby a settlement cannot be finalized until the court has approved the settlement, such as in the case of unascertained, underage, or mentally incapable beneficiaries. In such cases, any minutes of settlement signed at the mediation session would have to include the provision that the agreement is "subject to the approval of the court."

Confidentiality to Persons Outside the Mediation Session

As indicated above, confidentiality is a key aspect of mediation because it encourages par-ties to be candid with each other without fear of compromising their case beyond the mediation session. In the confidentiality clause of a mediation agreement the parties agree to keep all communications at the mediation session, and connected with the mediation session, confidential from any persons not taking part in the mediation. This agreement includes everything contained in the mediation briefs and any other documents that are generated in connection with the mediation. The confidentiality provisions prevent a party from putting forth evidence of what transpired in relation to a mediation in court without the written consent of all parties to the mediation and, similarly, prevents a party from even discussing what took place at the mediation with any persons other than his spouse and members of his legal team, including his representatives, agents, and expert witnesses. The confidentiality clause may also include a provision that the mediator cannot be sum-moned to testify in relation to the case. It should be noted that there are exceptions to the confidentiality provisions. Naturally, any memorandum of settlement or minutes of settlement can be disclosed as evidence of a settlement and, as indicated above, a court may in rare circumstances allow some mediation communications to be introduced into evidence in order to determine the existence or the scope of a settlement agreement where some question relating thereto arises after a mediation session. The mediation agreement also often includes a provision indicating that evidence of what transpired at the mediation will be provided to a court if it is required by law—for example, where threats of violence or other illegal acts take place during the mediation session itself. In such cases, the exception to the confidentiality rule does not arise from the agreement but from the law. Nevertheless, most mediators believe that it is appropriate to bring the parties' attention to these limits of confidentiality. Finally, the confidentiality clause may also be subject to a provision allowing the mediator to testify in order to disprove a claim or complaint of professional misconduct filed against himself.

Confidentiality within the Mediation Session

During the course of the mediation session there are often times when the mediator will be speaking alone to one of the parties and his legal representative. Such discussions will take place when the parties are caucussing or meeting privately with their respective legal advisers and the mediator in a room apart from the other parties. During these discussions, a party may reveal weaknesses about his case that he does not want the mediator to share with the other parties. The mediator usually establishes with the parties beforehand, often in the mediation agreement itself as in the example provided, that she will keep such revelations confidential from the other parties but only if so instructed. This "confidentiality within the mediation" provision of the agreement puts the onus on the party revealing the sensitive information to notify the mediator during the caucus meeting that she needs to keep that information confidential.

Other Participants in the Mediation Session

Parties often wish to bring spouses, other family members, or friends to mediation sessions for guidance and moral support. This practice is not normally discouraged because having such people present at the mediation can mean the difference between a session that results in a settlement and one that does not. On the other hand, the presence of such people can sometimes be viewed as an aggravating factor by the other parties in the mediation session. Typically, a mediator will allow such non-party participants to attend the mediation session if all other parties agree. If non-party participants do take part in a mediation session, they must sign the mediation agreement so that they too are bound by its provisions, especially those pertaining to confidentiality. As in the example provided, the mediator reserves the right to exclude such non-party participants if in the mediator's opinion those persons are negatively affecting the mediation process.

Other Clauses

Other clauses included in most mediation agreements pertain to the mediator's fees, including his hourly rate and who is responsible for payment, and an indemnity clause specifying that the mediator is indemnified by the parties from any causes of actions against him provided that he conducts the mediation in good faith.

Mandatory Mediation

As indicated in the introduction to this chapter, mandatory mediation applies only in the City of Toronto, the City of Ottawa, and the County of Essex (Windsor). It is, however, conceivable that the rules will be expanded over time to include other jurisdictions in Ontario. Accordingly, it is probably worthwhile for lawyers and law clerks whose practice is not carried on within those jurisdictions to develop an understanding of such rules. In addition, as indicated below, the rules for mandatory mediation of estate matters closely mirror the rules for court-ordered estate mediations, as provided for in rule 75.2, and such mediations can be ordered to take place in any jurisdiction of Ontario.

Rule 75.1, which is entitled "Mandatory Mediation—Estates, Trusts and Substitute Decisions," was drafted alongside rule 24.1, which is entitled simply "Mandatory Mediation." While there are exceptions to what kinds of actions are subject to mandatory mediation under rule 24.1, it is applicable to most civil cases in the named jurisdictions. A comparison of the subrules under rule 24.1 and those under rule 75.1 reveals that mandatory mediation of estate litigation matters requires its own set of rules for two reasons. The first is that, unlike "standard" litigation, which clearly commences when a party issues a statement of claim or a notice of application, estate litigation is commenced in a variety of different ways—for example, statements of claim, motions for directions, notices of objection, or applications to pass accounts. This means that the triggering mechanism for mandatory mediation is more complex in estate litigation and rules are needed to accommodate this complexity. The second reason why mediation of estate litigation requires its own set of subrules is that, unlike most "standard" litigation where the parties are clearly defined, there are often several persons whose rights are affected by an estate, including the estate trustee himself, and rules are needed to determine which parties must take part in a mandatory mediation. The following discussion should be taken to apply to the jurisdictions of Toronto, Ottawa, and Windsor.

What Kinds of Estate Disputes Are Subject to Mandatory Mediation

For the purpose of specifying which matters falling under the category of estate litigation are subject to mandatory mediation, rule 75.1.02(1)(b) provides a list. As it turns out, the list includes virtually every kind of court dispute that arises with respect to an estate or a power of attorney. The list is as follows:

- contested applications to pass accounts under rule 74.18;
- proceedings for the formal proof of a will under rule 75.01;
- objections to issuing certificates of appointment under rule 75.03;
- proceedings for the return of a certificate of appointment under rule 75.05;
- claims against an estate under section 44 or 45 of the *Estates Act*[2] and rule 75.08;
- dependant's relief claims under Part V of the *Succession Law Reform Act*;[3]

---

2 RSO 1990, c E.21.

3 RSO 1990, c S.26.

- proceedings under the *Substitute Decisions Act, 1992*;[4]
- proceedings under the *Absentees Act*,[5] the *Charities Accounting Act*,[6] the *Estates Act*, the *Trustee Act*[7] or the *Variation of Trusts Act*;[8]
- proceedings under subrule 14.05(3) (the rule specifying matters that may be commenced by way of application), if the matter relates to an estate or trust; and
- spousal elections under the *Family Law Act*.[9]

One exception to the list of estate litigation matters that must be mediated is set out in rule 75.1.02(2), which provides that if an estate or trust is made a party to a proceeding by virtue of the fact that a party to an ordinary action has died and his estate is added to the action in his place, that is not a sufficient issue to trigger mandatory mediation.

How a Mandatory Mediation Is Set Up

Motion Respecting the Conduct of a Mediation

Although the court provides the rules requiring mediation to take place, it does not perform the actual tasks necessary to set up the mediation. That job, at least initially, falls on the person commencing the proceeding. Under rule 75.1.05, the person commencing the estate litigation proceeding—that is, the "applicant"—must bring a motion for directions respecting the conduct of a mediation within 30 days of receiving the notice of appearance from the other party in the case. On its face, this rule implies that all estate litigation proceedings are commenced by way of application, which may not always be the case. For example, sometimes a party commences the proceedings simply by issuing a statement of claim. Regardless of how the proceeding starts, whatever party brings the proceedings in the first place should bring the motion for directions respecting the conduct of the mediation once the other side takes an official step toward resisting or defending the proceeding. Obviously, if no notice of appearance is served on the party commencing the proceeding, there is no dispute and no need for a mediation.

Notwithstanding the above, where a proceeding commences by way of an application for directions or where a judge orders a trial of issues in a passing of accounts hearing, a judge can make an order respecting the conduct of a mediation on her own. In such a case, the applicant need not bring the motion respecting the conduct of the mediation unless the judge orders otherwise. It should be noted as well that rule 75.1.05(3) allows the motion for the conduct of a mediation to be brought at the same time as an application for directions under rule 75.06. In other words, if a person is commencing the estate litigation proceeding by way of application for directions she does not need to wait 30 days, or wait for a notice of appearance from the other side, before bringing the motion for directions respecting the conduct of the mediation.

---

4   SO 1992, c 30.
5   RSO 1990, c A.3.
6   RSO 1990, c C.10.
7   RSO 1990, c T.23.
8   RSO 1990, c V.1
9   RSO 1990, c F.3.

At the motion respecting the conduct of the mediation, the judge will order which person in the matter is to be the **party with carriage of the mediation**. From that point, it will be this person's job to perform some of the organizational tasks for the mediation as outlined below. Every other party who is to take part in the mediation is referred to in the rules as a **designated party**. The other items that the judge will order pursuant to the motion respecting the conduct of the mediation are as follow:

- the issues to be mediated;
- within what times the mediation session will take place;
- which parties are required to attend the mediation session in person;
- how the persons required to attend are to be served with notice of the mediation;
- whether notice of the mediation is to be given to parties who have submitted their rights to the court;
- how the cost of the mediation is to be apportioned among the parties; and
- any other matters that may be desirable to facilitate the mediation.

Note that any party can seek an order of the court under rule 75.1.04 exempting himself from the need to take part in the mediation session and a court can make such order on its own accord. Obviously, a compelling reason would have to exist for this relief to be granted.

Choosing a Mediator

The procedure for choosing a mediator is set out in rule 75.1.07. This rule provides that within 30 days of the order giving directions respecting the conduct of a mediation, the parties are to choose a mediator. The choice is made from a list that is maintained by a person in the jurisdiction known as the mediation coordinator. The mediation coordinator is defined under rule 24.1 as a person designated by the Attorney General for a particular jurisdiction (Toronto, Ottawa, or Windsor) who is responsible for the administration of mandatory mediations within that jurisdiction. There is also a mediation committee in each jurisdiction, one member of which is a judge or a case management master. One of the committee's tasks is to maintain a list of qualified mediators in each area and to monitor the performance of the individual mediators. It is worthwhile noting that in selecting a mediator from the list, the parties should be cognizant of the fact that only some of the mediators on the list will have considerable experience with estate matters as the list is maintained for all mandatory mediations in the area.

If the parties cannot agree on a mediator from the list but all agree on a mediator who is not on the list, that mediator can be used for the mandatory mediation. However, that mediator but must comply with all rules that a mediator on the list would have to comply with, as discussed below. If the parties cannot agree on a mediator, the mediation coordinator can assign a mediator at the request of any one party. If 30 days have passed and no mediator has been agreed on and no party has requested that the mediation coordinator assign a mediator, the party with carriage of the mediation must request an assignment of a mediator in Form 75.1A.

Once a mediator is chosen, the party with carriage of the mediation must supply the mediator with a copy of the order giving directions respecting the conduct of the

party with carriage of the mediation
the party in a dispute heading to mandatory mediation who is appointed by the court to assume the responsibility of carrying out certain organizational tasks

designated party
any party in a dispute who is ordered by the court to attend a mediation

mediation. The mediator then sets a date for the mediation, usually in consultation with the parties and their lawyers, and serves notice of the time and place of the mediation session on the parties. The notice is in Form 75.1B and states that the parties must each file a statement of issues and must attend. An example of the notice is in Figure 17.2. The notice must be sent to the parties at least 20 days before the date set for the hearing. The mediation session will take place at a location selected by the mediator in consultation with the parties. The chosen location could be at the mediator's office, at the court, or any other location acceptable to the parties.

Conducting the Mandatory Mediation

Pre-Mediation Materials for Mandatory Mediation

At least seven days before the mediation, each party must prepare a statement of issues in Form 75.1C identifying the factual and legal issues in the case and setting out each party's position and interests. The statement should be as concise as possible and any document that the party thinks has "central importance" should be attached. A blank Form 75.1C appears as the attachment to Form 75.1B in Figure 17.2.

If the mediation cannot be conducted because a party has not prepared and served her statement of issues, the mediator will cancel the mediation and immediately file with the court a certificate of non-compliance in Form 75.1D

Mandatory Mediation Session

The mediator is in charge of the process to be followed at the mediation session. The mediator may choose to have the parties in a room together for the entire mediation or may caucus the parties into separate rooms or use a combination thereof. Again, the mediator is not an adjudicator but will assist the parties in exploring ways to settle the issues in dispute.

The parties do not have a legal obligation to settle the case or even to compromise their respective positions—though most settlements are achieved through some form of compromise—but they do have an obligation to attend on time and take part in the mediation session in good faith. This means that the parties must accept the mediator's authority over the process of the mediation and must not conduct themselves in a way that frustrates the process. The mediator may have the parties sign an agreement to mediate. If the mediator feels that the session is not productive, he can end the mediation any time; but the parties themselves have an obligation to remain for the length of the mediation, which can be up to three hours (unless all parties wish to extend the mediation, after which point it turns into a purely voluntary process).

Only the parties and the mediator have a right to attend a mediation session; but under rule 75.1.09(2), if a party needs someone else's approval before agreeing to a settlement that person shall arrange to have "ready telephone access to the other person throughout the session."

If a party has not arrived within the first 30 minutes of the start of the mediation session, and the mediator is of the view that the party's non-attendance makes it impractical to conduct the mediation, the mediator will cancel the mediation and immediately file a certificate of non-compliance with the court.

If an agreement is reached at the mediation session, on some or all of the issues, it shall be signed by the parties or their lawyers in accordance with rule 75.1.12(3).

FIGURE 17.2   Notice by Mediator (Form 75.1B)

Court file no. *18-76545*

ONTARIO
SUPERIOR COURT OF JUSTICE

IN THE ESTATE OF Amit Gabai deceased,

late of *the* City of Ottawa,

occupation: musician,

who died on January 29, 2016.

NOTICE BY MEDIATOR

TO: **Dima Malcah**

AND TO: **Fadi Gabai**

~~I am the mediator whom the mediation co-ordinator has appointed to conduct the mediation session under Rule 75.1.~~ *(Delete this paragraph if mediator was chosen by designated parties under clause 75.1.06 (1) (a) or (c).)*

The mediation session will take place on *February 14, 2018*, from *10:00 a.m.* to *1:00 p.m.*, at *12 Giacomina Avenue, Ottawa, ON, K1P 3R3*.

You are required to attend this mediation session. If you have a lawyer representing you in this proceeding, he or she is also required to attend.

You are required to file a statement of issues (Form 75.1C) by *February 7, 2018*. A blank copy of the form is attached.

When you attend the mediation session, you should bring with you any documents that you consider of central importance in the proceeding. You should plan to remain throughout the scheduled time. If you need another person's approval before agreeing to a settlement, you should make arrangements before the mediation session to ensure that you have ready telephone access to that person throughout the session, even outside regular business hours.

YOU MAY BE PENALIZED UNDER RULE 75.1.10 IF YOU FAIL TO FILE A STATEMENT OF ISSUES OR FAIL TO ATTEND THE MEDIATION SESSION.

January 11, 2018   *Margarid Anahit*
                                      12 Giacomina Avenue
                                      Ottawa, ON
                                      K1P 3R3
                                      Tel: 613-555-5555
                                      Fax: 905-555-5556

                                      (Name, address, telephone
                                      number and fax number, if any,
                                      of mediator)

RCP-E 75.1B (November 1, 2005)

FIGURE 17.2 CONTINUED   **Blank Statement of Issues (Form 75.1C)**

Court file no. *18-76545*

ONTARIO
SUPERIOR COURT OF JUSTICE

IN THE ESTATE OF Amit Gabai deceased,

late of the City of Ottawa,

occupation: musician,

who died on January 29, 2016,

STATEMENT OF ISSUES

(To be provided to mediator and designated parties at least seven days before the mediation session)

1. Factual and legal issues in dispute

The undersigned designated party states that the following factual and legal issues are in dispute and remain to be resolved.

(Issues should be stated briefly and numbered consecutively.)

2. Party's position and interests (what the party hopes to achieve)

(Brief summary.)

3. Attached documents

Attached to this form are the following documents that the designated party considers of central importance in the proceeding: *(list)*

(Date)   *(party's signature)*

(Name, address, telephone number and fax number, if any, of lawyer of party filing statement of issues, or of party)

NOTE: Rule 75.1.11 provides as follows:

All communications at a mediation session and the mediator's notes and records shall be deemed to be without prejudice settlement discussions.

RCP-E 75.1C (November 1, 2005)

Confidentiality of Mandatory Mediation

Regardless of the outcome of the mediation, rule 75.1.11 provides that all communications at a mediation session and the mediator's notes and records are deemed to be without prejudice to settlement discussions. In other words, the parties and the mediator must keep the communications taking place in the mediation, including what is contained in the mediation summaries, in the strict confidence indefinitely subject only to order of the court, which occurs only in extremely unusual situations. By necessary implication, if an agreement resolving some or all of the issues is signed at the mediation session, the agreement is not subject to confidentiality.

Post-Mandatory Mediation

Mediator's Report Pursuant to Mandatory Mediation

Within 10 days following the date of the mediation session, the mediator will provide a report to the parties and to the mediation coordinator pursuant to rule 75.1.12(1). The report will of course not provide details as to what transpired at the mediation session but will confirm whether a settlement of some or all of the issues was reached.

If Certificate of Non-Compliance Filed Regarding Mandatory Mediation Session

If a mediator files a certificate of non-compliance in Form 75.1D, the party with carriage of the mediation must bring a motion for further directions in accordance with rule 75.1.10(1). If the party with carriage of the mediation does not do so, any other party may do so within 30 days of the cancelled mediation.

At the motion for further directions, the judge (or case management master as the case may be) may make any of the following orders:

- establish a timetable for the proceeding;
- strike out any document filed by a designated party;
- order a designated party to pay costs; or
- make any other order that is just.

Mediator's Fees in Mandatory Mediations

It is also incumbent on the parties following the mandatory mediation session to ensure that the mediator's fees are paid. The mediator's fees are set in accordance with the regulation establishing the mandatory mediation rules and will depend on the number of parties present at the mediation. The mediator is entitled to charge by the hour, including one-half hour of preparation time per party and up to three hours of mediation time, depending on the length of the mediation session. The mediator's overall fee for the mandatory session, however, will be subject to a cap as set out in O Reg 43/05, depending on the number of parties in the mediation session. If the estate trustee is to take part in the mediation session, she will be counted as a party for the purposes of determining the appropriate hourly rate. Table 17.1 outlines the maximum fees chargeable by the mediator.

NUMBER OF PARTIES	MAXIMUM FEES
2	$600 plus HST
3	$675 plus HST
4	$750 plus HST
5 or more	$825 plus HST

Under the regulation, each party is required to pay an equal share of the mediator's overall fee for the mandatory mediation, unless the court orders otherwise, and one party's failure to pay does not obligate the other parties to pay that party's share. On the other hand, if a mandatory mediation is cancelled because of non-compliance by a party, the fee incurred to that point in time will be payable by the party whose non-compliance caused the cancellation. If two or more parties cause the mediation to fail for non-compliance, these parties will equally pay the cost of the mediation.

It should be noted that if the parties reach the end of the third hour of a mandatory mediation session and still wish to continue, the balance of the mediation session will proceed as if it were a privately arranged mediation. This means that the mediator's fees for the balance of the session, and how they are to be paid, will have to be agreed on by all parties and the mediator prior to continuing.

If Partial or Full Agreement Reached at Mandatory Mediation Session

If the parties reach an agreement on all of the outstanding issues, the party with carriage of the file must file a notice with the court indicating the settlement within ten days after the agreement is signed. If the settlement is conditional on the occurrence of an event, the party with carriage of the mediation is to file the notice within ten days of the event occurring. If the event does not occur, then there is no settlement. In addition, if one of the parties is under a mental or legal disability such that court approval is necessary, the notice must be filed within ten days of the court's approving the settlement.

Moving On If No Agreement or Only a Partial Agreement Is Reached at a Mandatory Mediation Session

If no agreement is reached on some of the outstanding issues, the matter will proceed with any directions already provided by the court for the litigation of the matter. If no order for directions has been given as of that point in time, a motion for directions under rule 75.06 should be commenced as soon as possible by one of the parties.

Similarly, if a partial agreement is reached, after the party with carriage of the mediation notifies the court of the partial settlement, the matter will proceed on the remaining issues in accordance with any existing order giving directions for the litigation of the matter. Again, if no order giving directions exists, a motion for directions should be brought respecting the remaining issues.

In the event that none of the issues are settled, or only some of them, an additional mediation can be ordered under rule 75.1.13(1) but only with the consent of the designated parties.

Failure to Comply with Agreement Reached at a Mandatory Mediation Session

If an agreement is reached on some or all of the outstanding issues, and a party does not comply with the agreement, any other party may bring a motion to a judge under rule 75.1.12(6)(a) for judgment on the terms of the agreement. Alternatively, the other parties may continue with the proceeding as if there had been no agreement pursuant to rule 75.1.12(6)(b).

Court-Ordered Mediation

Apart from the fact that mandatory estates mediation only occurs in Toronto, Ottawa, and County of Essex (Windsor), the essential difference between mandatory estates mediation and court-ordered estates mediation is that the former occurs in every case and the latter occurs only in cases in which a judge determines it to be appropriate. Nevertheless, the rules for court-ordered estates mediation under rule 75.2 follow the same pattern as those for mandatory estates mediation under rule 75.1 with the exception of some minor differences that are noted below.

Choosing a Mediator

As indicated above, under the mandatory mediation rules, the parties either agree on a mediator or the mediation coordinator for the jurisdiction assigns one from the list maintained by the committee for that jurisdiction. Under court-ordered mediation, there is no mediation coordinator and no list of mediators kept for that jurisdiction. If the parties in court-ordered mediation cannot agree on a mediator, it is up to one of the parties to bring a motion to the court to have the court assign a mediator. Regardless of whether the mediator is chosen by the parties or assigned by the court, rule 75.2.04(4) requires that the mediator comply with the rules for court-ordered mediations.

No Party with Carriage of the Mediation

Under the rules for court-ordered mediation, there is no rule explicitly providing for one of the parties to be the party with carriage of the mediation. Thus, while under mandatory mediation the party with carriage of the mediation must provide the mediator with a copy of the order giving directions respecting the conduct of the mediation. Under court-ordered mediation, no person explicitly has that duty.

Similarly, if there is a cancellation of the mediation because of non-compliance with the rules, under the mandatory mediation rules it would be the party with carriage of the mediation who has the initial responsibility of bringing a motion for directions within 15 days of the cancellation. Under court-ordered mediation, however, it is the applicant who has this initial responsibility.

Finally, if there is an agreement reached at a mediation session resolving some or all of the issues, in court-ordered estates mediations it is the applicant who has the responsibility of filing notice with the court within ten days of the agreement being finalized.

It should be noted that under rule 75.2.03(4), the court may give any order pursuant to the conduct of a court-ordered estates mediation that it could also give in a mandatory mediation jurisdiction. This suggests that if the judge deems it appropriate, she could order one particular party to have carriage of the mediation even though it is a court-ordered mediation.

Court-Ordered Mediation Does Not Have a Rule for Exemption from the Mediation

The final difference between mandatory estates mediations and court-ordered estates mediations is that the former has a rule—namely, rule 75.1.04—allowing a party to bring a motion seeking an order that he be exempt from the mediation and the latter does not. Presumably this is because, in a court-ordered mediation, a party has an opportunity to bring this request before a judge while he is considering whether to order a mediation to take place.

KEY TERMS

caucussing, 369
designated party, 381

mediator, 368
party with carriage of the mediation, 381

REVIEW QUESTIONS

1. What are the advantages of mediation over litigation?

2. Why are mediations confidential?

3. Where is mediation mandatory in estate litigation matters?

4. What kinds of estate litigation cases must be mediated in the mandatory estates mediation jurisdictions?

5. What are the duties of the party with carriage of the mediation?

6. What is a designated party under the mandatory mediation rules?

7. If there is a good reason for a person not to take part in a mandatory mediation, is there a way for that person to be exempt from taking part in the mediation session?

8. What is a mediation coordinator?

9. What is a certificate of non-compliance in the mandatory or court-ordered mediation rules?

10. What is the grace period for getting to a mandatory or court-ordered mediation late?

11. What if there is a settlement reached at a mandatory mediation but one of the parties is under a disability?

Glossary

#

21-year deemed disposition rule of trusts rule that every 21 years a trust is deemed to have disposed of all of its capital property at fair market value

A

abatement diminishment of a gift under a will to satisfy debts of an estate

ademption situation that occurs when the object of a specific gift does not exist or is not owned by the testator at the time of his death

administration bond of indemnity promise by the estate trustee to administer the estate properly and promise by the estate trustee and a third party, such as an insurance company, to indemnify any creditors or beneficiaries prejudiced by the failure to do so

allowance compensation paid to the trustee for administering the trust

alter ego trust a particular kind of *inter vivos* trust, which is used to suspend the 21-year deemed-disposition rule in the *Income Tax Act* and to suspend capital gains tax until the death of the settlor

alternate beneficiary a beneficiary who becomes a beneficiary by taking the place of a previously named beneficiary, most commonly as a result of the death of the previously named beneficiary

anti-lapse provisions rules designed to allow gifts to certain relatives of deceased beneficiaries that would otherwise lapse

application to terminate statutory guardianship of property application to end the guardianship of the Public Guardian and Trustee

B

beneficiary person for whom trust property is held

C

capital cost allowance amount that can be deducted from income each year by a business for depreciation of its capital property

capital disbursements lump-sum payments made out of the estate other than those that are revenue disbursements

capital receipts money coming into the estate in lump sums

care and management fee compensation paid to the estate trustee for administering an ongoing estate

caucussing separating parties in a dispute, along with their legal representatives, into separate rooms

certificate of appointment of estate trustee with a will document from the court setting out the name of a deceased with a will, identifying the estate, and giving the name and address of the estate trustee

charitable trust trust that is set up for a charitable purpose

claw back provisions (in the context of dependant's relief claims) statutory provisions allowing the court to order that certain assets, normally falling outside the estate, be paid to a dependant

clearance certificate Canada Revenue Agency document that confirms that all income taxes on an estate have been paid and the estate trustee is discharged from further responsibility for the estate with respect to such taxes

codicil formal document that amends a will

contingent conditional

contingent beneficiary person who, if a particular condition is satisfied, becomes a beneficiary of a trust

court-appointed guardianship scheme under which substitute decision-making for an incapable person is possible

creditors of the estate those to whom debts of the estate are owed

D

declaration of transmission sworn statement by one or more of the estate trustees that sets out the particulars of the deceased and, if necessary, confirms that the deceased is the same person whose name appears on a stock certificate or in a transfer agent's records; used to direct the transfer agent to put the stock directly into the name of the estate or a beneficiary

deemed disposition rule rule that states that any capital gains that would have been earned by the deceased if he or she had disposed of all of the capital property in the last year of life must also be reported on the terminal T1 tax return

demonstrative gift gift of a sum of money from a specifically identified source

dependant's relief financial support ordered to be paid by an estate to a dependant of the deceased pursuant to Part V of the *Succession Law Reform Act*

designated party any party in a dispute who is ordered by the court to attend a mediation

devise a specific gift of real property in a will

disposition clause instructions regarding how an estate is to be distributed among the beneficiaries

E

elective tax returns separate tax returns that cover the same taxation period as the terminal T1 return; allowed in certain specified situations

escheat the forfeiting of ownership to the Crown for lack of heirs

estate accounting process of communicating to the residual beneficiaries of the estate how the amount representing their share of the estate was arrived at

estate trustee with a will person chosen by testator to oversee the administration of her estate

even hand principle principle according to which a trustee must not act in the best interests of one beneficiary to the prejudice of another beneficiary, even if that other beneficiary is unborn or unascertained; this principle can be modified by the terms of the trust document

excluded property property which, under the *Family Law Act*, is not included in the calculation of net family property on the breakdown of a marriage or upon the filing of an election by a surviving spouse

executor's compensation compensation paid to the estate trustee for administering the estate

F

factum formalized statement of the facts, issues, and law in a case composed by a lawyer and submitted to the court to aid in the proper disposition of a matter in issue

final accounting accounting after which the estate trustee can wind up the estate

formal accounting passing of accounts

G

general power of attorney for property power of attorney for property that gives unrestricted powers over the grantor's assets to the attorney(s)

gift over alternate gift to another beneficiary in the event that the first beneficiary predeceases

H

Henson trust trust created for the benefit of a beneficiary who is receiving regular government assistance under the Ontario Disability Support Program while protecting the beneficiary from being cut off from such benefits

holograph will handwritten will

I

informal accounting accounting made by letter to the beneficiaries or their representatives that requires obtaining releases from them

***inter vivos* trust** trust that is activated while the person setting up the trust is still alive

interim accounting accounting made during the course of estate administration that allows the estate trustee to pay the beneficiaries and concentrate on the remaining unadministered part of the estate

intestacy state of dying without a valid will

investment account account that sets out the principal amount that was paid out by the estate trustee to invest funds for the estate and the principal amount that was received back from the investment

J

joint partner trust essentially, alter ego trusts for spouses

joint will rare form of will that is signed by two persons with respect to the disposal of their property after death

jurat attestation paragraph

L

lapse fail; the situation that occurs when a beneficiary specified in a will is not alive at the time of the testator's death

legacy gift under a will of personal property or money

letter of direction for transfer and sale of shares standard direction that serves to confirm to the transfer agent that the estate trustee agrees to the sale of the shares

M

mandatory memorandum binding memorandum that is made before the will is executed and is referred to in the will

matrimonial home a residence in which a person has an interest and which is normally occupied by him and his spouse

medallion signature guarantee guarantee of the signatures of estate trustees by a bank or trust company

mediator a neutral third party whose role is to facilitate a negotiation among the parties in a dispute with a view to reaching a settlement of some or all of the issues

memorandum document added to the will that lists beneficiaries of specific items

motion for directions motion to the court for guidance on how to proceed with a determination of the matters in issue

multiple or split wills two or more wills that are intended to govern an estate concurrently

N

notice of objection form that is filed setting out the basis of an objection to the issuing of the certificate of appointment of estate trustee with a will and the objector's interest in the estate

O

obligee entity to which an administration bond of indemnity is owed (the court)

over-the-counter passing of accounts uncontested passing of accounts (without a hearing)

P

party impugning the will party in litigation who is seeking to set aside the will

party propounding the will party in litigation who is seeking to uphold the will

party with carriage of the mediation the party in a dispute heading to mandatory mediation who is appointed by the court to assume the responsibility of carrying out certain organizational tasks

passing of accounts accounting that passes through the courts, either with a hearing before a judge or without a hearing

per capita form of distribution to surviving descendants of a predeceased beneficiary whereby each survivor receives an equal share of the original gift

per stirpes form of distribution to surviving descendants of a predeceased beneficiary whereby the original gift flows downward by representation

person who appears to have a financial interest in the estate person who can demonstrate that she is likely to have a personal stake in the estate

power of attorney document in which a person grants power over her assets or personal care to another person

precatory memorandum non-binding memorandum that is made after the will is executed and may or may not be referred to in the will

preferred beneficiary election election that can be filed by a disabled beneficiary to report any income that is accumulating in the trust to the benefit of the beneficiary

Q

qualifying spousal trust trust that qualifies for advantageous capital gains tax treatment under the *Income Tax Act*

R

recapture of income what must be reported as income on the terminal T1 tax return if the undepreciated capital cost of the last asset in a class of depreciable capital assets is lower than its fair market value

request for further notice a request made by a beneficiary of an estate who is not objecting to the estate accounts, but who wants notice of any further step or document in the application to pass accounts, including any requests for costs or requests for increased costs, and which gives the person requesting further notice the right to take part in a hearing on the issue of increased costs

residual gift gift to a beneficiary that is left over in the estate after the debts and the gifts to other beneficiaries are paid

revenue disbursements money spent for the purpose of maintaining an asset that earns income

revenue receipts money or payments earned by the estate during the accounting period

rollover situation where capital property is transferred to a beneficiary upon the taxpayer's death without immediate tax consequences, deferring income tax until the recipient becomes liable for the tax

rule against perpetuities rule that prevents a trust from being open-ended indefinitely with respect to its potential beneficiaries

S

secret trust form of testamentary trust that does not appear in the will and may or may not be in writing

settlor person who sets up an *inter vivos* trust

specific gift gift of a particular object of personal property, lease, or assignment of debt

spendthrift trust trust that names a trustee to manage the gift to a beneficiary until the beneficiary reaches a specified age

stock power of attorney special kind of power of attorney in which the estate trustee is the grantor and the attorney is the transfer agent or an employee of the transfer agent

sums certain specific bequests; amounts that do not depend on the decisions made by the estate trustee in administering the estate

surety third party to an administration bond of indemnity

T

terminal loss what can be deducted from income on the terminal T1 tax return if the undepreciated capital cost of the last asset in a class of depreciable capital assets is higher than its fair market value

testamentary trust trust that is set up by the will of a testator and commences after the death of the testator, provided that the preconditions under which the trust is to be set up exist

testator person who makes a will (traditionally the male term; now used for all genders)

testatrix the traditional term for a female person who makes a will

transfer by personal representative a transfer of real property by an estate trustee to a third party

transmission application application requesting the land registrar to amend the parcel register to show the owner of the property as the estate trustee or the estate

trust means by which money or property can be held by an individual or an institution (the trustee) for the benefit of another (the beneficiary) according to the rules governing the trust

trustee person to whom trust property is transferred

U

unascertained beneficiary a theoretical beneficiary who does not yet exist—or who does not exist as a beneficiary—but who would become a beneficiary of a trust upon being born or upon the happening of a specified event

undepreciated capital cost percentage of the value of a depreciable asset that has not yet been depreciated by a business

undue influence improper pressure exerted on the testator

V

valuation date day before the date of death or the date on which the spouses separated with no reasonable prospect of reconciliation

vested settled upon

voucher acknowledgment of receipt of payment

W

will document that sets out a person's wishes and directions with respect to the disposal of his property after death

Index

Credits

CHAPTER 1

Figure 1.3: © 2000-2016, The Law Society of Upper Canada.

CHAPTER 8

Figure 8.8: © Queen's Printer for Ontario, 2017. Reproduced with permission. The materials listed are current to 2017 and are subject to change without notice. The most current version can be found on the web site of the Ministry of the Attorney General at http://ontariocourtforms.on.ca/en. The Government of Ontario and The Ministry of the Attorney General had no role in the creation of the publication.

CHAPTER 9

Figures 9.1, 9.3, 9.5, 9.6, 9.7: © Queen's Printer for Ontario, 2017. Reproduced with permission. The materials listed are current to 2017 and are subject to change without notice. The most current version can be found on the web site of the Ministry of the Attorney General at http://ontariocourtforms.on.ca/en. The Government of Ontario and The Ministry of the Attorney General had no role in the creation of the publication.

CHAPTER 11

Figure 11.3: © Queen's Printer for Ontario, 2017. Reproduced with permission.

Figures 11.5 and 11.6: Reproduced with permission of the Minister of Public Works and Government Services Canada, 2017.

CHAPTER 14

Figures 14.1, 14.2, 14.4, 14.5, 14.7, 14.8: © Queen's Printer for Ontario, 2017. Reproduced with permission. The materials listed are current to 2017 and are subject to change without notice. The most current version can be found on the web site of the Ministry of the Attorney General at http://ontariocourtforms.on.ca/en. The Government of Ontario and The Ministry of the Attorney General had no role in the creation of the publication.

Figure 14.6: © Queen's Printer for Ontario, 2017.

CHAPTER 15

Figures 15.1, 15.2, and 15.3: © Queen's Printer for Ontario, 2017. Reproduced with permission. The materials listed are current to 2017 and are subject to change without notice. The most current version can be found on the web site of the Ministry of the Attorney General at http://ontariocourtforms.on.ca/en. The Government of Ontario and The Ministry of the Attorney General had no role in the creation of the publication.

CHAPTER 16

Figure 16.1: © Queen's Printer for Ontario, 2017.

CHAPTER 17

Figure 17.2: © Queen's Printer for Ontario, 2017. Reproduced with permission. The materials listed are current to 2017 and are subject to change without notice. The most current version can be found on the web site of the Ministry of the Attorney General at http://ontariocourtforms.on.ca/en. The Government of Ontario and The Ministry of the Attorney General had no role in the creation of the publication.